LIVING WITH HATE IN AMERICAN POLITICS AND RELIGION

LIVING WITH HATE IN AMERICAN POLITICS AND RELIGION

HOW POPULAR CULTURE CAN DEFUSE INTRACTABLE DIFFERENCES

JEFFREY ISRAEL

Columbia University Press
New York

Columbia University Press
Publishers Since 1893
New York   Chichester, West Sussex
cup.columbia.edu
Copyright © 2019 Columbia University Press
All rights reserved

Library of Congress Cataloging-in-Publication Data
Names: Israel, Jeffrey, author.
Title: Living with hate in American politics and religion : how popular culture can
defuse intractable differences / Jeffrey Israel.
Description: New York : Columbia University Press, 2019. | Includes
bibliographical references and index.
Identifiers: LCCN 2018040882 | ISBN 9780231190169 (cloth : alk. paper) |
ISBN 9780231548755 (e-book)
Subjects: LCSH: Religion and politics—United States. | Popular culture—United
States. | Emotions—Political aspects. | Political psychology. | Political
science—Philosophy.
Classification: LCC BL65.P7 I87 2019 | DDC 201/.720973—dc23
LC record available at https://lccn.loc.gov/2018040882

Columbia University Press books are printed on permanent
and durable acid-free paper.

Printed in the United States of America

Cover design: Julia Kushnirsky

FOR MORRIS AND SOLOMON

How could he leave? How could he go? Everything he hated was here.

—Philip Roth, *Sabbath's Theater*

CONTENTS

FOREWORD

MARTHA C. NUSSBAUM

Jeff generously invited me to play a speaking role in his brilliant book about comedy, a book in which his own comic sensibility and his own personal reactions as a Jewish man are a constant presence. An honor, surely, but also a problem: what role can I play? Unfortunately, there is no such role as the ex-shiksa, not really. Being a shiksa is a fate as inexorable as taxes. So even now, on this fiftieth anniversary year of my conversion to Judaism, I am doomed to occupy some shiksa role. I definitely do not want to be one of Philip Roth's shiksas, mere objects of anxious male narcissistic objectification. So let me assume the role of Margaret Dumont, that snooty WASP foil of the Marx brothers, who sneakily collaborates in their joking and whose frosty above-it-allness gets taken down to earth in so many delightful ways, definitely with her own connivance. This from *Duck Soup*:

> GROUCHO: I suppose you'll think me a sentimental old fluff, but would you mind giving me a lock of your hair?
> DUMONT: A lock of my hair? Why, I had no idea you . . .
> GROUCHO: I'm letting you off easy. I was gonna ask for the whole wig.

This exchange, both a little rough and totally delightful, illustrates a central thesis of Jeff's book: that people, especially people in society's dominant groups, love to define themselves as above the flawed physicality of the merely human (here aging, thinning hair)—and these people improve, while greatly enjoying themselves, when someone refuses to let them stay on those Olympian heights—when that other sees them, and makes them see themselves, as flawed and embodied. Dumont's initial response is lofty sentimentality: she clearly sees herself as a fine lady before whom a smitten knight has just made a declaration. But Groucho refuses to go there: instead he teases her by seeing through her pretensions. She actually wears a wig, and he knows it. The pleasure for her is being seen with all her imperfections; the pleasure for the audience is seeing pomposity taken down a peg, but then, also, being reminded that we are all wearers of wigs, people who cover our imperfections and yet at the same time long to be seen as we are. (For Jewish audience members, another dimension to the joke is the suggestion that Mrs. Teasdale is really Jewish and her wig is a *sheitel*, surely an identity that the fictional Mrs. Teasdale would cover yet more anxiously than she covers baldness.) Yet another level to the joke involves recognizing that the two actors have cleverly connived at this moment. Dumont's characters are certainly not treated well in the plots of the movies; but Groucho always publicly acknowledged Dumont as a valuable collaborator in play, and she remained devoted to "Julie" (as she preferred to call him) throughout her career. So the audience also knows that Dumont the comic actress is playing along with the game and reveling in her character's earthy takedown. I'm happy to assume that role for the rest of this foreword, saying some serious things that will no doubt end up in the soup.

Where exactly does Jewishness enter the picture in this exchange? As Jeff points out with impressive historical analysis, Jewish humor, especially American Jewish humor, is obsessed with the body, and the recovery of the body as the self, in a puritanical WASP culture obsessed with rising above the bodily and determined to stigmatize the Jew as dirty. This WASP culture is not just missing a lot of fun, it is also lacking resources to confront social divisions, since a powerful way in which polarized people can come together is on the terrain of common bodily humanity. So American Protestant culture needs, perhaps more than many, the delightful comic takedown exemplified in Groucho's remark as well as by so many cases in this extremely funny book.

The connection of the helpful and delightful takedown to Jewish identity is contingent (Aristophanes did some similar things in ancient Greece), but it is helpful to think with. And it suggests valuable insights not only for the personal life but also for the political life.

The general thesis of this book is that American Jewish humor and its analogues (but really, in America more or less all humor is Jewish humor) contribute to the stability and success of American political life by helping our society negotiate and defang (at least to some extent) hostile emotions that, unaddressed, threaten to derail it. In general, Jeff argues, liberal societies with high ideals (here Jeff kindly turns to my version of the Capabilities Approach, though not without insightful discussion of Rawls) are always threatened by "remainders"—by fears and hatreds that lurk beneath their civilized surface. If we don't confront them, they fester and threaten the success of the liberal project. But if we simply vent them, the violence of our emotions threatens that project directly.

What to do? We should not, Jeff argues, confront these remainders through politically imposed censorship: then the liberal project would undercut itself. And indeed, he believes, there is not much that law and politics can do directly to affect the problem of lurking negative emotions. But there is a way to address them in what Rawls called the "background culture"—the informal nonpolitical set of interactions that have large effects on the formal political parts of our lives. This way is to explore the ugly sentiments at one remove, by framing them as play. Seen under the quotation marks of play, particularly when gifted comic writers or actors render the exchange delightful, the ugly sentiments are, to an extent, transformed, defanged, and perhaps, as in Lenny Bruce's greatest routines, just trail off into sheer nonsense. Here, again kindly, Jeff refers to the role of play on my capabilities list, but he is really doing something totally original and different. My capability of Play was meant to signal a duty on the part of government to provide spaces for recreation, leisure, and self-cultivation. Jeff agrees with that, and he does offer an insightful discussion of public cultural activity; but in the main he is not talking about government action and he frames his whole exercise as one that must surge up from the background culture—though preferably without government interference of the sort that dogged Bruce's footsteps.

Play, as Jeff argues, is a type of activity, and it typically involves interaction between performers or authors and an audience whose members are not passive at all, even though they may seem so, but are connecting, responding to, even objecting to the comic performer or author. Israel argues that play is intentional but noninstrumental, not done for a specific purpose. And it has a frame: all the participants accept the idea that their activities within the play frame may mean something quite different from what they mean the rest of the time. This line drawing makes it possible, he argues, for play to explore what could not easily be explored outside the frame. In fraught societies, the play frame makes it possible for us to explore the remainders of historical grievance and injustice people carry with them that would be too threatening and destabilizing outside the play frame. And although play is set apart from the rest of life, it can have large effects on people's general self-understanding. Because the lingering grudges that never really go away come out into the open, people are able to laugh at them together, and this can significantly affect how they function in real life. It's important that this is not a catharsis thesis: Jeff does not imagine that venting anger creates less anger. It's basically a cognitive thesis: by seeing our anger within the frame of play, at a distance, we acquire self-understanding, a measure of self-detachment, and new motives for change.

Even put in this general way, without the detailed argument that fills the book's central chapters, that's an impressive thesis. I think it is basically true, and political theory in the liberal tradition can surely stand to be enriched by an understanding of the political role of humor and comedy. But exploring the thesis further requires a set of concrete cases. For humor, as Jeff sees (citing aptly the work of our late colleague Ted Cohen) is always intimate, requiring for its success a particular social context and an audience of people in the know. So Jeff focuses on just one society, the U.S., and on what he both knows and viscerally inhabits, American Jewish humor. Although the book discusses many examples and, along the way, offers its readers a rich grounding in the history of Jews in America, Jeff works out his argument in three rich chapters: on Lenny Bruce; on Philip Roth's *Portnoy's Complaint*; and on the TV sitcom *All in the Family* (whose characters are not Jewish but whose creator, Norman Lear, is, and Jeff makes a strong case for reading the sitcom as part of the Jewish humor tradition he investigates).

I've said that I find the thesis persuasive and the execution brilliant. But at this point I want to enter a skeptical objection or at least a question. And it was Jeff's hope and expectation that I would talk back to him critically, exemplifying an ideal of scholarship as dialogue, the printed word as a snapshot in an ongoing critical conversation. The book is strong enough to invite one's deepest views about life, both personal and political, and what else could Margaret Dumont do but give a serious lecture? The book will survive it, and maybe I'll even earn a comic send-up.

For psychoanalyst Donald Winnicott, whose account of play, in the main, I follow, play is valuable if and when it is *going somewhere*—in particular out of narcissism toward greater understanding of the inner worlds of others, toward greater respect for those worlds, and, if all goes well, toward a greater *capacity for concern.* A child begins as a narcissist, unable to connect to others or even to see them as fully real. Through imaginative play, she learns, with delight, that there are many worlds and that those worlds too contain vulnerability and agency. Gradually her attitude toward real people in her world undergoes a corresponding shift: she sees them no longer as her slaves, or as thwarting objects to be met with rage, but rather as centers of thought and feeling who can make demands on her just as she will make demands on them. She then moderates her demands in the light of that understanding, eventually becoming capable of adult reciprocity. Obviously this progress is immensely important in the political life, and that is really why play is important in the political life. (Winnicott insisted on this and made that a linchpin of his case for a political role for the arts. And Winnicott is important to Jeff's account.)

There is, however, a type of play that is not going anywhere. It is narcissistic, it says "me me me" all the time, it does not lead outward toward any greater understanding of the worlds of others. We might say that it is infantile play, play stuck in the narcissism of the insecure infant. It is not a given that American Jewish humor always exemplifies the Winnicottian rather than the narcissistic type of play. Jews, heaven knows, are quite capable of narcissism, and capable, correspondingly, of a kind of humor that is me-me-me and self-enclosing.

I find that Jeff's book lurches somewhat uneasily between these two types of humor without distinguishing them—in part through the fiction that the "remainders" in the self are immutable. No, not really. They are changed by learning to think from the point of view of others. In the end, they may even laugh themselves out of existence.

Lenny Bruce seems to me to exemplify quite remarkably the first going-somewhere type of play, the type that really does conduce to a more robust and stable democracy. I'll leave you to examine Jeff's brilliant and convincing chapter, but will say only that the spectator is not static in Bruce's routines. By being moved out of her comfort zone, she is changed. Not once for all, to be sure. That is why the humor thrives on repetition: we still have our old habits of thought and give them up only gradually and with long relearning. But we are definitely going somewhere, and Bruce's embrace of the body is a large part of that journey.

Philip Roth seems to me very different, at least in *Portnoy*, the one work Jeff considers. I grant that Roth is a great writer and I also grant that he is so complicated that any such critique might be totally mistaken. (Jeff's chapter points to the dizzying metaperspectives that Portnoy's narrative invites.) I also believe that in some works, particularly *American Pastoral*, Roth attains a depth of insight into other worlds that for the most part he doesn't. (Not coincidentally, *American Pastoral* is the rare case where a leading male character makes a serious effort to imagine the world of a female. Jeff does not pose enough questions about women to Roth. In one telling note he asks what a female reader would make of his Roth interpretation—but then he waves that question away by a brief discussion of Erica Jong's silly novel, which he reads as a female response to *Portnoy*.) In *Portnoy's Complaint*, and not there alone, Roth's text is narcissistic, misogynistic, and *going nowhere*. Women are unreal, in general other people are unreal; all that exists is the ego. To encourage this sort of venting in a society—venting that is static, enclosed, and without a window onto other worlds—is surely not to render that society more stable. Even Roth represents his entire me-me novel as a prelude to psychotherapy, which begins as the novel ends. I wish that Jeff, rather than endorsing both Bruce and Roth, had tried to come to grips with what seem to me very significant differences between them.

As for *All in the Family*, I can't comment, because I never liked that show and never watched it, but I have the suspicion that it is more static and narcissistic than Winnicottian and transitional. But let me, instead, comment on a TV show that is both significantly Jewish and clearly transitional, indeed a program that has probably changed our democracy more than any other piece of popular culture, and one that I happen to love: *Will and Grace*. The society into which Max Mutchnick and David Kohan launched their amazingly durable sitcom in 1998 was a society in which hostile stereotypes of gays and lesbians reigned unchallenged. The closet meant that a large proportion of the population believed they had never met a gay or lesbian person. The sitcom depicts the deep and long-loving friendship of Grace Adler (Debra Messing) and Will Truman (Eric McCormack), who dated in college, but then realized it would never work out between them when he admitted to himself and to her that he was gay. But here's the thing: it *did* work out between them, as he became her rock and her source of abiding love amid all the unsuitable men who are so easy for a high-achieving woman to find and sleep with. Even the love of her life, Leo (Harry Connick Jr.), is unstable, and in the show's successful revival, starting in 2017, he has simply disappeared. The same narrative holds for Will, *mutatis mutandis*: unsuitable men turn up one by one, and one, Vince (Bobby Cannavale), is better than the others; still, they never offer one part of the deep responsiveness and steady love that Grace does. (In the revival, Vince marries someone else, and as the two conduct a postmortem of their relationship we see how Will did not really see him the way he sees and loves Grace.) The show is very cleverly plotted and wittily written, so through play the audience comes to love the two protagonists, to identify with their search for happiness, and to admire their reciprocal love.

If this were all, one would suspect the creators of sentimentalizing gay life in order to win over the squeamish: look, gays are not promiscuous, they are just like straights. They really want lasting love and marriage. But here is the real genius of the show: it also includes two edgier characters, one gay and one bisexual, who in a sense enact the stereotype of the flighty gay man and the unreliable lesbian, but written and acted with such charm (by Sean Hayes and Megan Mullally) that the stereotype itself becomes play. The audience is going somewhere: in this case, from blank ignorance into a pretty nuanced imaginative participation in different types of same-sex (and some straight) lives.

Jeff will now ask, "But where is the hate?" And indeed the show is conspicuous for its avoidance of antigay hate as a theme. (After all, it's set in New York.) But the hate always lay in the obtuseness, in what Ralph Ellison's protagonist in *Invisible Man* called "a peculiar disposition . . . of [the] inner eyes," on the part of people who refuse to look and see. So the hate is/was in the relationship of same-sex lives to audience (or nonaudience), and the show seduces people into looking, with a gaze of genuine curiosity and kindly concern. It plays with the hatred of obtuseness, subverting it, making it laugh at itself. For me, one of the great features of the gay rights movement has been a belief that love could conquer hate if only people would actually look and see. The rapid change of attitudes among younger Americans seems to bear out this bold conjecture.

I would say, too, that *Will and Grace* contains what Lenny Bruce's routines contain, and what I suspect *All in the Family* does not: a portal onto a general human truth that we might call quasi tragic, meaning one that is difficult, but one all must face or remain superficial. In the case of Bruce, there are many such truths. One is about shame and stigma: everyone has some stigma of their own that they are trying to cover, and life with stigma is painful. In the case of *Will and Grace*, it is a profound truth about love: that the world being what it is, you do not always get to sleep with the person you love, for one reason or another, but you also do not stop loving the person you don't sleep with. Running away from that complexity is endlessly tempting, as Grace's cavalcade of lovers shows us. (And, good heavens, now she is with David Schwimmer, who at least has comic timing and is Jewish, as her previous lovers have not been—though Connick had a Jewish mother.) But here she is, in 2019, still faithful to Will, after her fashion. How silly. How wise.

Will and Grace changed the U.S. It was quite possibly one of the largest single causes of rapid attitudinal shifts toward gays and lesbians that have taken place in American culture. And it did this, I claim, in virtue of its virtuosity in comic play, but also, at the same time, its genuine depth of feeling, its clearly Winnicottian and non-narcissistic embrace of different lives. We don't need it any longer to create a bridge to unknown worlds, but we do need it still: for, in a sense, the most unknown world of all is the world of love.

I hope Jeff will investigate this distinction in his next book, and maybe even my example of TV play-going-somewhere. There are so many wonderful applications for his thesis. Or, possibly, he will just say "Horsefeathers" to my distinction and show why it isn't pertinent.

After that big question—for it really is a question put to Jeff—there remain just three further observations: about the Capabilities Approach, about anger, and about religion.

Jeff suggests that my version of the Capabilities Approach doesn't confront problems of fraught societies, particularly in America. Now Americans are all too inclined to the narcissism of saying me-me-me all the time, but the fact is that many other nations exist. The Capabilities Approach is the creation of a multinational group of scholars and activists. The Human Development and Capability Association contains members from over eighty countries. Its main purpose is to provide a highly abstract template for thinking about measures of development in developing countries. It is not inapplicable to rich countries, but that has never been its focus, given our connection with the United Nations Development Programme. Furthermore, each of these nations has its own history and resources, and any sensible approach ought to recognize both these differences and the autonomy and agency of the people in these nations. In crafting my own distinctive version of the approach, I deliberately leave the main categories abstract because I defend a principle of "local specification": we should allow people in each nation to think things through on their own and choose the version of the approach that fits their own history and current problems. And I also insist on a nonpaternalistic idea of implementation: the approach is a template that ought to be implemented by each group of citizens in and for their own nation. So that is why my philosophical versions of the approach do not allude to the particular struggles of any one nation: it's up to them to make that connection.

But I do also take a deep interest in the connection between abstract template and fraught reality. Although I, of course, am American, I am also a scholar of Indian law and politics, and in crafting my version of the approach I have focused particular attention and long (often collaborative) research on India: *Women and Human Development* (2000) uses that nation as its focus in thinking about gender equality and capabilities. I have also written about political polarization and division in India in the 2007 book *The Clash Within: Democracy, Religious Violence, and India's Future.* Although there are many pitfalls in making claims about the political life of a nation not one's own, I wrote that book at the urging of Indian scholars who felt that their own warnings about the danger of Modi and the Hindu right were not getting heard in the U.S. I continue to write extensively about Indian politics, particularly issues concerning academic freedom and the politics of sexual orientation, often with Indian collaborators or even coauthors. And, as scholars living in India face increasing threats to academic freedom and even physical safety, I write things in the Indian press that I can say and they perhaps cannot. So that is my "fraught society" and my focus. One of my great heroes is the architect of the Indian constitution, B. R. Ambedkar, a *dalit* who figured out how to adapt abstract ideas to the particular fraught situation of India's multiple exclusions: of the lower castes, of women, and of Muslims. And, although he never wrote about sexual orientation, Amedkar is repeatedly cited as an authority in Indian court judgments overturning those unjust laws.

Further, since it is obviously a useful thing to put our heads together and compare different types of prejudice and stigma, I've been involved in a binational project on stigma and prejudice in India and the U.S. that was just culminated in a book entitled *The Empire of Disgust: Prejudice, Discrimination, and Policy in India and the U.S.*, edited by Zoya Hasan, Aziz Huq, Martha C. Nussbaum, and Vidhu Verma (two Indians and two Americans), deriving from a conference at the University of Chicago Center in Delhi in 2016 (published by Oxford University Press, Delhi, in 2018, and soon by Oxford University Press in New York). Here we examine, for example, the uncanny similarities but also the profound differences between racism in the U.S. and the caste hierarchy in India; but we also look at gender, age, disability, sexual orientation and transgender, class, and prejudice against Muslims, all through a binational lens. As for humor, I have a profound interest in the fiction and dramas of Rabindranath Tagore, which contains many elements of play that would make an apt parallel to Jeff's discussion of Jewish humor.

Next anger. Jeff makes my view seem a bit sentimental and passive, saying that I argue that anger needs to be replaced by love and hope. What I say is that we need to give up *the retributive element in* anger, which is present as an element in all the major definitions of anger in both Western and Indian thought, but we need to keep the element of outrage and protest. And there is one borderline species of anger, which I call Transition-Anger, which is from the beginning free of the retributive wish. Its entire content is: "How outrageous that is. Something must be done about that." (We often see this type of anger in parents toward their children: they are outraged, but they do not seek payback in the spirit of the *lex talionis*.) I argue, following Martin Luther King Jr., that the retributive part of anger, which pretends emptily to alter the past, must be replaced by future-directed hope and work, but that the outrage part, which leads to acts of courageous protest, is politically valuable and should be retained. King made this point by saying that when anger brought people to his movement that anger had to be "purified" and "channelized." (I document this in my essay in the excellent new collection *To Shape a New World: The*

Political Philosophy of Martin Luther King, Jr., edited by Tommie Shelby and Brandon Terry.) My view may still have defects, but not the one of failing to take outrage and protest seriously.

Finally religion. I won't even begin about the Constitution and the religion clauses, since this is a foreword, not a book. But on the general topic of religion and Judaism: surely religion is not the entirety of Judaism, but it would be perverse to deny that it is a very important part. Jeff doesn't have much use for that part; I do. So let me conclude by giving some reasons why. Reform Judaism, as I know and participate in it, is a set of moral practices in which belief in God is optional. This has always been so: the founder of the seminary where rabbis are trained to this day, Isaac Meyer Wise (1819–1900), was openly a Spinozist. The moral law, Reform Jews believe, is central. OK, why do we need a religious gathering to be moral? Well, we are weak. Having rituals and communal practices focused around altruism and generosity strengthens us in our weakness. Kant said exactly this about the reason why people have a duty (as he saw it) to join a church. Reform Judaism is basically a Kantian religion. I don't think everyone has a duty to join a church or synagogue; I just think that it is very helpful for many people. Our synagogue has the largest food garden in the U.S. that provides fresh produce to the poor. It's hard to engage in such an ongoing project without the moral impetus and the organizational capacity of something like a synagogue. And when I sing there it really is different from singing in a secular recital, because it is about ethical meanings that we have agreed to take extremely seriously. And of course, since it is a Jewish synagogue, there is also much delightful humor. Jeff would perhaps have a hard time resisting our cantor David Berger, a hilarious and gifted gay man (married to a Conservative rabbi and raising an African American child). If he heard Berger sing a doo-wop version of "I Have a Little Dreidel" in a Jerry Lee Lewis falsetto he would see that we religious Jews definitely do not leave play behind. Next time he is in Chicago, perhaps on a book tour for this marvelous book, I will invite him.

Mazel tov, Jeff.

ACKNOWLEDGMENTS

Living with Hate is the result of many years of conversations, reading books, accepting invitations to play, and thinking while sitting in chairs. I have benefited especially from the supportive environment at Williams College. In 2017, I participated in the Manuscript Review Program at the Oakley Center for Humanities and Social Sciences at Williams. I received enormously helpful comments from Edan Dekel, Jacqueline Hidalgo, Martin Kavka, Mark Reinhardt, and George Shulman, all of whom graciously agreed to read a draft of the whole manuscript and dig into it with me at the center. I also participated in an Oakley Center Discussion Seminar in 2017 on psychoanalysis in the humanities and social sciences. I am grateful for comments on chapters of the manuscript provided by participants in the seminar: Jennifer French, Tom Kohut, Bojana Mladenovic, Gail Newman, and Jana Sawicki.

I am grateful to be surrounded by supportive and engaging colleagues at Williams, and I appreciate every little moment of compassion and intellectual excitement shared in our little New England town. Special thanks go to Denise Buell, Justin Crowe, Edan Dekel, Jackie Hidalgo, Jason Josephson-Storm, Tom Kohut, Mark Reinhardt, Neil Roberts, and Christian Thorne, who have directly buoyed my efforts to write this book with invaluable guidance and critical engagement.

I started to developed the ideas that appear in this book while in graduate school at the University of Chicago. I will always be indebted to Paul

Mendes-Flohr, who brought me to the university, taught and encouraged me in the study of modern Jewish thought, and commented on an earlier version of the ideas expressed here. I am grateful to Robert Gooding-Williams, who read and provided crucial comments on an earlier version of these ideas while I was at Chicago and profoundly deepened my appreciation and understanding of Frantz Fanon.

As my doctoral adviser at the University of Chicago, Martha Nussbaum encouraged me always to think carefully, read widely, write sincerely, and, most important, to cultivate my own distinct judgments about political ethics. She was always eager for good arguments, open to criticism, quick to reconnect our intellectual work to the ongoing crisis of political injustice, and equally ready to appreciate the intrinsic beauty and gravity of classic texts and ideas. For comments on numerous iterations of ideas in this book, for always emboldening my individuality, and for years of supportive mentorship, I will be forever grateful to Martha.

Intellectual and professional support came at key moments in my career from Jeff McMahan and Val Vinokur. I am thankful to Wendy Lochner and Susan Pensak for guiding me through the publishing process at Columbia University Press with encouragement and insight.

I am grateful for many years of good, long conversations with friends who have argued with me and joined with me in intellectual play, which has significantly impacted my thinking: Howard Berkowitz, Ryan Coyne, Rob Goldberg, Sarah Hammerschlag, Michael Kessler, Ben Klein, Jal Mehta, Eric Nuñez, Joshua Safran, Michael Schaffer, and Joe Schwartz.

I was extraordinarily lucky to grow up with parents, Diane and Warren Israel, and an older sister, Rebecca Sarett, who have always made me feel loved and appreciated. My parents have supported me, worried about me, talked with me, cheered for me, and comforted me over many years of navigating an academic career and now, finally, publishing my first book. My gratitude to them is boundless.

Above all, I am grateful to my wife, Dina, who believes in me, talks through ideas with me, pushes through each day's challenges with me, and whose love and commitment have made it possible in countless ways for me to write this book. The great gift of my life is to be able to share it with someone that I respect, admire, and passionately love.

This book is dedicated to my sons, Morris and Solomon. Your gentleness, compassion, curiosity, and playfulness make me proud every day. I hope you will radiate these virtues into the world throughout your lives. And I hope you will feel that America's problems are your problems, that the American story is your story, and that you can help to make it a story about the pursuit of justice.

LIVING WITH HATE IN AMERICAN
POLITICS AND RELIGION

INTRODUCTION

Loving and Hating America Since the 1990s

Sometime in the early 1990s, when I was a teenager, my high school hosted a "café night." I performed by reading Allen Ginsberg's poem "America" aloud. I had long hair and I wore green gabardine pants, a green-collared shirt, a green suede vest, and a maroon and forest green paisley bowtie. I was a beat poet wannabe for the night, for some reason dressed like I'd just arrived from the Emerald City. The first line of the poem must have sounded ridiculous coming out of my teenage mouth. "America I've given you all and now I'm nothing." What had I given? I didn't even have any interesting nothingness to boast of. Undoubtedly, the big draw for me was the fifth line. What could be more thrilling than to declare before the gathered teachers, parents, and students, "Go fuck yourself with your atom bomb." I identified with Ginsberg's irreverence toward American piety, the sense of outrage, his evocations of a Jewish-Marxist pedigree, his hints of Jewish resentment: "America I still haven't told you what you did to Uncle Max after he came over from Russia." But that wasn't the whole story.

By pedigree, I was really more Neil Diamond's son than Allen Ginsberg's. Ginsberg: "America when I was seven momma took me to Communist Cell meetings." When I was seven we listened to Neil Diamond on long car rides in the station wagon from Baltimore to Columbus, Ohio, to visit my grandparents. "Coming to America" was a favorite (also the duet with Barbra Streisand, "You Don't Bring Me Flowers"). "On the boats and on the planes, / They're coming to America, / Never looking back again, / They're coming to America." To this day I love to blast "Coming to America" in the car, on the road with my own kids, screaming at the top of my lungs, welling up: "Home, / To a new and a shiny place, / Make our bed and we'll say our grace, / Freedom's light burning warm, / Freedom's light burning warm." Sentimental 1970s third-generation Jewish immigrant patriotism. It's deeply embedded in my kishkes, in my guts.

Ginsberg and Diamond. An unlikely couple perhaps, the fathers of my earliest political emotions. Irreverence, disappointment, and outrage about America, but sentimentality too. When the time came for college applications, I applied to one place only, Oberlin College, because of its artistic and intellectual culture and its historical association with radical politics. Ginsberg had proved decisive. I arrived at Oberlin in the fall of 1995. The public mood around college life was evident at the movies: *Higher Learning*, *PCU*, the film version of David Mamet's play *Oleanna*, *Reality Bites*, *Kicking and Screaming*. Arguing about "identity politics," "political correctness," "slackers," and "postmodernism" was de rigueur. This was the era of Bill Maher's late-night talk show *Politically Incorrect*. The Oklahoma City bombing was in April of 1995. The O. J. Simpson murder trial began that year, with the not-guilty verdict delivered in October. Louis Farakhan's Million Man March was held the same month.

At Oberlin it was very clear that patriotic emotion was for jingoistic rednecks and deluded bourgeois saps. I couldn't pass as the former even if I tried. But I was haunted by the possibility that I was, in the end, an incorrigibly deluded bourgeois sap, that it's Neil Diamond all the way down. I was still sentimental about the American project. I was still easily moved by the great moments when America has seemed to live up to its promise. And yet I remained deeply worried that the promise has been a ruse.

Why not, after all, assume that the whole thing has been a ruse? Born amidst the colonial domination of native peoples, white supremacy, patriarchy, economic exploitation, and Protestant Christian cultural hegemony, is it entirely unreasonable to suspect that the political ideals expressed in founding documents like the Declaration of Independence and the U.S. Constitution are mere ideological tripe, contrived precisely to perpetuate injustice? The poison at the root of American history is evident from a variety of critical perspectives: Marxist, feminist, antiracist, to name a few. As a college student in the 1990s trying to develop into a grown-up engaged intellectual, it was very clear to me that whatever schmaltzy, sentimental feelings I may still have had about America were ultimately bereft of intellectual and moral credibility.

What is more, the particular reasons not to love or trust America eventually came to count, for me, as merely symptoms of a deeper problem. A problem with the fundamental ideas that animate the American political project. A problem with the idea of a modern liberal state. As a graduate student of religion, focusing on modern Jewish thought and political ethics, I spent much of my time studying early Jewish sentimentality and outrage about the modern liberal state. I recall Hermann Cohen, the great German-Jewish neo-Kantian philosopher writing sentimentally just a couple of decades before the rise of Hitler, "In perfect equanimity and harmony of soul, we feel as secure in our German patriotism as in our Jewish religion"[1]—deluded bourgeois sap!

Cohen's "perfect equanimity and harmony of soul" in Germany in 1916 is haunting. But it is not just his now cringeworthy German patriotism that rankles. His sense of security in "our Jewish religion" also came to bother me. Cohen accepted and indeed advocated the truncating of Jewishness into a modern "religion" on the model of German Protestantism. He was following in a line of Jewish liberals who hoped to prove themselves eligible for modern state citizenship by claiming that Jewishness is only a matter of each individual's private faith. Count Stanislas de Clermont-Tonnerre had famously argued on behalf of Jewish emancipation to the French National Assembly in 1789, "The Jews should be denied everything as a nation, but granted everything as individuals."[2] And Jewish liberals like Cohen have since then been at pains to show that they are indistinguishable upstanding citizens whose private, respectable, moral, rational religion just happens to be in a Hebrew font. It's hard to blame them—the count also said, "if they do not want this, they must inform us and we shall then be compelled to expel them."[3]

There seemed to be at the core of the liberal project a demand for standardization that intrudes deep into Jewishness and compels conformity to an inevitably Christian paradigm of what it means to be a rights-bearing person.[4] Already in 1854, the traditionalist Rabbi Samson Raphael Hirsch chafed at this intrusive narrowing. Against what he saw as the excessive accommodations made by liberal Jewish reformers, he wrote, "Judaism is not a religion, the synagogue is not a church, and the rabbi is not a priest. Judaism is not a mere adjunct to life."[5] In a different spirit, Hermann Cohen's student Franz Rosenzweig expressed similar concerns.[6] He condemned in 1920 any further revival of "that old song, already played to death a hundred years ago, about Judaism as a 'religion,' as a 'creed,' the old expedient of a century that tried to analyze the unity of the Jewish individual tidily into a 'religion' for several hundred rabbis and a 'creed' for several tens of thousands of respectable citizens. . . . God keep us from putting that old cracked record on again."[7]

A lot of what I read as a graduate student at the University of Chicago in the early 2000s exacerbated my growing suspicion that modern liberal states in the West inevitably compel non-Christians to convert what makes them different into something that looks like Protestant Christianity.[8] For a contemporary example, consider the way that the tax-exempt status of religious institutions in the United States requires the IRS to decide what counts as a religion and what does not. Jonathan Z. Smith explains, "the unproblematized use in tax law of terms such as 'church,' 'sect,' 'religious organization,' 'religious orders,' 'ministers,' 'sacerdotal,' and so forth suggests that the features of other religions are routinely being matched against some Christian prototype."[9] There is a clear incentive here: the IRS will reward you if you can make your enterprise recognizable as a "church" with a "minister." The much-lauded ideals of liberal citizenship and religious freedom that folks like Hermann Cohen had thought so promising started to look to me in graduate school like a sneaky way to turn Jews into Protestants. And knowing what happened to so many respectable citizens who were as secure in their truncated liberal "Jewish religion" as they were in their German patriotism makes this trick all the worse.

It was easy, then, for me to fall into deep cynicism about the core ideas in the liberal tradition. Max Nordau seemed to understand the situation far better than Cohen when he addressed the First Zionist Congress in 1897. He suggested that Jewish emancipation in France over a hundred years earlier was a mere logical deduction from the philosophies of Jean-Jacques Rousseau and the Encyclopedists. "The emancipation of the Jews was proclaimed in France," he said, "not out of fraternal feeling for the Jews but because logic demanded it."[10] The formal but not substantive inclusion of Jews as citizens in the modern nation-states of Europe was a failure at best—it was probably just a ruse all along!

"For one or two generations the Jew was allowed to believe that he was merely a German, Frenchman, Italian, and so forth, like all the rest of his countrymen," Nordau recalled.[11] But this didn't last long. Again, Nordau is writing in 1897, almost two decades before Hermann Cohen pronounced his patriotic equanimity in Germany: "All at once, twenty years ago, after a slumber of thirty to sixty years, anti-Semitism once more sprang out of the innermost depths of the nations of western Europe. It revealed to a mortified Jew, who thought anti-Semitism was gone forever, the true picture of his situation."[12]

There is a particular Jewish political anxiety in Nordau's words. The anxiety that the goyim will always hate the Jews. They will always long for the world finally to admit that the Jews are the real problem and to get rid of them once and for all. But there is also a more general worry expressed here about the modern liberal state. This is the worry that every person in a liberal state will have who is not a member of the core group that is largely taken to represent the quintessential citizen—the quintessential German, Frenchman, American, etc. It is the worry of the patriotic member of society, descended from colonized native people, people who were enslaved, and immigrants, that he does not see "the true picture of his situation."

Philip Roth captures this worry brilliantly in his novel *The Plot Against America*, which I devoured when it came out in 2004. In the book, Charles Lindbergh becomes president rather than FDR in 1940. As in real life, Lindbergh accepts a medal from Nazi air force commander Hermann Göring in 1938 for his famous transatlantic flight and rejects calls to return it after *Kristallnacht*. Also as in real life, he is a spokesman for the isolationist America First Committee, which opposes using American military force against Hitler, and he makes a speech in Des Moines in 1941 claiming that "the Jewish people" (sometimes "the Jewish race") is pushing the country to war because of "their own interests"; "but we must look out for ours."[13] The clear implication, of course, is that the interests of Jewish Americans are not the interests of *real* Americans.

When Lindbergh becomes president in Roth's alternative history, he quickly establishes the "Office of American Absorption," which starts the "Just Folks" program: ostensibly "a volunteer work program introducing city youth to the traditional ways of heartland life."[14] As the narrator (an alternative "Philip Roth" who grew up in this period) explains, "It was the intention of Just Folks to remove hundreds of Jewish boys between the ages of twelve and eighteen from the cities where they lived and attended school and put them to work for eight weeks as field hands and day laborers with farm families hundreds of miles from their homes."[15] The point, according to Philip's father in the book, is to separate Jewish kids from their parents so that the Jewishness that led Jewish Americans to support FDR and his call to join the fight against fascism would not be reproduced in the next generation. It seems apt to me, given my suspicions about liberal Judaism, that the appointed federal director of the Office of American Absorption is the pompous Rabbi Lionel Bengelsdorf, who was known to give popular sermons and talks, frequently quoting Theodore Roosevelt: "There can be no divided allegiance here. Any man who says he is an American, but something else also, isn't an American at all."[16]

Roth shows how plausible it is to imagine an alternative American history in which the Second World War does not reveal an America willing to define itself against fascism, but demonstrates instead an America just as ready to double down on the primacy of its founding "core group": white Anglo-Saxon Protestants of "the heartland."[17] The true picture of the situation we are allowed to imagine in *The Plot Against America* is that Jewish Americans are not and never will be seen as real Americans by the Christian majority.

This anxiety is still potent for many Jews in America today, no matter that they are more secure than any Jewish population in twenty-five hundred years of Jewish history.[18] Jews in America tend to be prosperous and highly educated, and yet the paranoia persists. How much more potent must be the anxieties of Americans descended from people who were enslaved, colonized native people, and non-European immigrants? Indeed, as I write this in the summer of 2018, reasons to be anxious are piling up like the books on my desk.

Donald Trump was elected president of the United States in 2016 after a campaign designed to exacerbate the anxieties and aggression of white Christian men, especially those who have limited education. Whipping up fear and rage against Hispanics and Muslims, passively encouraging the support of white supremacists and neo-Nazis, it cannot be merely historical coincidence that he adopted "America First" as one of his slogans. However reassuring the elections of Barack Obama in 2008 and 2012 may have been, the political ascension of Donald Trump has equally reinforced the haunting unpredictability of history captured so well in *The Plot Against America*. Americans who are not white, heterosexual, Christian men are rightfully seized by "the terror of the unforeseen" that "the science of history hides."[19] It is more than ever unimaginable that historically stigmatized people in America can ever trust that they see "the true picture of their situation."

So where does this leave us? Why not just say to America—even the very idea of America—*Go fuck yourself with your atom bomb!* Why not tell America to fuck off and be done with it? Why not just settle in with our contempt and abide in this country begrudgingly, without real allegiance? Or, why not "blow up the system" and hope that whatever comes next is better than what we've got? In the chapters that follow, I argue that it is still worth daring to love America. But this is not a call for old-fashioned jingoistic patriotism. Nor is it an attempt to revive Martin Luther King Jr.'s powerful call for us to "transform the jangling discords of our nation into a beautiful symphony of brotherhood."[20] Neither of these visions will do.

I present a vision of political love that does not seek to deny, minimize, or erase the legacy of America's historical injustices, but instead expects the unforgivable to remain unforgiven. Mine is a vision of political love that endures despite chronic pain, despite open wounds that cannot heal. In this vision, the deeply embedded historical grudges, paranoia, resentment, intergroup antipathies, and other nasty emotions that divide people in the U.S. are not presumed somehow to wither away over time. Instead, I imagine these nasty emotions *thriving* along with political love and enriching that love in the process. Loving America will be imaginable if we can imagine loving and resenting, loving and condemning, loving and not forgiving—all at the same time. As it turns out, this kind of political love also animates Allen Ginsberg's "America." My setup, starkly contrasting Ginsberg and Diamond, doesn't quite hold because Ginsberg's poem is not merely an expression of radical outrage. It also expresses a deep love for America. As I will show, Ginsberg's poem plays with love and outrage with distinct virtuosity. The love that I hope to theorize and enlarge in this book is meant to sustain the feeling that America is contemptible or worse, just as it is meant to sustain the occasional indulgence in Neil Diamond's fantasy of a "new and a shiny place."

But let me be clear about what I do and do not mean to evoke when I use the term *love*. I do not have in mind anything theological or highly conceptual. There is nothing pure, miraculous, "freely given," or "Christ-like" in the love that I have in mind, for example. Nor does love, as I am thinking of it, require the feelings of sustained affection, attraction, or delight that characterizes some of what is associated with love. Instead, I'm picturing a father rushing frantically to make breakfast, pack lunch, and get his kids out the door to school in the morning. I have in mind long-term adult relationships that are quietly haunted by the low burning flame of resentment and occasional bursts of fiery anger, which nevertheless endure and deepen into a profoundly shared life. I have in mind the way you love your parents and appreciate all that they've done for you even though they sometimes annoy the crap out of you. I have in mind the not always articulated but consistent sense that someone really matters to you, the willingness to endure a certain amount of drudgery, the readiness to take action if there is an emergency, the unshakable sense of responsibility that sometimes comes with a grumble and a grimace.

I am trying to make imaginable a love of this sort, albeit on a much larger scale, that can hold us together in the United States of America despite our irreconcilable grievances as we try to make America more just. It is a distinctly *political* love—a love that involves caring about the flourishing of the nation as a whole and the flourishing of every person in it as an essential part of your own flourishing.[21] I'm offering a vision of political love for an America whose population—each and every person in it—is presumed to be a product of historic injustice, whether as victims, beneficiaries, or both. Such people will carry interminable anger and resentment, dark moods and perverse emotions, obnoxious self-indulgent fantasies, and silly delusions. How it is possible to love each other *as a nation of such people* is what I hope to make imaginable in this book.

But wait, you may be thinking, shouldn't we spend a bit more time on the telling-America-to-fuck-off option? Why should people who identify as Chicana, Cherokee, Navajo, or Sioux in America be interested in any ideal that concedes the legitimacy of the settler-colonial state still occupying their ancestral land? Why should descendants of enslaved people from Africa, who are subjected to mass incarceration, police brutality, and structural racism, be interested at this particular moment in a new take on why we should love America? Why should queer people who are watching a wave of reinvigorated stigmatization gather under the banner of "religious freedom" or want to entertain a new ideal of love for a nation so ready to deny them precisely that? For that matter, why should a white guy who thinks, "Hey, this country was founded by and for people like me and for all people who share faith in Jesus Christ"—why should *he* be interested in an idea that will ultimately displace his story from the center of the American story?

I recognize that there are innumerable reasons to resist the kind of argument that I am making and as many positions within and around American society from which to look upon it with grave suspicion. Even in formulating the questions in the previous paragraph I am merely projecting what I imagine might make people suspicious given their different locations in the structures of power that shape American life. Worse still, I artificially imply that people with suspicions that are worth taking seriously fit neatly and singularly into bounded groups, when in fact many people sit uneasily with their presumptive groups or face bewildering challenges at the intersection of multiple groups. The truth is that I don't really know where people are coming from, what it's like to be in this situation or that situation, and I won't pretend to. I do know, however, that as people living in the United States we are, in a very real sense, in the same boat. And this is the basis for the level of generality at which this book is pitched. It is a book written primarily for people who live in the United States of America at the beginning of the twenty-first century.[22] And this is an audience of people who are divided even within their divisions and divided even further still—who are divided and divided and divided.

Thus I offer no incontestable reason why you should suspend the cynicism that you may harbor and consider what I envision here. I know that I can't quell preemptively the variety of suspicions you may have as a result of how you are positioned on this teetering ship. Nor do I presume to offer "what anyone who is reasonable will obviously accept," or "what all serious and mature people will recognize as laudable," or "what any rational being must endorse," or "what could only be rejected by someone who is pathological or an ideological extremist." Instead, my model is the good, long conversation that you have with a friend that you hope and expect is only one of many more to come.

As in a good, long conversation, I will try over the course of this book to expose myself fully, to express what I really care about, and to reflect self-critically on the contingencies that lead me to think and feel the way that I do. I imagine that you will talk back to me in your mind or with a pencil in the margins as you read. (All my own favorite books, perhaps especially those with arguments that I largely resist, are so congested with my marginalia that they look like tractates of Talmud.) After finishing the book, I do not aspire for you to say, "well, this problem has now been solved." I don't suffer from that particular delusion. I hope, instead, that you will walk away with some new thoughts and sensitivities, which you will respond to in your own scholarship or everyday life, and that your response, and responses to you in turn, will help us get closer to a vision of America we can all share.

Accepting my invitation to imagine an America worth loving will mean being outfitted with some gear that may look silly or dubious to you at first glance. It will involve entertaining controversial premises: that it is worth holding onto the nation and the state as appropriate horizons of political thought, that individual persons are the basic units of moral reasoning, that there ought to be time and space that is set aside for people to make choices and pursue activities in which government is loath to intervene, that it is worth trying to make the United States of America more just rather than abiding in it with contempt, tearing the whole thing down, or trying to dominate it through sheer will to power. Accepting my invitation will also mean artificially isolating problems that we face in the U.S. from their imbrication with problems around the world. And it will mean allowing yourself to see *the way things are* from a particular perspective, according to which we do not live in a "normal" world or a world that is "roughly as it should be"—we live in a world that is the morally grotesque offspring of injustice. Instead of arguing for these and other key premises before laying out my vision, I invite you first to sit for a while with the vision itself, to keep reading, to inhabit my responses to concerns that we may share, and then to reconsider whether or not these premises might be worth accepting pragmatically on behalf of the overall vision. To be sure, there are many reasons to resist even the few premises that I just mentioned. Cultivating national consciousness of any kind is worrisome given all of the bloodshed that has resulted from nationalist fervor in modern history. When a modern state is widely believed to serve a particular nation, there are inevitable exclusions and structures of majority/ minority conflict that are very troubling. Furthermore, thinking in terms of nations and states threatens to render invisible concerns that would be easier to appreciate from a perspective focused on the history of European colonialism and empire, which might divide the world instead into a global North and global South. Separating domestic problems of injustice in the U.S. from the larger problem of global injustice (in which the U.S. is deeply implicated) likewise risks missing the forest for the trees. And moral individualism notoriously threatens the conservation of cherished groups and traditions and is easily coopted by those who promote a "market mentality" that reinforces class hierarchies and straitjackets human potential. I'm asking you to trust that I am acutely aware of these concerns. I will do my best to address them and other related concerns as I go.

At the same time, I want to be straightforward about the fact that there will be fundamental limits to the persuasiveness of my argument for some readers. There are elements of the liberal tradition that I maintain, including some of the premises listed previously, that will never be acceptable to readers who are critical of liberalism from either the left or the right. I hope this is not a conversation stopper. And I admit that I am particularly keen to keep the conversation going with critics of liberalism from the left. This is not another book of liberal bravado presuming to scold the contemporary left over purported excesses of identity politics or political correctness. It is a sincere attempt to offer a chastened and reconstructed liberal vision of America that responds with sensitivity to fundamental challenges diagnosed in many cases by critics of liberalism from the left.

I do not expect that my responses will satisfy readers who are already committed critics of liberalism, but I deem the effort worthwhile nevertheless. In 2018 liberal democratic ideals in America are often invoked cynically, exploited by everyone from politicians to university administrators in the service of *neo*liberal norms. That is, terms like *justice* and *equality* are intoned as a hollow benediction before promoting the application of market values (efficiency, profitability, consumer satisfaction, unlimited growth, etc.) to all spheres of human life and the cultivation of a polity that cannot even imagine evaluating anything in any other way.[23] Liberal democratic thought in America is in grave danger of total

eviceration as a result of the encroaching normativity of neoliberal values. I submit to left critics of liberalism that it is better to have an earnest
and robust liberal democratic ally to stand with against white Christian
nationalism and economic exploitation in America than to wager on the
ultimate political triumph of the left over the right in a narrowly two-sided
confrontation.[24] This book offers a vision of liberalism that is meant to
help point the way toward such an alliance. I respectfully invite suspicious
readers to keep reading as a gesture of noncommittal unwarranted optimism about this possibility.[25]

Let me tell you more about the overall vision and where it comes
from. At some point in my twenties I started to read the work of Martha
Nussbaum. Here was a genuinely robust approach to political ethics that
resonated with my lingering liberal intuitions but also corrected fundamental problems at the heart of the liberal project. Nussbaum's capabilities approach to political justice had that elusive ring of plausibility for
me. With Nussbaum's approach, I could articulate with far greater clarity
and resolve *why* I thought America was not yet a just society. It equipped
me with a rough-and-ready ideal—the goal of a society where everyone is
guaranteed a lifetime of opportunities to exercise a set of fundamental
human capabilities at a basic level—that I could use to orient myself in
opposition to the status quo. I will explain Nussbaum's approach in detail
in subsequent chapters. It will suffice now simply to say that the capabilities approach reinvigorated my sense that we should stick with our modern liberal states and strive to make them more just and that we should
stick with the United States of America and try to make *it* more just.
Nussbaum's approach is the philosophical backbone holding up the vision
I present here, and I believe it is likewise the source of much of its strength
and courage.

And yet the ideal of political love that Nussbaum advocates, which she
persuasively argues is key to the just society that we should pursue, does
not sufficiently account for legacies of historical injustice, which will persist even in the best American society that we can realistically imagine.
Or, at least, this is what I argue in the chapters that follow. So my vision
builds on the theoretical foundation laid by Nussbaum: I imagine an
America where we see our neighbors and ourselves as vulnerable, dependent, human animals who long to flourish in a common life together

amidst institutions that guarantee the exercise of the fundamental human capabilities at a basic level.

But I add some distinctly explicit premises: America was born through injustice; racial, gender, sexual, class, and other forms of oppression have been the rule, not the exception in American history; every person in America should be presumed to be a product of historic injustice. My understanding of the importance of these additions reflects my engagement with the work of philosopher Charles Mills, who will also be a guiding presence throughout much of this book. Mills has undertaken a trenchant critique of liberalism over the past couple of decades, paying particular attention to its disavowed acceptance of the racially hierarchal status quo. His constructive call to "occupy liberalism!" is an inspiration to me, and I have tried to keep his critique of liberalism at the forefront of my vision in this book.[26]

Along with these additions to Nussbaum's approach, I add further that flourishing for people in a fraught society like the United States, even under the best possible circumstances, requires time and space *to play with* the legacies of historic injustice we carry. Furthermore, in the America I envision we are always on the lookout for examples of people playing in ways that illustrate how it is possible to hold onto interminable grudges and share political love at the same time. In my vision, we celebrate this sort of playing as part of what makes us a nation. The kind of playing that I have in mind is foreshadowed in Ginsberg's "America."

Early in the poem, Ginsberg evokes Walt Whitman, who famously reveled in the texture and embodiment of the American nation.[27] Ginsberg, likewise, identifies with America's worldly perfection instead of the perfection of some imagined Kingdom of God: "America after all it is you and I who are perfect not the next world." One can also hear Whitman when Ginsberg absorbs America into himself, when he hears himself—as America—singing, just before the first stanza break: "It occurs to me that I am America. / I am talking to myself again."[28] There is certainly disappointment and woe in the poem: "America why are your libraries full of tears?" But there is also strong identification. Ginsberg loves America in this poem. It is his own, and he cares about it as a part of himself even though its injustices, about which he is indignant, have been wildly out of his control: Tom Mooney, Sacco and Vanzetti, the Scottsboro boys.

It is in the context of this simultaneous love and indignation that Ginsberg does something that may seem incongruous to readers today. Toward the end of the poem, after he has reminisced about his childhood experiences at Communist cell meetings, he addresses the sense of impending conflict with Communist Russia and China that was potent in 1955–1956, when the poem was written. In order to understand what Ginsberg is doing here, it is important to consider the way in which he read this poem aloud in public for the first time at the Town Hall Theater in Berkeley, California. He read it to uproarious laughter. The "unfinished" version he read differs somewhat from the one that is later published in *Howl*. It goes like this:

> America you don't really want to go to war.
> America it's them bad Russians.
> Them Russians them Russians and them Chinamen. And them
>   Russians.
> The Russian's are power mad. The Russia wants to eat us alive.
> She wants to take our cars from out our garages.
> Her wants to take our factories.
> Her wants to corrupt our college girls.
> Her wants to put us all in slave labor camps.
> Her wants to emaciate us like skeletons.
> Her wants Malenkov or Bulganin or somebody to be our boss.
> Her wants to dictify us.
> Him big bureaucracy running our fillingstations.
> That no good. Ugh. Him make Indians learn read. Hah. Him
>   need niggers. Hoh.
> Her make us all work sixteen hours a day. Help.[29]

Commenting almost forty years later, he explained: "This first reading sounds like a stand-up comedy routine, and the audience response frames a cultural profile of the mid '50s."[30] In fact, Ginsberg was in the vanguard when he did his "stand-up" reading of "America" in 1956. Mort Sahl, who contributed significantly to the emergence of stand-up as a form, and whose comedy was groundbreaking in its biting political irreverence, was only just developing his sensibility hanging around Berkeley in 1955.[31] And Ginsberg is particularly ahead of the curve when he takes on the persona, as he reads the poem, of the kind of person who presumably *would* really want to go to war: the jingoistic anti-Communist. "America it's them bad Russians" marks the shift into this voice. Ginsberg's emphasis is on "bad," which he slightly elongates—"it's them baad Russians." The use of "them" also signals that his character is an uneducated person who speaks English poorly. I suspect that Ginsberg is trying to evoke an image that he has in his mind of an intellectually unsophisticated, white, Christian, conservative.

The vaguely pejorative "them Russians" morphs quickly into some kind of monstrous animal, "The Russia," that "wants to eat us alive." This compounds the stigmatizing language that is already mounting in his reference to "them Chinamen," a term that he has played with already in the poem: "Asia is rising against me. / I haven't got a chinamen's chance." The horrible creature is coming after our bourgeois comforts—our cars—and also our factories and our "college girls." And it wants to enslave us, turn us into emaciated victims of European totalitarianism, and subject us to the rule of Soviet dictators.

The slip into grammatically incorrect "them Russians" slips further into the even more jarring, because it is no longer even colloquial, "Her wants" litany. Then there is an abrupt gender switch, with "Him big bureaucracy running our fillingstations." I can't discern much significance in the gender switch, other than perhaps an indication that the preceding use of "her" is arbitrary. "That no good" then functions semantically as a summary judgment on the threat that he has just delineated, but with its "pidgin" syntax it also functions as a segue into "Him make Indians learn read." This line raises the stakes of Ginsberg's evocation of stigmatizing language about "them Russians" and "them Chinamen."

"Him make Indians learn read" connects fear of Communism to fear about what might happen if the empowerment of the oppressed were to disrupt the racial hierarchy in America. And it simultaneously mocks the way that Native Americans are caricatured in popular culture—this is Tonto from *The Lone Ranger* or some other such character. Ginsberg is mocking middling American anti-Communist hysteria and racism in American popular culture.

"Him need niggers" follows as a crescendo. It really deserves an exclamation mark given the emphasis that Ginsberg puts on the repugnant last word when he reads it. This is confirmed by the fact that the later published version exacerbates the implication that he's referring to large scary animals, "Him need big black niggers." This is how we talk and think and feel in America in 1956, says Ginsberg. This is what we print in our newspapers, what we project on our television screens, and presumably on our movie screens and in our magazines and in the other venues of our racial fantasyland.[32]

By taking on the persona of a bigoted "quintessential American" and in that role enunciating nasty racial stereotypes and epithets for both satirical and comic effect, Ginsberg is doing something that will not really become recognizable as a distinct cultural phenomenon in American stand-up comedy until Lenny Bruce emerges a few years later.[33] In a performance of his "How to Relax Your Colored Friends at Parties" routine at the Gate of Horn in Chicago in 1962, for instance, Bruce takes on the persona of a well-intentioned "white guy" at a party. The jazz musician Eric Miller, Bruce's personal friend and his partner in the bit, plays a "black guy." The white guy awkwardly introduces himself to the black guy and, after a pause, he barks—"that Joe Louis's a hellavu fighter!" He presumably lifts his glass, "Here's to Bo Jangles!"[34]

Then he reflects aloud, deciding that the black guy must know people in show business, and asks if he knows Aunt Jemima or the man on the Cream of Wheat box. Then he says, "Ya' know, I do a little construction here, and these Hebes—you're not Jewish are ya?—no offense, ya know what I mean, someone call me a Hebe I'll knock 'em right on their ass . . . I mean, I don't know how you feel about that integratin' stuff, I mean, I don't care what the hell a guy is as long as he keeps in his place, ya know what I mean?" There is a pause. "Here's to all the colored people!"

The bit turns on the incongruity between the white guy's intentions and his bungled actions. He clearly assumes that a compliment paid to a black sports icon will translate as a gesture of overall appreciation for black people, as if to say: "don't worry about me, I'm not a racist, I admire Joe Louis." The audience laughs at this remark because the first move of the well-intentioned white guy, who wants to "relax" his new "colored friend," is to call attention to his blackness, and to the issue of race, under the guise of banal sports conversation.

He bypasses the individuality of the man in front of him in order to treat him hospitably as "a black guy"—it is as if he is anxious to show his "hospitality to black guys" more than he wants to be hospitable to this particular guy. Bringing up "Hebes" makes the white guy look all the worse, as if he is willing to find a connection with the black guy on the basis of their common distaste for Jews. The bit is particularly funny here since the audience knows that Lenny Bruce is Jewish and uses his Jewishness frequently in his comedy. I will return to this routine in chapter 6.

What Ginsberg accomplishes in "America," and Lenny Bruce develops into an enduring cultural form, is to use a moment that is specifically set aside for art or entertainment—a poetry reading or stand-up comedy routine—to evoke nasty stereotypes and epithets in a comic mood and thereby give these materials a meaning that is entirely different from what they mean when they are used naively or instrumentally out in everyday life. This kind of rough play, I will argue, is what ought to be the fate of the hard feelings that will persist in even the best America that we can realistically imagine. Time and space that is set aside for this kind of play with the elements of culture that may be indefensible, crude, irrational, or unreasonable is crucially important to living well with the interminable emotional legacies of historic injustice.

To be clear, though, this is emphatically not a purgation theory. The idea is not that societies need to release the tension of historical grudges from time to time in poetry, comedy, and other contexts that are especially set aside. I am not making the trite suggestion that we allow people to "blow off some steam" from time to time. Nor am I suggesting that playing is a necessary palliative, like "bread and circuses," to subdue people stuck living in an unjust society. And I am not suggesting that we need opportunities for crude satire in order to target certain social and political problems for critique, but that once the problem is resolved we can retire the crude satire. Instead, the idea is that flourishing—living well—for many of us will involve activating, engaging, performing, expressing, and otherwise perpetuating nasty, rancorous words, ideas, and emotions in the context of play.

Consider Purim. For many Jews, a life that is going well, a flourishing Jewish life, will include the yearly celebration of Purim. On Purim the tradition is to read the Book of Esther, which recounts the plot of the Persian royal official Haman to exterminate the Jews. Celebrating Purim usually means reading the story aloud, blotting out the name of Haman with boos and noisemakers when it is read, and reveling in his execution at the end. But it's not just that Haman is executed at the end: the Jews in the Book of Esther rejoice in vengeful mass slaughter of their enemies and have Haman and his ten slain sons impaled on stakes.

And yet Purim is so essential to a flourishing Jewish life, according to the great medieval Jewish philosopher and legal authority Moses Maimonides, that in the messianic era, when we will no longer read the Prophets or the Writings in the Hebrew Bible, we will nevertheless continue to read Esther and celebrate Purim.[35] Maimonides describes the messianic era as a future time ruled by a Jewish king descended from King David, when there will be an abundance of all necessary resources, no war or envy or competition, and Jews will truly be free to live a life of Torah and wisdom.[36] But the most essential feature of the messianic era he describes as follows, quoting the ancient rabbinic sages: "[the emancipation] from our subjugation to the [gentile] kingdoms."[37] Nevertheless he writes, "Although all memories of the difficulties [endured by our people] will be nullified . . . [the celebration of] the days of Purim will not be nullified."[38]

For Maimonides, Purim is not a yearly opportunity to blow off steam for a paranoid people scarred by historical persecution. It is an essential part of a flourishing Jewish life. It is not a purging of energy that is produced by frustrating and stressful circumstances, which would be unnecessary under better circumstances. It is an essentially worthwhile activity that would be worth doing even under the best possible circumstances. It is what Jews will do even if all hostilities between Jews and gentiles are permanently ended and all that's left to do is live the Good Life in the utopian messianic era.

I assume that historically oppressed people in America will ritualize, fictionalize, perform, or otherwise play with Purim-like fantasies of victimization, revenge, superiority, grief, and much else, *even in the most just American society that we can realistically imagine.* And so will those people who will lose power and privilege as America becomes more just. In the vision of America that I present, we are held together by political love even as we persistently revive legacies of historical injustice in the times and spaces that are set aside for our "Purim" rituals.

Now, it is worth noting that Purim has long infuriated Christians. The Byzantine emperor Theodosius II, in an edict of 408, forbade Jews from burning Haman in effigy on a wooden post, assuming that Haman was really just a stand-in for Jesus who was being mocked on the cross.[39] In

1543, Martin Luther noted that Jews "love the book of Esther, which so well fits their bloodthirsty, vengeful, murderous greed and hope."[40] Legislation targeting Jews promulgated by Frederick the Great of Prussia in 1750 included a proviso that "they must refrain from all improper excesses in their festivals, particularly during the so-called Haman or Purim festival."[41] Predictably, some Jewish liberals by the end of the nineteenth century sought to get rid of Purim.

Claude Montefiore, a founder of liberal Judaism in England, wrote in 1888: "for those who regard Judaism as a religion pure and simple, and the Jews as merely the members of a religious brotherhood, any festival which . . . lacks inward and essential religious justification presents serious difficulties and objections. Such a festival is Purim."[42] He concluded by indicating that he would not be unhappy to see it eventually drop off of the Jewish calendar altogether.[43] In the liberal English society that Montefiore desired, undignified historic grievances would be carefully shorn. The Jew qua respectable adherent of liberal Judaism has no need for such barbaric rites. In my vision of America, by contrast, Jews feel welcome to indulge their Purim perversity and everyone else feels welcome to indulge their equivalent.

In fact, as I imagine progress, the better we do at building just institutions in America, the more rage, vulgarity, and horror we are likely to see in the times and spaces that are set aside for play. I'm talking about nasty stuff that's gonna be racial, sexual, sadistic, masochistic, nauseating, bewildering, hilarious, cacophonous, and creepy in ways that will make a lot of us uncomfortable. This is not necessarily the sort of stuff that one usually expects would thrive in the very best American society that we can realistically imagine. So this is a risky vision. And I promise to worry about its risks with you as the argument unfolds. I am personally worried about the risks and I am very aware that a person's tolerance for the unpleasant ways that other people play will depend significantly on the extent to which that person feels respected outside of the play frame.

But while I recognize that it is a risky vision, I still believe it is a compelling long-term vision for America, and one that is also particularly suitable to the current political moment. Since the election of Donald Trump to the presidency, it is especially easy to imagine that there are rural white Christian Americans who harbor deep distrust and resentment toward blacks, Jews, Hispanics, gays, transgender people, Muslims, and others and fantasize about an America where they have all somehow disappeared. It is likewise easy to imagine that there are black, Jewish, Hispanic, gay, transgender, Muslim, and other Americans who harbor deep distrust and resentment toward rural white Christians and fantasize about an America where *they* have all somehow disappeared. And then there are the nasty ideas that some black people harbor about Hispanics, and some Hispanics harbor about Muslims, and some Muslims harbor about gays. And there are ugly internecine and intersectional hopes, too: wishing for the final supersession of the black church over all minority black religions, wishing for the final eradication of Jewish conservatives, wishing for Mexican Americans to count as the presumptive representatives of the homogenizing category "Hispanics," and so on. Of course, there are also people who fit into and blur multiples of these and other clunky categories and are stuck in and across their fault lines. After all, a person can be black, Hispanic, Muslim, and transgender all at the same time. I offer a vision of America where we can forge bonds of political love through just political institutions, even as our unforgiving emotions, perverse fantasies, and ambivalent identifications are able to thrive when we are at play.

This vision depends heavily on the idea of psychosocial processes of "framing." As the sociologist Eviatar Zerubavel explains, "Framing is the act of surrounding situations, acts, or objects with mental brackets that basically transform their meaning by defining them as a game, a joke, a symbol, or a fantasy. . . . A frame is characterized not by its contents but rather by the distinctive way in which it transforms the contents' meaning."[44] Erving Goffman, in his groundbreaking work on frame analysis, explains how a person can "key" activities with interactional conventions that drastically transform the meaning of those activities. "A keying," Goffman writes, "performs a crucial role in determining what it is we think is really going on."[45] It is because of keying that an observer can view an activity that might look troubling, like fighting, and answer the question "What is it that's going on here?" with the answer "They're only playing."[46]

For my vision to seem plausible we will have to be able to imagine that people who live in America can switch continuously between at least two frames. Within one frame, the "political frame," they see themselves and each other as "citizens" (according to a modified version of Nussbaum's idea of the citizen): vulnerable, dependent, compassionate, human animals who have a profound stake in choice, whose good includes the good of every other, and who carry a legacy of historic injustice. As will become clear, by using the term *citizen* I do not mean to differentiate between people who have U.S. citizenship and those who do not. The concept of the citizen that I refer to here is a guiding contrivance meant to help clarify how we might see ourselves and others in the best version of American society we can realistically imagine. If it is a helpful contrivance, it will guide the way we approach every person living within the United States regardless of their official citizenship status.

Within the other frame, the "play frame," people should be able to see themselves and each other through a lens colored by whatever ideas and emotions they need and want to, however perverse they might be.[47] I will elaborate on how this works extensively in subsequent chapters, where I explain the "domain of play" and how it relates to the "domain of the political." What is crucial to appreciate here is this: if we dare to pursue a more just society, then we should be prepared to find that the historically oppressed, when they are empowered by justice, will never forget their historical oppression. We should also be prepared to find that those who lose power as a result of a society becoming more just will never forget the loss. If we can imagine these fraught memories thriving together in the domain of play (where people see each other within the play frame) while simultaneously political love thrives in the domain of the political (where people see each other within the political frame), then we can imagine a society that is worth pursuing and worth loving.

This kind of playing can be rough. It can be *nasty*. And we would have to learn as a society how to differentiate between what belongs in the domain of play and what belongs in the domain of the political. The 2016 election suggests that many of us do not yet know how to do this well. But if we can make room for our irreconcilable emotions and perverse habits of play in our vision of America, then I believe we can open a new path toward broadly shared political love.

To be sure, I will have to explain why rough play and political love do not ultimately contradict each other sufficiently to render the whole project self-defeating. One reason to think that it is indeed a project worth pursuing is already right in front of us: Ginsberg's poem. It is full of resentment, indignation, distrust, mockery and satire, and some plain goofing off. But it is no less full of love, and concern, and commitment. Unlike a solely vengeful Purim celebration that we might conjure in our minds (Purim is not nearly as vengeful as it could be in America these days, since it is so often meant to be family-friendly), Ginsberg's poem is as loving as it is excoriating. In both versions the poem ends:

> America is this correct?
> I'd better get right down to the job.
> It's true I don't want to join the Army or turn lathes in precision
>   parts
> factories, I'm nearsighted and psychopathic anyway.
> America I'm putting my queer shoulder to the wheel.

Without negating the resentment, indignation, satire, and so on in the rest of the poem, Ginsberg ends by expressing that *he cares*. This country, America, is *his* problem. And he's prepared to get serious. Perhaps not like the conventional image of the patriotic hero would have it: as a soldier in the Army. Instead, he will put his queer shoulder to the wheel. He will write his poetry and show us how it is possible for *us*—for *our particular nation*—to hold together, all at the same time, genuine political love and genuinely interminable historical grudges, intergroup antipathies, and so on. Instances of play that show us how this is possible are the key monuments to the new political love. The poets, comedians, artists, performers, and thinkers of all kinds that can play this way are its heroes.

The argument of this book will unfold as follows. Chapter 1 explores the clashing emotions between groups in America and the need for political emotions that we can all share. I turn to Martha Nussbaum's account of political emotions as just the sort that we need. I explain and endorse her account of political love, but I also suggest that it is not sufficient. It is not sufficient because it does not account for what I call "the fact of fraught societies." Chapters 2 and 3 are devoted to explaining this idea. The fact of fraught societies is the fact that three irresolvable problems will persist even in the best America that we can realistically imagine. I call these the problem of remainders, the problem of reproduction, and the missing link problem.

Chapter 2 focuses on the problem of remainders. This is the problem that nasty words, epithets, stereotypes, and caricatures will linger interminably in the popular culture of a free society and will forever exacerbate distrust and resentment between groups. The problem of reproduction, which is addressed in chapter 3, is that people will see it as part of a good and meaningful life to reproduce historical grudges and intergroup antipathies even when they are prosperous and secure in American society. Indeed, some people will actively strive to impart these emotions to future generations as essential to their heritage. Chapter 3 also addresses the missing link problem: our incorrigible desire for the "perfect justice" of angels, which is forever doomed to clash with our interminable status as products of historical injustice. A dangerous temptation will always exist to set oneself up as the "missing link" between the dark past and a perfectly just future, to imagine that we can eradicate the fraught emotional legacies of history. This temptation poses a constant threat to political love in America.

The problem of remainders, the problem of reproduction, and the missing link problem together amount to the fact of fraught societies and reinforce each other in multiple ways. The point of chapters 2 and 3 is to show that an ideal of political love in America will be realistic and worth striving for only if it can be sustained despite the fact of fraught societies. In chapter 4, I turn to the role of "play" in making political love sustainable under such conditions. I present my own political conception of play that draws from a wide range of fields, including philosophy, psychology, and anthropology. I situate my account of play within Nussbaum's list of central human capabilities. Guaranteeing the capability of play, I argue, ought to include affording genuine opportunities for people to build, enter, abide, and flourish in the domain of play.

In chapter 5, I explain how the domain of play and the domain of the political are presumed to relate to one another. The key to their dynamic relationship is the idea of the "public cultural critic." The public cultural critic offers, from her perch in the domain of the political, interpretations of what bubbles up from the domain of play and makes a case for what this sort of playing *means* for who we are as a nation. We should aspire for everyone in America to feel empowered to take on the role of the public cultural critic. In my view, this is a significant justification for expending public resources to bolster the humanities in higher education. The public cultural critic helps to narrate the moral history of the nation and construct an ever-contestable sense of "we" in the process of interpreting how we play. Chapter 5 also clarifies how we can differentiate between play and politics in everyday life. And it addresses the specific ways that play mitigates each of the three problems that constitute the fact of fraught societies. It concludes with a brief discussion of the distinctive mitigating role of humorous play.

In chapters 6, 7, and 8 I take on the role of the public cultural critic and frame as play a set of materials produced by Jewish Americans after the Second World War. Why this time period and these examples? In the 1960s, Jews found themselves in a distinct position in American economic, cultural, and political life. Those who were born in the U.S. and were children during World War II would likely have sensed (or have experienced directly) the intensified stigmatization of Jews as a racial threat to white America. And they would have been aware of the persecution of Jews as a racial menace in Europe. But by the 1960s, these same Jews were more welcome than ever to live as respectable citizens of "white America." Jews in this period hovered uneasily between the allure of whiteness and memories of nonwhiteness, between privilege and paranoia, between appreciating public gestures of "interfaith" respect for Judaism and resenting the marginalization of secular Jewishness.

In this position, they were confronted directly with the question: what should become of our historical grudges, distrust, and anxiety now that we seem to have such an open invitation to thrive? Many Jews responded by plumping in one direction or another. For instance, by diving into whiteness or Judaism—they didn't want to hover. Chapters 6, 7, and 8 interpret a different response: playing with stigmatized Jewishness, idealized Americanness, identification with blackness, resentment toward the goyim, whiteness, privilege, paranoia, and much else, within the institutions of American popular culture that flourished after the war. These chapters focus on popular virtuosic play that emerged from the distinct position of Jews in this period. On my interpretation, these are examples of play that evoke our capacity to hold together, all at the same time, genuine political love and genuinely interminable historical grievances.

In chapter 6, I interpret the stand-up comedy of Lenny Bruce as inviting his mixed (Jewish and gentile) audiences into sophisticated play with human animality, Jewish resentment, fraught group differences, derogatory epithets, and much else—all the while cultivating a distinct, albeit transient, intimacy. I argue that the simultaneous intimacy and humorous framing of fraught materials that Lenny Bruce provoked intones a note of hope about our capacity for political love despite the fact of fraught societies.

In chapter 7, I show how Philip Roth's *Portnoy's Complaint* plays similarly. But Roth's book is a massively popular American novel. And as a remarkable work of literary fiction, the playing that it invites is far more sophisticated than what Bruce was able to solicit on stage and on his records. From my perch as public cultural critic, I argue that *Portnoy's Complaint* ought to be fastened as an enduring point in the public political culture of America. That is, we should treat it as an important snapshot of play that we return to over and over again in order to play *together* with the fact of fraught societies. I claim that treating it this way would contribute to our becoming a "we" that is capable of sharing political love despite the fact of fraught societies.

In chapter 8, I narrate the groundbreaking television program *All in the Family* into the moral history of America as a massively popular instance of play with potent emotions that boiled over in the 1970s. I connect *All in the Family* back to Lenny Bruce. Norman Lear, who created the show, noted in an interview in 1972 to the *Los Angeles Times*, "If you're looking for where *All in the Family* began in American life . . . it began with Lenny Bruce."[48] While the show famously included satire of bigotry and "politically incorrect" language, I argue that it was important because it exhibited a desire and capacity to have feelings of love, anger, and resentment all at the same time about America's original core group—its white, Anglo-Saxon, Protestant "fathers." Reflecting back on it now, we can build from it a collective self-awareness that we, Americans, desire and are capable of having these feelings all at the same time.

In a concluding epilogue, I summarize the vision of the book and explain briefly what I imagine will happen to religion in the America that I think we should strive to become. I suggest that we stop distinguishing between religion and nonreligion in laws and policies, as well as when we perceive ourselves and others within the domain of the political. I claim that the distinction between religion and nonreligion impedes our capacity to cultivate political love despite the fact of fraught societies. When taking a political perspective, we would do better, in my view, to differentiate only between the pursuit of political justice, the pursuit of "nonpublic projects" (which can overlap with the former), and play.

1

JEWISHNESS, RACE, AND POLITICAL EMOTIONS

There is a classic scene in Spike Lee's 1989 film *Do the Right Thing* when Mookie, played by Lee, tries to talk to his coworker Pino, played by John Turturro, about his racial hypocrisy. Mookie is black and works at Sal's pizzeria in Brooklyn with Pino, who is Italian. Mookie presses Pino to explain the fact that all of his favorite sports figures and entertainers are black, given that he constantly expresses racist attitudes: "Pino, all you ever talk about is nigger this, nigger that, when all your favorite people are so-called niggers." The conversation goes nowhere, and the scene breaks off in frustration. Then there is a cut to Mookie, facing the camera directly, unloading in a slur-filled rant about Pino: "You dago, wop, guinea, garlic-breath, pizza-slinging, spaghetti-bending, Vic Damone, Perry Como, Luciano Pavarotti, Sole Mio, non-singing motherfucker!"

Then we cut to Pino facing the camera ranting: "You gold-teeth-gold-chain-wearing, fried-chicken-and-biscuit-eating, monkey, ape, baboon, big thigh, fast-running, high-jumping, spear-chucking, three-hundred-sixty-degree-basketball-dunking *titsun* spade *moulan yan*! Take your fucking piece of pizza and go the fuck back to Africa." Then Stevie, who is Puerto Rican: "You little slanty-eyed, me-no-speaky-American, own-every-fruit-and-vegetable-stand-in-New-York, bullshit Reverend Sun Myung Moon, Summer Olympics '88, Korean kickboxing son of a bitch!" Then the white cop, Officer Gary Long: "You Goya bean-eating, fifteen in a car, thirty in an apartment, pointed shoes, red-wearing, Menudo, *mira-mira*, Puerto Rican cocksucker. Yeah, you!" Then Sonny, who is Korean: "'It's cheap, I got a good price for you!' Mayor Koch, 'How I'm doing?' chocolate-egg-cream-drinking, bagel-and-lox B'nai B'rith Jew asshole!" The barrage of rants only stops when radio DJ Mister Señor Love Daddy, who generally presides over the film with wisdom, intervenes: "Yo! Hold up! Time out! Time out! Y'all take a chill! Ya need to cool that shit out! And that's the double truth."

Do the Right Thing is a landmark of rough play in American public culture. With this film and others, especially his post-9/11 film *25th Hour*, Spike Lee has established himself as one of the artistic heroes of the new political love. In the scene I have just described, the juxtaposition of Mookie, Pino, Stevie, Officer Long, and Sonny screaming racial slurs and stereotypes at the camera has the simultaneous effect of highlighting the fraught differences between these characters and what they share in common. Whatever their differences, each character has simmering in his gut some set of nasty, unfair, dehumanizing thoughts and emotions about people in another group. I will investigate the ultimately humanizing effect of this verbal collage of dehumanization in chapter 5. For the moment, though, I want to focus on the shift in mood and language from Mookie's attempt at an earnest discussion about race with Pino to his unrestrained rant and the rants that follow.

When the conversation between Mookie and Pino starts, over the cigarette machine in *Sal*'s, it has an intimate quality. The lighting is soft, and so is the contemplative jazz score in the background. When the conversation breaks off, the music shuts off too, and we're in the street with Mookie spouting furiously. We see Mookie reaching out to Pino with curiosity and generosity. Then we see him enraged, attacking Pino with derogatory language about Italians. The rant is functionally a monologue to the film's audience, but I do not think we should interpret it as revelatory of Mookie's singular authentic self. Neither earnest Mookie nor ranting Mookie is "the true Mookie." He is both. And his capacity for love and friendship across group boundaries is not incompatible with the derogatory resentment that he carries with him about Pino and maybe all Italians in the Bedford-Stuyvesant neighborhood of Brooklyn.[1] Like Radio Raheem, who wears the words spelled out on enormous rings, one on each hand, Mookie carries *both* love and hate ready at hand.

The search for political love in America is the search for the earnest-ness, curiosity, generosity, and solicitousness we can share despite the grudges that we will inevitably harbor against each other. It is a readiness to slip into the mood of the contemplative jazz sax that plays while Mookie reaches out to Pino.[2] But political love, like the soft mood in the film just before the rant scene, must have an emotional basis that is different from the emotions that ultimately burst out as derogatory rage. The core argu-ment of this book is that broadly shared political love is possible if all kinds of Americans can cultivate it together in the common domain of the polit-ical, even as we express our divisive unmitigated rage creatively in the domain of play. In this chapter I will explain what I mean by "political emotions," how they differ from other kinds of emotions, and why we need to cultivate political love in particular. I rely heavily on Martha Nuss-baum's overall approach to political emotions and political justice. Though at the end of this chapter I will argue that her account is not yet sufficient and requires additional elements, which I will develop in the subsequent chapters.

A key element of Nussbaum's account is that emotions involve cogni-tive processes of perception and judgment and always relate directly to something that is important to the individual having the emotion. If I am hiking in the woods and I hear breaking sticks and rustling leaves, my judgment that it is a charging bear and that my life—which is very important to me—is in danger constitutes the emotion of fear. I may *feel* feverish and hysterical or cold and inert, but the emotion is the percep-tual judgment of a dangerous object threatening something I care about. This is important because emotions, on this account, centrally involve how we perceive the world and others in it. I heard the noise *as* a threat-ening bear. If I heard it, instead, *as* a gentle fawn then I would not have the same emotion.

When Mookie reaches out to Pino, he sees him as a person who might be able to open up, might be willing to have an earnest, self-critical con-versation. When Mookie is ranting at the camera, by contrast, he sees Pino as a "dago, wop, guinea, garlic-breath," etc. This shift in perceptual judg-ment is also an emotional shift. Emotions involve *seeing-as.* The broadly shared political love that I promote in this book is, then, a way of seeing—or, more generally, a way of perceiving and judging. When I describe it as "political," I mean that it is supposed to be a way of perceiving and judging oneself and others that is open and inviting to all members of society regardless of however else they perceive and judge themselves and others.

I will explain this sense of "political" at length in what follows. What is important to register here is that there is no natural or neutral way of seeing the world and others. We shift around in response to context. But we are not mere passive respondents to context; we can also change it. And we can cultivate habits of perceptual judgment in certain contexts, while recognizing that we will see things differently in other contexts. We can shift the way that Mookie shifts. Since we are born from injustice, we will likely wear the ring of resentment on one hand, but this doesn't mean that we can't also wear the ring of political love on the other. If we want to live well together, then we should try to develop a way of seeing each other and ourselves—an American vision—that we can all share.

SEEING IN BLACK AND WHITE

There are a lot of good reasons to think that calling for such a vision is naive. After all, liberals have long counseled a posture of dignified civility and patience while deep structures of racial, gender, and other kinds of injustice remain intact. How can one be sure that the vision I'm offering is not yet another liberal ruse that ultimately functions to distract the historically oppressed from "the true picture of their situation"? In this section I will investigate a major reason to be skeptical about the possibility of cultivating widely shared political love in America: the integral role of white supremacy in our core political institutions and the tight hold that white supremacy has on how we perceive and judge each other.

A serious reckoning with and critique of white supremacy is a prerequisite for any legitimate American ideal. But more than this is needed if we would dare try to move forward together as a nation. Moving forward requires a bold shift of attention to new and compelling political emotions—a shift to Mookie's solicitous way of seeing Pino. As we will see, a "shift of attention" is needed because an absolute repudiation and eradication of emotions that are tainted by the history of white supremacy is

impossible. The meaning of these fraught emotions is simply too conten-
tious and too wrapped up in who we are and what we care about. We
need a political ideal of love to pursue together precisely because, inevitably, we will sometimes shift back to seeing each other according to the
ugly visions that haunt us and ranting about each other with Mookie,
Pino, Stevie, and the others on the street.

A skeptic about the prospect of broadly shared political love in America will rightly worry about the disturbing dissonance between the institutional "progress" claimed by liberals and the actual ways that people
continue to perceive and judge each other. If we have made great strides
in civil rights, in making sure that everyone is equal before the law, America is nevertheless still a place where racial oppression is pervasive. The
political philosopher Charles Mills has pointed out that in societies where
citizens are formally recognized as equal before the law, and minorities
are ostensibly protected from discrimination, there is a tendency to see
continuing racial animus as a mere remnant of retrograde attitudes that
will soon disappear.[3] But Mills explains that the very basis of our faith in
formal equality as a value, the idea of a "social contract," has functionally
served *from the very beginning* to establish and perpetuate a racially hierarchical way of perceiving and judging. According to Mills, continuing
instances of racial violence and exploitation are not merely lingering detri-
tus but are part of what liberal democracies in the West were designed to
protect. The social contract was designed to promise equality while perpetuating white supremacy.

The social contract is a classic idea in liberal political theory that says
we can best understand the rights and obligations of a society's members
once we decide what would be fair, mutually beneficial rules for cooperation in a society where every member is free, equal, independent, rational, and self-interested and resources are scarce for all. This is an idea at
the very root of American political thought, and it continues to inform
popular "common sense." Mills argues that we see only one side of the
coin when philosophers, political thinkers, activists, and others point to
the idea of a social contract in order to justify their political demands. The
social contract has always been integrally related to an equally deeply
rooted "Racial Contract"—the other side of the coin. The racial contract
is a set of assumptions that affirm the fundamental legitimacy of the

racially hierarchical status quo in which whites have disproportionate power nationally and globally over nonwhites.[4] It is usually unacknowledged and often disingenuously or delusionally disavowed.

According to Mills, the social contract tradition that animates the Declaration of Independence and the Declaration of the Rights of the Man and of the Citizen, and is echoed when people today "insist on their rights and freedoms and express their outrage at not being treated equally," was and remains presumptively for white men, by white men.[5] On this view, wherever the ideal social contract has threatened genuinely to overturn the racial contract it is the social contract that has relented. As long as the racial contract is upheld, the moral power of the social contract tradition will be constrained to benefit the racially hierarchical status quo—that is, to benefit white supremacy.

Mills argues, further, that white supremacy is significantly perpetuated by the fact that white people, who generally lack self-critical awareness of the racial contract, are apt to live in "an invented delusional world, a racial fantasyland."[6] This is very important because it impacts how we see each other. James Baldwin captured powerfully the dissonance between what white people in America tell themselves and what black people have witnessed in his 1962 essay, "Down at the Cross." "The American Negro," he wrote,

> has the great advantage of having never believed that collection of myths to which white Americans cling: that their ancestors were all freedom-loving heroes, that they were born in the greatest country the world has ever seen, or that Americans are invincible in battle and wise in peace, that Americans have always dealt honorably with Mexicans and Indians and all other neighbors or inferiors, that American men are the world's most direct and virile, that American women are pure. Negros know far more about white Americans than that.[7]

Mills has analyzed at length the social epistemology of "white ignorance": the cognitive blinders that allow white Americans to see their world, which is characterized by white dominance and nonwhite disadvantage, as a good and natural world where America is unproblematically worthy of admiration as a historical beacon of liberty.[8] In the "racial fantasylands" where white people imagine they live, Mills explains, there will be white mythologies, invented Orients, invented Africas, invented Americas, with a correspondingly fabricated population, countries that never were, inhabited by people who never were—Calibans and Tontos, Man Fridays and Sambos—but who attain a virtual reality through their existence in travelers' tales, folk myth, popular and highbrow fiction, colonial reports, scholarly theory, Hollywood cinema, living in the white imagination and determinedly imposed on their alarmed real-life counterparts.[9]

Mills decries these phenomena as central to the racial contract, "which requires a certain schedule of structured blindness and opacities in order to establish and maintain the white polity."[10]

For a good example of the kind of blindness and fantasy that I imagine Baldwin and Mills have in mind, let's go back to Neil Diamond. The song "Coming to America" opens the 1980 film *The Jazz Singer*. The opening scene captures exactly the sentiment that the song has always provoked in me: floods of people, funneling through New York City, in different kinds of clothes, with different kinds of faces, from around the world, but Americans all. This is the America that I was so proud of when I was a kid, the America of Ellis Island and the Statue of Liberty and the Lower East Side—the Jewish American homeland that is also the port where so many others have docked to join this great nation of immigrants.[11]

It never really occurred to me as a kid that the American immigrant story, which provoked such patriotic emotion, rather conspicuously excludes those who were brought to America as slaves, those who were here before the first European settlers arrived, and those who were swallowed up by the Texas annexation and the Treaty of Guadalupe Hidalgo. It certainly never would have crossed my mind that *The Jazz Singer* and *Fiddler on the Roof* and *Grease* and the *Rocky* movies—all staples of my childhood—were part of a "relocation of normative whiteness from what might be called Plymouth Rock whiteness to Ellis Island whiteness," as Matthew Frye Jacobson has argued.[12] In the 1970s, Jacobson writes, "there arose a new national myth of origins whose touchstone was Ellis Island . . . whose most far-reaching political conceit was the 'nation of immigrants.'"[13]

Jacobson offers an interpretation of *Rocky* that makes it an exemplary representation of the kind of "racial fantasyland" that Charles Mills describes. In *Rocky*, the grubby, endearing, underdog boxer, the "Italian Stallion" Rocky Balboa, rises up to take on the black, hot-shot reigning champ, Apollo Creed. It is the "white ethnic" Rocky who is underprivileged, struggling against the odds, in the film. Apollo Creed has all the spotlight, glamour, and power. Jacobson notes the emotional resonance of the film with the California Supreme Court's decision in *Bakke*, which ruled on behalf of a white medical school applicant who claimed that he was rejected unconstitutionally as a result of affirmative action. It was 1976, the same year that *Rocky* appeared in theaters.

"The *Bakke* case and the boxing film shared more than a historical moment," Jacobson writes, "they shared an ethos, a way of understanding the respective meanings of 'whiteness' and 'blackness' in post–Civil Rights America. If the white applicant had unjustly become an underdog under Title VI admissions practices, as the California court held, Rocky Balboa dramatizes precisely that underdog status in his titanic struggle to unseat the flashy and arrogant black champion, Apollo Creed."[14] The film ends with the inelegant Rocky making it through to the very last round against Apollo by virtue of sheer heart and chin. When it is announced in the background that Apollo wins by a split decision, Jacobson's analysis demands the conclusion that it is offered to the audience as an unjust decision.[15]

Rocky can thus be read to represent a post–civil rights racial resentment switcheroo in which it is whites who are legitimately aggrieved and unfairly disadvantaged under a regime of "black privilege."[16] As Jacobson notes, the absurd notion of "black privilege" was perpetuated through the 1980s by Ronald Reagan's mythic "Welfare Queen" rhetoric and by other such tropes.[17] These are the "white mythologies" that Mills writes about. Many more examples could be provided to bring us up to the present day.

From Mills's perspective, the exclusionary "nation of immigrants" ideal in the opening song of *The Jazz Singer* and the white resentment in *Rocky* look like clear examples of the ever-changing rationalizations provided by popular culture for the perpetuation of the racial contract. The situation, finally, amounts to this:

> Both globally and within particular nations . . . white people, Europeans and their descendants, continue to benefit from the Racial Contract, which creates a world in their cultural image, political states differentially favoring their interests, an economy structured around the racial

exploitation of others, and a moral psychology (not just in whites but sometimes in nonwhites also) skewed consciously or unconsciously toward privileging them, taking the status quo of differential racial entitlement as normatively legitimate, and not to be investigated further.[18]

The implication of Mills's critique is that contemporary political thinkers who are concerned with injustice but do not confront the racial contract directly are merely running in circles on the track of white supremacy. There can be no forward movement until the critique of the racial contract is finally devastating and becomes foundational for all future political thought. I agree. It is morally repulsive to suggest that the current overwhelming power of Europeans (in Europe, in its former colonies, and beyond) is anything like a reasonably just historical outcome. The current distribution of power around the globe is a result of grotesque historical injustice, including racial injustice, and any political theory that fails to acknowledge this at its core, foregrounding it, is morally illegitimate.

Nevertheless, Mills does think forward movement is possible. He thinks that genuinely constructive political thought can emerge and make headway after the racial contract is truly exposed and repudiated. Mills's project is ultimately "pro-Enlightenment"—"it criticizes the social contract from a normative base that does not see the ideals of contractarianism themselves as necessarily problematic but shows how they have been betrayed by white contractarians."[19] Mills has recently called on critics of white supremacy to "occupy liberalism," arguing that "liberalism should not be contemptuously rejected by radicals but retrieved for a radical agenda."[20] In search of a "black radical liberalism," Mills is now ready to ask: "What principles would you choose . . . to dismantle a racialized basic structure and a racialized social ontology founded on a racial contract?"[21] Justifiably unforgiving about America's history of racial exploitation and the "racial liberalism" that has lent it legitimacy, Mills has not given up on the pursuit of justice in America and a black radical liberalism that can guide us toward it.[22]

A more despairing view can be found in what Frank Wilderson describes as the approach of "Afro-pessimists" who insist, "though Blacks are indeed sentient beings, the structure of the entire world's semantic field . . . is sutured by anti-Black solidarity."[23] Unlike Mills, whose analysis is structured around a white/nonwhite dichotomy, Wilderson, as an

Afro-pessimist, views the fundamental dichotomy as white/black, or, more precisely, as Human/Black. "The race of Humanism (White, Asian, South Asian, and Arab)," he writes, "could not have produced itself without the simultaneous production of that walking destruction which became known as the Black. Put another way, through chattel slavery the world gave birth and coherence to both its joys of domesticity and to its struggles of political discontent; and with these joys and struggles the Human was born, but not before it murdered the Black, forging a symbiosis between the political ontology of Humanity and the social death of Blacks."[24]

According to Wilderson, a historical process of forming what we now call humanity started in the thirteenth century with the broadly agreed upon negation of African people as the "Blackness," the nothingness, against which human social and political reality would be made possible.[25] Whatever conflicts over power and resources may have marked interactions between whites, Asians, and Arabs since that time, these members of "the Human" have always maintained their unspoken "anti-Black solidarity." Wilderson writes, provocatively, that "the essence of *being* for the White and non-Black position" is finally (quoting Frantz Fanon), "simple enough one has only not to be a nigger."[26] This, he explains, is "ontology scaled down to a global common denominator."[27]

Wilderson has no interest in alliances or coalitions that unite nonwhite people against white supremacy. In the United States, "Latinos and Asians," for instance, "stand in *conflictual relation* to the Settler/Master . . . They do not register as antagonists."[28] For Wilderson, the human/black dichotomy is simply the master/slave dichotomy and we should "think of today's Blacks in the United States as Slaves and everyone else (with the exception of Indians) as Masters."[29] Disputes that pit Latinos and Asians, for example, against whites are merely "conflicts" between those who enjoy the presumption of humanity. Only the ontological opposition between black and nonblack, which is the deep foundation of American social and political reality, is a truly fundamental "antagonism."[30] On these grounds, Wilderson likewise refers approvingly to Frantz Fanon when he "dismisses the presumed antagonism between Germans and Jews by calling the Holocaust 'little family quarrels,' recasting with this single stroke the German/Jewish encounter as a conflict rather than an antagonism. Fanon returns the Jew to his or her rightful position—a position *within* civil society animated by an ensemble of Human discontents."[31]

From Wilderson's perspective, to toil in the "little family quarrels" between whites, Asians, Latino/as, Arabs, Jews, Germans, gays, straights, men, women, and so on, is to evade and continue to exploit the deeper antagonism between human and black.[32] Indeed, Wilderson's approach commits him in principle to offer no positive vision or prescription of any kind for the future. Instead, drawing again from Frantz Fanon, he urges his readers "to start 'the end of the world,' the 'only thing . . . worth the effort of starting.'"[33] His task is only to proclaim, "we *must* be free of air, while admitting to knowing no other source of breath."[34] The racial fantasylands and systematic blindness that Mills identifies as key features of the racial contract are structures we can work to demolish on behalf of political ideals that we can meanwhile try to improve. The ontology of humanity/blackness that Wilderson perceives, by contrast, leaves us mired in our inertia, whether human or black.

I side with Mills and share his assumption that it is still worth promoting liberal ideas, as long as we build into them vigilant recognition and intolerance of the racial contract and other prominent ideological obstacles that stand in the way of justice. This means, in part, rejecting the comforting notion that it is merely the lingering prejudices of unenlightened individuals that still pose a problem. The Racial Contract, as I think of it, is the system of laws, policies, voting districts, policing methods, real estate practices, economic structures, educational establishments, and other institutions, which, altogether, consistently affirm the fundamental *tolerability* of disadvantaged, invisible, suffering nonwhite people. And it is also the way of seeing oneself and others that makes this system tolerable. The ideal of political love I want to conjure will have to be embedded in an overall political view that makes this tolerability intolerable.

But the critique of white supremacy alone is not a sufficient basis for a broadly shareable ideal of political love. If we are ready to look together for an American vision that we can all share—and I recognize that it's a big "if"—we need more than the diagnostic tools of criticism. The critique of white supremacy is absolutely essential to identifying major obstacles in the way of justice. But I think we also need a rough-and-ready vision of what these obstacles impede. To be sure, it is a general characteristic of critical thought that it focuses on what we presumptively oppose and often leaves unanswered questions about what we should support. But there is also a problem with too singular a reliance on the binary terms that characterize the critique of white supremacy.

In the early 1990s, Kimberlé Williams Crenshaw brought this concern into focus with her groundbreaking work on intersectionality.[35] Crenshaw explains how antiracist advocacy could sometimes work at cross-purposes with feminist advocacy, and that mainstream antiracist and feminist positions taken together were often structurally blind to women of color. In the case of political activism surrounding sexual violence, she writes, "The primary beneficiaries of policies supported by feminists and others concerned about rape tend to be white women; the primary beneficiaries of the Black community's concern over racism and rape, Black men. Ultimately, the reformist and rhetorical strategies that have grown out of antiracist and feminist rape reform movements have been ineffective in politicizing the treatment of Black women."[36] The light of antiracism alone is not sufficiently illuminating to see all of the injustice in America. Nor is it enough simply to add the light of feminism. We desperately need both, but we need more too.[37]

Patriarchy, Christian hegemony, heteronormativity, class exploitation, and critiques thereof relate in complex and sometimes contradictory ways to each other and to the critique of white supremacy.[38] I assume that these and other oppressive ideologies are built into America's core political institutions and present a constant threat to justice. It is a central task of contemporary political thought to further understand how they work and how to thwart them. But no single framework of ideology-critique can be trusted to dominate our assessment of American injustice or our imaginations when we imagine a more just America. After all, as scholars of intersectionality have amply shown: no one is ever situated comfortably on only one side of one binary like black/white, and some situations are not binary at all.

When a single critical perspective is allowed to dominate our collective efforts to envision a more just America, it is inevitable that somebody's situation or some group will be left out of the vision. As it turns out, for instance, too narrow a focus on the critique of white supremacy elides the complexity of Jewishness in American culture. It also reinforces the tendency of modern societies with Christian majorities to demand that Jews either contract and contort themselves into a pious "religious minority" or disappear as a distinctive population altogether. I will explain this elision and demand in the next section. But I will also readily admit that I do not come to the defense of threatened Jewishness as a disinterested theorist testing the limits of ideology-critique. I have a special concern for Jews and Jewishness in America. I'm a Jew. And that's the kind of Jew I am.

And while it turns out that I have some defensible reasons to save my own fourth-generation Jewish immigrant kitsch from repudiation by the critique of white supremacy, I still have to admit that these will not be reasons that everyone can accept. Even if I think that there are good reasons to make visible the complex Jewishness that the critique of white supremacy often renders invisible, I can't expect others to make this a top priority. Indeed, my prioritization of Jewishness will undoubtedly look perverse, or like an egregious disavowal of privilege, from a variety of perspectives. What is more, as I will explain, sometimes the way that I see Jewishness *is perverse*. That is, I have no good reason to believe others will want to see it the way I do and significant reasons to believe others will judge my way of seeing it unfair, obscene, or otherwise unjustifiable.

The crucial point here is that what counts as a blind spot, disavowal, fantasyland, or fundamental antagonism in an individual's point of view, and how we should rank these according to egregiousness, is irresolvably contestable. The picture of political love that I want to offer will have to somehow oppose the institutional reproduction of racial and other forms of injustice, while nevertheless allowing our conflicting or even perverse ways of seeing each other and our society to persist without resolution.

DISAPPEAR, BE RELIGIOUS, OR BE A PROBLEM

Let's return again to Neil Diamond's "Coming to America." What was once my childhood anthem of Jewish American immigrant patriotism, after Jacobson's critique looks more like an anthem of Jewish succession into American white supremacy. If we accept this critique, we might think that in order to avoid perpetuating white supremacy *The Jazz Singer* must be fundamentally repudiated. It must be dumped into a pile that presumably includes D. W. Griffith's *The Birth of a Nation* and other artifacts of oppression that are viewed with embarrassment and scorn.

But there are alternative interpretations of the cultural meaning of "Coming to America." Jonathan Freedman, in *Klezmer America:*

Jewishness, Ethnicity, Modernity, recounts the use of the song at mass rallies across the country against anti-immigration legislation, which were led and populated largely by Latino/a Americans in 2006. Drawing on an article in the *Los Angeles Times* by Ann Powers entitled "Latinos Give New Voice to Neil Diamond Anthem," Freedman explains that the song found its way to these activists through its use in the 1987 Cheech and Chong movie *Born in East L.A.,* "where it serves as an ironic musical counterpoint to a comic scene portraying a mad rush of Mexicans across the border."[39]

Some activists apparently opposed using the song, wanting instead to use music that is more closely associated with the struggles of demonstrators gathering to rally.[40] Among those opposing the song, some also wanted to distance themselves from Ellis Island whiteness and the Jewish focus and complex racial politics of *The Jazz Singer* movies (in the original 1927 version the main character infamously uses blackface in his routines).[41] On the other hand, advocates for the song saw a great advantage in connecting their struggle to the emotionally potent Ellis Island narrative—both in terms of inspiring the protestors to make their claim as *real* Americans and in terms of the effect on the white majority audience that would see coverage of the rallies.[42] Regardless of which view one takes, the point made by Freedman is that "these marchers remind us that the process of culture making at its most elemental and dynamic proceeds through virtually innumerable such acts of appropriation, revision, counterrevision, and outright theft, ones whose ends are never wholly predictable from their origins."[43]

On this reading, "Coming to America" is not a stable reinforcer of Ellis Island whiteness, but a pliant cultural substance that can be shaped and shifted in unpredictable ways. Of course, from Wilderson's perspective, the use of the song will indicate the ease with which cultural capital can be transferred among nonblacks, despite their "conflictual relations." Or it will show how some Latino/a Americans are, in fact, embracing the politics of "becoming white." But what Freedman brings to our attention is that a stark white/black or white/nonwhite framework of analysis renders almost entirely invisible the complex uses, iterations, and revisions of Jewishness in America.

While Friedman does not, in the end, contest "the narrative of Jews' accession to whiteness," he nevertheless wants to make visible all that is

left out of this narrative and to make more imaginable alternative varieties of Jewishness that are otherwise foreclosed by the presumption of tele-
ological whiteness.[44] He points specifically to the association of Jews
with the Near East, the exotic, and the erotic, as well as gender ambiguity
in the representation of Jewish men, the fraught connection of Jews to the
Holy Land, and prevalently attributed Jewish melancholia.[45] He sets as his
task to showcase Jewish American cultural expression that affirms and
promotes "all the things that their rejection of Orientalizing ascriptions
forced Jews to jettison: exoticism, foreignness, alterity, queerness in both
the original and the current sense of the word."[46]

In his attempt to rescue the Jewishness that is otherwise erased by the
black-white dichotomy, Freedman boldly goes against the nearly overwhelming forces that have long pressed Jews to repudiate their own sense
of difference and admit that they are just white people in America. As Eric
Goldstein recounts in *The Price of Whiteness*, Jews have faced severe pressure to accede to whiteness from white America since the nineteenth
century and from black America since the 1960s.[47] And yet, while Jews
have mostly buckled under this pressure, and have often exploited their
access to whiteness, the discomfiting truth is that Jews in America have
mostly understood themselves to be a "racial" group.[48] As Goldstein
explains, "the ultimate loss of 'race' as a term for self-description rendered
inarticulate some of their deepest feelings of group solidarity and difference," and the general Jewish embrace of whiteness "resulted in alienation,
communal breakdown, and psychic pain as surely as it produced the
exhilaration of acceptance in non-Jewish society."[49]

Up until the turn of the twentieth century, whites in America had
mostly seen Jews as members of the "Great Caucasian family."[50] That is,
"Native-born whites during this period tended to see Jews' economic success and their perceived links to 'civilization' as characteristics that
affirmed their membership in the dominant racial grouping."[51] While
indigenous Jewish ideas of peoplehood long predate and fit awkwardly
with modern racial categories like "Caucasian" and "white," Jews nevertheless embraced the idea of themselves as an ancient branch on the Caucasian family tree, as one of the venerable so-called white races. Using
this particular nineteenth-century American idea of "race," Jews could
articulate their collective sense of history and fate in a way that was recognizable and not threatening to the white majority. On the other hand,

the popular image of the Jew as "Oriental" indicates that Jews seemed like rather distant relations to their white neighbors. Lurking suspicions remained about the authenticity of Jewish whiteness.

The Reform rabbinate in the mid to late nineteenth century, mostly led by Jews who had emigrated from Central Europe, officially sought to avoid racial differentiation. They reassured their white Christian neighbors that there was no racial difference at all between them. Jews differed only in their confessional devotion to the Jewish "faith." This was the American version of the German Jewish liberalism mentioned in the introduction. But if this was the official stance, many major Reform leaders and other establishment elites continued frequently to refer to the virtues of "the Jewish race," and this remained the de facto terminology among most Jews.[52] Neither Jews nor their neighbors were clear or confident about how exactly to describe the difference between Jews and gentiles. But both groups shared the suspicion that the difference was somehow racial.

By the turn of the twentieth-century, America's white gentile majority was increasingly gripped by anxiety about modernization and started to cling ever tighter to the stable, comforting persistence of the dichotomous black-white racial hierarchy. This is especially evident in the South with Jim Crow. But it was a national phenomenon. Lurking suspicions about Jewish racial ambiguity exerted newly intolerable pressure given the widespread desire for racial clarity, especially among "poor urban dwellers, displaced agrarians, and disillusioned patricians."[53] As in Europe, Jews emerged in the public imagination as an unassimilable group distinguished not by their religion at all, but by their role as the quintessential carriers and beneficiaries of modernization. As Goldstein explains, the instability of Jewishness "interfered with white Americans' attempt to construct a stable racial hierarchy, ultimately threatening their own claims to the power of whiteness. For until white Americans could define the Jew and the forces of modernization he represented, they could not clearly define themselves."[54]

The huge influx of Eastern European Jews between 1880 and 1920 complicated matters even further. These Jews were initially far less susceptible to the lure of whiteness than the Jews who had been in America already for decades. Eastern European Jewish immigrant merchants saw no reason to avoid living or selling among African Americans, the Yiddish press often used the language of "pogroms" to describe violence against blacks, identifying their own experience with the black American experience, and Jewish labor often embraced black labor.[55] A 1920 study of "Americanization" noted, "Jewish tradition and with it the Jewish masses speak neither in terms of 'race' or 'religion.' Both of these terms are imported from the Western World and are foreign to the Jewish spirit as terms descripti[ve] of Jewishness."[56]

The most popular indigenous terminology, as Goldstein indicates, was *dos yiddishe folk*—the Jewish people.[57] What is more, the Eastern European Jews who arrived in the U.S. during this period had long been responding creatively to modernization and Enlightenment thought in their own way. By contrast to Western European Jews, the differing political environment in the East did not lead most Jews to convert their Jewishness into a matter of private faith so that they could seem eligible for citizenship in a modern liberal state. Instead, as Laura Levitt explains, "Here modernization was not a matter of becoming bourgeois; in fact, for many Eastern European Jews, poverty and political disenfranchisement led to more radical forms of enlightened politics. These Jews became involved in socialism and communism as Jews. They accentuated their Jewish particularism even as they participated in these larger political movements. In Eastern Europe, Jews used the languages of socialism, communism, and nationalism to envision their own transformed versions of modern Jewish communal life."[58] Nevertheless, these Jews, like those who came before them, soon felt the enormous pressure of an increasingly concrete demand from the white majority: disappear as a distinctive group (especially through intermarriage with "other whites"), identify as white adherents to a minority religion, or be a problem.[59]

From the 1920s through the 1940s, the idea that "the Jews" presented a major problem gained significant prominence in public conversation and political argument.[60] This is the period depicted in Roth's fantasy *The Plot Against America*, when in fact Henry Ford did publish *The International Jew*, the enormously popular Catholic radio preacher Father Charles Coughlin did rail against a global Jewish conspiracy, Charles Lindbergh did support the America First movement, and an American Nazi rally did fill Madison Square Garden. It is during this period that whites in America start to talk about Jews as *kikes,* a term "used most often to refer to the Jews as members of a distinct race who were dangerously powerful and influential, rather than marginal, in the white world."[61] When students, alumnae, and administrations of elite colleges and universities sought to restrict Jewish admission, they were trying to prevent the kikes from infesting "white men's colleges."[62]

While some Jews in this period responded by embracing racial difference and amplified their identification with the situation of black Americans (vocal Jewish support for the Scottsboro Boys is a good example), by the end of the Second World War the pressure on Jews to disappear into whiteness, identify as a white religious minority, or be a problem was never greater. Most Jews chose the first two options. The U.S. government heavily promoted the second—the "religion" option. In fact, government efforts to promote tolerance during the war focused specifically on "religious" tolerance and served mostly to integrate Catholics and Jews into the white mainstream while studiously avoiding the white-black racial hierarchy.

As Kevin Schultz has shown, it was during the war and afterward that a new ideal of "tri-faith America" was advanced by government institutions and widely embraced by the public.[63] This vision—captured well in the title of Will Herberg's 1955 classic in the sociology of religion, *Protestant-Catholic-Jew*—conjured an America divided benignly among the great religions of the "Judeo-Christian tradition" (a term that also emerged at this time). The idea of a tri-faith America contrasted starkly with Nazi intolerance. This contrast was important since Americans increasingly thought of their military triumph in moral terms, and it was extremely inconvenient that the period immediately before and during the war was the height of American anti-Semitism. The idea of tri-faith America also distinguished the U.S. from the "godless" Soviet Union. As Shultz explains, "It permitted the United States to claim a victory for pluralism without having to address the concerns of racial minorities."[64]

Embracing the religion option after the war, Jews helped to realize the idea of tri-faith America and, thereby, exploited its further marginalization of racial minorities. Many Jews longed for the benefits of unambiguous whiteness and feared the consequences of being seen as dirty kikes. Thus masses of upwardly mobile Jews moved to the suburbs and donned the white mask of religion as a cover for their still quasi-racial sense of themselves as dos yiddishe folk. There was a major boom in synagogue membership in the suburbs, and many of the Jews who joined were joining a synagogue for the first time.[65] Rabbis were thrilled. They eagerly made the case that adherence to the religion of Judaism ought to be what makes Jews Jewish in America. Levitt quotes the Conservative Rabbi Robert Gordis, writing in 1952 in the inaugural issue of the journal *Judaism* (which was conceived precisely to bolster Jewish religious identification): "The only enduring type of pluralism which the structure of American life envisages lies in the field of religion. . . . It is within the rubric of religious pluralism, therefore, that the basis for permanent survival of the Jewish group as an indigenous element of American Life is to be sought."[66] But most Jews did not take at all seriously the religion that was the purported raison d'être of the synagogues they increasingly joined.

As Hasia Diner recounts, at these suburban synagogues Jews "used the cover of religion to express social instincts. Which congregations families opted to join probably had little to do with theological or halachic concerns. In this peculiar type of secularism, American Jews differed from their Protestant and Catholic neighbors."[67] Goldstein makes the same point, "Jews often defined themselves publicly as a religious group while privately pursuing Jewishness as a tribal phenomenon. If they sought to become undifferentiated Americans on the suburban frontier, they often restricted their most intimate contacts to other Jews. They gathered primarily in synagogues, but usually to socialize rather than to pray."[68]

Under the cover of religion, Jews could enter the American mainstream as white people who happen to pray on Saturday rather than on Sunday, while nevertheless continuing to see themselves as primarily a quasi-racial group and praying barely at all. Jewish identification with liberal politics served a similar function. Participation in civil rights advocacy and other liberal causes enabled Jews "to identify as part of the white mainstream's political culture without making them feel as if they had abandoned their legacy as a persecuted minority group."[69] Many Jews who thought of themselves as taking the first option in response to the demand that they "disappear, be religious, or be a problem," actually perpetuated their quasi-racial Jewish consciousness under a mask of liberal or leftist commitment. If Jews who sought to be distinguished in public life only by their religion in fact tended to maintain exclusively Jewish social environments, Jews who sought to be distinguished in public only by their ideological commitment to liberalism or the left likewise tended to preserve some sense of themselves as motivated by a history of Jewish persecution. In both cases, there is an effort to join the white majority while maintaining a difference (religious affiliation, liberal politics) that serves as a proxy for suppressed quasi-racial Jewish consciousness.

In the 1960s some conservative Jewish critics argued that those Jews who embraced liberal or left politics as the best way to channel Jewish identification had actually chosen this path as a capitulation to the demand that Jews disappear. For instance, in his major address to a symposium, entitled "Changing Race Relations: Impact and Implications for Jewish Agencies," Arthur Hertzberg argued in 1965 that Jewish activists were fighting for "further entry into the white majority" when they were fighting for black civil rights.[70] The bourgeoning Jewish right, at this time, argued that Jews should focus on their own survival as a distinct—usually "ethnic"—group, rather than sacrifice their group distinctiveness for the sake of being seen as white by whites and as *good* whites by blacks.[71] And yet, these conservative critics can themselves be described as promoting the "Ellis Island whiteness" that I discussed earlier. Goldstein makes the irony clear: "Although born from a desire to assert their difference from the white power structure, the ethnic revival became for some Jews (as well as for some other ethnics) the vehicle for a new, conservative politics that denigrated blacks and affirmed their own membership in the white mainstream, even as it highlighted their distinctiveness."[72]

If postwar Jews felt pressure to be white from the white majority, and indeed exploited most opportunities to be white, they never quite gave up on their quasi-racial Jewish consciousness. But by the late 1960s they felt a new pressure to be white from black activists and intellectuals. For instance, James Baldwin wrote in his essay of 1967 "Negroes Are Anti-Semitic Because They're Anti-White" that when a Jewish person reflects on the Jewish historical experience in order to think about the black experience in America, he needs to understand that "he has absolutely no relevance in this context as a Jew. His only relevance is that he is white and values his color and uses it."[73] "The Jew," Baldwin writes, "does not realize that the credential he offers, the fact that he has been despised and slaughtered, does not increase the Negro's understanding. It increases the Negro's rage."[74]

Whatever psychic "pressure" or discomfort Jews have felt while enjoying the benefits of whiteness—which they have sometimes enjoyed at the direct expense of blacks—just looks like another white fantasy, or even a particularly egregious disavowal, from the black side of the black-white racial hierarchy. For black critics like Baldwin and Harold Cruse, Gold-stein concludes, "the Jewish desire to straddle the black-white divide undermined the very basis of their quest for integrity and clarity. These competing visions are what underlay the last three and a half decades of conflict and tension between blacks and Jews."[75] When the critique of white supremacy is framed in terms of a stark black-white or white-nonwhite dichotomy, Jewishness must ultimately be sacrificed on the cross of racial justice. Jews face a familiar choice, then, from a different direction: disappear, be religious, or be a problem.

David Hollinger has argued that Jewishness fares similarly in the context of academic multiculturalism. "The key point about multicultural-ism," Hollinger writes, "is that there has been almost no place for Jews. Multiculturalism has been organized largely on the basis of the ethnora-cial pentagon, our mythical, five-part structure with cultures ascribed to color-coded communities of descent, often in recent years labeled African American, Asian American, European American, Hispanic or Latino, and Indian or Native American. On this map of culture in America, Jews are invisible."[76]

Hollinger describes the intellectual-political project of academic mul-ticulturalism from the 1970s to the 1990s as showing almost no interest in religious difference, strongly emphasizing color, largely dismissing linguistic and historical differences within each pentagonal group, and prioritizing groups on the basis of their demographic size and dispropor-tionate lack of access to power.[77] "All this is to suggest," Hollinger writes, "that the story of how Jews found their way in America could come across, in the 1980s and 1990s, as a distraction, if not a threat. The Jewish case was just plain inconvenient."[78] As a result, by 1998 the editors of a volume on American Jews and multiculturalism could write, "it is no secret that Jews confront contemporary multiculturalism with great ambivalence, trepidation, and even hostility."[79] Hollinger's analysis of late twentieth-century academic multiculturalism highlights yet another theoretical framework in which Jews in America are asked to disappear, be religious, or be a problem.

Critical reflection on Jews and race in the U.S. reveals some of the major historical blind spots that are required for critics of white supremacy to see *only* in black and white—or in white and nonwhite. Given these blind spots, I am suspicious of the suggestion that I must repudiate my sentimentality about "Coming to America," *The Jazz Singer*, Ellis Island, the Lower East Side, and the Statue of Liberty in order to pursue a more just America. If these elements of my godless American Jewishness defy the demand that I disappear or be religious and make me a problem, then so be it. I'm happy to be a problem.

However, when I turn the lens of critical reflection on myself, I have to admit that my resistance is not really a matter of intellectual integrity. After all, the critique of "Ellis Island whiteness" still seems important and insightful to me, even if there is a part of me that revolts against it. You can probably hear a shift in my earlier attitude—I'm getting worked up, agitated, and a note of bravado is swelling in my tone. I think this is because my Jewish American sentimentality is rooted so deeply in my sense of who I am: it feels like an axial feature of my own interminable Jewishness. To repudiate it, to cut this pound of flesh from myself, would surely be a mortal wound.

What can I do if the bedrock of my self-understanding is so deeply implicated in historical and ongoing injustice from the perspective of the critique of white supremacy? How can I genuinely love others as equal participants in the American project if the *Jazz Singer* fantasy—with all of its blind spots and exploitation—is so deeply ingrained in me? How can others dare to reach out to me in the spirit of political love if they find my fantasies repugnant or see me as a carrier of white supremacy because of them? It will not do to say that the critique of white supremacy is basically comfortable with the disappearance of dos yiddishe folk and is therefore discredited on that basis. Every framework of ideology-critique has its blind spots. I don't want to throw out the baby with the bathwater.

In order to answer these questions, it will be helpful first to paint an even more vivid picture of those aspects of my self-understanding that will seem repugnant and perverse to others. These are moods, emotions, myths, fantasies, and "ways of seeing" that may seem like clear disqualifiers for participation in a genuinely inclusive project of political love. Once these aspects of myself are exposed, I will then try to convince you that they need not, in fact, be disqualifiers. The kind of political love that I think we should cultivate can endure despite the persistence of the perverse ways of seeing that are so important to many of us.

SEEING IN JEWISH AND GOYISH

As I have suggested, I am apt from time to time to indulge in moods of unabashed sentimentality and self-justifying nostalgia: "Coming to America" is playing, I remember pilgrimages as a kid with my family to Katz's Deli on the Lower East Side, I think of Feival Mousekewitz singing "Somewhere Out There" in the 1986 animated ode to the immigrant nation, *An American Tail*. This is my 1970s third-generation Jewish immigrant patriotism. These moods are connected to another mood that I have when my sense of Jewishness is particularly heightened. I think of Jews (really I have in mind specifically Jews descended from the Eastern European Yiddish-speaking milieu) as an exceptional group of people who have seized the opportunities given to them in America with distinctive determination and brilliance. When I am in this mood, I certainly do not see the world in terms of a racial hierarchy that runs along a white-nonwhite or white-black axis. Nor do I see it as a complex grid of intersecting lines of identification. Instead, I see the world in Jewish and goyish.

There are Jews, who are inherently intellectual, funny, socialistic, and committed to the Moral Law, who uphold *"the virtue of powerlessness, the power of helplessness, the company of the dispossessed, the sanctity of the insulted and the injured,"*[80] and who have fled peaceably from persecution to persecution since the first century C.E. (hey, it's my fantasy—don't interrupt!). And then there are the goyim, who value conquest and physical strength, who obsess over respect for their manliness and honor, and who believe in religious nonsense. At any given point in history, there are powerful goyim who ruthlessly oppress and exploit less powerful goyim. But the less powerful goyim would be just as ruthless if given the opportunity.[81] Meanwhile, the Jews, for millennia, huddle with our books or in our shops hoping that the goyim will "not oppress Israel overly much."[82]

Now, I don't expect other people—including other Jews—to endorse this as a good or true way of seeing the world. But I wouldn't quite be me if I didn't see the world and talk about it in this way from time to time. My favorite bit of writing that expresses this mood is in Philip Roth's 1969 best seller *Portnoy's Compaint*. The main character, Alexander Portnoy, is reflecting on how he was raised to distinguish Jews from goyim in terms of the *chazerai*, the junk, that they can eat (by contrast to kosher food, of course):

> Let them eat eels and frogs and pigs and crabs and lobsters; let them eat vulture, let them eat ape-meat and skunk if they like—a diet of abominable creatures well befits a breed of mankind so hopelessly shallow and empty-headed as to drink, to divorce, and to fight with their fists. All they know, these imbecilic eaters of the execrable, is to swagger, to insult, to sneer, and sooner or later to hit. Oh, also they know how to go out into the woods with a gun, these geniuses, and kill innocent wild deer, deer who themselves *nosh* quietly on berries and grasses and then go on their way, bothering no one. You stupid *goyim!* Reeking of beer and empty ammunition, home you head, a dead animal (formerly *alive*) strapped to each fender, so that all the motorists along the way can see how strong and manly you are. . . . They will eat *anything*, anything they can get their big *goy* hands on! And the terrifying corollary, *they will do anything as well*.[83]

Is this a reasonable description of one particular variety of non-Jewish American? Absolutely *not*. There is nothing reasonable or fair-minded about it. It is the worst kind of stereotyping. It is cruel and pretentious. But in a certain mood, I find it utterly delectable to think it, feel it, and believe it. At the same time, I am equally thrilled, sometimes even more so, to savor this passage:

> Because I am sick and tired of *goyische* this and *goyische* that! If it's bad it's the *goyim*, if it's good it's the Jews! Can't you see my dear parents, from whose loins I somehow leaped, that such thinking is a trifle barbaric? That all you are expressing is your *fear*? The very first distinction I learned from you, I'm sure, was not night and day, or hot and cold, but *goyische* and Jewish! But now it turns out, my dear parents, relatives, and assembled friends who have gathered here to celebrate my bar mitzvah, it turns out, you schmucks! You narrow-minded schmucks!—oh, how I hate you for your Jewish narrow-minded minds!. . . it turns out that there is just a little bit more to existence than what can be contained in those disgusting and useless categories! And instead of crying over he-who refuses at the age of fourteen ever to set foot inside a synagogue again, instead of

wailing for he-who has turned his back on the saga of *his people*, weep for your own pathetic selves, why don't you, sucking and sucking on that sour grape of a religion! Jew Jew Jew Jew Jew Jew! It is coming out of my ears already, the saga of the suffering Jews! Do me a favor, my people, and stick your suffering heritage up your suffering ass—*I happen also to be a human being!*[84]

I should admit to another way that I often see the world too: in Jewish/black/goyish. I sometimes imagine that the singular moral protagonist of the American story is really African Americans. Jews, in this story, are their Old World, elderly neighbors in the special albeit secondary role of wise long-suffering outsiders ready to lend a hand against the domineering goyim. This way of seeing the world undoubtedly derives, in part, from my upbringing in a neighborhood of northwest Baltimore that was almost exclusively Jewish and black. Even if we hardly ever spoke a word to each other across the black-Jewish divide, looking out from Park Heights Avenue there were the Jews and the blacks, and then there were the goyim—a fantasy landscape captured well in Barry Levinson's film *Liberty Heights* (1999).

I also very early absorbed the idea of a historic "black-Jewish alliance" and I relished the Jewish names of activists in the civil rights era when I was old enough to learn about them. We read Martin Luther Kings Jr.'s "I Have a Dream" speech at the end of the seder every Passover when I was a kid. I bought Michael Lerner and Cornel West's *Jews and Blacks: Let the Healing Begin* immediately when it appeared in 1995 and attended their National Summit on Ethics and Meaning in Washington, D.C., a year later in order to take up the call for healing.

Of course, there are good reasons to make African American suffering and struggle central when telling the American story. But it is important for me to be honest with myself and acknowledge that I have not come to my own sense of this centrality through a rigorous process of historical analysis. The mood in which I see a Jewish/black/goyish America is just as much a contingency of my background and personality as the more Manichaean mood in which I see only Jewish and goyish. Indeed, the preponderance of black political thought in this book, every bit as much as the even greater preponderance of Jewish references, undoubtedly results from such contingencies as much as it does from genuine intellectual warrant. For the same reason, the experiences of Native Americans, Latino/a Americans, Asian Americans, and many, many, many others do not receive the attention that they deserve.

These moods are just some of those that overtake me at different times and at different levels of intensity in a manner that I assume is common to most people. I assume that everyone will have some "default settings" that intuitively demarcate the groups that populate their world, their relative importance, what these groups are like, and which emotions they provoke. Each person will likewise have her own thrilling bits of perceptual meanness or his own propensity to righteous indignation. As I have come to observe my own shifting moods and "settings" over time, I have come to appreciate how important it is to avoid the tempting presumption that one's kishkes are a good source of serious political perception. This is not because I lack options for satisfying my deepest intestinal desires. A Jew in 2018 has options. Here is another persistent mood: throughout my life I have toyed with a kind of strident paranoid Zionism. Indeed, somehow along with my schmaltzy bourgeois patriotic sentimentality and my artsy leftish outrage, I also brought to my Oberlin College dorm room in 1995 an Israeli flag, 5′ x 8′, that took up an entire wall during my freshman and sophomore years.

I had my share of aliyah fantasies as an adolescent and younger man, imagining that I would move to Israel, accept the citizenship offered me by my birth, and live behind laws and walls that finally separate and protect the Jews from the goyim. I spent about two years in Israel between 1997 and 2002. My aliyah fantasies were never really motivated by a sense of physical insecurity in the U.S. I worried more about gentile America killing the Jews with kindness. Even if Jews would never really be threatened physically in the United States, I thought, the prospects for Jewishness in America are grim.

Concede that Jews are just a barely distinguishable variety of "white people" and be dissolved into the American cultural mayonnaise? Concede that Jews are "white ethnics" like Italians or Poles (who, by the way, were not differentiated from their countrymen back in Italy and Poland, where Jews were segregated and persecuted for centuries)? Concede that Jews are a "religious" minority and play along with superstitious rituals for the rest of my life in order to keep alive some vestige of Jewishness? No thanks. Only in Israel, where everyday life happens in Hebrew and the national religious holidays that most people ignore or celebrate at the beach are Jewish, is it possible for a godless Jew like me to flourish.[85] Listen to me getting worked up again. I have these thoughts.

Zionism, in the most general terms, is a political view that holds a modern Jewish nation-state in the historical land of Israel to be the ideal political order for Jews. In many of its iterations, it also exemplifies a normative political view that is tightly bound to a singular framework of ideology-critique: the critique of anti-Semitism. Zionism waits with open arms for the Jewish American who is finally overwhelmed by anxiety about "the vanishing American Jew" and the goyim who are all too happy for him to vanish.[86] While there are many varieties of Zionism, most envision an ideal political order that is organized around the Jewish/goyish dichotomy. Zionism presents the opportunity to turn *ahavas yisroiel* (love of the Jewish people) and anxiety about the goyim into a real-life, tanks, taxes, and passports political project. I resist this temptation to indulge my fantasy of living in a total comprehensive Jewish/goyish political order precisely because I still believe that it is possible to forge an enduring and genuinely inclusive ideal of political justice and political love in America.[87]

My own way of seeing the world evidently shifts depending on my mood. I may savor Portnoy's contempt for the Jews or for the goyim, be drawn into a Zionist fantasy one day, and imagine myself a cosmopolitan Jewish intellectual in Kafka's castle wandering amidst the paradoxes of modernity the next. Most of the time I couldn't possibly ask anyone else to see the world in the perverse and ridiculous ways that I do. But one thing is for sure, I am not letting go of "Coming to America" and I will never agree to a way of seeing the world as Frank Wilderson does, in which the Holocaust—including the systematic execution of nearly two million Jewish children—is merely a "little family quarrel" among white people. I do not begrudge Wilderson this view. But we are going to have to find a way to live together that does not require us to reconcile on this particular point.

What is needed is a way of seeing each other—an American vision—that the critic of white supremacy and the occasionally paranoid Jewish chauvinist (who also wants to be a critic of white supremacy) can pursue together. If there is a way of seeing each other that we can both accept, then we need not merely abide in America cynically, flee for some promised land, or, god forbid, blow up the world with the hope that a better world will magically arise from its ruins. This is a tough sell, to be sure. And I recognize that no such vision can be acceptable from a perspective that sees only an ontological antagonism between human and black, which is perpetuated merely through "conflictual" political action.

But I have no idea what would accomplish the needful ontological revolution on such a view or why anyone would have sufficient reason to assume that the postrevolutionary order would be any better than the current one. By contrast, as I have already suggested, I see openness to a new vision in Mills's critique of the racial contract. The challenge is to conjure a liberal vision that fundamentally acknowledges and repudiates the racially hierarchical status quo, in which it is presumptively tolerable that whites have disproportionate power nationally and globally over nonwhites. This vision would have to recognize that we do not live in a "normal" world or a world that is "roughly as it should be." It would have to see our world as the morally grotesque offspring of injustice and include a profound reckoning with this fact.

Given the historical record of liberalism, if the new vision of America is going to be an acceptable liberal vision, it will have to be transparently *not* rigged to perpetuate the racial contract and other oppressive ideologies through processes that are hidden and disavowed. It will have to address directly the blind spots and fantasylands that preserve our antagonisms. It will have to show that a liberal vision need not be a ruse.

Making matters still more complicated, if it is truly a vision for all of America, it will have to be acceptable to those in America who have been victims of injustice, to those who have been both victims and beneficiaries, and also to those who have benefited from injustice. It will have to be acceptable to the black critic of white supremacy, the occasionally paranoid Jewish chauvinist, and to the white Christian "core group" too: to the blue-collar white Catholic who is fed up with "political correctness," to the pious white New England Protestant who thinks that reason and forgiveness will eventually allow us to transcend our benighted prejudices, and even to the Southerner who dresses up like a Confederate soldier every year to reenact the Battle of Gettysburg. Now that is a tall order.

Thus the first step toward our new vision is to differentiate between the kind of vision that stands a chance at broad acceptability and the kind that is clearly unacceptable. My Jewish/goyish way of seeing America is obviously not likely to be broadly acceptable, nor is my Zionist fantasy or my cosmopolitan Kafka fantasy. Furthermore, as I have explained at length, we cannot expect to derive a positive, broadly shareable vision from any single framework of ideology-critique or even from a set of such frameworks. The crucial work to be done is to figure out how to construct a vision that aspires to be broadly acceptable despite its refusal to repress or disavow the interminability of those ways of seeing that are not broadly acceptable and the historical grudges and antagonisms they carry. The political philosopher John Rawls, in the latter part of his career, developed an innovation in liberal thought that can help us to take the first step toward such a vision. Though we will ultimately have to step far beyond Rawls if we want to conjure a vision that reckons sufficiently with historical injustice and its legacy.

POLITICAL LIBERALISM AND THE NOT UNFORTUNATE CONDITIONS OF HUMAN LIFE

John Rawls is a divisive figure. Some view his general approach and his specific idea of justice as essential to all serious thought about politics and demand that his concepts and terminology be used with mathematical precision in order to be used well. Others consider his theory of justice to be an elaborate disembodied evasion of urgent political reality and the dominance of his work as reflective of the homogenous population of white elites that has dominated academic political philosophy since the 1970s. I have a large black and white photograph of Rawls hanging on the wall in my office. It was taken by the photographer Steve Pyke for his series Philosophers. It's a close-up of Rawls's face, which is slightly tilted to his right. He has a narrow face, with a somewhat pointy nose. He wears big square glasses with black trim at the top, translucent on the bottom. His brow is knitted with concern. But he doesn't look stern. Something about his gently closed mouth, which is not at all pursed, conveys warmth rather than severity. This is the Rawls that has been an enormous part of my intellectual life since graduate school—a thoughtful, imaginative person who offers flawed but enduring insight into how all of us living in America can investigate the possibility of justice.

I suspect that for many people who are attracted to Rawlsian political philosophy it is easy to be intoxicated by the feeling that you might just be able to work out profound questions of political life as if they were logic problems or the neat models used by economists. But we do not have to relate to Rawls in this way. What is important to me is his lifelong intellectual struggle to think clearly about justice and his willingness, in the latter part of his career, to reconsider fundamental aspects of his own approach. His thought process and some of the ideas that he developed at this stage will prove very helpful in my own effort to envision an America that we will all feel is worth striving toward together.

In the latter part of his career, Rawls decided that his vision of a just society, which had made him famous, was not sufficiently realistic. He was still trying to produce a normative political ideal—to provide a goal and measure that can orient our collective pursuit of justice and help us to evaluate how well or badly we're doing. But he increasingly came to appreciate the importance of including certain interminable human limitations into his ideal so that it would be more plausible. He understood that only a genuinely plausible ideal, only an ideal designed for *us*, would seem worth pursuing. With this in mind, he built into his vision the assumption that fundamental conflicts about religious, philosophical, existential, metaphysical, and other such questions would persist even in the most just society that we could realistically imagine. He called this the "fact of reasonable pluralism" and he states explicitly that it is "not an unfortunate condition of human life."[88]

It is not, strictly speaking, unfortunate for the simple reason that one cannot lament what is known to be necessary and inevitable even in the best-case scenario.[89] In the new vision that Rawls promotes, citizens remain divided by their irreconcilable "comprehensive doctrines" (he usually seems to have in mind religions and elaborate philosophical systems when he uses this term), even as they share a set of ideas about what makes their core political institutions just. In the same way that Rawls hoped to present an ideal of society that could win the allegiance of citizens regardless of their otherwise conflicting comprehensive doctrines, I hope to present a vision of America that is attractive to most of the people who live here regardless of our otherwise conflicting views about history, interminable grudges, moods of in-group exceptionalism and out-group contempt.

The important step to take with Rawls is to acknowledge that many of our ideas and emotions—for instance, the way that I think and feel when I see the world in Jewish vs. goyish—are not broadly acceptable. I should not expect you to think that my intuitions about the goyim when I am in a particularly ridiculous chauvinistic mood are a good basis for the way that everyone should see each other in America (or the way that *I* should see my neighbors when I am, for instance, sitting on a jury). It behooves me, then, to try to formulate some ideas and emotions that do not depend on my particular prejudices and preoccupations, but are instead designed to be accessible on the basis of something that we share. Rawls's term for the set of ideas and emotions that we can all share as members of a single political society is a "political conception of justice." He imagined that in a society that is going well most people will share one among a variety of compatible political conceptions of justice, which together function as the "mutually recognized point of view from which citizens can adjudicate their claims of political right on their political institutions or against one another."[90]

Rawls does not imagine that people will take this point of view all the time. Instead, he suggests that this is the point of view that we should take when we relate to each other as citizens, especially when we are trying to determine and interpret fundamental rights and duties. Crucially, we should also expect this to be the point of view of core political institutions like the legal system, law enforcement, mandatory educational institutions, the tax system, laws and policies that provide and regulate work, and electoral procedures—which Rawls labels "the basic structure of society." In the ideal society, for Rawls, everyone will be able to look at the basic structure of society and feel satisfied that it is generally animated by a worthy political conception of justice and receptive to ongoing criticism and correction on the basis of this conception.

Rawls offers his own political conception of justice—"justice as fairness"—as a model. It is an elaborate architectural blueprint. It specifies key values like reasonableness and reciprocity. It clarifies core principles like liberty and equality and how they should relate. And it includes guiding conceptions, such as Rawls's political conception of the person as a citizen. The political conception of the person as a citizen is perhaps the most important component of any political conception of justice. It requires some further explanation. It is the answer to the question: *who* is the political conception of justice *for?* A political conception of the person as a citizen is what we decide to see in others, and what we hope others will decide to see in us, that gives us a shared stake in the prospect of justice.

Anyone trying to offer a vision or ideal of collective human life will have to make some general assumptions about what it means to be a person. After all, it's not so obvious. What are people like? Are people inherently selfish? Are we sinners all? Are people inherently benevolent? Are people motivated by a desire to express their individuality, to have safe and predictable lives, to dominate others? Are people susceptible to rational justifications or only to promises of pleasure and the threat of pain? Are people essentially black or white, Jewish or goyish, gay or straight? Or are people not *essentially* anything at all? It is impossible to make any proposal or judgment about collective human life that does not depend on some set of assumptions about what people are like. A political conception of the person as a citizen is a proposed set of assumptions about what "we" are like that is meant to be shared by everyone in our society, even as we all retain other conflicting assumptions as a result of our conflicting comprehensive views.

Some of the time you might see me as a stiff-necked Jew who is desperately in need of Christ's salvation or submission to the mercy of Allah. Or you might see me as just another privileged white guy, who is probably unwilling in the end to cede the power that he disavows, or as a sexually depraved socialist Jewish intellectual or as a guy with a distracting mole on the tip of his nose. But when you see me in the context of the basic structure of society, and when you assess how these institutions impact me, Rawls's idea is that you should shift to seeing me in the image of a political conception of the person as a citizen that we can all share. Rawls, for instance, would have us see each other in this context as free, equal, rational, independent, motivated to live in a just society, and invested in diverse ideas of a life well lived that a just society would allow us to pursue. There are problems with this particular image of the citizen, but I will return to them later.

It is important first to be clear that Rawls's expectations about how people can shift between points of view—that people can shift back and forth from the point of view of the political conception of justice to the other points of view that they are predisposed to take—is not an exotic expectation. It is the same kind of expectation that we have of people all the time in everyday life when we expect them to adhere to formalized or stylized norms. I assume, for instance, that you expect your doctor to exclude or "bracket" his sexuality when he interacts with you. It seems appropriate to expect your doctor to see you from a medical point of view, not from a sexual or financial point of view or from the point of view of mere disinterested scientific curiosity. Now, this doesn't always work. Doctors are occasionally found sexually abusing their patients, or male doctors are found discounting what women have to say about their experiences and symptoms, and we have a massive structural problem with our healthcare system, which compels doctors to see their patients from a financial point of view.[91] But this just means that medical schools should stay vigilant in their efforts to provide training in medical ethics, and we should try to fix the healthcare system so that it promotes medical care over profit.

There is, then, a way of seeing others that is appropriate to medical interactions, medical institutions, and medical reasoning. We can say that this is a medical point of view and that it applies to the medical domain. I'm sure that there are competing ideas out there about how precisely to define the medical point of view and the domain to which it applies. And there are certainly hard cases that blur the boundaries between the medical and other domains: for instance, an Orthodox Jew might want her doctor to be sensitive to considerations of Jewish law that contradict conventional medical assumptions about how to relate to patients. But I assume that most people living in America today recognize a distinct medical domain and that there should be an ongoing effort to develop the best possible norms for guiding distinctly medical practice (even if there is no perfect set of norms and there will always be limit cases that require some finagling).

The key idea that I borrow from Rawls is that we should recognize a distinct domain of the political where we decide to see each other according to a political conception of the person as a citizen and to judge how well we're doing as a society on the basis of a political conception of justice. Political interactions, political institutions, and political reasoning (Rawls will call it public reason) are appropriate to the domain of the political in the same way that medical interactions, institutions, and reasoning are appropriate to the medical domain. This is Rawls's special sense of the political: what is political in this sense is designed specifically to be justifiable, as a regulatory ideal for the basic structure of society, to people who are and will forever remain divided by their irreconcilable comprehensive views.

The political love that I am searching for in this book is meant to be political in this sense. What I am trying to promote is an emotion—a way of perceiving and judging—that all of us who live in America today can share, even as we remain divided by our interminable grudges, chauvinism, and aversions. It is an emotion that is meant to characterize how we see each other within the domain of the political, even if we see each other very differently beyond this domain—in what Rawls refers to as "the background culture." In my vision of an America animated by political love, it is not, strictly speaking, unfortunate that our interminable historical resentment lingers in the background culture. I assume these divisive emotions will persist even in the best America we can realistically imagine, just as Rawls presumed irreconcilable comprehensive doctrines would persist even in the best society that he could imagine. Modeled on the fact of reasonable pluralism, I will call this assumption "the fact of fraught societies."

I will explain the fact of fraught societies at length in chapters 2 and 3. But first I need to lay out the particular political conception of justice that will animate the basic structure of society in my vision of America and the political conception of the person as a citizen that will inhabit it. As it turns out, Rawls's preferred ideal, justice as fairness, replicates many of the loopholes in classical liberalism that have made it possible for people over the past few centuries to hold liberal views while remaining unperturbedly complicit in racial, gender, and other forms of domination. By contrast, Martha Nussbaum has set out explicitly to devise a political conception of justice that will do better. I will adopt her approach, though I want to amend and amplify it.

LAYING THE GROUNDWORK: THE CAPABILITIES APPROACH

Having leapt from my incorrigible moods and emotions to Rawls's abstract idea of a political conception of justice, I want to return now to Ginsberg's "America," which can help us find a more balanced reflective stance.

"America when will you be angelic? When will you take off your clothes? When will you look at yourself through the grave?" These three questions, which come eight lines into "America," represent an important sequence of thoughts. "When will you be angelic?" seems, initially, to express a utopian aspiration: that we should strive to be as pure as angels. But "When will you take off your clothes?" suggests, if it is not a non sequitur, a connection between our utopian aspirations and who we are when we are naked human bodies. And if this question is connected to the next, it then takes us beyond the ken of the angels to the grave where our naked human bodies inevitably reside.

Ginsberg's questions provoke us to connect our highest national aspirations to awareness of ourselves as naked, mortal, human bodies. Martha Nussbaum raises precisely these questions when she makes her case for an ideal political vision, a vision of the "angelic," that nevertheless incorporates the vulnerability of naked human embodiment and mortality—how we look with our clothes off and "through the grave." Her overall view is called the capabilities approach. She frames her approach as "political," in Rawls's sense, so we can say that she offers a distinct political conception of justice.[92] As we will see, the core of her approach is a set of central human capabilities, which every person should be enabled to exercise at a basic level. We will also see that her political conception of the person as a citizen has far more in common with Ginsberg than with Rawls.

Nussbaum's approach starts with the idea that every human being is precious and of equal worth.[93] The kind of life that is suitable for a human being, she suggests, is one that honors human preciousness—it is a life "worthy of human dignity."[94] But human dignity is profoundly vulnerable: a minimally good life is inextricably dependent upon the variability of external conditions. This means that much of what is valuable to a person is beyond his or her control. Governments, according to Nussbaum, are the human institutions that are ultimately responsible for cultivating citizens and external conditions that are conducive to dignified human life. [95]

Governments should therefore cultivate a set of central human capabilities in every person and ensure external conditions that will allow for these capabilities to be exercised at a threshold level. Nussbaum has offered her own list of ten central human capabilities, which she has devised to serve as "the philosophical underpinning for an account of core human entitlements that should be respected and implemented by the governments of all nations, as a bare minimum of what respect for human dignity requires."[96] The list includes, for example, bodily health, use of the senses, imagination, and thought, and practical reason. The capabilities list is the centerpiece of Nussbaum's political conception of justice.

Nussbaum's political conception of the person as a citizen specifies that citizens will care about each other's opportunities to exercise the central human capabilities. "The good of others," she writes, "is not just a constraint on this person's pursuit of her own good; it is part of her good."[97] This is the idea of fundamental human sociability: human beings are presumed to seek and find "deep fulfillment" in their relationships with others, including in political relationships and, in particular, "relations characterized by the virtue of justice."[98] One way that such citizens are presumed to relate to each other is through political compassion: the perception that another person (or oneself) has been deprived of a central human capability and the judgment that this amounts to a serious injustice perpetrated against someone who matters *to me*. Nussbaum suggests that governments should cultivate citizens who have a predisposition to make appropriate judgments of political compassion in the right circumstances.[99] Political compassion is, therefore, an indispensable political emotion specified by Nussbaum's political conception of justice.

Nussbaum's political ideal, then, includes citizens educated to make judgments of compassion based on the list of central human capabilities (at least when legislating, interpreting laws, making claims in political life, and evaluating the claims of others in political life). But human beings, according to her conception, are not only connected by a shared motivation to live in thriving political relationships characterized by the virtue of justice and appropriately directed compassion. Human beings, according to Nussbaum, are also connected by human embodiment—by the fact that to be a human being is, among other things, to be a human body. This means that citizens, since they are human beings, should be presumed to have lives that are characterized at multiple phases, and sometimes throughout, by "asymmetrical dependency."[100] As a baby, as a result of illness or calamity, in very old age, or because of inborn impairments, human beings are largely dependent creatures.

Thus sociability, compassion, and animality (being an animal body) are key features of Nussbaum's political conception of the person as a citizen—how she suggests that people should see themselves and others in the political domain.[101] In addition, they should also recognize their own and everyone else's "deep interest in choice."[102] This should not be mystified as the ethereal autonomy of perfectly rational beings or anything like that. Nussbaum has in mind the "garden variety practical reasoning" that human animals share with every other kind of animal that makes daily choices to avoid danger, pursue pleasure, store food, build nests and other shelters, etc. Every such animal has a stake in opportunities to make good choices. The kinds of opportunities that we want are just these sorts of opportunities, of the human variety.[103]

Accepting Nussbaum's capabilities conception of political justice going forward means that we should see governments as moral institutions that are responsible for guaranteeing each and every person subject to their governance a lifetime of opportunities to exercise her or his central human capabilities at a minimum threshold level. Furthermore, when a person thinks of herself or himself or others as a "citizen," this should not evoke the free, equal, independent, rational, self-interested being imagined by Rawls and the social contract tradition. It should evoke the vulnerable, dependent, compassionate human animal who has a profound stake in choice and whose good includes the good of others.

These elements of Nussbaum's view already significantly disrupt features of the social contract tradition that perpetuate the presumptive legitimacy of the unjust status quo, including the racial contract. Instead of trying to construct an idealized conception of justice and the citizen that allows us to avoid thinking about real, embodied human beings, Nussbaum provides an ideal that requires us precisely to confront human animality, sociability, dependence, and vulnerability.[104] I take this to be a significant intervention into pervasive liberal contentment with the status quo because I agree with Nussbaum that the stigmatization of groups often derives from pathological denial that we are vulnerable, dependent, animals.

For Nussbaum, "acceptance of our animality involves an uphill battle against denial of animality and stigmatization of those whom a dominant group of humans view as quasi-animal."[105] This "anthropodenial" obstructs the formation of appropriately directed compassion, and does so most notably by generating the emotion of disgust along with what Nussbaum calls "primitive shame."[106] Nussbaum provides an account of how these emotions are typically generated in human beings that is drawn from a range of philosophical, literary, and psychological sources. Her account is particularly informed by the psychological theory of D. W. Winnicott and others in the object-relations tradition.[107]

It unfolds as follows. Human infants are born into a state of extreme physical helplessness, which, with a rapidly emerging capacity to discern objects in their environment, very soon produces painful frustration.[108] The frustration that arises with the infant's experience of unmet needs is forever contrasted to an antecedent experience of "blissful completeness": the undifferentiated experience of a universe governed harmoniously by the infant's needs, where the infant is the sun around which all else revolves. Primitive shame describes the judgment that a failure to control one's environment—to govern the external world like the sun governs its gravitational empire—is a "shortcoming or inadequacy in the self."[109] This judgment then typically motivates or otherwise causes an aggressive response from the infant: the external world's stubborn noncompliance is blamed for the frustrating and painful experience of helplessness and becomes the target of the infant's howling rage.

The environment and relationships that characterize the infant's subsequent experiences and development significantly determine what happens next. In the process of maturation, as the child becomes more independent, the intensity of primitive shame may lessen and the child may come to see others as centers of experience in their own right who are worthy of genuine concern *for their own sake*.[110] But primitive shame typically lingers. And by the age of two or three it becomes entangled with the emerging emotion of disgust—a "very strong negative emotion" that, in this case, specifically targets the child's own bodily waste products.[111] What the child and later the adult eventually identifies as "disgusting" in his environment is connected in an important way to this initial disgust, which targets his own bodily waste.[112]

Our antecedent and ongoing disgust toward our own bodily waste is what animates our disgust toward oozy smelly animals: they are reminders of our uncontrollable, untidy, bodily nature. This is further compounded and intensified once an awareness of mortality develops, once we "realize that we are truly helpless in the most important respect of all."[113] When our bodily nature, already subject to the judgment of disgust, comes also to stand for our helplessness in the face of our inevitable demise, then the intensity of our disgust rises and encompasses anything that smacks of biological decay or death. According to Nussbaum's account, it is from this psychological nexus of primitive shame, disgust toward our own bodily waste, and mortality-distress that the injustices associated with stigmatization arise in human societies.[114] And it is in recognition of precisely this condition that Ginsberg, as I read him, pleads to America, "When will you be angelic? When will you take off your clothes? When will you look at yourself through the grave?"

Within the framework of Nussbaum's approach, whatever exacerbates an aversion to dependence and vulnerability, or the denial of animality and mortality, obstructs our capacity to see ourselves as citizens in the right way and thereby assaults a core basis of political justice. The historical and psychological evidence that such denial and its projection has in fact been integral to obvious circumstances of injustice (related to anti-Semitism, racism, and misogyny, for example) reinforces the attractiveness of her political conception of the person. Nussbaum reviews social psychological research on a number of these cases.[115] In each, it is clear that stigmatization tends to involve the attribution of animalistic, decay, or disgust features to the stigmatized.

How, then, does Nussbaum imagine that human societies can be transformed from places where anthropodenial is exacerbated and stigmatization is rampant to places where appropriately directed compassion animates public life? Prominent among her suggestions are her guidelines for education policy: "public education at every level should cultivate the ability to imagine the experiences of others and to participate in their sufferings."[116] In particular, this involves bolstering the place of the arts and humanities at every level so that "children gradually master more and more of the appropriate judgments and become able to extend their empathy to more people and types of people."[117] Pride of place in this curriculum goes to tragic narratives.

Students learn appropriately directed compassion when they come to care about tragic protagonists who suffer gravely and undeservedly.[118] Through tragic novels, plays, films, and other media, students can confront dilemmas, pain, and loss in ways they might not yet have experienced and may not ever experience. What is more, the fact that they "experience" such confrontations through the exercise of their imagination in a safe environment, which is appropriate to emotional and intellectual experimentation, is important in its own right. It is important that people at an early age learn to engage in such "narrative play."[119]

A strong arts and humanities curriculum in every school, with a special focus on tragic narratives, is designed to ward off the resurgence of "seething jealousy, a demand to be the center of the world, a longing for bliss and comfort, a consequent desire to surround oneself with 'normals' and to stigmatize vulnerable people and groups": the goal is to create "a 'facilitating environment' for the emotional health of . . . citizens."[120] From our current standpoint, that means promoting a society that allows its members to be vulnerable, experimental, dependent, and creative. For Nussbaum, instituting educational environments that provide ample space for narrative play and tragic spectatorship is the first step in this direction.[121]

Despite these bold aspirations, Nussbaum is not naive about progress.[122] She acknowledges that the habits of seeing that are involved in stigmatization require vigilant effort to be transformed. "Every time we find ourselves seeing the object in the old, defective way," she writes, "we have to work to shift our perception and substitute a different way of seeing."[123] And it is crucially important that this different way of seeing makes visible the nation as a whole, through vivid imagining of its particular history as a political collective striving for justice.

Here we arrive at the kind of political love for one's own nation that a state can justifiably cultivate in its population. Nussbaum argues that governments should narrate the nation—the story of the polity—through public rituals, songs, symbols and other forms of expression that employ "named individuals (founders, heroes), physical particulars (features of landscape, vivid images and metaphors), and, above all, narratives of struggle, involving suffering and hope."[124] When people identify with these particulars, especially with particular instances of the unending struggle for justice, they can come to see themselves as equal contributors to a national story. This means including prominently in the national imagination particular stories of those who have suffered and continue to suffer under injustice in America, along with particular stories that valorize the determination to persevere in the struggle. Stories that have been historically suppressed are particularly important to include, and the national story should expand and deepen as these silenced stories are heard. This is one way that each person is invited to adjudge, "this is *my* nation" and "I am *personally* committed to promote it becoming a *just* nation."

The shift from seeing others as threatening or subhuman to seeing them—and yourself—as vulnerable, dependent, human animals who long to flourish *with you* as equal members of a just nation requires a corrective to the imagination. It requires a vivid, compelling alternative. Merely pointing to abstract moral principles is not going to do the trick.[125] What is needed is a national narrative that tells the story of common struggle highlighting the dignity of the historically oppressed, a narrative through which people who see themselves as citizens can "embrace one another as a family, sharing common purposes; thus stigma is overcome (for a time at least) by imagination and love."[126] Nussbaum provides historical examples of great figures—Abraham Lincoln, Martin Luther King Jr., and Gandhi, for instance—who have narrated the moral history of their nations in such a way as to accomplish this process of humanization through imagination and love.[127]

She also reads Walt Whitman as a great poet of democracy who celebrated the human body and rejected prevalent attitudes of disgust toward human animality, desire, and vulnerability. Whitman portrayed precisely such disgust as the deeply concealed source of racial hatred and social hierarchy in American society during his lifetime. As a stark alternative, Whitman conjures an America "healed of disgust's self-avoidance and therefore truly able to pursue liberty and equality."[128] While Nussbaum warns us against Whitman's occasional intimation that we can eradicate disgust entirely, she celebrates his call to ennoble a vulnerable, embodied America. This is the call that Ginsberg echoes when he puts his queer shoulder to the wheel.

WHY THE CAPABILITIES APPROACH IS NOT YET SUFFICIENT

Using the capabilities approach as a measure of the basic structure of American society means feeling consistently *outraged*. It is simply not the case that every baby born in America can expect stable opportunities to develop and exercise her central human capabilities at a threshold level. Worst of all, especially for the prospects of broadly shared political love, capability depravation continues to be disproportionately acute among the descendants of those who were colonized and enslaved by the founding of the nation. We have not yet converged on the common denominator of political compassion or love.

A huge amount of work needs to be done to assure that every person living in the United States of America has real and enduring access to the entitlements that they deserve. This work will involve crafting and winning support for better labor, health, education, and other laws, policies, and institutions. My suspicion is that the most important task is to strip economic forces entirely of their capacity to decide the extent to which a person is able to exercise her capabilities at a threshold level. Forces that decide who can sell what to whom for how much, and the prestige and monetary compensation assigned to particular skills and professions, should have *no impact whatsoever* on a person's opportunities to exercise her central human capabilities.

Scholars and political actors that have the necessary expertise must determine the precise combination of laws, policies, and institutions that can accomplish this protection of people from economic forces. There is also a huge amount of work to do in order to produce an inclusive national narrative—one that truly integrates the particular stories of the historically oppressed into the more general story of our national struggle for justice. Crucially, this means highlighting, promoting, and producing dignified images of people who have been and continue to be stigmatized, just as Nussbaum suggests.

So why isn't this enough? Why isn't it enough to pursue this vision, accepting the ongoing challenge to redouble our efforts when we are inevitably set back by the tendencies of shame and disgust. It is not enough because it is not yet realistic about the interminable, irreconcilable grudges, fantasies, and blind spots that will persist even in the best America that we can realistically imagine. Nussbaum has not yet built into her view something like the fact of reasonable pluralism for historical anger, fear, distrust, and resentment.

Where she addresses anger, she claims that—like disgust—it is never an appropriate political emotion. Anger, as she describes it, is the judgment that a serious wrong has been done to someone or something that you care about *and it would be good if the wrongdoer were to suffer as a result.*[129] In personal and political life, she argues, a healthy, rational person will shift quickly from anger to a more productive future-oriented emotion. Thus anger "quickly puts itself out of business, in that even the residual focus on punishing the offender is soon seen as part of a set of projects for improving the offender and society—and the emotion that has this goal is not so easy to see as anger. It is more like compassionate hope."[130]

Nussbaum argues that anger should never characterize the point of view of the political.[131] When injustice provokes anger, people who see themselves as citizens and political institutions should quickly convert it into compassionate hope. With Martin Luther King Jr. and Gandhi, she calls for a revolutionary politics of nonanger: "a mental revolution in which people look at their goals and at their oppressors with new eyes, in a spirit of love and generosity."[132] And what about all the historical grudges, revenge fantasies, and blind spots we carry as a result of historical conflicts and oppression? Nussbaum does not explain what she expects to happen to this stuff as a society becomes more just. Will our perverse emotions just fade away? Is it enough simply to expect people and institutions to resist anger on behalf of love, generosity, and compassionate hope?[133]

I don't think so. For many people, including the historically oppressed, thriving with all capabilities secured will mean expressing, memorializing, and even ritually reenacting one's historical grievances. Let me illustrate this by returning to my own darker moods of Jewish paranoia and chauvinism. In one such mood, I feel like the goyim will always find a reason to hate the Jews. The Jews are either arch-communists or craven capitalists. They are deracinated cosmopolitan interlopers exploiting the good people who belong to the land, or their "Zionist state" is the last holdout of nationalist chauvinism that must be overcome in order for global justice to be possible. One way or the other, the goyim will find a way to hate the Jews. Or so I muse to myself when I've soured as a result of some troubling news item or overheard conversation.

In this mood, Amalek, the ancient and eternal guardian of Jew-hatred among the goyim, only changes its mask through history.[134] Leon Wieseltier describes this way of thinking, what he calls "Amalekization," at the turn of the twenty-first century: "And so Amalek became Haman (who actually was an Amalekite), who became the Romans, who became the

Crusaders, who became Chmielnicki, who became Petlura, who became Hitler, who became Arafat. The mythifying habit is ubiquitous in the literature of the Jews."[135] In his article—it has a great title, "Hitler Is Dead: Against the Ethnic Panic of the Jews"—Wieseltier reflects on the dissonance between this way of seeing the world, which may have been understandable under some historical conditions of Jewish life, and the conditions of Jewish life in America today. "One method for relieving the dissonance," he explains, "is to imagine a loudspeaker summoning the Jews to Time Square. In the absence of apocalypse, we turn to hysteria."[136] Wieseltier suggests that there may be deep in the psychology of some Jewish Americans a perverse desire to hear the loudspeaker calling them to gather, to be registered, to be put on a list—presumably the same desire holds the attention of many Jewish readers of *The Plot Against America*.

While he is focused on the Jewish case, Wieseltier connects Jewish paranoia to a broader American phenomenon of "ethnic panic." "In America," he writes,

> ethnic panic has a certain plausibility and a certain prestige. It denotes a turn to "realism" and to roots. A minority that has agreed to believe that its life has been transformed for the better, that has accepted the truth of progress, that has revised its expectation of the world, that has taken yes for an answer, is always anxious that it may have been tricked. For progress is a repudiation of the past. Yes feels a little like corruption, a little like treason, when you have been taught no. For this reason, every disappointment is a temptation to eschatological disappointment, to a loss of faith in the promise of what has actually been achieved.[137]

Ethnic panic is attractive. It has the appeal of a certain kind of heroism. The cynical hero who sees through every facade, every kindness and source of vulnerable connection, and defies it—this is the relevant sort of heroism. It also has the appeal of authenticity. The hero of ethnic panic and defiance has no ambivalence, no competing loyalties, no internal contradictions or ambiguities. He is the quintessential man of his group, animated at the core of his being by its fate. Everyone not in his group is under suspicion, the goyim, white.

Particularly notable in Wiesletier's account is that ethnic panic arises not from increasingly bad conditions but from increasingly *good* conditions. Progress itself produces this hysteria.[138] And this is because progress seems to portend a diminution of the past. Whether described as assimilation, amelioration, reform, or otherwise, progress can feel like it threatens to leave behind much that has seemed important. In this sense, ethnic panic is both a distrustful fear of others and a fear and distrust related to the integrity of the group itself as well as membership in the group. Progress toward justice, therefore, presents a particularly paradoxical threat to those who have come to self-understanding through the struggle for justice.[139]

The thrust of Wieseltier's article is to suggest that Jews in America should be able to get over their paranoia. A normal existence in a liberal society, especially when one is prospering, requires giving up on lingering distrust and resentment. From this perspective, we might lament the publication of a book like *The Plot Against America*. It only feeds and perpetuates emotions that we should hope will die out and disappear. I agree with Wieseltier that the Jewish-goyish divide is an absolutely inappropriate set of categories for serious thinking about political life. The menacing instrumentalization of Amalek-hatred among some populations in contemporary Israel exemplifies the problem.[140] Nevertheless, something important would be lost if the kind of people who perversely relish *The Plot Against America* are meant to disappear with progress. And I'm not just saying that because I'm one of them. I really can't imagine sincerely endorsing an ideal vision of American society that has no room in it for people like me and I don't expect any other people to endorse and pursue a vision of American society that will have eradicated *them* when it arrives.

Furthermore, this is not just about the guilty pleasures of ethnic panic. The traditional Jewish ritual calendar is a litany of opportunities to keep Amalek at the forefront of one's mind: Hanukkah recalls Jewish resistance against imperial domination by ancient Greeks, Purim recalls Haman's attempt to annihilate the Jews, Passover recalls enslavement in pharaonic Egypt, Yom HaShoah recalls the Nazi war against the Jews, and Tisha B'Av recalls the destruction of the Temple in Jerusalem by the Romans and numerous other sad occasions in Jewish history. A Jewish person might repeat this calendar of ritual recollection every year, over and over again, for his entire life. And this is not even to mention the daily recitation of the Aleinu prayer, which praises God for choosing Israel by contrast to other nations "who bow down to vanity and emptiness and pray to a god who will not save," or the tradition that every morning a Jewish man should thank God for not making him a non-Jew.[141]

Of course, there is usually much more to Judaism than this history of grievance and contempt. And many, many Jews experience their Jewishness as a loving and moral, outward-reaching, open-armed, altogether happier tradition. But there does seem to be an unspoken imperative underlying many variations of Judaism and Jewishness, which is: *never give up on your resentment!* And we might imagine that even the happiest Jews fall into a foul mood from time to time and perhaps on such occasions dig into their tradition's ample reservoir of complaint.

Are we to imagine that it is only the Jews that have given up entirely on their resentment that are meant to constitute the Jewish population of our ideal society? As it stands, the ideal society envisioned by the capabilities approach does not yet explicitly make room for the positive, which is to say affirmed role of anger, fear, distrust, and resentment in being some kinds of people. The blackness that will never forgive the history of white supremacy, the way of being Native American that will forever mourn when others celebrate Thanksgiving, the way of being Chicana that will not stop loudly yearning to resurrect Aztlán, the way of being a woman that will forever resent the history of patriarchy and the laissez-faire acceptability of sexual intimidation—should we imagine that these kinds of people will not exist in the society that we are striving together to become?[142] Wouldn't this amount to asking some people to strive to achieve a society where they will not be welcome?

Let me be very clear about something: there is a difference between justifiable indignation about ongoing capability depravation (injustice) and the kind of resentment that I have in mind, which can be presumed to linger indefinitely after the capabilities are securely guaranteed. There is also a difference between the distrust that I have in mind and the serious political judgment that core institutions are in danger of veering toward severe decline or existential crisis. In fact, one of the extraordinary accomplishments of *The Plot Against America* is to make vivid the terrifying uncertainty involved in trying to determine if you are just indulging in ethnic panic or indeed watching your deepest fears come to life. For many people in the United States, this terrifying uncertainty is newly acute after the election of Donald Trump in 2016.

And yet if we decide not to give up on America then we must be ready to imagine an America that it is worth striving to become, which means we have to be realistic about the emotions that will linger even in the best possible circumstances. If anything, the election of Donald Trump should be a wake-up call to anyone who somehow believed that the ugly emotions that are baked into American lives are quickly dissolving. And there is a big difference between striving to become a nation bound by political love *because we have eradicated* the perverse emotions and ideas that have divided us historically and abetted injustice and striving to become a nation bound by political love *in spite of the persistence of* the perverse emotions and ideas that have divided us historically and abetted injustice. I argue for the latter.

But recognizing that it is part of a good and flourishing Jewish life never to forgive the scourge of Amalek and generally to divide the world into Jewish vs. goyish can only take us so far in recognizing the divisive emotions that will linger even in the best version of America that we can realistically imagine. In the next two chapters I will explain, in depth, the fact of fraught societies. Just as Rawls hoped to make his vision of justice more realistic by assuming the fact of reasonable pluralism, I hope to make Nussbaum's vision of political love more realistic by building onto it an assumption of the fact of fraught societies. This will include adding to her political conception of the person the explicit assumption that each of us carries a legacy of historical injustice. Once the fact of fraught societies is clearly elaborated, I turn to the key resource that will enable political love to endure despite the fact of fraught societies: the capability of play.

2

THE FACT OF FRAUGHT SOCIETIES I

The Problem of Remainders

I have suggested that perverse ideas and emotions about others forged under conditions of conflict and injustice cannot be presumed to disappear as political institutions become more just. Even if the central human capabilities were increasingly guaranteed by the basic structure of American society, and people began to see each other and themselves according to the capabilities conception of the citizen, we should nevertheless expect irreconcilable grudges, antipathies, and fantasylands to persist. This is the fact of fraught societies. In this chapter and the next I explain the three problems that constitute the fact of fraught societies: the problem of remainders, the problem of reproduction, and the missing link problem. In the process, I begin to explain in detail why the fact of fraught societies is not an obstacle to political love. To the contrary, broadly shared mature political love is possible *only* when the fact of fraught societies is appropriately acknowledged.

THE PROBLEM OF REMAINDERS

Ugly stereotypes, cruel epithets, and false beliefs about various groups saturate American popular culture. Think of the NFL Redskins logo or the mammy caricature on display with Aunt Jemima pancake products. Then there are the stock characters that reappear in movies and TV shows like the black thug, the Jewish shyster, the Latina domestic, and so on. Periodic public outbursts of nasty epithets by celebrities exacerbate the fear that something ubiquitous but hidden is being revealed. It is impossible not to wonder who else might use words like *nigger* and *faggot* or talk about the "fucking Jews" behind closed doors.[1] The rise in public expressions of hateful language like this with the election of Donald Trump in 2016 only confirms the long-standing everyday assumptions of the historically oppressed in America.

What is more, historical stigmatization is built into the American cultural landscape. There are apparently about fifteen hundred memorials to the Confederacy, including names of public schools and state holidays, throughout the United States.[2] Canonized literary works—*The Adventures of Huckleberry Finn* being the most famous and controversial— carry old stereotypes and slurs into the cultural future. Even seemingly benign family favorites do their part. I remember sitting down with one of my kids to watch the old Disney *Peter Pan* cartoon, which I loved as a child, only to find that I had entirely forgotten about its offensive depiction of Native Americans gleefully dancing around singing, "What Makes the Red Man Red?"

Even where derogatory terms, stereotypes, and prejudices are not made explicit, watching American television and movies, listening to popular music, or exploring products sold at American malls can still give the impression that to be a "normal" American is to be white and middle class, to celebrate Christmas and desire only members of the opposite sex, and to be largely unperturbed by the political status quo. Fantasies that are about people who fit this description, or are suitable to their tastes, still dominate television and the movies.

The problem of remainders is that any effort to eradicate or police these elements of culture threatens to extend the power of the liberal state too far and infringe upon the entitlement to expressive capabilities of some of its citizens. Thus constrained, liberal states are unable to prevent stereotypes, prejudices, and demeaning epithets from lurking in popular culture. And they are likewise limited in their capacity to interfere legitimately with norms that proliferate in private life and consumer culture. The problem of remainders is therefore a deep structural feature of any liberal political order and, under a variety of descriptions, it has rightfully been identified as a likely conduit through which racial and other forms of oppression are perpetuated.

I will investigate the problem of remainders as it has been diagnosed in the work of two major critics of liberalism: Leo Strauss and Frantz Fanon. They are perhaps strange bedfellows. Strauss is often described as a conservative critic of liberalism from the right, while Fanon is described as a radical critic from the left. Nevertheless, I will show their critiques to be complimentary. Only once we have considered Strauss and Fanon together can we fully appreciate the distinctive features of what I am calling the problem of remainders.

In the process of interpreting their diagnoses of liberalism, I will also show that these two masterful diagnosticians longed for something that can, in fact, be accommodated by a revised liberal ideal that we can strive toward in the United States. I will show how the concerns of both Strauss and Fanon can be assuaged by a capabilities conception of political justice that differentiates between the domain of the political and the domain of play. Strauss and Fanon were right that the problem of remainders is an interminable problem for liberal states. The challenges they posed deserve a convincing response.

LEO STRAUSS'S CHALLENGE

Let's go back to Max Nordau's lament in 1897: "For one or two generations the Jew was allowed to believe that he was merely a German, Frenchman, Italian, and so forth, like all the rest of his countrymen" only later to find anti-Semitism surging again, showing "to a mortified Jew, who thought anti-Semitism was gone forever, the true picture of his situation." Leo Strauss, born two years after Nordau's speech, had similar concerns. Strauss was raised in a traditional Jewish family in a conservative German town on the outskirts of Marburg, a city whose university "stood as a central symbol of enlightened German humanism."[3] He matured intellectually amidst a surge of unprecedented German Jewish freedom and creativity. German Jews at that time spoke of a symbiosis between German humanism and modern Judaism.[4] When the Weimar Constitution was established in 1919, German Jewish liberals hailed the long-awaited political instantiation of the German humanistic tradition with which they identified. During the Weimar years, Strauss completed a doctoral dissertation under Ernst Cassirer, taught at Franz Rosenzweig's Freies Jüdisches Lehrhaus, published a paper on Hermann Cohen's reading of Spinoza's biblical criticism in Martin Buber's journal *Der Jude*, and held a research fellowship at the Hochschule für die Wissenschaft des Judentums in Berlin.[5] It was a heady moment for German Jews, including Strauss, even if it coincided with a tidal swell of anti-Semitism.

Luckily, scholarship brought Strauss westward at the age of thirty-three. He was a naturalized citizen of the United States by the time he turned thirty-nine. Only a few years later, Strauss's former German neighbors began lining up Jewish men, women, and children to be shot. Later they would pile Jews into the sealed cargo hulls of trucks rigged so that the exhaust from the engine would be funneled in and everyone inside would suffocate to death. Eventually, Strauss's former *landsmen* brought whichever Jews they could catch—men, women, and children—from far and wide, to centralized camps for wholesale extermination by poisonous gas in execution chambers dressed up to look like open showers. Of the 240,000 Jews still left in Germany and Austria by the time the "final solution" was implemented in 1942, non-Jewish Germans murdered an estimated 210,000 (90 percent).[6]

Strauss dodged the Nazi menace. But as a political philosopher he would never escape the sense that liberal democracy had been proven profoundly unreliable. Weimar could only ever be remembered as the "sorry spectacle of justice without a sword."[7] It had brought legal equality to Jews. It did not, however, reflect or establish any deep sense of shared political destiny and community between non-Jewish Germans and German Jews. According to Strauss, "as a demand of reason it had no effect on the feelings of the non-Jews."[8]

Like Nordau, Strauss thought that Jewish liberals had been duped. The German humanistic tradition, with which liberal Jews identified so strongly, was not a "universal ethos" at all—it was a Christian exclusivist ethos. Strauss quotes Goethe to illustrate his point. In an infamous passage from *Wilhelm Meisters Wanderjahre*, Wilhelm Meister and the "world league" are setting out to build an enlightened utopia in America. The authorial voice proclaims that in such a place

> we instruct our children from their youth on in the great advantages which [the Christian religion] has brought to us; but of its author, of its course, we speak to them only at the end. Then only does the author become dear and cherished, and all reports regarding him become sacred. Drawing a conclusion which one may perhaps call pedantic, but of which one must at any rate admit that it follows from the premise, we do not tolerate any Jew among us; for how could we grant him a share in the highest culture, the origin and tradition of which he denies?[9]

According to Strauss, Jews that found spiritual kinship with Johann Wolfgang von Goethe, Johann Gottfried Herder, Immanuel Kant, or Gotthold Ephraim Lessing thought that they were welcome to grow among the humanistic branches of the German Enlightenment tree without the nourishment and stability of its Christian roots. To the contrary, even when the law tolerates and protects the diverse individuals who live on German land, to be a *real* German would always be an evaluation decisively justified by German Christian norms. What is more, for Jewish Germans, "political dependence was also spiritual dependence."[10] Having embraced German humanistic thought as foundational, as the ultimate model and measure of their liberal brand of Judaism, they internalized their own self-repudiation. In this sense, Jewish liberals suffered a deep internal distortion that is not unlike what we will see in "the colonized" described by Fanon.

A liberal constitution, thus, could guarantee political equality for individual Jewish citizens, but it could have no authority to justify the claim that Jews could be *real* Germans. This is partly a result of the problem that Nordau recognized decades earlier. According to Strauss, the problem is that liberal states are designed to protect discrimination in the "private sphere," even as they seek to prevent discrimination in the "public sphere." The result is that discrimination is in fact *fostered* by the liberal state.[11] "The liberal state cannot provide a solution to the Jewish problem," Strauss writes, "for such a solution would require the legal prohibition against every kind of 'discrimination,' i.e., the abolition of the private sphere, the denial of the difference between state and society, the destruction of the liberal state."[12]

For Strauss, then, liberalism is constrained by a kind of formalism not to interfere with the persistence and proliferation of prejudicial practices, ideas, stereotypes, and so on. It can grant formal equality among citizens in public, but it can do nothing to protect people in the private sphere from being subject to substantive discrimination. Thus, in the end, liberal democracy actually facilitates the tyranny of the majority. As far as Strauss was concerned, "in the absence of a superior recognized equally by both parties the natural judge on the Germanness of the German Jews was the non-Jewish Germans."[13] And given their preexisting "private" antipathy toward Jews, it is not surprising that non-Jewish Germans ultimately judged their Jewish neighbors to be incapable of legitimate Germanness altogether.

The "Jewish problem" that Strauss refers to can be phrased like this: what should be the fate of the Jews now that the medieval theological-political order has been shattered? Strauss claims that the liberal state cannot provide a solution to the Jewish problem because liberalism ultimately has recourse to no authority greater than the whim of the majority.[14] Where the majority is predisposed to Jew-hatred, a liberal constitution has no defense against an anti-Semitic populist movement propelled by a charismatic demagogue. But even when someone decisively exceptional like Adolf Hitler does not emerge to take the reins of sovereignty left dangling by liberal democracy, the lack of a final authority to which all members of society are existentially bound—that is, bound to the core of their being—leaves any detested minority politically and socially dependent on those who detest them.

So, if the liberal state cannot provide a solution to the "Jewish problem," then what is to be done? In his 1962 lecture "Why We Remain Jews," Strauss reflected on a provocative answer to this question: why not simply cease to be Jews? This possibility is all the more powerful now that we've learned from Mills, Jacobson, Wilderson and others that, by being able to pass as white, Jews are free to escape the status of a vulnerable minority. But why be satisfied simply with being white? Why not free oneself of Jewishness entirely? Strauss identifies the poet Heinrich Heine with this leading question—or, more specifically, with the idea that "Judaism is not a religion but a misfortune."[15] Why not come to this conclusion, given liberalism's incapacity to prevent "private" discrimination and the distorting impact that liberal culture (for instance, German humanism) has already had on Jewishness?

Strauss notes the various ways that people do in fact draw this conclusion. They change their names, they marry and assimilate into non-Jewish families, they don't have children.[16] But he thinks that for most people who were born and raised to see themselves as Jews this is not an attractive option. For these people, he concludes, "It is impossible not to remain a Jew. It is impossible to run away from one's origins. It is impossible to get rid of one's past by wishing it away."[17] People whose Jewishness is sufficiently integral to their self-understanding, like a vital organ, will not readily excise it from themselves—nor will they feel much allegiance to a social or political order that implicitly or explicitly recommends this certainly fatal procedure.

If a significant number of Jews will find it impossible not to remain Jews, and the liberal state will leave them forever vulnerable to discriminatory ideas, emotions, and social networks that remain in the private sphere, then perhaps they need to find a liberal state that is not populated by a non-Jewish majority. Why not build a Jewish nation-state with a Jewish majority? How about Zionism?

Strauss's first thought when he considers the Zionist response to the "Jewish question" is political Zionism, which he identifies with Leo Pinsker and Theodore Herzl. Political Zionism, he explains, was "the movement of an elite on behalf of a community, constituted by common descent and common degradation, for the restoration of their honor through the acquisition of statehood and therefore of a country."[18] But political Zionism was only a rescue mission. It merely meant to relocate Jews to a modern liberal nation-state in which they would be the majority and therefore not subjected to the judgment of a non-Jewish majority about their place in the private sphere of society.

Strauss tells an interesting story about his own early involvement with political Zionism that will prove important:

Political Zionism was a very honorable suggestion, but one must add that it was also merely formal or poor. I would like to illustrate this. I was myself (as you might have guessed) a political Zionist in my youth, and was a member of a Zionist student organization. In this capacity, I occasionally met Jabotinsky, the leader of the Revisionists. He asked me, "what are you doing?" I said, "Well, we read the Bible, we study Jewish history, Zionist theory, and, of course, we keep abreast of developments, and so on." He replied, "And rifle practice?" And I had to say, "No."[19]

Strauss wasn't interested in being part of a rescue mission. He didn't really want to become a "rifle practice" kind of guy, like the militant Jabotinsky. His early engagement with Zionism was invigorating because of the exciting textual engagement with the Hebrew Bible, because of the chance to join other Jews in wrestling with big questions about Jewish history, the Jewish people, and the Jewish fate. Political Zionism was ultimately unattractive because "the mind was in no way employed, or even the heart was in no way employed, in matters Jewish."[20] The natural next step was then to consider cultural Zionism.

The key premise for this option is that "Jewish heritage" is a culture, the "product of the national mind, of the national genius," and a Jewish state with a Jewish majority is the only place for such a culture to thrive.[21] But the cultural Zionism option conceals the same secret that Goethe's German cultural humanism concealed. Strauss explains, "the foundation, the authoritative layer, of the Jewish heritage presents itself, not as a product of the human mind, but as a divine gift, as divine revelation."[22] Just as Goethe's utopia was ultimately rooted in Christ, the cultural Zionist would inevitably discover that the Jewish heritage is ultimately rooted in the revelation at Sinai. This is a problem: how can the "cultural" Jew, who believes in "the national genius" but *not* divine revelation, have a share in the highest culture, the origin and tradition of which he denies?

At this point, according to Strauss, one must entertain the possibility of religious Zionism: the idea of a Jewish state that is fundamentally justified by the revelation at Sinai. But religious Zionism, too, cannot be sustained. If one is to defer to Torah, Talmud, and halacha, one "must regard as blasphemous the notion of a human solution to the Jewish problem."[23] The State of Israel may be lauded as an important event in Jewish history, but it cannot be regarded as "the arrival of the messianic age, of the redemption of Israel and of all men."[24] If, however, it seems like it might be good enough to change Jewish history drastically by creating a state with a Jewish majority, despite the fact that it cannot ultimately be justified by Torah, Talmud, and halacha—well, then we're back to political

Zionism, and then cultural Zionism, and then religious Zionism again, and so on.

In the end, Strauss resigns himself to the conclusion: "Finite, relative problems can be solved; infinite, absolute problems cannot be solved. In other words, human beings will never create a society which is free from contradictions. From every point of view it looks as if the Jewish people were the chosen people, at least in the sense that the Jewish problem is the most manifest symbol of the human problem insofar as it is a social or political problem."[25] As Strauss sees it, the liberal state does not solve the Jewish problem, nor does political Zionism, cultural Zionism, or religious Zionism. Neither can the Jewish problem be solved by a communist revolution that erases the public/private divide: "we have empirical data about this fact, the abolition of a liberal society and how it affects the fate of Jews."[26]

In the end, the Jewish problem and the fundamental human political problem are irresolvable because "a nation is a nation by virtue of what it looks up to."[27] Recall that it was "the absence of a superior recognized equally by both parties" that left Jews vulnerable to the perverse will of the non-Jewish Germans in the 1930s and 1940s.[28] The fundamental human political problem that is exemplified by the modern Jewish problem, for Strauss, is the lack of a definitive, absolute sovereign law, revealed by an unimpugnable lawgiver who is recognized as such by all members of the polity. This is a problem that reflects a deep conflict at the core of "Western civilization." It is a conflict between Athens and Jerusalem, between philosophy and revelation.

Only under a revealed law could the conflicting roots of Western civilization—Hebrew fear of the Lord and Greek philosophical wonder—be reconciled.[29] Strauss thought that Plato recognized this need in antiquity; but Plato foundered because he lacked the needful lawgiver. On the other hand, Strauss saw the medieval Jewish and Muslim rationalists— Maimonides and Alfarabi, especially—as representatives of the only historical age ever to have accomplished the reconciliation.[30]

Unfortunately, for Strauss, that "age of belief" has long since been displaced by the "modern Enlightenment," where the profound conflict between Athens and Jerusalem has been radicalized into a petty choice between atheism and Orthodoxy.[31] But really there is no way back to the law. Insofar as there is a choice at all, one has already revealed oneself not to be living under the law. Orthodoxy that is *chosen* and lived *against* the modern Enlightenment is not *fear of the Lord*.[32] To be sure, Strauss entertains the idea that an individual Jew might find his way back to the law.[33] But this is only a fantasy for Strauss. When he reflects, at the age of sixty-eight, on the question of where he stands between Jerusalem and Athens, he muses, "We are open to both and willing to listen to each. . . . By saying that we wish to hear first and then to act to decide, we have already decided in favor of Athens against Jerusalem. This seems to be necessary for all of us who cannot be orthodox."[34]

Where does this leave him? And, more important, where does this leave *us* as we look to Strauss in order to think deeply about the problem of remainders? He offers us this final word:

> There is nothing better than the uneasy solution offered by liberal soci-ety, which means legal equality plus private "discrimination." We must simply recognize the fact, which we all know, that the Jewish minority is not universally popular, and we must recognize the consequences which follow from that. We all know that there is in this country an entirely extralegal, but not illegal, what we can call "racial hierarchy" coming down from the Anglo-Saxons, down to the Negroes; and we are just above the Negroes. We must face that. And we must see that there is a similarity between the Jewish question and the Negro question.[35]

Despite his concerns, Strauss concedes that the liberal state is still the best that we can do. He simply does not accept "the premise that every problem can be solved."[36] And he sees clearly that the unsolvable Jewish problem is equally a problem for black Americans and presumably for all those who have historically been subjected to and unable to pene-trate the social and cultural power held by the American WASP core group. The "racial hierarchy" that he describes even resonates with the racial contract and other accounts of white supremacy maintained under the facade of legal equality.

How can we imagine that Strauss might want to live in such a flawed society, in a liberal state? I think that he would want to live with his mind and heart employed with matters Jewish. This is what invigorated him as a young Zionist, before Jabotinsky asked him if he was practicing to shoot a rifle. He would want to *live the conflict* between Jerusalem and Athens.[37]

I surmise that Strauss wanted to live a life in which he could *play* with Jewishness, Greek philosophy, Islamic political thought, Spinoza, Zionism, etc. And he was prepared to endure some "private" discrimination in the process, as long as he could also enjoy some of the fundamental legal protections provided by the liberal state. What Strauss could not imagine was a vision of the liberal state that would address forthrightly and embrace the very unsolvable problems that he merely bent to in an attitude of resignation.[38] This is precisely what I hope to offer.

FRANTZ FANON'S CHALLENGE

Strauss's suggestion that Jews and others simply endure the "private discrimination" perpetuated by liberal states sounds tone-deaf in America in 2018. For one thing, Strauss does not appreciate the distinct problems of color-coded discrimination in the United States and how Jews are protected from it by being white. His focus on discrimination also fails to address the deep systemic structures of oppression that have organized, for instance, race and gender within the basic structures of liberal societies. Racial and gender oppression have always run through the power circuits of liberal societies, crisscrossing and inverting the private-public divide in myriad ways. What is more, we are now apt to view the effects of "private discrimination" as much more serious in their own right than Strauss did. Whatever their contribution to the instability of liberal states, we might think that stereotypes and slurs cause profound harm in and of themselves.

A major obstacle to accepting the idea that perverse remainders will persist even in the best America that we can realistically imagine is if "misrecognition" is a fundamental harm. In the 1990s Charles Taylor expressed this concern paradigmatically when he wrote, "a person or group of people can suffer real damage, real distortion, if the people or society around them mirror back to them a confining or demeaning or contemptible picture of themselves. Nonrecognition or misrecognition can inflict harm, can be a form of oppression, imprisoning someone in a false, distorted, and reduced mode of being."[39] According to Taylor, it was Frantz Fanon who introduced the idea of misrecognition as a fundamental harm to modern political thought.[40]

As Taylor recounts, Fanon in *The Wretched of the Earth* centered his critique of colonialism on the distorted, inferior self-image that is forcibly ingrained into the way that the subjugated see themselves and others. Freedom, under such circumstances, requires that the distorted self-image be purged or revised.[41] If perverse remainders are responsible for perpetuating the distorted self-image, how can they be allowed to remain in the society that we hope to achieve? If a liberal view, like the one that I offer, accepts the problem of remainders as a permanent feature of democratic societies, doesn't it thereby accept the racial contract and other regimes of stigmatization as permanent features of society? Isn't this just the old liberal ruse? Fanon's answer to this question would, no doubt, be an emphatic *yes*. I must, then, examine the precise mechanics of Fanon's view if I am going to argue, plausibly, that perverse remainders can persist without constituting or perpetuating subjugation or injustice.

In 1943, at the age of eighteen, Frantz Fanon left his lower middle-class family on the island of Martinique to fight with the French army under General de Gaulle, to free France from German occupation.[42] Fanon seems to have been inspired to join the fight in Europe by a universalism that would later be the bane of his many revolutionary avatars. Reportedly, he justified his decision saying that when human freedom is at stake "we are all involved, white, black, or yellow."[43] He spent most of his time as a soldier in Morocco and Algeria. While there, his experience of the intense racism of French society was a "rude awakening."[44] After the war, in 1947, Fanon went to France and attended medical school, training as a psychiatrist.[45] He had grown up thinking of himself as French, even European of a sort; in the French army, and in France as a student, he realized that the French did not agree.[46] To them, he was merely "a black."

Fed up with French hypocrisy, he took a job as a psychiatrist at a hospital in Algeria in 1953; the revolution, with which he would be forever associated, was about to break out in earnest.[47] He helped the Front de Liberation Nationale (FLN) from the very beginning—all the while spending his days treating the French colonialists (a testament to his ethical commitment as a physician). After joining other doctors supporting the FLN in a strike, in 1957 he was expelled from Algeria and fled to Tunisia. There he wrote on behalf of the Algerian revolutionary cause in *El Moudjahid* and functioned as a diplomatic representative for the FLN abroad.[48] On December 6, 1961 Fanon died of leukemia, but not before he completed *The Wretched of the Earth*.

The book was unapologetically radical.[49] In it Fanon argued, among other things, for the intrinsic value of revolutionary violence and the overthrow of Europe's hypocritical global political order. Lewis Gordon writes, "Fanon, like Mao Tse Tung, Malcolm X, Huey Newton, Che Guevara, Fidel Castro, or Regis Debray, represented a frightening reality to the white world: people of color and people of developing nations who were willing to use violence in their struggle for freedom."[50] According to David Macey, one of his biographers, Fanon "came to be seen as the apostle of violence, the prophet of a violent Third World revolution that posed an even greater threat to the West than communism."[51]

The world depicted in Fanon's *The Wretched of the Earth* is defined by the dichotomy between colonist and colonized: it is "a Manichean world."[52] The colonist is manifested through his violent exploitation of the colonized, through which he also brings the colonized into being: "It is the colonist who *fabricated* and *continues to fabricate* the colonized subject."[53] In this respect, Fanon allies himself with Jean-Paul Sartre, who wrote: "it is the anti-Semite who *makes* the Jew."[54]

Because the harm that concerns Fanon is a deep distortion of self-understanding and not, say, lack of franchise or an unfair distribution of wealth and power, the remedy must effect a radical transformation of the colonized subject into something else: "the 'thing' colonized becomes a man through the very process of liberation."[55] But to "become a man" does not entail simply taking the place of the colonist or living the lifestyle enjoyed by privileged whites in, for instance, France or America. "After the struggle is over," writes Fanon, "there is not only the demise of colonialism, but also the demise of the colonized. This new humanity, for itself and for others, inevitably defines a new humanism."[56] This is Fanon's final plea: "we must make a new start, develop a new way of thinking, and endeavor to create a new man."[57]

In *The Wretched of the Earth*, he suggests that the life of this new man "can only materialize from the rotting cadaver of the colonist."[58] Only acts of violence against the colonists can transform the colonized into new men; "Violence can thus be understood to be the perfect mediation. The colonized man liberates himself in and through violence. This praxis enlightens the militant because it shows him the means and the end."[59] The violence of the colonized may function epiphenomenally as a means to political independence, but, more important, it is an end in itself: a transformative incitement of new humanity.[60] For Fanon, violence washes away the subjugated self-understanding of the colonized: "At the individual level, violence is a cleansing force. It rids the colonized of their inferiority complex, of their passive and despairing attitude. It emboldens them, and restores their self-confidence."[61]

Without violent praxis, argues Fanon, "there is nothing but a carnival parade and a lot of hot air. All that is left is slight readaptation, a few reforms at the top, a flag, and down at the bottom a shapeless, writhing mass, still mired in the Dark Ages."[62] The importance of violence to Fanon and his legacy should not be underestimated.[63] Neil Roberts puts it this way: "Fanon transforms the terrain of political theory with Copernican revolutionary insight by calling attention to the existence of intrinsic, metaphysical values in relation to violence."[64]

It is also important to clarify that, despite Charles Taylor's influential appropriation, Fanon does not see the relevant harm resulting primarily from a failure on the part of the colonizer to recognize *the culture* of the colonized and its worth. What Fanon opposes cannot be remedied through education—even if it showcases the stifled culture of the oppressed. "Colonialism," writes Fanon, "will never be put to shame by exhibiting unknown cultural treasures under its nose."[65] Similarly, Fanon had no patience for bourgeois Third World intellectuals who "go native" and try to glamorize what is supposed to be a suppressed traditional culture.[66] The point is made well by Anthony Appiah: "Frantz Fanon exposed the artificiality of nativist intellectuals, whose ersatz populism only estranges them from the *Volk* they venerate."[67] It was not enough that the history and culture of the natives be recognized and celebrated. For Fanon, "whatever proof there is of a once mighty Songhai civilization does not change the fact that the Songhais today are undernourished, illiterate, abandoned to the skies and water, with a blank mind and glazed eyes."[68] While malnourishment, illiteracy, and exposure are bad circumstances found among people well beyond the scope of Fanon's concern, the "blank mind and glazed eyes" are those of the colonized subject who can only be humanized through violence.

Sartre infamously amplified Fanon's view of violence in his preface to *The Wretched of the Earth*. He puts succinctly the fate of the colonizer and the colonized where this revolutionary violence is undertaken: "killing a European is killing two birds with one stone, eliminating in one go oppressor and oppressed: leaving one man dead and the other man free."[69] Sartre is not only writing about Europeans in Algeria. He writes to his own countrymen in France, "Europe is doomed. But, you will say once again, we live in the metropolis and we disapprove of extremes. It's true, you are not colonists, but you are not much better. They were your pioneers, you sent them overseas, they made you rich."[70]

Fanon is not solely concerned with the circumstances of institutional colonial occupation. It is in places like America and France where "Western values" like dignity and equality are most perfidious, insidious, and psychologically cruel. The experience of humiliation produced by a white child yelping, "'Dirty nigger!' Or simply, 'Look, a Negro!,'" which Fanon recounts in *Black Skin, White Masks*, is not specific to actual colonial occupation.[71] But this is the experience that exemplifies the harm that Fanon brought to the world's attention: "'Look, a Negro! *Maman*, a Negro!' . . . My body was returned to me spread-eagled, disjointed, redone, draped in mourning on this white winter's day. The Negro is an animal, the Negro is bad, the Negro is wicked, the Negro is ugly; look, a Negro; the Negro is trembling, the Negro is trembling because he's cold, the small boy is trembling because he's afraid of the Negro . . . the little white boy runs to his mother's arms: '*Maman*, the Negro's going to eat me.'"[72]

This powerful passage, in a book written a decade before *The Wretched of the Earth* while Fanon was completing his doctorate in psychiatry in France, illustrates Fanon's sense that wherever he is in the white dominated world, the black man's body always situates him beneath the gaze of racist white eyes.[73] There he is seen as a bad, mean, ugly animal, ready to eat you up. In this respect, the black man is worse off than the Jew, who, according to Fanon, is slave merely to the idea that others have of him, but not to the appearance of his body.[74] The Jew is also able to pass as white, whereas, as far as Fanon is concerned, a black person has no such option.[75]

At the same time, when Fanon describes the pervasive experience of being the target of aggression, which is characteristic of the black man's everyday life, he turns favorably to Sartre's description of the Jewish experience. "Certain pages of *Anti-Semite and Jew*," he writes, "are some of the finest we have ever read. The finest, because the problem they raise moves us to the very core."[76] In the pages he cites, Sartre portrays the Jew as a perverse contrivance whose every effort at liberation is tainted by the falseness of his condition. Sartre writes,

His life is nothing but a long flight from others and from himself. He has been alienated even from his own body; his emotional life has been cut in two; he has been reduced to pursuing the impossible dream of universal brotherhood in a world that rejects him. Whose is the fault? It is our eyes that reflect to him the unacceptable image that he wishes to dissimulate. It is our words and our gestures—*all* our words and *all* our gestures, our anti-Semitism, but equally our condescending liberalism—that have poisoned him. It is we who constrain him to choose to be a Jew *whether through flight from himself or through self-assertion.*[77]

This is the fundamental crime perpetrated by Europe against the Jews, according to Sartre. He therefore concludes: "the Jewish blood that the Nazis shed falls on all our heads."[78]

The Jew, here, is caught in a maddening, terrifying panic of flight from himself and others, with no exit in sight. The promise of redemption through universal values, which he clings to desperately, is the perfidious projection of an anti-Semitic social universe. Thus he is left hopeless, betrayed, despairing, and unmoored. And he is in this position because his society needs him to be in this position. Fanon affirms this view, arguing that Christian Europe's feeling of superiority requires an "inferiorized" scapegoat,[79] and in this respect "what others have said about the Jew applies perfectly to the black man."[80] The anonymous character of "the black" in *Black Skin, White Masks*, who has had many of Fanon's personal experiences, flails manically as he tries to affirm his own humanity in a world where to be human is presumptively to be white.

Lewis Gordon explains that in *Black Skin, White Masks*

each chapter represents options offered the black by modern Western thought. In good faith, then, the black hero attempts to live through each of these options simply as a human being. But the black soon discovers that to do so calls for living simply as a white. Antiblack racism presents whiteness as the "normal" mode of "humaness." So, the black reasons, if blackness and whiteness are constructed, perhaps the black could then live the white construction. . . . Each portrait is, however, a tale of how exercising this option leads to failure.[81]

Fanon, thus, theorizes the crisis of the inferiorized, who are stuck flailing from one aborted flight to another, in terms of a "paradox of failure."

Gordon writes, "although Fanon the quasi-anonymous hero of the text, the black, constantly fails (misses his mark), Fanon the critic of Western discourses of Man, Fanon the revolutionary theorist who demands systemic and systematic change, succeeds (by identification of each failure). Paradoxically, if the hero of the text wins (that is, achieves his aims), the hero of thought (the theorist) fails, and vice versa."[82] *Black Skin, White Masks* draws us into the embodied trauma of "the black," whose grasping for humanization necessarily fails under white supremacy. At the same time, Fanon's theoretical insight into this failure succeeds. But Fanon's successful theoretical questioning of white supremacy is, then, yanked from under him by a world that still looks down on him as a "black." Even an intellectual genius like Fanon, as a black man, is caught in a merciless cycle that always comes back to failure.

How is it possible to get out of this terrible situation? Fanon writes, "in order to break the vicious circle, he [the black man] explodes."[83] He can only break the vicious circle if he explodes, and it is precisely this that perfidious liberalism denies him. Fanon explains, "the white man says to him: 'Brother, there is no difference between us.' But the black man *knows* there is a difference. He *wants* it. He would like the white man to suddenly say to him: 'Dirty nigger.' Then he would have that unique occasion—to 'show them.' But usually there is nothing, nothing but indifference or paternalistic curiosity. The former slave wants his humanity to be challenged; he is looking for a fight; he wants a brawl."[84] This desire for a palpable difference, the desire to hear it cursed in his face so that he can explode, is what Fanon calls the "alterity of rupture, of struggle and combat."[85] But it is not forthcoming when liberal-minded whites feign innocence and with politeness and civility squelch every opportunity for creative emotional outburst. At the same time, the kind of creativity that Fanon hopes for cannot really be "reactive" at its core.[86] It must fundamentally result from a self-determined leap.

"My life must not be devoted to making an assessment of black values," he writes, "There is no white world; there is no white ethic—any more than there is a white intelligence. There are from one end of the world to the other men who are searching. I am not a prisoner of History. I must not look for the meaning of my destiny in that direction. I must constantly remind myself that the real *leap* consists of introducing invention into life. In the world I am heading for, I am endlessly creating myself. I show solidarity with humanity provided I can go one step further."[87] Fanon rejects the idea that he is tasked to cultivate "black values" in order to counter "white values." He recognizes that his own Manichaean impulse to separate the world into black and white is part of his distorted self-understanding. He writes, "it is by going beyond the historical and instrumental given that I initiate my cycle of freedom."[88]

The cycle of freedom is the circular process of success and failure, affirmation and negation, which becomes combustible as it accelerates. When the cycle heats up sufficiently to induce frenzied bewilderment, these combustible elements can cause the friction needed to ignite genuinely free action. And then freedom is just *to leap*.[89] But genuinely free action is not necessarily violent performance in *Black Skin, White Masks* as it is in *The Wretched of the Earth*. I agree with Judith Butler that at the end of *Black Skin, White Masks* Fanon seems to entertain a nonviolent version of the self-innovation necessary to achieve a new humanity.[90]

He cries out against dehumanizing instrumentalization and subjugation. He longs to be able to desire and discover a humanity that is overwhelmed by racialization. He writes, "The black man is not. No more than the white man. Both have to move away from the inhuman voices of their respective ancestors so that a genuine communication can be born."[91] But first, he says, there needs to be a heightened critical self-awareness, "an effort at disalienation" that includes "self-consciousness and renunciation."[92] Then, with just the right touch, something new can emerge that has nothing to do with hierarchy: "Superiority? Inferiority? Why not simply try to touch the other, feel the other, discover each other? Was my freedom not given me to build the world of *you*, man?. . . My final prayer: O my body, always make me a man who questions!"[93]

If in *The Wretched of the Earth* Fanon prescribes rage violently unleashed, in *Black Skin, White Masks* he longs for the curious, solicitous touch of equals who are leveled by a life of questioning—of two blind would-be lovers flirtatiously feeling their way to new perceptibility. Fanon's central insight, in both cases, is that our efforts to articulate moral ends discursively will fail because of our corrupt language and ideas, and this requires a "turn to the body." This means that new practices of bodily interaction and performance must take hold and change our language before we can start to articulate a truly human morality. Though, to be sure, we cannot open these bodily possibilities without initiating the cycle of freedom through theoretical questioning. If we synthesize Fanon's view in both books, we can imagine the cycle of freedom exploding in an orgiastic revolution of sensuality that mixes violence, tenderness, and eroticism in a frenzied hope to produce some never before heard howl of humanity.[94]

This may be an attractive vision for some. But Fanon can offer no limits to what would be acceptable amidst such an explosion. His commitment to a radical break with distorted subjectivity and tainted values demands that he allow violence of any kind, and that we let it speak for itself. He can offer no moral constraints on the revolutionary violence that ensues.[95] None of us can judge the legitimacy of revolutionary violence or its effectiveness at producing a new humanity because we are not yet equipped to recognize the new humanity when we see it—we are, after all, citizens of the *old* humanity! If all our norms and ideas of the good derive from our irreparably distorted minds, then we can only have blind faith that transgressive bodily outbursts will result in a world that is somehow better than the one we've got.[96]

At this point Fanon starts to sound, to me, a lot like Augustine of Hippo in his *Confessions*. Augustine lived in the fourth century in what is now Algeria. In his *Confessions*, he narrates a personal story of crisis amidst the intellectual fashions and decadence of his time, of being whipped around by tortuous skepticism and false values. He tried mightily to make sense of his thoughts and desires, but his own mind was as corrupt as the world around him—every effort to think his way through the crisis was self-defeating.

So he started to yearn for something beyond the wretched contingencies of his world. Then he received the message: "Why are you relying on yourself, only to find yourself unreliable? Cast yourself upon him, do not be afraid. He will not withdraw himself so that you fall. Make *the leap* without anxiety; he will catch you and heal you" (my emphasis).[97] Struggling against himself, weeping, he hears a voice from afar. He hears, "pick up and read."[98] He picks up Paul's Letter to the Romans and reads a passage that calls on him to leave the contingent world behind, "but put on the Lord Jesus Christ and make no provision for the flesh in its lusts."[99] He leaped, and something wholly Other met him halfway—"All the shadows of doubt were dispelled."[100] My response is the same to both Fanon and Augustine: I am profoundly moved by the diagnosis, but the cure is not one that I (and presumably many other people of all kinds) can reasonably be expected to accept.

Nevertheless, some readers will at this point demand that the leap of intrinsically valuable revolutionary violence remain an option. To recoil from the radical challenge of *The Wretched of the Earth* and embrace the perhaps tamer bodily and discursive experimentalism of *Black Skin, White Masks* is surely the cowardly defensive tactic of a deluded bourgeois sap.[101] Maybe. But I suspect that the thrill of winking at revolutionary violence in contemporary America (or France, for that matter) is equally likely to derive from a pathology of the bourgeoisie. It tickles a longing for vitality, transgression, even the "festival of cruelty" that has enticed bourgeois readers of Friedrich Nietzsche and others since the nineteenth century.[102]

I will return to the attraction of Fanonian violence and how it relates to what is attractive about Nietzschean amoral self-creation—and the attraction to the wholly Other—when I address the missing link problem. At this point, though, I am prepared to move forward with my argument on the assumption that, in principle, there can be no acceptable *reasons* to accept Fanon's call to violent praxis: the force of Fanon's call to violence is not the force of reasons and argumentation. I am not, therefore, persuaded that we ought to hope for the emergence of Fanonian violence as the best response to the hypocrisies and failures of liberal democracy. Readers who are moved by Fanon to enact violence with the hope of transformative catharsis will have already put this book down and be on their way. I hope they are stopped.

THE PROBLEM OF REMAINDERS
FOR STRAUSS AND FANON

Both Strauss and Fanon are outraged by the weakness and lies of liberalism. Stereotypes, racial hierarchies, and social exclusion will persist in the society of a liberal state because, as Strauss indicates, liberal states must be as committed to protecting "private discrimination" as they are to guaranteeing protection from "public discrimination." Equality before the law in a liberal state coexists indifferently with inequality beyond the law, in the "private sphere." Under such circumstances, a powerful core group that is seen as culturally representative of the national majority (i.e., *real* Germans, *real* Americans) will always retain the prerogative to define social norms. In an America where this powerful core group is white and Christian we can expect white Christian fantasies and blind spots to dominate the private sphere. Were the formal pretenses of liberal institutions ever to pose a real challenge to the fundamental hegemony of this core group, as Strauss sees it, there is nothing to stop them from bursting their faux constraints and reasserting their sovereign will.

Fanon directs us specifically to the profound *racial* dehumanization that a liberal state leaves unchecked, and indeed circuitously defends, in its private sphere. Subjected to the downward-looking eyes of the white core group, "the black" is always a problem. He inhabits a threatening and uncomfortable "zone of nonbeing"; he is a kind of encroaching, nauseating nothingness.[103] Ways of seeing and representing "the black" that are perpetuated by the problem of remainders render him a "pure exteriority." As Gordon describes this condition, it is "the phenomenon of being seen as a thing, a mechanistic effect governed purely by causal forces, a being without an inner life and self-control."[104] This condition is not improved by mere formal equality. Instead, formal equality is an alibi for the white core group. They can use it when they are on the defensive to defend the deeper racial order.

Reading Strauss and Fanon, it is hard not to decide that the problem of remainders is a deal breaker. A liberal state like the United States will necessarily reproduce discrimination and racial hierarchy in its private sphere, even as it congratulates itself for whatever strides it makes toward public equality. And yet I have suggested that we should accept the problem of remainders as a feature of the fact of fraught societies—a fact that should be presumed to characterize even the best America that we can realistically imagine. How is this not another liberal ruse?

To start, Rawls made it very clear that as far as he was concerned "political" liberalism does not replicate the classical liberal public/private divide. In the ideal society that Rawls imagines, the basic structure of society always recognizes every person as a citizen—and therefore as entitled to political justice—wherever he or she may roam. "The principles defining the equal basic liberties and opportunities of citizens," he explains, "always hold in and through all so-called domains."[105] There is no preexisting private realm of sovereignty, legitimacy, or ownership to which the basic structure of society must defer. For instance, "the family" is not presumed to be a venerable natural formation with its own preexisting normative legitimacy that is merely protected and benefited by the state. Instead, the family is presumed to be an institution of the basic structure of society, to be shaped and constrained like any other.[106] And where I have written "the family" in the previous two sentences, I could just as easily have written "property ownership" or "work." From the perspective of political liberalism, all relationships in society should be shaped and constrained by political justice to some degree, even if sometimes at a great distance and with a light touch.

But this is not a sufficient response. After all, Rawls is still expecting that a well-ordered society will include people thriving side by side who have diverse ideas about what constitutes a good life. The whole point of political liberalism is to try to imagine a society that is just and stable despite the persistence of *preexisting* and *inevitable* irreconcilable conflicts about ultimate concerns. As Nussbaum explains, even if it is not precisely the public/private divide of classical liberalism, "the general structure of political liberalism requires a sphere of ethical choice outside of that which is politically compulsory."[107] This is why the problem of remainders abides: if this sphere of choice is a domain where diverse ways of life are allowed to thrive, then it has to be a place where people can enact the preexisting incorrigible drives, obscene longings, and unappeasable grudges that make them different from one another. It should also be a place, I hasten to add, where one can curate one's own audience or be alone. Recognizing the flaws in the classical liberal idea of a private sphere should not prejudice us against the profound importance to a good human life of reliable time and space that is *unwatched* and *mine*.

So, Rawls did not really close the loophole created by the public/private divide. Perverse remainders can be constrained on behalf of political justice, but these constraints must themselves be constrained by the need to allow robust diversity and choice. "But wait!" Rawls might exclaim, "I can close the loophole with an argument from the social bases of self-respect." Self-respect, for Rawls, means having confidence that you are capable of a human life worth living and having the conviction to pursue it.[108] Rawls thought that in an ideal society the "social bases of self-respect" would be guaranteed to all as a "primary good"—something that all citizens are presumed to want and deserve, regardless of whatever else they might want or deserve.[109]

But it is doubtful that Rawls's claim to guarantee the social bases of self-respect in all domains of society can do the trick. The social bases are just "things like the institutional fact that citizens have equal basic rights, and the public recognition of that fact."[110] To say that a society guarantees the social bases of self-respect is really just another way of saying that in that society everyone sees themselves and each other, and is seen by the basic structure of society, as a citizen (regardless of however else they might see themselves and each other).

But, as I indicated in the last chapter, Rawls's conception of the citizen is problematic. The efforts of well-intentioned liberals to see themselves and others as free, equal, independent, reasonable, and rational, and to get the basic structure of society to see everyone this way, have coexisted too comfortably for too long with oppressive ideologies (white supremacy, patriarchy, Christian hegemony, heteronormativity, etc.). Rawls is basically saying: trust me, this time it's going to work! Let's take a moment to look more closely at the problem. Rawls's political ideal perpetuates a kind of societal mind-body dualism, as I shall call it, which is integral to racial and other oppressive hierarchies. From this dualistic perspective, members of the empowered core group presume themselves fundamentally to be independent *minds*—they understand the meaning and value of liberal rights and hope to extend them to others. By contrast, the beneficiaries of these extended rights ("the black," women, homosexuals, "savages," etc.) are presumed fundamentally to be a mass of *bodies*.[111] The liberal promise has always been that the beneficiaries of newly extended liberal rights will now be individuated and seen as minds too.

This idealization of the citizen as a disembodied, independent mind is a fantastical projection of invulnerability built upon a state of denial about human animality. In this respect, Nussbaum offers a crucial corrective to Rawls. She points in the opposite direction. Rather than promise yet again that liberal rights can be extended to newly recognized independent minds, she suggests that we all see ourselves as vulnerable, dependent bodies who long for a thriving life in common. Instead of trying to raise us to an ideal of the free cooperative mind, she wants to immerse us in the common denominator of dependent embodiment.[112] Nussbaum defies

Marx's charge, made long ago, that liberalism always reproduces a distorted picture of human beings as disconnected, egoistic individuals who consent to participate in society only to the extent that it benefits their individual interests.[113] Nussbaum offers a liberal view that rejects the societal mind-body dualism that Rawls perpetuated with his still generally egoistic contractarianism.

The person who imagines himself to be an independent mind, who deigns to extend liberal rights to new populations, is the white man in *Black Skin, White Masks* who says to "the black," "Brother, there is no difference between us." The object of his gaze, "the black," has special knowledge: "The black" knows that there is a difference between them because he knows that the white man's magnanimity is founded on a self-aggrandizing fantasy that comes at the expense of "the black." The fantasy is that he, the white man, is an independent mind, a mind capable of granting mindedness to what looks like just a mass of bodies. The old liberal ideal invites the already empowered white bourgeoisie to smile broadly, stand proudly with dignified posture in fashionable clothes and sharp haircuts, with athleticism and all the vigor of youth bound for success, and asks only that they be ready to invite others—"minorities," people who are "diverse"—to join the posh alumni cocktail party.

The capabilities conception of the citizen, which is also a liberal ideal, asks something very different. It asks you to expose yourself. It asks you to admit that you were a helpless little baby once, that you used to piss and shit all over yourself, and somebody had to feed and clean and protect you to usher you into childhood. It asks you to admit that you are a body that sometimes smells, that sometimes fails, with hidden oddities, idiosyncratic sexual yearnings, and other secrets. Admit that you are afraid, that you need others, that you need to be loved. Admit that you will piss and shit all over yourself again! Maybe at the end of your life. Maybe before. Admit that your brain and bones will decay, that your flesh will droop, that your corpse will rot like any other dead animal in the ground. Admit that you have a secret shame. Admit that you have been lucky. Admit that you have benefited from the suffering of others. Admit that you harbor prejudices and perverse fantasies. Admit. Expose. Reveal. Give up your dignified pretensions and meet me in the muck of our common indignity. Instead of "Brother, there is no difference between us," say "I question what I have, what I do, who I am—I only know that I want us to love each other." Take up Fanon's prayer: "O my body, always make me one who questions!"

My hope is that the capabilities conception of political justice, by cultivating citizens that relate to themselves and each other in this way, can contribute to a solidarity of vulnerable, dependent, human animals that will enable us to endure the problem of remainders together. It is true that an aspect of Strauss's critique still applies to the vision that I propose: my vision does not organize political life by distinguishing between a public sphere and a private sphere, but it does acknowledge the need for time and space that is set aside for thinking, acting, and feeling in ways that are not directly constrained by political obligation. And this means accepting the fact that cultural legacies of historical injustice will flow into these times and spaces even in the best America that we can realistically achieve. The problem of remainders remains.

My hope is that the effect of these remainders would be mitigated if all members of American society came to see each other—even if they see each other in myriad other ways too—as vulnerable, dependent human animals who long for a thriving life in common. This will only be possible to the extent that all members of society are seen this way by the basic structure of society: it is a prerequisite that everyone in America is *institutionally* guaranteed the entitlements that ensure their ability to exercise the central human capabilities at the threshold level. Thus monumental efforts are still needed in the realms of policy and public culture: to guarantee the capabilities and cultivate this new way of seeing ourselves. But to strive for this ideal is not just to make the ever-broken liberal promise yet again. This is a new goal for us to strive for.

And yet, as I indicated in chapter 1, Nussbaum's approach is also not sufficient. The capabilities conception of the citizen would have us see each other in a way that redresses directly the societal mind-body dualism that Fanon diagnosed so profoundly as a feature of racial hierarchy. But Fanon called for something more. Those who have historically been on the body side of the societal mind-body dualism yearn for rupture, long to explode or touch tenderly, to break free or come close, to burst from the vicious circle. A satisfying response to Fanon will emerge only after this need is addressed. Only then will it be clear exactly how the historically oppressed could possibly be asked to endure the problem of remainders in particular and the fact of fraught societies more generally. I will address this need at length in chapter 4.

But now I turn to the problem of reproduction. It is not only the public/private loophole identified by Strauss that compels us to put up with the problem of remainders. The problem of remainders is exacerbated in a crucial respect by the problem of reproduction. An investigation into the problem of reproduction will clarify the necessity of accepting the problem of remainders as a permanent feature of even the best society that we can realistically imagine.

3

THE FACT OF FRAUGHT SOCIETIES II

The Problem of Reproduction and the Missing Link Problem

THE PROBLEM OF REPRODUCTION

Sometimes it is very important to members of a group to remember their historical suffering as a group. Many Jews, as I noted earlier, yearly memorialize the enslavement of the Israelites by ancient Egyptian Pharaohs, the destruction of the Second Temple in Jerusalem by the ancient Romans, and the mass murder of nearly half of all living Jews by Nazis and other Europeans during World War II. I suspect that the memory of the multiple massacres perpetrated by the U.S. government and brutal assimilationist policies at boarding schools is an important part of identification as Cherokee or Choctaw for many people who identify as such. Identification as African American or black may similarly include strong memories of enslavement and discrimination by whites. And identification as a woman may include strong memories of repression, exclusion, and unchecked sexual intimidation by men. All of these American oppressions are ongoing, so they are especially easy to remember.

But even if we did far better than we are doing right now at institutionalizing justice in America, flourishing as a Jew, African American, Native American, a woman, and so on, might nevertheless still include memorializing, feeling, and expressing anger and resentment toward gentiles, the U.S. government, whites, men, and so on. The problem of reproduction is this: sometimes the part of justice that assures each person opportunities to flourish as the kind of person that she takes herself to be also thereby assures the reproduction of smoldering grudges and antipathies that carry a disturbing legacy of historical injustice. If a legacy of intergroup antipathy and oppression becomes inextricably attached to identification as a certain kind of person, and a thriving life for some people includes identifying as this kind of person—such that they will want their children and their children's children to identify as this kind of person—don't political conditions that allow these people to thrive *also* unacceptably perpetuate the legacy of injustice?

Matters get even more complicated if we assume that some of the "kinds of people" with which a person might identify are inherently damaged or distorted by historical oppression and ongoing misrecognition, as Strauss and Fanon have suggested. And the situation is complicated even further still by people whose flourishing includes memorializing the experiences of those that others see as their historical oppressors: in the epilogue I will consider southerners in the United States who yearly reenact the Civil War as Confederate soldiers.

I have already explained that I think every person in America ought to see herself and everyone else as a vulnerable, dependent, embodied human animal, who is marked by a legacy of historical injustice and longs for a thriving life in common with others, and who is owed equal respect through the guarantee of core entitlements by the basic structure of a democratic society. The problem of reproduction is that seeing oneself and others in this way, and sharing the kind of political love that comes with it, may be contradicted by some of the other ways that a person might see herself and others if she is genuinely welcome *to be herself*. Should we imagine that broadly shared political love is only possible where everyone has already given up on their historical grudges and antipathies? Must we limit the kinds of people that are included in the ever-expanding American national story to those that are *not* characterized by anger, fear, distrust, and resentment toward other kinds of people?

The answer has to be no. If I am inviting you to join me in the pursuit of an America characterized by broadly shared political love, there should not be fine print at the bottom of the invitation that reads: "valid only if you are willing to give up on the historical resentment that makes you the kind of person that you take yourself to be." You might want to mourn while others celebrate Thanksgiving. You might want to live mostly secluded with your group while others mix and mingle. You might not want to forgive or forget. These cannot be disqualifiers if we have already agreed that all of us are marked by legacies of historical injustice. If we are trying to get to a place where we can all thrive together, we have to accept what thriving looks like for people who have been forged through conflict and oppression (this is actually *all people*, whether they know it or not).

It is worth spelling out the connection here to the problem of remainders. Nasty stereotypes and epithets, exclusionary rituals and social networks, will linger in a liberal society because of the public/private loophole, but also because the kinds of people who want to use, laugh about, and enact these remainders will be reproduced as a result of the problem of reproduction. Remember that passage from *Portnoy's Complaint* that I referred to in the last chapter? The one full of vicious and hilarious contempt for the goyim? Well, much of *Portnoy's Complaint* is an exercise in savoring the vim and vinegar of self-destructive Jewish resentment toward the goyim. This aspect of the book is intertwined with cruel and outrageous ideas about women, especially Alex Portnoy's Jewish mother and the shiksas (gentile women) that he chases. Of the latter, he explains to his therapist: "What I'm saying, Doctor, is that I don't seem to stick my dick up these girls, as much as I stick it up their backgrounds—as though through fucking I will discover America. *Conquer* America—maybe that's more like it."[1] This is the problem of remainders: these ideas about gentiles and women will be carried into any future America that does not ban and burn all of its copies of *Portnoy's Complaint*.

On the other hand, we might want to say that the kinds of people who are raised in a more just society would have no interest in such nastiness. If this is the case, then we can imagine that artistic works that are animated by an emotional legacy of historical injustice like *Portnoy's Complaint* will simply recede into an archive of unreadable historical curiosities. To claim that the aesthetic merit of the book would save it from oblivion is fallacious. Much of the artistry of the book is precisely in its use of this emotional legacy. To maintain an appreciation of a work like *Portnoy's Complaint* without appreciating its use of sexually charged contempt and resentment toward the goyim would be like maintaining an appreciation of Rembrandt without appreciating his use of color.

The problem of reproduction is that to be a certain kind of Jewish American male is to find Roth utterly hilarious and moving. If the America that we are striving to become is a place that is genuinely hospitable to Jewish American men of this sort, then it will have to be a place where they can flourish in the enjoyment of their literary canon. This obviously applies equally to Jewish American canons that are more compelling to Jewish women, and it applies to the Jewish religious canon, which also includes its share of contempt for the goyim. Of course, there are books, songs, rituals, styles of dancing, forms of speech, clothing fashions, manners of bodily comportment and much else that have this same quality of perverse uptake for varieties of African American, Hispanic, and Native American men and/or women. And the same is true for the "Southern" canons of American whites.

The point is that any invitation to an America characterized by broadly shared mature political love must be addressed to *us*. It must be addressed to the full range of embittered, cynical, and distrustful people who live in America today. And it must invite us to thrive as the kind of people we are, not only as some future us that is noble, upright, and smiling, for whom all is forgiven and forgotten. The problem of reproduction is that inviting people who carry legacies of historical injustice to thrive in a better society means inviting their constitutive grudges and antipathies to thrive too—and to be passed down to future generations. As in the case of the problem of remainders, I assume that the problem of reproduction is the expected outcome of life under reasonably just institutions. Thus I hope ultimately to present a picture of broadly shared political love in America that is plausible, attractive, and indeed worth striving for, despite the problem of reproduction. Much will depend, then, on whether or not we can imagine people who see themselves and others according to a widely acceptable conception of the citizen while *at the same time* they continue to see themselves and others in ways that they could never expect anyone else to accept.[2]

VICISSITUDES OF SELFNESS AND GROUPNESS

The problem of reproduction relates to the kinds of people we take ourselves to be and the value that we attach to reproducing features of these "kinds" in future generations.[3] An explanation of the problem of reproduction will require a plausible story about how and why people value reproducing the kinds of people that they take themselves to be, even when this means reproducing anger, fear, distrust, and resentment between groups. Toward this end, it will be helpful for me to incorporate into my argument terminology developed by the sociologist Rogers Brubaker. The relevant terms are *self-understanding, groupness,* and *identification.* I will add to these the term *selfness,* which I believe will further clarify matters. Brubaker has set out to provide analytical terms that avoid the fallacy of "groupism": "the tendency to take discrete, bounded groups as basic constituents of social life, chief protagonists of social conflicts, and fundamental units of social analysis."[4] In *Ethnicity Without Groups,* he warns scholars to "avoid unintentionally *doubling* or *reinforcing* the reification of ethnic groups in ethnopolitical practice with a reification of such groups in social analysis."[5]

Following his lead in this regard means undertaking a shift in our folk-sociological talk away from "ethnic groups," "racial groups," "national groups" and toward "ethnicization, racialization, and nationalization as political, social, cultural, and psychological processes. And [this] means taking as a basic analytical category not the 'group' as an entity but groupness as a contextually fluctuating conceptual variable."[6] Brubaker describes groupness as a quality of self-understanding that a person can have to a greater or lesser degree variably throughout her life. As Brubaker explains it, self-understanding is "one's sense of who one is, of one's social location [where one fits in society], and of how (given the first two) one is prepared to act."[7] The groupness quality of self-understanding is "the sense of belonging to a distinctive, bounded, solidary group."[8]

Groupness can range from high to low variably throughout one's life. When I read *Portnoy's Complaint,* or reports of anti-Semitism in the Jewish press, or when I feel nostalgic about standing at the Western Wall in Israel with my late grandfather, I feel very Jewish—my Jewish groupness is heightened. Likewise when I feel adrift in a sea of gentiles and I miss being in the company of Jews. On the other hand, when I'm immersed in Jewish community life, I am inevitably infuriated by the sanctimonious rabbis, the hypocrisy of the more-Jewy-than-thou types, the crass communal obsession with wealthy benefactors, the bourgeois decadence, the limousine liberalism, the willful blindness to Arab humanity among the Israel *über alles* types, and the desperation for self-indictment among the Israel *unter alles* types. Then my Jewish groupness plummets. I also experience groupness as an Oberlin alum—Obie groupness. I frequently have a high degree of groupness that makes me feel like scholars, philosophers, and poets from every time and place are "my people." I suppose this is a sort of humanist groupness. And I experience groupness as an American, which is a special kind of groupness that I shall return to in the next section. Any particular person will have a variety of propensities to groupness, which increase and decrease as a result of various triggers over the course of her life.

According to Brubaker's account of self-understanding, "both the bounded self and the bounded group are culturally specific rather than universal forms."[9] This parallelism suggests to me that an additional term ought to be introduced into his analytical toolkit: *selfness* can be used in order to specify the quality of self-understanding that accounts for one's sense of being a distinctive, bounded individual. Like groupness, selfness should be presumed to admit of degrees. Indeed, we can say that in certain societies at certain times selfness is pervasively heightened, while in other societies at other times selfness might generally be very low.

Let's try to imagine what shifting selfness and groupness looks like. Sometimes a person is driven by a very clear conception of himself as a unique individual and is agitated, even enraged, by any effort to subsume him into a group and thereby blur the line that separates him from others. I have witnessed people thrilled at a baseball game losing themselves in the mass intonation of the national anthem and other people repulsed at the same prospect. Indeed, the same person might respond one way today and another way next week. Some people go to great lengths—think of tattoos and piercings and such—to be permanently and unmistakably individuated, while others tend to resist differentiation from the crowd.[10]

We can imagine that there are some people who endure, at least some of the time, in a relatively passive state wherein psychological continuity depends on a quite diffuse and amorphous collage of vague memories, inarticulate feelings, habits, addictions, etc., which are only barely contained in a self-conscious, coherent sense of "me." To speak of "degrees" of selfness marks the distance between, at one extreme, foundering passively in this way, fuzzy-headed, propelled forward only by the relentlessness of time and, at the other extreme, striving energetically and consciously at nearly every moment to *be* a clearly envisioned and individuated individual.

We should not assume that there is an inverse relationship between selfness and groupness. It is not the case that as groupness is heightened selfness is lowered (or vice versa). All sorts of combinations are possible. The despairing "fuzzy-headed" person may have both low selfness and low groupness. A person with a highly groupist self-understanding may think of herself as uniquely destined to be the charismatic leader of her group and therefore be driven, at the same time, by heightened selfness.

Furthermore, levels of groupness and selfness will be valued differently at different times and places. In some contexts a person who spends much of her time in a state of low selfness might be described as depressed (or repressed), while ambitious people ever striving to achieve the selves that they want to be are described as healthy (or free). In another context, low degrees of selfness might be seen from a positive perspective: from the admiring perspective of some Buddhist traditions, perhaps. The ambitious person with high selfness might be seen, in some contexts, as pathetically beholden to the false neoliberal god of "success." Henceforth, I will use self-understanding to refer to the most basic sense of who one is, one's social location, and how, by virtue of these factors, one is prepared to act, *which remains relatively constant as degrees of selfness and groupness (and their respective meanings) vary situationally.*[11]

Before moving on, it is important to clarify how groupness (and presumably selfness) emerges. According to Brubaker, it emerges through processes of identification. When one is called upon "to characterize oneself, to locate oneself vis-à-vis others, to situate oneself in a narrative, to place oneself in a category," it is the process of identification that produces a relevant response.[12] In the last instance—"categorical identification"— one identifies oneself "by membership in a class of persons sharing some categorical attribute (such as race, ethnicity, language, nationality, citizenship, gender, sexual orientation, etc.)."[13]

Categorical identification describes the expressive ways that people render themselves recognizable to others (and to themselves) as members of a categorically defined set of persons. Of course, one might also be categorically identified by others and categorically identify others too. A helpful account of how the process of categorical identification works is in

Anthony Appiah's *The Ethics of Identity.* Appiah describes "collective identities" as kinds of person that provide "scripts" to live by: "narratives that
people can use in shaping their projects and in telling their life stories."[14]
We might say, then, that categorical identification is the process by which
people follow these scripts in their life pursuits.[15]

A person who identifies with a group will measure her life by what is
appropriate for a member of that group—for *that* kind of person. Sometimes taking oneself to be a member of the group will function as a
"parameter": a contour that benignly shapes what flourishing will look
like. In other cases, it will function as a "limit": an obstacle to flourishing. Appiah sees fluidity in the process of identification that partakes of
both limit and parameter.[16] He is careful to point out, in any case, that
identification is neither ever "wholly scripted for us nor wholly scripted
by us."[17]

Going forward, we should keep in mind the vicissitudes of selfness and
groupness, which we can presume to characterize every person's life. Every
person will be raised to identify with some groups and not others and, at
the same time, to distinguish herself from all others as an individual. Over
the course of a life, external conditions will sometimes heighten a person's
groupness and other times heighten that person's selfness (though, as I've
said, these are not mutually exclusive). For some people, intense groupness of a particular kind will be a very great good. And here's the crucial
bit: for some of these people, the intense groupness that they value will
include smoldering historical grudges and anger, fear, distrust, and resentment toward other groups.

The problem of reproduction results from the fact that every person
in the U.S. (as conceived according to our political conception of the
person) is entitled to pursue his own best life, even when that life includes
grudging, resentful, and irrational groupness. This is the same as the
fact that every such person is entitled to pursue his own good, even when
that good includes divisive "religious" assumptions, like the assumption
that other citizens are fated to burn in hell for eternity. The next step in
my argument, then, is to show how the picture of self-understanding that
I have developed from Brubaker and Appiah, with its varying degrees of
selfness and groupness, maps onto a moral psychology of the person as a
citizen that I have developed within the framework of political liberalism.

THE IDEA OF COMPREHENSIVE GROUPNESS

Brubaker's account of self-understanding is compatible with what John Rawls has described as our "moral identity" or our moral "conception of ourselves." [18] I will refer to this simply as our moral self-conceptions. Rawls differentiates between a person's institutional and noninstitutional self-conceptions. In the United States, a citizen's Social Security number is a label that is affixed to her *political institutional self-conception*. She might change her name, voting district, political party affiliation, marital status, gender, and many other things. Nevertheless, her Social Security number remains the same and she makes herself institutionally identifiable throughout her life whenever she provides it. The rights and duties that apply to anyone with a Social Security number are the rights and duties that apply to citizens of the United States. Thus, a person's political institutional self-conception is that person's conception of herself as a citizen according to the laws and policies relating to citizenship of an actual state like the United States of America.

A person's *moral self-conception*, on the other hand, is not (and should not be) registered with state institutions; it is a noninstitutional self-conception. Crucially, it has two aspects: a political aspect and a nonpolitical aspect, each of which comes with its own "aims and commitments." [19] Remember, here *political* has a very special meaning. It means: contrived to be a framework within which people can pursue a good life together, even though they disagree about big questions related to theology, the purpose of human life, and so on. Among the aims and commitments of the political aspect of a person's moral self-conception are "the values of political justice," which she presumably wants to see "embodied in political institutions and social policies." [20] The central human capabilities are designed to be values of this sort. Thus, the political aspect of a person's noninstitutional moral self-conception is the *moral measure* of her institutional political self-conception. That is, she will want the rights and duties that accrue with her Social Security number to be justifiable according to the values of political justice that she maintains as part of the political aspect of her moral self-conception. To the extent that they are not, she has a good reason to work toward political institutional reform. [21]

Now, she will also have a nonpolitical aspect to her moral self-conception. This is an aspect of herself that is *not* specifically designed to be a point of overlap with people who disagree with her about the meaning of history, deities, the purpose of human life, etc. And she will presumably work on behalf of various aims, commitments, and values in the background culture, sometimes pursuing the ends of associations to which she belongs.[22] Part of the nonpolitical aspect of her moral self-conception will be her so-called comprehensive doctrine, which I described earlier.[23] Her comprehensive doctrine is a view that she will likely share with others in associations that are organized around a shared comprehensive goal.

I am suggesting that we distinguish another part of the nonpolitical aspect of her moral self-conception, which is her "comprehensive groupness." Comprehensive groupness is best defined negatively: it is groupness that is not *political* groupness. The best example of political groupness is the patriotism that Nussbaum promotes, which I develop further and advocate in this book: one's sense of oneself as a member of a distinct, bounded, democratic nation, with a particular history of suffering and hope, that one loves as one's own. By contrast, comprehensive groupness is a sense of oneself as belonging to a group that one may not expect other reasonable members of a democratic society to be able to accept as a group at all (let alone an admirable group).

According to Rawls, citizens will be compelled for a variety of reasons, at various times, to "adjust and reconcile" the two aspects (political and nonpolitical) of their moral self-conceptions.[24] "It can happen," he writes,

that in their personal affairs, or in the internal life of associations, citizens may regard their final ends and attachments very differently from the way the political conception supposes. They may have, and often do have at any given time, affections, devotions, and loyalties that they believe they would not, indeed could and should not, stand apart from and evaluate objectively. They may regard it as simply unthinkable to view themselves apart from certain religious, philosophical, and moral convictions, or from certain enduring attachments and loyalties. These two kinds of commitments and attachments—political and nonpolitical—specify moral identity and give shape to a person's way of life, what one sees oneself as doing and trying to accomplish in the social world. If we suddenly lost them, we would be disoriented and unable to carry on. In fact, there would be, we might think, no point in carrying on.[25]

Rawls already appreciates that, along with his comprehensive doctrine, or perhaps correlated with this doctrine, a citizen may also have "affections, devotions, and loyalties" that he "would not, indeed could and should not, stand apart from and evaluate objectively." It may be as "unthinkable" for him to see himself at a distance from these "enduring attachments and loyalties" as it would be for him to see certain of his "religious, philosophical, and moral convictions"—that is, his comprehensive doctrine—from a relativistic point of view. One kind of partiality of this sort might be family bonds, or perhaps even bonds of romantic love. But I think it is particularly important that we include among these affections, attachments, devotions, and loyalties those that are involved in comprehensive groupness. Part of the nonpolitical aspect of a person's moral self-conception may be his sense of himself as belonging to a particular "racial" or "ethnic" group, for instance. What is more, it is wholly arbitrary to include here only positive descriptors of partiality like affection, attachment, devotion, and loyalty. This list must also include negative descriptors of partiality: the specific aversions, grudges, suspicions, and antipathies that it may be "unthinkable" to detach oneself from if one is, for instance, scarred by historical conflict and stigmatization.

When, elsewhere, Rawls describes the three main kinds of conflicts that set citizens at odds, he explains that his focus will be on those deriving from irreconcilable comprehensive doctrines.[26] But he notes that racial and ethnic conflicts also set citizens at odds. With respect to comprehensive doctrines, he assumes that "even though our comprehensive doctrines are irreconcilable and cannot be compromised, nevertheless citizens who affirm reasonable doctrines may share reasons of another kind, namely, public reasons given in terms of political conceptions of justice."[27] In the case of racial and ethnic conflicts, by contrast, he writes: "once we accept reasonable principles of justice and recognize them to be reasonable (even if not the most reasonable), and know, or reasonably believe, that our political and social institutions satisfy them, [this] kind of conflict need not arise, or arise so forcefully."[28]

But I think we should assume that the attachments and aversions that constitute irreconcilable differences resulting from comprehensive groupness are just like irreconcilable comprehensive doctrines. The case of Judaism exemplifies the problem with Rawls's assumption. Even if we could isolate a comprehensive doctrine called Judaism, it would most often include comprehensive groupness that separates people into Jews and goyim. Anyway, for most people who identify as Jews in America it is their Jewish groupness that is central; their adherence to something called "Judaism" is mostly nominal.

Rawls seems to base his idea of comprehensive doctrines on a modern paradigm of "religions," which he thinks of as belief systems or doctrines that anyone might affirm or deny. He follows in a long tradition of valorizing "universal religions" or "world religions" over *mere* "national religions" or "race religions."[29] Emblematic of this tradition, Immanuel Kant once wrote: "Strictly speaking Judaism is not a religion at all but simply the union of a number of individuals who, since they belong to a particular stock, established themselves into a community under purely political laws."[30] Because he has this idea of "religions" in mind, Rawls unnecessarily privileges doctrinal conflicts over conflicts that result from irreconcilable groupness. I suggest, instead, that the attachments and aversions that constitute irreconcilable differences resulting from comprehensive groupness are among those things one may not be willing to compromise, but which do not preclude the capacity to "share public reasons given in terms of political conceptions of justice."

In fact, Rawls already suggests that the kinds of irreconcilable differences which presumably abide between groupists add to the weight of the so-called burdens of judgment. These are eternal epistemological problems that prevent complete human agreement from ever being a possibility. Consider Rawls's description of the fourth source of the burdens of judgment:

> To some extent (how great we cannot tell) the way we assess evidence and weigh moral and political values is shaped by our total experience, our whole course of life up till now; and our total experiences must always differ. Thus, in a modern society with its numerous offices and positions, its various divisions of labor, its many social groups and their ethnic variety, citizens' total experiences are disparate enough for their judgments to diverge, at least to some degree, on many if not most cases of any significant complexity.[31]

Thus, among the "reasonable disagreements" between citizens are those that arise from their "ethnic variety." Such disagreements are among those that reasonable people can have. Reasonableness, for Rawls, centrally involves a willingness "to recognize the burdens of judgment and to accept their consequences for the use of public reason in directing the legitimate exercise of political power in a constitutional regime."[32] So recognition of the fact of ongoing disagreement as a result of ethnic variety is a basic aspect of reasonableness. And since "ethnic variety" is never only the benign multiplicity of positive partialities, but seems always also to include negative partialities (even if only with respect to past group relations and emotional judgments about history), the consequent irreconcilable differences of groupness can be presumed to be among the tolerable sources of the burdens of judgment.

So, if a person has *reasonable* comprehensive groupness as part of the nonpolitical aspect of her moral self-conception—or even if she merely comports her unreasonable comprehensive groupness *reasonably*[33]— then she is presumably open to public reason and to seeing herself as a citizen, *however else she might see herself and others.* If this is right, then it is fair to assume that some irreconcilable conflicts between ostensible groups are the predictable long-term result of a society under just institutions. These conflicts may relate, for instance, to group boundaries, how history is recounted, who was to blame for what, who owes what to whom, which emotions are appropriate when we relate to each other, and so on. The reproduction of these conflicts is simply an aspect of reasonable pluralism.

We cannot, of course, predict the variations, transformations, and novelties of groupness that might thrive in an American society where opportunities to exercise the full range of central human capabilities over the course of a complete life are genuinely guaranteed to all. By assuming that the problem of reproduction is a part of the fact of fraught societies, I do not mean to suggest that we should expect the categories and kinds of people that currently exist to be reproduced forever. Some categories and kinds have existed for millennia, others for mere decades. It is not the business of the political domain to judge which sorts of comprehensive groupness ought to persist, emerge, or decline. As we will see in the next chapter, *the dynamic relations between the domain of the political and the domain of play leave open an unpredictable horizon of newer forms of life.*[34]

To be sure, in a society characterized by political justice, those varieties of comprehensive groupness that a person can have while at the same time having political groupness will find particularly fertile soil in which to grow. Varieties of comprehensive groupness that are directly contradicted by an institutionally embedded liberal political conception of justice might have more difficulty thriving. The pursuit of a more just society according to a politically liberal ideal is not a commitment to neutrality: it is a moral pursuit devoted to building a good life with others despite the persistence of profound irreconcilable conflicts. People who are not devoted to this moral pursuit will find life in a society characterized by liberal political justice inhospitable or oppressive.

Luckily, there is almost no comprehensive self-understanding (whatever its constituent varieties of doctrine, selfness, or groupness) that is not compatible with the capabilities conception of political justice that I offer here. This will sound like hubris. Didn't communitarian theorists in the 1990s like Michael Sandel and Alasdair MacIntyre show that liberalism is inhospitable and oppressive to those who want to live an integrated life? Isn't it quintessential liberal presumption to assume that everyone will want to live a life divided between anemic public concerns on the one hand and ultimate concerns that are relegated to the private sphere on the other?

I suspect that a critic who asks these leading questions will probably have in mind a picture of a person who is religious. The assumption is that political liberalism is ultimately hostile to religion and religious people. I will address this concern directly in the epilogue, so I will not take up too much time with it here. For now, let me simply suggest the following. First, the picture of the religious person that is so crucial to this critique is deeply problematic. It relies on a conception of religion that has rightfully been eviscerated by contemporary scholars engaged in the academic study of religion. Second, the related notion of a distinctive religious psychology, which is hermetically sealed and abhors division, is likewise untenable. But let me be clear: the ideal advocated in this book—an American society characterized by political justice and broadly shared political love—is not a secular ideal. It is an ideal that rejects the religious-secular dichotomy altogether. I will explain this at greater length in the epilogue.

Still, the problem of remainders and the problem of reproduction do provoke a nagging feeling that is related to the "religious" critique of political liberalism. Why should we settle for a society that is contaminated by the cultural legacies of past injustice? Why not try to initiate an entirely new order of human life cleansed of past moral failings? These questions put pressure on a core weakness in the project of political liberalism, a weakness that is often exploited by the so-called religious critique. Political liberalism strives only for the narrow ideal of political justice. It does not strive for cosmic justice, the redemption or salvation of humanity, total human emancipation, or even to aspire to becoming an indisputably best human society. But why should we let ourselves be limited in this way? Why should we put up with imperfection? This brings us to the missing link problem.

THE MISSING LINK PROBLEM

The missing link problem is a hazard that comes with the very project of trying to imagine and promote a just society. It is this: we will inevitably long for a vision that is cleansed entirely of the legacy of injustice; we will be tempted by the thought that we can somehow eventually cross a threshold into a society unmarred by perversity. But if the goal is a society where *we* can flourish despite our differences, then the problem of remainders and the problem of reproduction make this impossible. Perverse legacies of historical injustice will be in the DNA of even the best society that we can imagine—if it is to be a society *for us*. Thus, our incorrigible desire for the "perfect justice" of angels will always inevitably clash with our interminable status as products of historical injustice.

Frustration with our fundamental imperfectability can produce dangerous reactions. This problem is related to the perpetual threat of primitive shame and projective disgust that Nussbaum describes. The deep desire to dominate that comes from primitive shame is related to the feverish desire for purity that is provoked by frustration with one's own and others' incapacity to transcend historical injustice. Others who seem morally retrograde or otherwise represent the intransigence of human perversity may come to be identified as cancerous elements that must be purged, just as others who come to represent human mortality and decay may be stigmatized as disgusting elements that must be cleansed. The emotions of the leftish, urban sophisticate at a rural county fair—the feeling that these macho, evangelical, Trump-loving, gun-nuts are just repugnant!—are disturbingly related to the feelings of the Progressive era liberal who recoiled with disgust from people with mental and physical impairments. Both reflect a dangerous perfectionist desire for purity. We are all susceptible to this kind of desire. I *was* that leftish guy at the rural county fair. I have to admit, expose, reveal!

I suspect that wide adoption of Nussbaum's conception of the citizen would already go a long way to palliate the effect of the dangerous reactions that the missing link problem tends to provoke. Recall that she sought to mitigate the threat of projective disgust caused by primitive shame by building into her view a conception of citizens who vigilantly and compassionately reaffirm each other's vulnerability, dependence, and animality. I will claim in the next chapter that the idea of a domain of play, and citizens who can toggle between a play frame and a political frame, further ameliorates these threats. In order to explain how, though, I need first to dig deeper into the missing link problem itself and describe in detail the precise threats that I think it provokes.

THE WILDERNESS GENERATION

While the problem of remainders and the problem of reproduction become salient as modern problems for the liberal state in particular, core elements of the missing link problem are already articulated in the Exodus narrative of the Hebrew Bible. Michael Walzer highlights the key contribution of this narrative to modern radical and revolutionary politics in *Exodus and Revolution*. His analysis illuminates the missing link problem and the responses that it evokes. In the narrative, the Israelites, having been freed from Egyptian bondage by the deity Yahweh (through the action of Yahweh's representative on the ground, Moses), must make their way to the Promised Land. But they must travel through a desert wilderness for forty years in order to get there. Walzer quotes Moses Maimonides, the great medieval rabbinic authority, interpreting these forty years in the wilderness as follows: "the deity uses a gracious ruse . . . in causing [the people] to wander perplexedly in the desert until their souls became courageous . . . and until, moreover, people were born who were not accustomed to humiliation and servitude."[35] On Maimonides' reading, the Israelites need some time wandering in the desert in order to overcome the slavishness that has been inculcated in them as a result of enslavement, to shed their tolerance for humiliation and servitude and become courageous.

Then Walzer turns to Karl Marx, reflecting on 1848, who echoes this interpretation, writing, "The present generation is like the Jews whom Moses led through the wilderness. It has not only a new world to conquer, *it must go under* in order to make room for men who are able to cope with a new world" (my emphasis).[36] Walzer notes the difference in emphasis between Maimonides and Marx: "Maimonides writes of those who will be born, Marx, more harshly, of those who have to die."[37] Indeed, the deep element of the missing link problem that echoes from the Exodus narrative might be summarized, in the words of Frank and Fritzie Manuel writing about utopian thought, as "that irksome interim when the old man was not yet dead and the new one had not yet been fully formed."[38]

And there is certainly death in the wilderness. The Israelites receive a new law in the desert, which is meant to govern their lives and their relations with Yahweh, who views them as indebted to him for bringing them out of Egypt. When many among the Israelites nevertheless revert to the worship of other deities, Moses enlists the tribe of Levites (who apparently had not so reverted) to execute them. They execute three thousand people, after which Yahweh tops off the massacre by sending a plague. Walzer describes this as "the first revolutionary purge."[39] He explains that Moses enlisting the Levites "divides the community, creates a subgroup—we might call it a vanguard—whose members anticipate, at least in their own minds, the 'free people' of the future. In fact, they become the magistrates of the future, the priests and bureaucrats. And meanwhile, in the present, they rule by force; they are the enemies of 'graciousness' and gradualism."[40]

The generation that is brought out from Egypt is crippled by slavishness and a propensity for idolatry. The Exodus narrative can be understood to respond to the missing link problem by proposing that time can do the work of linking the generation that grew up under slavery to the generation that is suitable to enter the Promised Land: time for the older generation to have new experiences under new conditions "in the wilderness," time to shed some of the psychological damage done by enslavement in Egypt, time to give birth to a new generation that will not be reared in slavery, and, most important, *time for the older generation to die-out* before the Promised Land is reached.

Indeed, Lincoln Steffens, in his Marxist reading of the Exodus story, claims that the entirety of the generation of the wilderness has to die before the Israelites can enter the Promised Land. According to Steffens, God's view in the Exodus story is that *"the grown-ups must die. . . .* He knew that old people, who have lived and been formed on the earth as it is yet, are not fit for the kingdom of heaven; they must be put to death; and the children, the unspoiled, the untaught, the unformed—they alone can go over—and even they must first pass through the purifying experience of the natural conditions of the desert."[41]

While some of the older generation may be allowed simply to die out, others must be purged. The Exodus narrative presumes a vanguard that does the work of purgation. To be sure, the revolutionary vanguard is not allowed simply to run amok with purgative zeal. It is bound by the new law that is revealed to Moses and, more fundamentally, by obedience to Yahweh. This law is propagated by Moses and the rest of the Israelite leadership. Walzer explains, "If there is a Leninist reading, there is also . . . a social-democratic reading—which stresses the indirection of the march and the role of Moses as the pedagogue of the people and their defender before God (and which de-emphasized the story of the golden calf)."[42] But we are left to wonder, with Walzer, "Was it the purging or the teaching that made the decisive difference?"[43]

Walzer supports the social-democratic reading and views it as the normative Jewish interpretive tradition.[44] In fact, *Exodus and Revolution* generally assumes a predictable social-democratic posture of superiority over Leninist and New Left radicalism: social democrats present themselves as serious people who are ready to undertake the gradual process of making real change in the real world of political institutions, which requires tolerance and compromise. Leninists and New Left radicals, by contrast, are presented as pathologically predisposed to violence and magical thinking.[45] I admit that I have a tendency to take on this social-democratic posture as well—I became a regular reader of *Dissent* at Oberlin, where I could read a hard copy for free in the periodicals section of Mudd Library. Walzer and Irving Howe have shaped my intellectual sensibility significantly. As I suggested in the introduction, the vision that I am offering in this book does not pretend to derive from natural or obvious premises that are self-evidently acceptable to all good and reasonable people. It is offered out of my own idiosyncratic sensibility, combining a variety of influences, as part of the continuing effort among scholars and intellectuals to imagine a just America that we can pursue together.

But let's return to the Exodus narrative, because the way that the story continues, especially as Walzer recounts it, further illustrates the extent of the challenge posed by the missing link problem. Once in the Promised Land, the Israelites do not live happily ever after. Reversion to the corrupt behaviors that we might expect from the generation freed from slavery persist long after the Israelites have crossed the Jordan. Critics of the culture and political order that emerge in the Land of Israel, like the prophet Jeremiah, see it as a "second Egypt" from which the Israelites must be delivered.[46]

With the old law broken and corrupted, Jeremiah promises a new covenant—a new incorruptible law that Yahweh will put "in their inward parts, and write it in their hearts."[47] Jeremiah's promise, Walzer writes, "is a transformation of human nature or, better, the reappearance of the original Adam. . . . And then it is but a short and obvious step to bring him home, to make the goal of the second Exodus not Canaan but Eden. This is a crucial move in the development of a full-fledged messianism out of Exodus thinking. Once this move is made, the Exodus can be reinterpreted, first in Jewish apocalyptic literature and then in Christian writings, as an allegory for the final redemption of mankind."[48]

"Exodus politics," whether the social-democratic version or the Leninist version, always provokes the temptation of messianism. According to Walzer, "Messianism is the great temptation of Western politics. Its source and spur is the apparent endlessness of the Exodus march."[49] The endlessness of the Exodus march is the missing link problem. Walzer continues in a crucial passage,

> Ideologists and militants have not only dreamt of but actually reached for a kind of secular paradise, the perfection of humankind in a perfect

society: unity, harmony, freedom, eternal bliss. And they have done this in the firm expectation that paradise was the necessary and inevitable end of *our* history, a promised land, indeed, whether or not there existed a God capable of making promises. The end of history is also the abolition of history, the total destruction (not only of Canaanites but) of the familiar world and conceivably of most of the people in it—so that the surviving remnant can enter the new Jerusalem. If messianism outlives religious faith, it still inhabits the apocalyptic framework that faith established. Hence the readiness of messianic militants to welcome, even to initiate, the terrors that precede the Last Days; and hence the strange politics of *the worse, the better*; and hence the will to sin, to risk any crime for the sake of the End.[50]

Why is messianism so troubling? It is because it inevitably justifies any act that can bring the End. And because *it fails*. The messianic End never comes, and the march goes on. Once this is understood, the vanguard of the messianic time must tighten its authority. The messianic stories they tell inevitably function to reassure their authority as the End continues not to arrive. The proleptic legitimacy of the messianic vanguard becomes a basis for extreme purgative violence: those who are subject to their summary judgment, if they question the actions of the vanguard, can readily be told that they cannot possibly understand the reasons why the vanguard has to do what it does.

This is not the only way to think about messianism. Nevertheless, the missing link problem is, in part, the fact that messianic imaginaries—both edifying and profoundly dangerous—will necessarily persist and emerge in the best liberal democratic society that we can realistically imagine. This is because the very best we can do in a liberal society will inevitably feel *not that great*. And the temptation to be the messianic vanguard will always be there.[51]

"TERRORS THAT PRECEDE THE LAST DAYS"

It is worth meditating for a moment on Walzer's concern about the "terrors that precede the Last Days." We have already seen an indication that the problem of remainders produces a propensity to violence. Fanon offered us deep insight into the emotional life of a person who is institutionally and interpersonally subjected to the harsh glare of a distorting gaze when he described such a person's yearning for the "alterity of rupture," for the transformative effect of violence more broadly. Here I will show that Strauss also identifies an imminent threat of destabilizing violence in the structure of the liberal state, which is more directly related to the "terrors that precede the Last Days" in Walzer's formulation.

As we will recall, Strauss thought that the liberal state would always leave minorities vulnerable to private discrimination and, in general, would remain ever susceptible to overthrow by a charismatic demagogue. Both problems result from a lack of ultimate sovereign authority that is recognized by all. With respect to the latter problem, the susceptibility to demagogic overthrow derives from the fact that reason (the presumptive source of justification for liberal laws and norms), when it is not grounded in a revealed law (as it was for the medieval rationalists), inevitably reduces to the *will* of the rational agent. Reason itself proves insufficient as a justificatory basis for laws and norms because reason cannot, in and of itself, serve as a justification for the value of rationality.[52] Thus, for Strauss, reason is never the ultimate source of justification in the political order produced by the modern Enlightenment. The will that happens to lean toward rationality is the ultimate source.

According to Strauss, then, the liberal state establishes an environment in which the strongest will can at any moment overthrow the liberal regime and rule illiberally. Strauss could, therefore, explain the victory of national socialism as follows: "the man who had by far the strongest will or single-mindedness, the greatest ruthlessness, daring, and power over his following, and the best judgment about the strength of the various forces in the immediately relevant political field was the leader of the revolution."[53] Strauss saw the attraction of Nazism resulting from Hitler's fierce will, along with a romantic longing for the German Middle Ages (among other related longings) that pervaded the culture—the longing for a bold and willful Germany, one not yet humiliated by World War I and the Treaty of Versailles.[54]

Strauss, here, is pointing to a very deep element of the missing link problem that relates to a core premise of political liberalism. In my assessment of the problem of reproduction, I have already identified the way in which a person's comprehensive groupness functions just as Rawls imagined a person's comprehensive doctrine will function. The difference between a person's sense of being a member of a group and the doctrine(s) that a person might proclaim is murky indeed. The common denominator is that these are emotions, actions, and ideas that are *not* designed to be justifiable within the domain of the political. The idea of a separation between what is designed to be political and what is not comes out of a long liberal tradition of "separation." And the feelings of loss, disappointment, and longing that are inevitably provoked by this separation are a part of the missing link problem.

Mark Lilla describes as a "Great Separation" the shift in political thought, inaugurated by Thomas Hobbes in the seventeenth century, that provoked "a new approach to politics focused exclusively on human nature and human needs."[55] This approach abandoned the aspirations of "political theology," which offers "a way of thinking about the conduct of human affairs" that is connected to loftier thoughts "about the being of God, the structure of the cosmos, the nature of the soul, the origin of all things, the end of time."[56] According to Lilla, a distinctive feature of the modern West is the ubiquitous unspoken assumption that this Great Separation is a permanent historical fact and the aspirations of political theology have lost their appeal forever. But he views this as a deeply troubling delusion: "In the West people still think about God, man, and the world today—how could they not? But most seem to have trained themselves not to take the last step into politics. We are no longer in the habit of connecting our political discourse to theological and cosmological questions, and we no longer recognize revelation as politically authoritative. This is a testament to our self-restraint. That we must rely on self-restraint should concern us."[57]

As far as Lilla is concerned, we must vigilantly remind ourselves that political theology is always appealing to human beings because of its *comprehensiveness*.[58] This means that we will always need to be reminded to redouble our commitment to the Great Separation.[59] The way that I think of it is this: there was a historical process that unfolded in the early modern period in Europe that involved a small number of people, mostly intellectual elites, starting to think seriously about the kinds of governing values, rules, and ideals that might be viewed as legitimate by people who are otherwise divided by profound, irreconcilable disagreements. The legacy of this process resounds whenever we make the judgment that the best we can do with the political institutions that govern human affairs is to guarantee fundamental entitlements that come with moral personhood (which we define in terms of a provisional political conception of the person as a citizen—like, for instance, Nussbaum's vulnerable, dependent, human animal). The worry that I share with Lilla is that if this is the best that we can do, then political institutions will always feel too limited.

Political institutions that are limited in this way can promise great heights of national emotion through the expression of political love, but they cannot promise a political order that is tightly and coercively structured according to the map of your own particular emotional, ideological, groupist, cosmological, and other prejudices.[60] Nor can they promise to fulfill the utopian longings that these prejudices often produce (or derive from). Foreswearing comprehensive satisfaction means that everyone in a liberal society agrees to be something of a political schlemiel, a political loser—everyone in a liberal society is doomed to live with disappointment in political life.[61] Conceding this limitation is what Rawls called "the fact of oppression": political institutions that demand adherence to a single comprehensive doctrine can only be stable as a result of the "oppressive use of state power."[62]

Looking at the same period that Strauss wrote about, Lilla points to longings associated with political theology that emerged at the turn of the twentieth century, and were radicalized by the failed attempt of liberal theologians in Germany to deliver on their core promise: that bourgeois life in the society of a liberal state could be ultimately, indeed comprehensively, satisfying.[63] Of course, since it was designed precisely not to be comprehensive, the liberal state could never have delivered on what theologians like Ernst Troeltsch and Hermann Cohen promised. Thus "it was a time when educated Germans who were nominally Christian or Jewish explored the margins of religious experience—the occult, theosophy, yoga, nudism, vegetarianism—in hopes of escaping a modern civilization they considered soulless."[64]

A new generation of Jewish and Christian theologians called on their contemporaries to break radically from the civic piety and boring moralism of liberal religion.[65] They saw their moment as a time of profound crisis and called for decisive willful action of the soul in order to provoke an immediate redemptive experience of the divine. The sense of crisis, the longing for transformative willful action, the desire for the End should sound familiar given my analysis of Strauss, Fanon, and Walzer. While they did not cause or endorse the political reverberations of their ideas, Lilla suggests that the new theologians like Karl Barth and Franz Rosenzweig "did unwittingly help to shape a new and noxious form of political argument, which was the theological celebration of modern tyranny."[66]

It is not surprising, therefore, that some of Barth's intellectual epigones would find it easy to embrace Hitler and Nazism.[67] "The generation that Karl Barth's *Romans* helped to form," Lilla explains, "had no taste for compromise with the culture that their liberal teachers celebrated and that committed suicide in the Great War. They wanted to confront the unknown God, the 'wholly other,' the *deus absconditus.* . . . They wanted to experience the moment of absolute decision and to have that decision determine the whole of their existence."[68] Here again is the craving for comprehensiveness. But it is important to see that this craving is not only a matter of rarefied theological disputes among German Protestant and Jewish intellectuals in the Weimar period.

The new theologians and those they inspired shared this craving with movements emerging throughout Europe at the start of the twentieth century. Among other things, these movements were enthralled by a style of thought that views "the West" as a cartoonish villain, eventually rendering everyone and everything associated with it a legitimate target for violence. Ian Buruma and Avishai Margalit have called this style of thought "Occidentalism."[69] It draws essential elements from German philosophical and literary responses to French imperial rule at the dawn of the nineteenth century. "The West" in the eyes of twentieth- and twenty-first-century Occidentalists is genealogically descended from "the Enlightenment/the French" as it looked through the eyes of nineteenth-century German Counter-Enlightenment Romantics.[70]

The Counter-Enlightenment Romantic sees cold, rational, mechanistic, fragmented, self-alienating rules and ideas imperialistically eradicating the warm, emotional, organic, holistic, authentic life of *our* group, in *this* land, which courses through *our* veins. He yearns for harmony and is "forever haunted by the constant longing for lost unity."[71] The emblem of what must be resisted, and perhaps its secret engine, is frequently "the Jew," who seems in the Counter-Enlightenment Romantic imagination to benefit most from this new corruption of humanity.[72] Thus, while Buruma and Margalit showcase violent and nonviolent Occidentalism among Russians, Japanese, Jews, Muslims, and others, the assault of Nazi Germany on democracies, "seen as artificial, rationalistic, racially hybrid, materialist, and lousy with greedy Jews, was a pure example of murderous Occidentalism in the heart of the European continent."[73]

Many participants in Occidentalist movements seemed to long to submit themselves to a totalizing reality that would finally relieve them of their shameful, desiccated, bourgeois individuality. Hannah Arendt describes this as part of the appeal of "totalitarian" mass movements:

> Insofar as individualism characterized the bourgeoisie's as well as the mob's attitude to life, the totalitarian movements can rightly claim that they were the first truly antibourgeois parties; none of their nineteenth century predecessors . . . ever involved their members to the point of complete loss of individual claims and ambition, or had ever realized that an organization could succeed in extinguishing individual identity permanently and not just for the moment of collective heroic action.[74]

These movements also offered the possibility of "total explanation," a "sixth sense" provided by the ideology enabling one to see a "'truer' reality concealed behind all perceptible things," and a "consistency that exists nowhere in the realm of reality."[75]

The total reality maintained through total explanation is also supposed to be totally pure and totally sealed, making corruption from the outside impossible. And in this way the longing to submit to a totalizing reality is a longing that is inextricably entangled with the dynamics of primitive shame and disgust that Nussbaum has identified. Nussbaum has written specifically about the centuries-old image of "the Jew" in Europe that was employed in response to the crisis that followed the First World War. "The Jew" had long been depicted as "disgustingly soft and porous, receptive of fluid and sticky, womanlike in its oozy sliminess."[76] After the First World War, "No doubt propelled by a fear of death and disintegration that could not help making itself powerfully felt at that time, many Germans projected onto Jews, as well as women, misogynistic disgust properties that they both feared and loathed. The clean safe hardness of the true German man (often praised in images of metal and machinery) was standardly contrasted with female-Jewish-communistic fluid, stench, and muck."[77]

As Nussbaum describes this period, the historical representation and treatment of Jews as disgustingly animalistic served merely as a convenient pretext for identifying a group (it could have been any group, on this account) to serve as the target for aggressive projections of intensified primitive shame and anthropodenial.[78] The important connection here is that the longing for a totally clean, hard, impenetrable Germany and German-ness that Nussbaum identifies was related to a longing to submit to a totalizing reality, which was provoked in part by disappointment about the limitedness and weakness of liberalism.[79] A dark mixture of the critique of liberalism as limited, weak, and perfidious, with exacerbated mortality distress and its consequent projective disgust, a celebration of amoral violence, a yearning for comprehensiveness, and an ideal of submission amalgamated into what is now, following Arendt and others, commonly referred to as totalitarianism. The fact of fraught societies—that is, the problem of remainders, the problem of reproduction, and the missing link problem taken together—makes totalitarianism a constant threat to the liberal project.[80]

The problem of remainders and the problem of reproduction assure that liberalism's historical failures and hypocrisies remain potent and present to mind. The eternal liability to tragedy, whether as a result of natural disaster or human fallibility, always presents the possibility of crisis and therefore exacerbates mortality distress and its consequent projective disgust. Furthermore, the problem of remainders and the problem of reproduction make it likely that people will feel caught in some "vicious circle," as Fanon described it, and want to explode with some kind of violent outburst. Finally, insofar as this longing for rupture yearns for a "wholeness" or "totality" on the other side of the explosion, it is reinforced by the frustrating structural noncomprehensiveness of political liberalism.

When liberalism, implicitly or explicitly, seems to ask citizens to be citizens *all the way down*, like the liberal theologians who produced the "stillborn God" that Lilla describes, it is apt to provoke a longing that is concomitant to Fanon's: a longing for willful decisive action, rupture, ecstatic confrontation with the "wholly Other," anything to break the deadening moralism of bourgeois civility. Liberal thought thus presents a grave danger when it seems to assure people that merely to be a good and dutiful citizen who is inoffensive, free to buy enormous varieties of T-shirts and toothpaste, will be enough to lead a worthwhile and satisfying life. It is only a small and pitiable bunch, indeed, that could find such a life ultimately satisfying, with no quiet desperation or yearning for what is transcendent, transgressive, explosive, or perverse. Thus the allure of violence will haunt the historically oppressed *and everyone else*, even when a liberal state seems to be doing rather well. The lure of submission, which sometimes converges as an aspiration with the yearning for explosion and ecstatic communion that is provoked by noncomprehensiveness, lurks ubiquitously for the same reason.

Recent American popular culture is rich with representations of a simmering desire for rupture among bored white professionals. Indeed, popular movies from the late 1990s took up this theme with notable vigor. Particularly iconic was the 1999 film *Fight Club*, in which low-level white-collar and service industry workers are drawn into a brutal underground boxing club where they can feel masculine, vigorous, and alive. The club ultimately morphs into a terrorist syndicate with cells around the country. The movie ends with a spectacular terrorist assault on a major American city, including the demolition of several towering skyscrapers. But popular movies from this period that seem more focused on the troubled relationship between technology and our experience of "the Real," like *The Matrix* (1999) and *The Truman Show* (1998), were also preoccupied with the not-enoughness of bourgeois life. In 1998 the Goo Goo Dolls had a hit song called "Iris" with a lyric that captures the American 1990s version of this longing: "When everything feels like the movies / you bleed just to know you're alive."

If these popular cultural representations appear benign, recent violence that seems to result in part from the missing link problem is perhaps more disconcerting. For instance, Olivier Roy has argued persuasively that people in Europe who pledge themselves publicly to "Islamic State" represent a nihilistic youth movement driven by fantasies of theatrical heroism, immersion in the cause of the group (in this case, the *ummah*), and violence. They are not renewing medieval hostilities between Islam and Christendom or offering a political response to third-world grievances. According to Roy, "terrorism does not arise from the radicalization of Islam, but from the Islamization of radicalism."[81] Most of the jihadists are young second-generation North African immigrants who are already captivated by the idea and emotions of revolt, along with white French converts who are likewise so inclined long before their conversions.[82]

Both types are drawn to ISIS, Roy explains, because they are looking for a label and coherent narrative for their rebellion.[83] Islamized radicalism is "the only supranational universal militant ideology on the market."[84]

I would add, furthermore, that it is a militant ideology with clear Occidentalist and totalitarian features, taking full advantage of the missing link problem.[85] The young jihadists that Roy describes are not educated or particularly interested in Islamic jurisprudence, institutional history, traditions of Koranic exegesis, poetry, or theology.[86] Nor do they move to Syria in order to do the humdrum work of founding an enduring Islamic political infrastructure. They move to Syria for the thrill of war. They are intoxicated by a romantic narrative of heroism, violence, and death. As Roy describes it,

> The narrative plays on the image of movie and videogame superheroes. A typical cliché is that of the future hero whose destiny is not at first clear, as he leads an empty or too-normal life. And then he receives the call (taken in its religious sense of a sudden vocation, but with reference to the popular video game "Call of Duty") and turns into an almost supernatural, omnipotent character. Not only does he save the suffering and passive *ummah*, but he also possesses great powers, including the power of life and death and sexual power.[87]

The jihadist is excited by the dirty work of the Levites, not the prospect of everyday life in the Promised Land. What ISIS is trying do, Roy explains, is "to create an international vanguard, it's not to establish a real local Islamic society."[88]

The very limited though consequential international appeal of Islamized radicalism exemplifies an important way in which social processes related to the modern category of "religion" aggravate the missing link problem. Second-generation immigrants drawn to Islamized radicalism tend to start out thoroughly immersed in a brash rebellious French youth culture—drinking, sex, social media bravado—and totally alienated from the traditional cultural life of their parents. They utterly reject the Islam of their parents, which seems like a bunch of boring, Old World familial obligations (or if their parents are successful professionals, like a soulless, apologetic performance designed to fit into the "respectable French society" against which they are set in youthful rebellion). What they ultimately embrace is not the multifaceted Algerian, Moroccan, or Tunisian Islamic culture of their parents, but the "pure religion" offered to them as "Islam," entirely detached from any particular regional or cultural context. "There has indeed been an intention right from the start of the jihadist movement," Roy explains, "to create a new type of *Homo islamicus*, removed from all national, tribal, racial and ethnic, even family and affective attachments, a man truly uprooted in order to create a new society from scratch."[89] In the U.S. the Tzarnaev brothers who bombed the Boston Marathon in 2013 fit Roy's description very well.

Roy has developed ideas of "deterritorialization," "deculturation," and "pure religion" extensively in his scholarship on religion among immigrant populations.[90] The key point, for my argument, is that immigrants in democratic societies like the U.S. are often incentivized to define themselves narrowly in terms of their religion, conceived as an identifying mark that is detachable from any particular regional, cultural, or national context.[91] Roy explains, "The religious marker is effectively often perceived as positive or, in any case (except for Islam after 11 September 2001), honorable; it also allows the individual to escape racialist classifications and move up the social ladder in countries like the United States where this marker [the racial marker] is very often negative: it is better to be Hindu than Indian, Buddhist than Asian, Greek Orthodox than Arab."[92] Through such processes of "religionization," new members of society are compelled to privilege their religion, which is thereby isolated from what is demoted as merely culture. I have identified how these processes religionized Jews, too, in America in the twentieth century.

Regional language and folklore, culinary and musical traditions, school affiliations and friendship networks, family history—all this is too cumbersome and complicated to explain. It is easier just to say, "I'm Hindu" and wait for your invitation to a local "interfaith" event as such. According to Roy, the "Hinduism" ("Islam," "Judaism," etc.) that emerges from this process of differentiation is constructed "in a space that is no longer territorial and is therefore no longer subject to politics."[93] Readily then, in books and pamphlets, on the Internet and through ecstatic communal experiences, religion entrepreneurs seize the uptake of deterritorialized and decultured religion among immigrant populations that are otherwise diverse and, stripping them of their previous geographical, national, linguistic, or other identifications, forge them into adherents of a single pure religion.[94]

The fact of fraught societies makes the process of reorganizing people into homogenized adherents of pure religions particularly troubling. Think of the lingering stereotypes, prejudices, and caricatures that characterize the problem of remainders. Think of the reproduced and reinforced historical grudges and intergroup antipathies that characterize the problem of reproduction. And think of the fundamental imperfectability of the liberal state, with its ultimately unsatisfying noncomprehensiveness that characterizes the missing link problem. In this context, deterritorialized, deculturated, pure religion emerges as an especially apt medium for violent Occidentalism and totalitarianism. When a Jewish kid from New Jersey who grew up in a "secular" or "culturally Jewish" family becomes a militant religious Zionist extremist and moves to the West Bank or an Algerian French kid moves to Syria to join ISIS, this is likely a key dimension of what is going on. In both cases there is an effort to reterritorialize the pure religion, to subject real people and real land to a religionized fantasy of heroism, immersion in the cause of the group, and violence.[95]

To be sure, not all dangerous movements wailing "the grown-ups must die!" and set on "forcing the End" are products of the specific processes of religionization. Similar fantasies of heroism, total immersion in the cause of the group, and violence were readily on display in the surge of neo-Nazi enthusiasm after the election of Donald Trump. Coverage of the white nationalist rally in Charlottesville, Virginia, in August of 2017—where a throng of white men solemnly walked with torches chanting "Jews will not replace us" and a woman was murdered, and dozens were wounded, when a sympathizer with the cause plowed his car into counterprotesters—made this particularly evident.[96] Here, perhaps, racialization is doing work similar to religionization. And I suspect that we would find similar fantasies of heroism, total immersion in the group, and violence among anarchists and other far-left activists who continue to crop up occasionally, seizing an option for total rebellion that is now over a hundred years old.

The nation that I think we should strive to become will have to find a way of mitigating the interminable totalitarian threat posed by the fact of fraught societies. It is impossible to know precisely what this threat will produce at any given moment. As I write this in 2018, it is absolutely ridiculous to worry about the possibility of an emergent ISIS-style caliphate in America. It is also unnecessary to worry too much about the emergence of some sort of leftist totalitarian state. What is truly worrisome—*keeps me up at night worrisome*—is the emergence of a permanent reactionary security state through weak spots in liberal democratic institutions, presided over by an intransigent fascist in the White House who is buoyed by white Christian nationalism, that scapegoats immigrants and feeds off of the fear produced by sporadic acts of global jihadist terrorism, sensationalized stories of leftist overreach on college campuses, and occasional rumbles between far-left and far-right activists in the streets.

The immediate threat of an enduring white nationalist Trumpocracy that exploits violent responses to the missing link problem in order to justify itself, and indeed offers itself as a resolution to the missing link problem, requires immediate political resistance. I am not in a position to offer strategies for the needed direct political action here. The task of this book is to offer a longer arc of thought, a vision that can help orient aspirations of political action far into the future. Roy actually seems to intuit my own sense of what we ought to strive for as a nation, so that progress toward justice can be reasonably stable despite the interminable dangers posed by the missing link problem. Societies, he explains, need their "implicit" and "unspoken" domains, where "marginal elements, deviances and otherness—from the brothel to the carnival" are able to thrive.[97] Societies need their "places of transgression (red-light districts), moments of transgression (holidays, carnivals), marginal elements, as well as private life and political opposition. There is no culture unless such spaces exist."[98]

Reterritorialized pure religion will be particularly oppressive and unstable because it demands that society cleanse itself entirely of these domains.[99] That is Roy's point. But the point also applies to liberal societies: they need time and space set aside for perverse ideas, emotions, performances, and rituals, along with fantasies of purity, comprehensiveness, and submission. This is not news. What we can only now appreciate, however, is that liberal societies need such time and space *because of the fact of fraught societies*. I will turn next to explain in detail the idea of a domain of play, which I offer as a way of conceptualizing the time and space we need to set aside, and how exactly we should expect it to mitigate the fact of fraught societies.

4

THE CAPABILITY OF PLAY

Despite the fact of fraught societies, I believe it is still worth trying to cultivate widely shared political love in America. This is because perverse remainders, reproduced grudges, longings for the End, and propulsion toward transgressive bodily outbursts can be redirected into the domain of play. This is my central claim. If we can imagine a nation where these elements of the fact of fraught societies are redirected into the domain of play, we can imagine a nation worth striving to become. It is now time to address the deferred question: what exactly is the domain of play? If we all started to see a domain of play, as I intend, how would it absorb the redirected elements of the fact of fraught societies? And how, precisely, would it relate to the domain of the political?

It is important, first, to clarify that the domain of play is not a territory that exists without our having a name for it like a landscape of mountains, forests, and lakes. Think instead of a map that labels the mountains, forests, and lakes, represents their relative size, shows where they are in relation to nearby territories, and situates them along the axes of a compass. The map is not a mirror image of the territory; it is a simplification. It represents relationships of proportion and kind and uses names to distinguish one place from another. Above all, the map reflects a relationship between human beings and the landscape. It is a human interpretation of the meaning of these mountains, forests, and lakes *for us*. It allows us to think about the landscape as a whole and makes it navigable.

Similarly, the domain of play is a designation on a moral map of social territory. This sort of map is sometimes called a "normative social theory."[1] The domain of play is designed to fit into the normative social theory proposed by Rawls in *Political Liberalism*, which I adapt to Nussbaum's capabilities conception of justice. Adapting Rawls's map to Nussbaum's view and adding the domain of play should provoke, in the words of Iris Marion Young, an "imaginative shift" that makes a new image of collective life "plausible to the imagination."[2]

If we want to imagine what an America governed by just institutions might look like, it is helpful to have a working picture of the kinds of institutions, spheres, and other features that make up the landscape of American society. As part of a political conception of justice, a worthy normative social theory will be a point of view that people can take when navigating political relationships and judging the degree of justice in their society. It should be designed to enable critical deliberation about how well we are doing and what is appropriate in different spheres of life. To be clear, though, a normative social theory is more like a blueprint for creating dams and bridges, designating protected forests and animal sanctuaries, and the like, than it is a geographical representation of a landscape. It has to be based on a realistic representation of the landscape, but it is ultimately a plan to alter the landscape.

In actuality, power dynamics, oppressive ideologies, and the forces of chance and human fallibility circulate throughout every part of American society and every body in it, defying whatever boundaries are thought ostensibly to separate distinct spheres and institutions. Scholars in various disciplines who analyze precisely how these forces actually circulate are doing crucial work—they are trying to capture what the landscape actually looks like. I am doing something different. I am offering a blueprint for altering the landscape, which strives nevertheless to be realistic about the landscape as it is. The blueprint that I offer is designed specifically to help us articulate *what is bad, wrong, or unjust* about the fact that these forces flow into this sphere, those power dynamics influence that institution, and so on.

I assume it is possible for us to influence the flow of power, oppressive ideologies, and other forces so that, for instance, the force of political justice is more ubiquitous and the force of nasty stereotypes is more confined to the domain of play. Of course, we will never really succeed entirely at directing each of the various forces that circulate throughout our society into their appropriate spheres (where appropriateness is defined by a political conception of justice). We are never going to color perfectly within the lines. But we can do better or worse. And a crucial first step to doing better is to cultivate a widespread propensity to see our society according to a common normative social theory that is tied to a broadly attractive vision of America. Part of my goal is to encourage people in the U.S., when they are assessing American life, to distinguish between a domain of the political and a domain of play and to valorize the capacity to know what is appropriate in which domain.

THE NORMATIVE SOCIAL THEORY OF POLITICAL LIBERALISM

In contemporary America, it is "commonsense" normative social theory to distinguish between a public sphere and a private sphere. People make this distinction without even thinking about it when they want to express a political grievance. It might even seem like a natural distinction to many people, instead of one that became colloquial in part as a result of influential books by liberal theorists like John Locke.[3] I have already discussed the flaws Strauss identified in this distinction and Rawls's rejection of it. Now I will turn back to Rawls in order to look more carefully at his preferred distinction between the basic structure of society and the background culture. The domain of play, as I will explain in depth, is located in the background culture.

THE PUBLIC POLITICAL CULTURE

Rawls describes the basic structure of society as "a society's main political, social, and economic institutions, and how they fit together into one unified system of social cooperation from one generation to the next."[4] This includes, as I have explained, the legal system, mandatory educational institutions, the tax system, laws and policies that provide and regulate work, electoral procedures, and the family.[5] The basic structure of society is the centerpiece of the domain of the political. A political conception of justice—like Rawls's conception of justice as fairness or Nussbaum's capabilities conception of justice—should be constructed to function as the moral basis for the design and criticism of these systems, institutions, and procedures.

The political conception of justice, itself, should be built out of intuitively resonant "fixed points" taken from the "public political culture" of American society. Rawls uses the term *public* to indicate that this is something that most people know about and that they know that everyone else knows about it. The public political culture is part of the basic structure. It includes the core political institutions of society and traditions of judicial interpretation, along with significant documents, texts, and other widely recognized representations of political justice.[6] The idea is that in the process of formulating a political conception of justice, the theorist will designate certain key sources as a way of grounding the conception in actually existing political values. The U.S. Constitution, the cumulative tradition of U.S. constitutional interpretation, and the Declaration of Independence are obvious choices. One might also include key touchstones like James Madison's "Memorial and Remonstrance Against Religious Assessments," Abolitionist writings by Frederick Douglass, and the speeches of Martin Luther King Jr.

By calling these writings and speeches fixed points in the public political culture, they are posited as broadly accessible references for widely shared convictions. They tangibly express the value of equality before the law, the importance of liberty of conscience, and the injustice of slavery. While the texts themselves are riddled with inconsistencies, and the convictions they are said to represent have only very rarely and selectively been applied in American history, they are still common reference points for people in different groups across the political spectrum when trying to justify political claims. They can thus function as a "shared fund of implicitly recognized basic ideas and principles" that we can draw from when trying to construct a political conception of justice.[7]

As part of the basic structure of society, the public political culture is among the institutions that we are meant progressively to reconstruct on the basis of a political conception of justice. According to Rawls, the basic structure will have "deep and long-term social effects and in fundamental ways shape citizens' character and aims, the kinds of persons they are and aspire to be."[8] Thus people come to see themselves according to a political conception of the person as a citizen, however else they might see themselves, in part by being exposed to the laws, policies, judicial interpretations, and widely treasured speeches, songs, literature, and more that constitute the public political culture.

Promoting a political conception of justice, like the modified version of Nussbaum's capabilities conception that I promote in this book, involves positing the constituents of our public political culture and offering guidelines for others to make additions or subtractions in the future. If I posit King's "I Have a Dream" speech as part of the public political culture, this means that I think it should be taught in public schools, celebrated in government-funded museums and events, etc.[9] The hope would be that building the speech into the basic structure of society will over time result in most people growing up to see themselves and others according to the political conception of the person as a citizen that I advocate.

THE BACKGROUND CULTURE

The public political culture is distinguished from what Rawls called the background culture. The background culture is best understood negatively: it is where people express their views *without* being morally constrained by "public reason." Rawls uses "public" in this phrase to designate what he usually designates with his special sense of "political." He writes, "In a democratic society public reason is the reason of equal citizens who, as a collective body, exercise final political and coercive power over one another in enacting laws and in amending their constitution."[10] Accepting the constraints of public reason means trying to make arguments that you hope others will be able to accept without having to endorse *your* comprehensive view as a precondition of acceptance.

Public reason is the way that people reason with each other when they see each other as equal citizens according to a political conception of the person as a citizen. With the conception that I advocate, then, public reason involves trying to make claims that will be acceptable to anyone who sees himself—however else he might see himself—as a vulnerable, dependent human animal with a profound stake in choice, one who carries a legacy of historic injustice and longs to flourish in a common life with others (where "flourishing" means being able to exercise all the central human capabilities at a threshold level). Political liberalism demands that arguments about constitutional essentials and matters of basic justice be made in conformity with public reason.[11] While Rawls thinks of public reason in terms of arguments made verbally or in writing, I think we should take a maximally expansive view of what might count as public reason. A peaceful march or sit-in that registers political opposition through the disruption of everyday life while simultaneously registering respect for political institutions *performs* public reason. There are innumerable ways that people can perform their commitment to public reason that go far beyond the verbiage that is preferred by professional intellectuals.[12]

The background culture, however, is set apart as a place where comprehensive doctrines are generally expressed for the benefit of one's particular associations or communities, where one needn't concern oneself with public reason. Since what people pursue in the background culture is not essentially defined by being "comprehensive" or "doctrinal," but by *not* being justified with recourse to public reason, I will refer to people's pursuits in the background culture as "nonpublic projects." Some of these are related to formally articulated comprehensive doctrines, but some may be ad hoc, idiosyncratic, or impossible to categorize well. I don't want to repeat Rawls's mistake of assuming that the background culture will necessarily be dominated by "religions" or institutions, movements, and ideas that look like "religions."

Institutions in the background culture can include churches, mosques, synagogues, BDSM clubs, sports leagues, colleges, universities, and professional associations. The reasoning that animates these institutions need not be public reason. And people need not see each other primarily as citizens when they are participating in the life of these institutions. The background culture is where citizens argue, perform, and abide according to their wont, so long as this is compatible with switching to public reason and seeing themselves and their fellow citizens as citizens when appropriate.

Think of Joseph Jastrow's picture of a "Duck/Rabbit."[13] When you look at it one way it looks like a duck, when you look at it another way it looks like a rabbit. It is fully and genuinely both, even if it never appears as both at the same time. In the background culture, people may see themselves or others as rabbits, but when it comes to what they, and others, are owed by the basic structure of society they see themselves as ducks. For our purposes, though, we have to imagine that only one image is stable. We can imagine, for instance, that everyone sees herself and everyone else as a duck, however else they might see themselves and others. The duck here represents the political conception of the person as a citizen. But every duck will have another aspect, too, so that the polity includes a duck/rabbit, duck/cow, duck/ant, duck/Smurf, duck/Odradeck, and so on. And it includes ducks that are also several other things and mixes of things. The hope is that everyone can toggle appropriately between seeing the "duck" aspect and seeing the variable other aspect(s).

The background culture should be imagined to be a site of ongoing struggle. An American society animated by increasingly just political institutions will look very different depending on which nonpublic projects permeate the background culture. Some people will want the background culture to be saturated with Christian symbols, themes, rituals, institutions, and ideals. Others may want a background culture in which naturalism, irreverence, experimental living, intellectuality, sexual liberation, and aesthetic achievement are pervasive values. Some people may want a background culture that is neatly organized into "religions," which interact through "interfaith" dialogues and initiatives. Others may prefer it to be neatly organized into "cultures." What the background culture of an increasingly just America will look like cannot be determined ahead of time. The basic structure of society will influence what it will look like, to be sure. In turn, the public political culture will be influenced by trends in the background culture. I will explain how these dynamics work at length in what follows. But it is important to recognize that the character of the background culture will be a matter of *ongoing struggle* even in the best America that we can realistically imagine.

WORK

One very important way that the basic structure of society and the background culture relate is through "work," that is, paid activity. In the normative social theory that I am advocating, I assume that most adults between the ages of twenty-two and sixty-five spend a significant amount of their time per week working. We should want all members of American society to have "opportunities for meaningful work," and the basic structure should be the "employer of last resort," as Rawls suggested.[14] Regulation of what happens in the workplace, whether in jobs provided by the basic structure or otherwise, is crucial to making this possible. Antidrudgery policies should encourage variety, opportunities for excellence and mastery, opportunities for individual creativity and initiative, and dignity in conscientious labor regardless of individual ambition. There should also be a regulatory perspective from which citizens think about the diversity of opportunities for flourishing at work. There is no reason for the majority of people in American society to be dragooned unnecessarily in some particular type of work (service, agriculture, management, sales, finance). Diverse work opportunities are assured, in part, by making sure that there are openings for individual initiative and innovation in the production of goods and services. This enables new developments in work diversity and exit options when work is not working out.

The economy, as part of the basic structure of society, should be orchestrated to produce resources that are necessary for the exercise of central human capabilities: food, shelter, books, newspapers, public buildings and parks, environmental sustainability, etc. The political conception of justice (in this case, the capabilities conception) functions as a justification for the variety of work options that the state can provide or guarantee (possibly in coordination with sole proprietorships or corporations) as "employer of last resort." Thus, along with jobs in law enforcement, mail delivery, and infrastructure building, government can justifiably use public resources to provide opportunities for care work (jobs in eldercare, care for people with disabilities, and childcare).

In these government jobs, people do work that assures opportunities for all members of American society to exercise the full range of their basic capabilities. And the jobs themselves contribute to this by availing those who perform them an opportunity for meaningful work. Access to meaningful work is, in fact, one of the central human capabilities—#10B on the list of capabilities that Nussbaum suggests are central is material control over one's environment: "Being able to hold property (both land and movable goods), and having property rights on an equal basis with others; having a right to seek employment on an equal basis with others; having the freedom from unwarranted search and seizure. In work, being able to work as a human being, exercising practical reason and entering into meaningful relationships of mutual recognition with other workers."[15]

Work should therefore be available to all members of society in jobs that help make it possible for everyone to have a lifetime of opportunities to exercise their central human capabilities. And these jobs should be provided by the government, initiatives undertaken from the background culture that are regulated by the government, or both in various combinations. In this way, everyone will have a chance to do "meaningful work": work we can presume that any person would be motivated to do by virtue of his desire to live well with others under conditions of political justice.

Work provided by the government should not, however, function primarily to promote any particular ideal of full flourishing. The government should not provide jobs that facilitate particular nonpublic projects or forms of play, like jobs as priests or baseball umpires. Because the economy will presumably facilitate property ownership and opportunities for individual initiative and innovation in the production of goods and services, people should be able to create and find jobs that promote their particular nonpublic projects. So there should be plenty of jobs that *could not* be justifiably provided by the basic structure of society.

A very complex task of the basic structure is to cultivate a critical mass of citizens who genuinely want to do meaningful work of some kind, while at the same time allowing ample and diverse opportunities for people to do work that is meaningful for nonpublic reasons. Still more complicated, there must be some wiggle room for people who will not be willing or able to work for various reasons. Figuring out how precisely to provide, manage, and regulate all these features of the economy is essential to political justice (but light-years beyond my own intellectual capacity!).

The point I mean to make here is that, in keeping with my conviction that we should strive for a reasonably realistic ideal, I imagine people will work in the society we ought to pursue. In other words, I do not think we should strive to build a "postwork society."[16] Before moving on, let me clarify the following with regard to the role of work in the normative social theory that I propose. Work is paid activity that is facilitated by the economy, which is part of the basic structure of society. Some work will directly promote political justice and may therefore be provided or bolstered by the government. Some work will promote nonpublic projects. Thus some work will happen in the domain of the political, while some work will happen in the background culture (which, however, is a product of and is regulated by the basic structure of society—remember, there is no "private sphere").

A person may therefore be paid to pursue her nonpublic project (and she may even be paid to play) in the background culture. Everyday life at work, regardless of what kind, should be regulated in such a way that respects each person's dignity as defined by the political conception of justice. The background culture (and, as we shall see, the domain of play within the background culture) is constructed, in part, *temporally* through government regulation of work. For instance, government can enforce the norm of a forty-hour workweek (and, given technological advances, this could go lower) to assure that all members of society have time to pursue nonpublic projects and play. Furthermore, each individual's accumulation of money through work is expected to enable her to participate in and change the life of the background culture as she sees fit.

THE MEDIATING INSTITUTIONS
OF A DEMOCRATIC SOCIETY

In addition to the basic structure of society and the background culture, Rawls's normative social theory also includes institutions that "mediate between" the public political culture and the background culture. He mentions newspapers, television, and radio specifically.[17] I would add the Internet and social media, along with the fictional and nonfictional book market, film, theater, and other such media. The most pertinent characteristic that they have in common is this: they function as venues for reporting, expressing, and criticizing content from both the background culture *and* the public political culture. And they are venues where these two cultures come into relation.

In some cases these media present content from the public political culture and make it available to be assessed from the various perspectives that constitute the background culture (i.e., the State of the Union Address being broadcast on major television networks and simulcasted on newspaper websites). In other cases, they present content from the background culture and make it widely available to be assessed from the perspective of the public political culture or the various views that inhabit the background culture (this accounts for most television shows, films, plays, etc.).

I assume that these media may justifiably be produced and maintained by governments or nongovernmental actors (nonprofit organizations, corporations, individuals) in various combinations (consider the differences between, for instance, PBS, HBO, and NBC). I will refer to these institutions as the mediating institutions of a modern democratic society.

We need not assume that these institutions are neutral with respect to the ongoing conflicts that divide members of modern democratic societies. Sometimes the medium itself will, of course, significantly determine the content that it produces. The meanings that are possible on television are different from the meanings that are possible in a novel. All the mediating institutions of society will include biases and blind spots and they are highly susceptible to commercial influences. These institutions are thus apt *themselves* to be criticized both from the perspective of the public political culture and from the various perspectives that constitute the background culture.[18] Governments may regulate these institutions on the basis of values and principles drawn from the public political culture, while nongovernmental actors may likewise regulate them (with boycotts, public condemnation, competition) on the basis of values and principles drawn from the background culture.

THE PUBLIC CULTURAL CRITIC

Mediating institutions are sometimes carriers of content from the background culture that can be plucked and fastened to the public political culture. Let me explain how this works. Sometimes mediating institutions function like a massive drive-in movie screen onto which the diverse views and practices of the background culture are projected for all members of society to see. In some of these cases, what makes it to the massive screen is ostensibly about the society as a whole, even though it is expressed from within one of the particular nonpublic perspectives that constitute the background culture. Think of any television show or movie or novel that has the implication: this is what *we* are like, this is *us*.

In these cases, the content expressed is meant in effect to stimulate the audience to see itself as an "us." The conception of "us" that it means to construct may not necessarily be formulated in order to be appropriate to the public political culture (and it may not be appropriate to it). But sometimes what emerges from the background culture and appears on the massive screen of mediating institutions actually presents a picture of "us" that *can* be included in the public political culture. To my knowledge, Rawls did not write about how precisely the content of the public political culture is determined. Presumably, he understood his own role as a political philosopher to include making assertions about what ought to be included. In order to fill this gap, I will add to Rawls's normative social theory the distinct role of the public cultural critic who engages in "public cultural criticism": the activity of observing what emerges from the background culture in order to make interpretive judgments about what ought to be included as part of the public political culture.

Public cultural criticism can be compared to what goes on in "the public political forum," which Rawls describes as having three parts: "the discourse of judges in their decisions, and especially of the judges of a supreme court; the discourse of government officials, especially chief executives and legislators; and finally, the discourse of candidates for public office and their campaign managers, especially in their public oratory, party platforms, and political statements."[19] The public political forum thus generally takes place in regulatory institutions empowered to coerce citizens. The discourses listed by Rawls should therefore observe the strict constraints of public reason (though Rawls does not take these three discourses to be subject to exactly the same standards of public reason all the time). On this basis we have good reason to be outraged when participants in these discourses make no effort to constrain themselves in this way.

Public cultural criticism is a discourse of the public political culture, which is facilitated by the mediating institutions of a democratic society. Among the concrete tasks of public cultural criticism is to identify cultural objects as they emerge from the background culture that can be recognized as part of the public political culture. Emma Lazarus's poem "The New Colossus," which is engraved on the pedestal of the Statue of Liberty, with its mild-eyed "Mother of Exiles," waiting with her warm glowing light to welcome and embrace "the wretched refuse," the homeless, the "tempest-tost," the "huddled masses yearning to breathe free," is a great example. Recognized as part of the public political culture, "The New Colossus" can function as a tangible representation of the political emotions and values that we hope to cultivate (if we hope to cultivate citizens who see themselves and others—when appropriate—as vulnerable, dependent human animals with a profound stake in choice, who carry legacies of injustice and long to flourish in a common life together, where "flourishing" means being able to exercise all central human capabilities at a threshold level).

Along with objects like "The New Colossus" that clearly express a political conception of justice, the public cultural critic should also be on the lookout for objects that capture something about the unresolvable conflicts and intransigent grievances that characterize our particular nation's struggle to be just. In these cases, the point is to illustrate, reinforce, and promote our capacity to affirm a shared political conception of justice, while at the same time never giving up on our resentments—the point is to show how it is possible that we can share in political love despite the fact of fraught societies. In retrospect, then, my reading of Allen Ginsberg's "America" in the introduction is an argument for this poem to be established as a part of the public political culture that does this work. Spike Lee's *Do the Right Thing* is a good candidate too.

So, prominent among the mechanisms that bring the basic structure of society and the background culture into dynamic relations is public cultural criticism that argues for objects in the background culture or in the mediating institutions of society to be established as part of the public political culture. The public political culture changes as it includes new content that emerges from the background culture. As part of the public political culture, new additions can be promoted through public school curricula, museum exhibits, monuments, reading clubs, stamps, and honored with awards like the Kennedy Center Honors and the National Medal of the Arts.

Given that every citizen will be exposed in some way to the public political culture, its contents will have "deep and long-term social effects and in fundamental ways shape citizens' character and aims, the kinds of persons they are and aspire to be."[20] This will, in turn, directly affect what emerges in the background culture. Thus the normative social theory of political liberalism, as I see it, is not a static two-dimensional map. It is more like a three-dimensional sculpture suspended in space that is breathing, dynamic, alive. It is constantly changing in unpredictable ways, sometimes becoming more just, sometimes becoming less just. I will revisit the dynamic relations between the basic structure and the background culture at the end of this chapter.

Let me summarize what I have portrayed as Rawls's normative social theory—the way that I think we should see society when we look at it as citizens. There are two major domains: the domain of the political and the domain of the background culture. At the center of the domain of the political is the basic structure of society. It is animated by the public political culture, which includes the public political forum, public cultural criticism, and the poems, paintings, plays, novels, and speeches that public cultural critics have successfully promoted. Rawls depicted the background culture as animated mostly by individuals, associations, and communities pursuing the goals prescribed by their comprehensive doctrines. But I suggest that we recognize within the domain of the background culture another domain entirely, where people do something very special: the domain of play.

THE CAPABILITY OF PLAY

My account of play is not a descriptive account that is meant to fit into prominent descriptions of play in anthropology, sociology, or psychology, though I will draw from these fields. Instead, I am arguing for a conception of play that is designed to fit into the normative social theory that I have endorsed and developed up to this point. Like the rest of this normative social theory, the domain of play will only materialize through our constructive effort to see it—through a process of intentional "seeing-as." Remember that I am offering a blueprint designed to change the political landscape of American life so that it is more just. The blueprint has to be based on a realistic map of the territory, but it is ultimately intended to help us alter the territory, how we see, and how we interact in it. Toward this end, I will describe play as a capability that all people should be enabled to exercise at a threshold level, playing as the exercise of that capability, and the domain of play as a way to frame playing in the background culture from the perspective of the normative social theory of political liberalism. An America where we recognize the importance of play and a boundary that separates the domain of play from the domain of the political would be an America that could sustain widely shared political love despite the fact of fraught societies. A key initial step toward this America, then, is to make play and the domain of play recognizable.

Before moving on, let me be clear about what is meant by a "capability." As I explained in chapter 1, according to the capabilities approach, governments are the human institutions ultimately responsible for culti-vating citizens and external conditions that are conducive to dignified human life. On Nussbaum's account, this involves the cultivation of both "internal capabilities" and "combined capabilities." Internal capabilities are powers that a person can activate almost regardless of the environ-ment in which she finds herself.[21] The cultivation of internal capabilities is largely the result of educational institutions, families, and surround-ing communities. Where a good education is available, along with a caring family and community, a person will be well situated to develop internal capabilities like the ability to speak a common language, to be a friend, or to make moral choices.

However, as Nussbaum explains, a person who is "well educated, well fed, and healthy" may find herself living under conditions that make the meaningful exercise of her internal capabilities impossible.[22] Combined capabilities, then, describe "internal capabilities *combined with* suitable external conditions for the exercise of the function."[23] Consider that, for instance, women in many parts of the world are enabled to develop inter-nal capabilities, but denied the political and property rights, and rights in relation to their own bodies, that would enable them to use their inter-nal capabilities fully.[24]

According to the capabilities approach, governments are responsible for producing combined capabilities for all of their citizens. But they should not be empowered to dictate how citizens choose to exercise combined capabilities once they are secured. "Government ought to give people a full and meaningful choice; at that point, the decision whether to take up a given opportunity must be their own. Respect for a person requires not dragooning that person into a particular mode of activity, however desir-able it might seem."[25] Paradigmatically, someone may fast in observance of a religious obligation, despite the availability of nutritious food. "There is, however, a large difference between fasting and starving, and it is this difference that the CA wishes to capture."[26] Furthermore, the capabilities approach does not assume that a person will be guided in the exercise of her capabilities by an imperative to make unique, creative, pleasurable or ambitious choices or by a necessity always to expose herself to as many choices as possible. She might just as easily value conformity, hierarchy, submission, anonymity, and asceticism in pursuit of a nonpublic project.

What minimal justice requires, from the perspective of the capabili-ties approach, is that governments maintain a minimum or "threshold" level of combined capabilities for each and every one of their citizens.[27] Strictly speaking, this is not a matter of providing some minimum quantity of resources. It is a matter of providing "opportunities for activity"— precisely how resources might be distributed to provide for these opportunities can vary greatly given the circumstances of different societies.[28] The approach thus provides only a "partial account of justice" insofar as it does not make any demands with respect to what people should do above the threshold of opportunities that are provided: once key combined capabilities are secured at a minimum level, it is not the business of the capabilities approach to judge how citizens choose to exercise them.[29]

While Nussbaum's list of central human capabilities has evolved over the years, one capability that has always been included on it is the capability of play. In its most recent iteration, her list portrays the capability of play as "being able to laugh, to play, to enjoy recreational activities."[30] Of course, as we have seen, she has also given significant weight to the play of the imagination through tragic narratives. Nevertheless, as far as I know, she has not related play in this sense to the capability of play. In what follows, I will offer my own account of the capability of play. I will also clarify the need to frame a distinct domain of play within the domain of the background culture, so that the capability of play is guaranteed as a *combined* capability.

In general, the central human capabilities are capabilities *without which* we cannot imagine "a life worthy of human dignity."[31] The importance of play to such a life, and to life in fraught societies, means that the capability of play must be assured, and a domain of play must likewise be available so that this capability can be exercised. I will proceed in my effort to imagine the play element in life as Nussbaum suggests: by drawing on my "intuitive and discursive" sense of what play entails.[32] I will also draw freely from scholarship in many fields that address the play element in life.

HOW TO RECOGNIZE PLAY

Brian Sutton-Smith has already done the painstaking work of sorting most of the ways that people have thought about play in his book, *The Ambiguity of Play*.[33] But in order to avoid getting tripped up in theoretical controversies between the many "rhetorics of play," as Sutton-Smith calls them, it seems best initially to conjure some images of play. First, think of a baby at play: the baby cuddles a stuffed animal, only to throw it suddenly on the ground and crawl over to retrieve it; she then sits contentedly alone manipulating, sometimes cuddling or throwing, sucking or biting it. Now let me add some monkeys: think of a bunch of monkeys swinging off of the top of a tall tree into water, each doing some distinctive maneuver mid-air, only to splash and run back up the tree to perform something new. And think of Mardi Gras: the grand parade winds through the streets of New Orleans amidst a revelrous throng. Think also of a stand-up comedian in a comedy club, pacing back and forth, arousing laughter in a complex interaction with the audience. Finally, add a few friends spread out on a golf course, each trying to get his best score. These are not meant to be fundamental paradigms of play. But they are images that I have in mind when I think of play.

Several important characteristics of play emerge from these vignettes. First, they are all active. Play is a category of activity, and playing is doing that activity. The audience of a stand-up comedy routine may appear less active than the others, but they can be described as active in at least two ways. First, the audience is interacting with the comedian by expressing consent, perplexity, disapproval, skepticism, and other messages on their faces. Hopefully, they will also laugh on occasion. Comics say that audience interaction makes a big difference in a performance.[34] Second, if they are indeed at play, all of the audience members will be involved in some mental activity, however nonresponsive they may appear. It is possible, after all, to watch comedy routines on television or listen to old comedy records with a glass of scotch after the kids have finally fallen asleep. In these instances, if it is actively at play, the mind is making connections and asserting itself creatively by making sense of the material perceived. The activity of play, then, can sometimes look passive: listening to Allan Sherman's *My Son, the Folk Singer* after a long day, daydreaming on a train, wandering aimlessly in a park, delighting in the presence of a painting or a sculpture or a dramatic production or the sights, sounds, smells, and textures of other people.[35]

There are many different kinds of activities, so play is not just any activity. It seems to be an activity that is done for its own sake. That is, when a person engages in a play activity, she is not trying to produce any state, experience, object, or effect or achieve any goal other than doing that play activity. The preeminent theorist of play Johan Huizinga identified this feature when he wrote of play, "it is an activity connected with no material interest, and no profit can be gained by it."[36] Thinking about playing games, like the example of golf, will make this clearer. It will also compel me to refine what I mean by "activity" and account for playing that does not seem to be done "for its own sake."

In his wonderfully playful book, *The Grasshopper: Games, Life, and Utopia*, Bernard Suits writes, "To play a game is to attempt to achieve a specific state of affairs, using only means permitted by rules, where the rules prohibit use of more efficient in favor of less efficient means, and where the rules are accepted just because they make possible such activity."[37] In the case of golf, the players attempt to achieve the state of affairs of a ball landing in a hole in the ground, but they agree not to walk up and drop the ball in the hole. They accept the rules of golf (far less efficient than dropping the ball in the hole) so that they can engage in "playing golf" rather than "trying to put a ball in a hole in the ground" (for which practical reason would demand the most efficient means).

We know that the players accept the rules so as to be able to play the game, because if we provided them with a more efficient means to get the ball in the hole they would not accept it: that would ruin the game. For some games, the state of affairs that the player wants to achieve is not a goal that would end the activity ("winning" in most competitive games corresponds to the achievement of a goal that does end the activity of playing the game). Suits suggests the example of rallying in ping pong, where a necessary condition of a good hit is that it keeps the ball in play, allowing the other player an opportunity for a good hit.[38] Suits calls these "open games." Again, we know this is done for its own sake because if the players were offered two machines capable of keeping the ball in play, they would not accept.[39]

Suits recognizes that playing in games is only one way of playing. He offers a stipulative definition of play per se as any activity done for its own sake. He then separates play from work (activity done for the sake of some external goal or "instrumental activity") and ultimately concludes that in a utopia, where no instrumental activity would be necessary, only playing (and specifically playing games) would be worth doing.[40] Since this is what we would do under circumstances where *we don't have to do anything*, according to Suits it must be the best life for a human being.

I think Suits offers an outstanding definition of games, which accounts for a lot of playing. But I do not think his stipulative definition of play is sufficient to characterize play fully. How does play, as activity done for its own sake, account for our jumping monkeys? Of course, it is possible to imagine that they are not playing at all, that they have something like an instrumental goal: to get wet and cool off, or to practice their jumping, or to exercise their muscles. But why not just get in the water without expression? Why add the midair theatrics to a rigorous climbing and jumping routine? I can't speak for monkeys. However, there is enough skepticism among scholars about the "use" of play for animals that Sutton-Smith devotes a section to it entitled "It Is Not Proven That Animal Play Is Adaptive."[41]

For Suits, playing in games is a kind of intentional action. This means it is bodily movement undertaken deliberately or self-consciously. And the motivation behind the playing is connected to a reason: what else is "its own sake" than a reason for doing something? His definition of play (activity done for its own sake) demands that *all players* must have reasons for playing. But I am skeptical of attributing reasons too confidently to monkeys and babies. On the other hand, it would be difficult to call any bodily movement "activity" (a period of continuous *action*), rather than just plain "movement" (a body in motion), without some attribution of a guiding consciousness.

The key point here is to separate the claim that an agent is doing an activity from the claim that the agent is doing that activity *for a reason* (or deliberately causing the bodily movement).[42] When I walk down the street daydreaming on my way to fetch my lunch, I am not deliberately or self-consciously placing one foot in front of the other. But I would deliberately and self-consciously move to the side upon seeing a steaming pile of dog shit. As Harry Frankfurt explains: "The behavior is purposive not because it results from causes of a certain kind, but because it would be affected by certain causes if the accomplishment of its course were to be jeopardized."[43] In Frankfurt's terms, this is the sense in which an action can be purposive, and attributable to an agent, but not necessarily performed deliberately or self-consciously (that is, intentionally).[44] A recognizable purpose may emerge when the agent interrupts the activity: the corrective interruption indicates what purpose has not gone right. Before any such intervention, we may posit that there is some kind of purpose to the action, but it is nevertheless indeterminate to our perception. This helps me to say that a person (monkey, baby) can be doing an activity (i.e., playing), even when no one is in a good position to identify a reason why the activity is being done (including the one doing the activity).

Now I can say, further, that an activity can be noninstrumental but not necessarily done for its own sake. I agree with Suits that an activity designed solely as a task to achieve an external goal (such that one would gladly accept the achievement of the goal without having to do the task) is never playing. So playing is always noninstrumental activity. It does not follow, however, that playing is always "for its own sake." When an animal, human or otherwise, is moving, and there is no decisive reason to say that the movement is instrumentally motivated or that it is wholly externally driven (not at all under the guidance of the animal), then it may be an instance of playing, even if we can't say that it is "for its own sake."[45] This way, playing is allowed to include both cases of noninstrumental activity undertaken for its own sake (i.e., playing games) and noninstrumental activity any reason for doing which—if it is done "for a reason" at all—is left mysterious (monkeys expressively jumping off of trees, babies manipulating blankets).

But there is a problem with my characterization of play thus far (as noninstrumental activity that is not necessarily done for its own sake). It may include merely inexplicable activities. If an otherwise anonymous subway rider sitting next to me suddenly, for no apparent reason, leaps from his seat, beats me over the head for a few seconds, and then starts running to the next car, I should not necessarily say, "He is playing." One more characteristic of play must be introduced in order to make it a distinguishable activity: playing seems to be noninstrumental activity that occurs in a circumscribed space/time within which all the participants acknowledge a difference between what things mean inside versus what they mean outside the circumscribed space/time.[46]

The frame that demarcates the space/time of play is acknowledged in one of three ways: 1. someone can "step into" play, adopting the appropriate attitude, perception, expectations, or rules for this sort of play, which requires acknowledgment of the line that must be crossed in order to start playing; 2. someone can "step out" of play, adopting a nonplay attitude, rule, goal, which requires acknowledgment of the line that must be crossed in order to stop playing; 3. an external observer can speculate about how participants transition into or out of the space/time of play and thereby posit the relevant line of demarcation. In every case, *all participants in play acknowledge the play "frame," whether on the way in, on the way out, or both.*

There is always a line surrounding play that separates it as play from nonplay. Of course, what counts as nonplay will depend on the way people think about play. Among theorists of play, nonplay is often work, serious, instrumental, real, productive, useful, adult, coerced, utilitarian, or absolute.[47] Within the play frame, the meaning of activities associated with nonplay can be reversed, exaggerated, destabilized, mocked, or rendered ambiguous. When looking into or entering the framed space of play, there is an enormous sign that reads "This is play."[48] Gregory Bateson called this sign a "metacommunication."[49] The metacommunicative frame around play claims: "These actions in which we now engage do not denote what those actions *for which they stand* would denote" outside the play frame.[50] It is worth noting that many other animals are as capable of the metacommunication required for play as we are. An extraordinary example of a giant polar bear playing with a Canadian Inuit dog has been captured in stunning photographs published in *National Geographic*.[51] There was tail wagging, grinning, bowing, and nonaggressive facial expression, resulting in what can only be called playing together among two normally antagonistic species. And, of course, humans play with their pets all the time.

Now it is possible to interpret the sense in which Mardi Gras in New Orleans is play or happens within a play frame. Mardi Gras has a long pre-American history, and the contemporary throngs on Bourbon Street are not participating in the Mardi Gras of François Rabelais.[52] Indeed, Victor Turner has written of modern Mardi Gras celebrations that they often resemble the "cultural debris of some forgotten liminal ritual."[53] Investigating what he means by this will shed more light on what distinguishes play. Turner found the term *liminal* in Arnold van Gennep's 1908 *Rites de Passage*, in which it was used to describe a particular phase in rite-of-passage rituals in tribal societies.[54] The term described the transitional phase between initial separation and later incorporation into the tribe. During this phase, adolescent boys are sometimes allowed to transgress the usual rules of the society by, for instance, stealing, pillaging, and adorning themselves at the tribe's expense.[55]

According to Turner, the sequestered adolescents are often compared to ghosts, gods, ancestors, and animals: "They are dead to the social world, but alive to the asocial world"; they exist in the sacred against the profane, in chaos against the cosmos, and in disorder against order.[56] During this phase, "the ritual subjects pass through a period and area of ambiguity, a sort of social limbo which has few (though sometimes these are most crucial) of the attributes of either the preceding or subsequent profane social statuses or cultural states."[57] For Turner, the ambiguity, limbo, separateness, and transgression in this transitional phase can be seen in a range of social phenomena in societies that have not been stamped by the Industrial Revolution; he describes these as liminal phenomena.[58]

Turner contrasted liminal phenomena in tribal societies to "liminoid" phenomena in societies that distinguish between work and leisure (mostly postindustrial societies). Liminoid phenomena are characterized by the participation of self-motivated individuals in a free society governed by reciprocal contractual relationships. Liminal phenomena, by contrast, are obligatory and serve a socially conservative function in hierarchical societies.[59] Mardi Gras in today's New Orleans is now recognizable, in Turner's terms, as a liminoid phenomenon animating the remains of a liminal ritual. People go to Mardi Gras in New Orleans voluntarily from all over the world. What makes Mardi Gras a liminoid phenomenon is that there is always a self-selective group of rowdy folks. In a liminal case "even the normally orderly, meek, and 'law-abiding' people would be *obliged* to be disorderly in key rituals, regardless of their temperament and character."[60]

What Turner adds to a vivid portrayal of play is the sense in which the play frame can surround large-scale rituals and activities that are not games: festivals, parades, or parties.[61] His work also suggests that it may be possible to see a play frame around certain places: New Orleans, Las Vegas, Cancun, comedy clubs, strip clubs, dance clubs.[62] A big red velvet rope surrounds these places, from which a sign hangs reading: "This is play." These are places where actions do not mean what those same actions would mean outside the play frame.

While Turner's account of liminoid play in the leisure time and space of postindustrial societies helps me to articulate why I wanted to call Mardi Gras an example of play, I am not entirely convinced by his distinction between liminal and liminoid phenomena. The distinction seems to rest on the optional character of liminoid phenomena seen as opportunities for individuality, compared to the obligatory character of liminal phenomena that conserve the normative order. Turner seems to suggest that only people in "free societies" really play. When people in traditional societies (that are "not free") do rituals in space/time segregated from the normative order, they are really doing the *work* of maintaining social cohesion and stability: turning boys into men, making chiefs out of commoners, cooling those hot from war.[63] This puts Turner in the company of many important theorists who have described play as necessarily voluntary.[64]

I dissent from this popular view. First, there has never actually been a "free society." All pockets of robust choice in societies that have actually existed, and those that exist today, structurally exploit people who do not have robust choice. Furthermore, the fact of fraught societies means that parameters on self-understanding—including how one wants to play—will always be marked by legacies of historical injustice. We do not always choose the ways that we are moved to play, and sometimes the ways in which we want to play are saturated with the legacies of historical injustice. But I also dissent because I think so much of play is *not* entered into deliberately or self-consciously. The cause or intention behind play is often ambiguous, even mysterious. It is easy to imagine babies *drawn into* the space of play rather than decisively *stepping into* the space of play. The same is true for all sorts of adult play activities: daydreaming, wandering, sexual flirtation, "losing oneself" in the flow of some task.[65] But how can I describe a space where I am neither founder nor finder?

On this point we need to return to Winnicott. I referred earlier to Winnicott's story about how frustration in the mother-infant relationship develops and is mitigated. This is a key source for Nussbaum's account of how primitive shame and projective disgust develop and why we need to resist anthropodenial. Winnicott's story also includes an etiology of play that begins at the earliest stages of human psychological development in an "intermediate area" between the inner reality of the bourgeoning individual and the outer reality of the external world.[66] He describes the process of learning to cope with the external world, which is stubbornly resistant to the will, as going something like this: in the murky beginnings of psychological structuring, an infant hungers for the mother's satiating breast and we imagine that there is a primordial phase where the hunger and the satiating breast are not distinguishable to the infant. At this point Winnicott posits that the breast is a "subjective phenomenon" of the baby.[67]

A "good enough mother," to use Winnicott's language, will begin her relationship to the infant by adapting completely to his needs (which allows the infant to feel a kind of omnipotence early on). But, he writes, "as time proceeds she adapts less and less completely, gradually, according to the infant's growing ability to deal with her failure."[68] The illusion of the subjective breast that magically fulfills desire gives way to disillusionment and the objective breast, the mother, who is real and demands an adaptive response from the baby.[69] This provokes a common progression among infants that starts with sucking on fists, fingers, and thumbs and moves to what he describes as an apparent "addiction" to some object: say, a stuffed animal or a tattered old blanket.[70] He calls them "transitional objects," hypothesizing that these objects "are not part of the infant's body yet are not fully recognized as belonging to external reality."[71] As we will see, the transitional object carries with it some of the magical illusion that is lost in the process of disillusionment and adaptation.

While we are accustomed to think of human beings as, on the most fundamental level, dwelling in an analytic distinction between "me" and "not-me," Winnicott suggests that there is an equally fundamental "third space"—an "intermediate area"—where the me/not-me divide is blurred and ambiguous. This is the space of "transitional phenomena." It is "an area that is not challenged, because no claim is made on its behalf except that it shall exist as a resting-place for the individual engaged in the perpetual human task of keeping inner and outer reality separate yet interrelated."[72]

Transitional phenomena represent the first moments of what he calls "the use of illusion," an activity that bridges but nevertheless preserves the distance between myself (with my desires) and the external world (with its frustrating not-me-ness). Further, he explains, "there is a direct development from transitional phenomena to playing, and from playing to shared playing, and from this to cultural experiences."[73] Huizinga also noted this connection, writing about the word *illusion* that it is "a pregnant word which means literally 'in-play' (from *inlusio, illudere* or *inludere*)."[74]

Consider the baby that I described at the start of this chapter, cuddling his stuffed animal. The activities of cuddling, throwing, sucking, and biting are foundational to human play, on Winnicott's account. The stuffed animal is neither "from without" (demanding compliance from the baby) nor a hallucination "from within" (brought into being by the intention of the baby).[75] The "illusory experience" of playing with such an object is, in some sense, constructed by the infant, but it is provided by the external world, which is associated with the mother. The association with the mother is evident in the suckling, biting, and grabbing, which are also involved in feeding. Playing with the transitional object *copes with* separation from the mother and, at the same time, is a circuitous interaction with the mother, a way of feeling close to her.

How then do we get from this kind of playing with the transitional object to so-called cultural experience? Winnicott explains that the fate of the transitional object is "to be gradually allowed to be decathected, so that in the course of years it becomes not so much forgotten as relegated to limbo. . . . It loses meaning, and this is because the transitional phenomena have become diffused, have become spread out over the whole intermediate territory between 'inner psychic reality' and 'the external world as perceived by two persons in common,' that is to say, over the whole cultural field."[76] He continues, "I am therefore studying the substance of *illusion*, that which is allowed to the infant, and which in adult life is inherent in art and religion. . . . We can share a respect for *illusory experience*, and if we wish we may collect together and form a group on the basis of our illusory experiences. This is a natural root of grouping among human beings."[77]

So the infant slowly withdraws her feelings from the stuffed animal or the blanket and begins to play with string or songs or organized games or stories. As the child develops, what she finds to play with—but also *founds by playing with*—is part of a third-space of "illusions" that she may now have the sense of sharing with a group.[78] The shared illusion of the older child, and finally of the adult, allows circuitous interaction between the individual and the group in the same way that the shared illusion of the infant allowed circuitous interaction between her and the mother. Winnicott writes elsewhere, "the provision of the opportunity of the individual to break away from the parents to the family, from the family to the social unit just outside the family, and from the social unit to another, and perhaps to another and another. These ever-widening circles, which eventually become political or religious groupings in society, and perhaps nationalism itself, are the end-product of something that starts off with maternal care, or parental care, and then continues as the family."[79]

I will return to the relationship between play and groupness in a moment. Crucial here is that Winnicott's account vividly portrays the indeterminacy of the space of play. Too voluntaristic an interpretation of play risks shutting it down by resolving its essential ambiguity. As we will see, Winnicott promotes something like a morality of play requiring that at play "a paradox is involved which needs to be accepted, tolerated, and not resolved."[80]

With Winnicott's corrective, it is possible to say that some contemporary play, which Turner might describe as liminoid, should not be differentiated by an alleged voluntary individual intention. People may be drawn to have twenty-first-birthday bashes or bachelor parties in ways that belie any suggestion that they have chosen to do so for their own personal, freely chosen, and independent reasons. And the social conservatism that Turner sees in the liminal is also plausibly part of more contemporary phenomena: "What happens in Vegas stays in Vegas" may be interpreted to mean that what happens there will serve, and not be allowed to penetrate or interrupt, the everyday norms beyond its borders. Acknowledging the indeterminacy of subject, object, and other, which Winnicott identifies in play, means abandoning the presumption of volunteerism that features in most theories of play.

Let me summarize my account of play again: play is noninstrumental activity that occurs in a circumscribed space/time within which all of the participants acknowledge a difference between what things mean inside and what they mean outside this circumscribed space/time. The same circumscribed space/time can also be an intermediate area where transitional objects facilitate ambiguous relations between internal and external, finding and founding, self and group. I have claimed that recognizing a domain of play and the importance of playing in American society will contribute to the possibility of widely shared political love that can endure despite the fact of fraught societies. Now I need to explain a bit more about the mechanics of how a person "carries" legacies of historical injustice and the way in which these legacies can be *carried into* the domain of play.

5

PLAYING IN FRAUGHT SOCIETIES

L et me begin with a reflective exercise. On Passover it is always a special pleasure for me to eat peanut butter and jelly sandwiches on matzah, matzah brei, gefilte fish, and definitely no bread (OK, maybe some bread, but not a lot!). I have vivid memories of enjoying these delights in the spring of every year at different phases of my life. But the memories from childhood are particularly strong. I can remember the plastic sandwich bag, packed by my mom, sticky with jelly, stuck to my fingers as I'd crunch down on the matzah over the white linoleum-covered tables in the cafeteria at school. It was a special time, different from other times when I'd eat whatever. But it wasn't special because it was the "religious holiday of Passover." It was special because it was the sticky-jelly-bag-crunchy-matzah time of year.

Childhood is a time when practices (like eating peanut butter and jelly sandwiches on matzah every spring), symbols, places, faces, joys, traumas, smells, objects, relationships, gestures, and all sorts of other stuff gets imbued with a kind of primordial importance, which defines what is important to a person later in adulthood. When I say that it has primordial importance to a person, I mean that it is what a person will spend his entire life compulsively repeating, hunting for, romanticizing, memorializing, rejecting, repressing, reeling about, transforming, fearing, and so on. This is evident to me in my own adult life. I can see it in often-recalled memories, objects that I carry from place to place, rituals that I do religiously. But I can also glimpse its legacy in relationship dynamics that I repeat, whatever seems intuitive to me and "rings true," and the things that are so sensitive that to touch upon them even slightly can make me angry, put me in a foul mood, or excite me. I see it in the places I go for refuge or rejuvenation, habits that are so basic to my sense of a normal life that I am barely aware of them and it takes someone else to point them out to me, and the stories that I tell about myself, others, and the world. I see it in many of the things that I simply could not do without in a life that I would consider good.

In chapter 3, I explained how the dynamics of groupness and selfness fit into self-understanding. The process of identification that eventually imbues self-understanding with a high degree of groupness actually starts with the forging of primordially important stuff during childhood. It is always initially idiosyncratic. That is, utterly specific to me, like my memory of eating matzah in the lower-school cafeteria as a child. First comes mom-made matzah sandwiches and linoleum-covered tables, *then* comes "believer in the religion of Judaism," or "member of the Jewish people," or "bearer of Jewish culture." There is always a transition from an intimate amorphous world brimming with the raw materials of primordially important stuff to identification of these raw materials as the basis of groupness. This transition can occur in a number of ways. But it often hinges on the use of a label that stimulates and organizes a person's groupness. Here I return to processes that will be familiar from my discussion of the problem of reproduction.

When a child is born, her parents may have long ago attached to the institutions or aims of a group and might, as this child grows, pass on membership to her by using certain labels in everyday life such as, "we are Jews, they are goyim." In this way, parents sometimes facilitate childhood experiences that instill a propensity to heightened groupness of a particular sort in their children. Though I assume that the outcome of their efforts is always unpredictable. One outcome might be that at some point the child, perhaps as a young adult, will begin to attach ideological significance to her experiences of groupness. That is, she will start to justify her actions and ideas using preexisting styles of thought that have intellectual and emotional salience in her society: "it is important for me to keep Passover *because it is part of my culture and it is good for a person to preserve her culture,*" or "it is important for me to keep Passover *because*

it is part of my religion and it is good for a person to practice her religion,"
and so on.[1] These justifications are far away from what actually moves me
to repeat my practice of eating matzah every year. In fact, I have dressed
my practice of eating matzah in various styles of thought over the years,
even as my motivation to do it, or think about it, or worry about it, has
remained constant. I am drawn to the activity of constraining myself to
eat only matzah every Passover; the question of why only ever emerges as
an afterthought.

Another example of how labels heighten groupness goes like this: the
unselfconscious everyday flow of a person's idiosyncratic life might be
interrupted at some point when someone imposes a foreign label on her
that locates her in a group. In this case, groupness becomes salient as a
result of the imposition. Too often, the label that is imposed is implicated
in historical and ongoing stigmatization (*kike, spic, nigger, bitch, faggot*).
The imposition may be relational: someone shouting an epithet at you
from across the street or dropping it casually in conversation. Recall, paradigmatically, the scene in *Black Skin, White Masks* when the child yells,
"Look, a Negro!"

Or, it may be environmental: invading the intimate experiences of
everyday life through the mediating institutions of society (on TV, in movies) or through categories used by other institutions (schools, courts). In
cases of environmental imposition, it is important to note that the "label"
may not be an actual slur or epithet; it may be a caricatured image, a distinctly patronizing attitude, or a conspicuous exclusion that functions in
the same way. In any case, something is evoked that compels a person to
think, "that is about people like me, people *in my group*." The effect is to
heighten groupness.

As I see it, regardless of your propensity to heightened groupness, you
will spend your entire life working through the meaning of your primordially important stuff. However, when a group label successfully fastens
onto this stuff, the consequent groupness, simultaneously and forevermore, feels like it "goes all the way down," like it just *is* who *you are*. It is
at this point that your self-understanding is hitched to a group that might
be defined in terms of ethnicity, race, or religion. You cannot escape it—
and you might not want to escape it—any more easily than you can escape
the other primordially important stuff that commands your attention
throughout your life.

The essential point, then, is that the deep meaningfulness to a person of groupness that is instantiated through categorical identification results from the attachment of a category to preexisting idiosyncratic elements of self-understanding. We are not born members of our groups, as though some natural essence were embedded in us. And yet it can feel that way when groupness has attached to the primordially important stuff of one's childhood. At the same time, we should not forget Fanon's insight into the difference between being seen as, say, a Jew and being seen as "a black." Being susceptible to immediate inferiorization on sight by another person as a result of phenotypical appearance adds an element of destiny to some categories of identification. In the U.S., this is especially acute with respect to race. When the institutions of the basic structure of society reinforce inferiorization through structural racial injustice, the fate of everyone who is perceived according to the stigmatized racial category is severely diminished.

Nevertheless, skin color, hair type, nose shape, and other phenotypical features do mean different things in different contexts within the U.S. and all over the world. As I have throughout this book, I will assume that the struggle for political justice in America, which includes racial justice as an essential constituent part, is worthwhile partly because racial oppression is not fundamentally insurmountable. Thus, while "racial identity" is now egregiously determinative of destiny, the hope is that under a just basic structure phenotype will function as a mere "parameter" rather than a "limit" of self-understanding, in Anthony Appiah's terms. I therefore assume that groupness organized around phenotypical features works just like other kinds of groupness. There is an important difference, however, when the basic structure of society is marked by racial injustice. But this is something that can change. And it *must* change.

Consider, then, the groupness that is forged when an individual begins sincerely to apply a group label to herself and, in doing so, identifies the raw amorphous stuff that is primordially important to her as constitutive of her membership in a particular group. Such a person may identify with a group that has been historically oppressed: as a Jew, black, a woman, gay, etc. Or, one might identify with a group that is seen by others as responsible for historical oppression: as Christian, white, a man, straight, etc. Most often, categorical identification puts a person at the intersection of complex conflicts: a person who identifies as Jewish but also white, a person who identifies as black but also as a conservative Christian, a person who identifies as a woman but also as white and Christian. In any case, a fraught legacy of historical conflicts and oppression will linger in the mutual saturation between your groupness and your primordially important stuff. Your primordially important stuff will thus be marked by the fact of fraught societies—this is what it means to "carry a legacy of historical injustice."

Now let's return to Winnicott. His account of "transitional phenomena" resonates deeply with some of what I have described as the primordially important stuff of childhood. While he generalizes from his observation of infants and children to an account of adult "groupings" and "illusory experience," I have worked my way back from reflection on adult groupness to a postulate about the childhood conditions for the possibility of highly groupist adult self-understanding. To my mind, the accounts "meet halfway" and mutually reinforce each other.

Following Winnicott, my developmental story can now be told with more psychological nuance. Groupness is maintained through transitional phenomena that connect back through a process of "direct development" to the first transitional objects that are found/founded in the "third space" of infant play. This accounts for the importance of the primordially important stuff of childhood: it is the stuff—the objects, rituals, symbols, gestures, smells, words, faces—that from the very beginning has functioned as a means of coping with separation from, but also a means of circuitously interacting with, important others (starting with one's mother or primary caretaker, but ending up, where there is heightened groupness, with the group itself).

I think I can fill in a gap for Winnicott here by offering a plausible description of how transitional phenomena come to be "a natural root of grouping among human beings." When transitional phenomena are absorbed into groupness through processes of identification like labeling, they become important means of both coping with separation from the group (the group is usually never actually assembled in its entirety to acknowledge and appreciate your membership) and circuitously interacting with the group (despite its only elusive presence).

Consider my matzah example. The matzah sandwiches that I would find in my lunch bag at school were connected in a chain of nourishing transactions with my mother that go all the way back to infancy. When you eat a special sandwich made by your mom at school, you are certainly interacting with her—especially when there is a smiley face in Magic Marker on your lunch bag or some unanticipated treat inside. But, where I went to school, other kids had matzah sandwiches too! Some were also protected in brown bags with affectionate smiley faces. We were not only eating the same thing, we were also simultaneously having very personal, albeit circuitous, interactions with our mothers (or whoever so thoughtfully packed our lunches that day). We didn't yet have any notion of "Jewish peoplehood," or anything so sophisticated. But we did share something that can, over time, through processes of identification, become a heightened overlapping groupness.

Crucially, though, no two people ever actually share the same primordially important stuff. It is always too idiosyncratic for that. There must be a process of categorical identification in order for us to represent our respective practices of eating matzah as the same practice (as "practicing our religion" or "expressing our culture"). Winnicott describes something similar: "Should an adult make claims on us for our acceptance of the objectivity of his subjective phenomena we discern or diagnose madness. If, however, the adult can manage to enjoy the personal intermediate area without making claims, then we can acknowledge our corresponding intermediate areas, and are pleased to find a degree of overlapping, that is to say common experience between members of a group in art or religion or philosophy."[2] In order for our intermediate areas genuinely to merge, neither of us can demand compliance from the other. However, if somehow they do merge, we can reflect together on something like "shared" primordially important stuff as the basis of our common groupness.

But, for Winnicott, playing is not only "a natural root of grouping among human beings." It is also the basis for a "sense of self." Bringing his vocabulary into line with the terms that I have already introduced, I will interpret Winnicott to mean by "sense of self" what I have called, drawing on Brubaker, a person's "self-understanding." Thus I will also assume that it corresponds to a person's "moral self-conception," in Rawlsian terms. This means that Winnicott's "sense of self" should have qualities of both selfness and groupness that admit of degrees. Most important, Winnicott describes a process by which *new* self-understanding can emerge through playing, without repudiating the play or ceasing to play that way. This is crucial to the way that recognition of the capability of play and its distinct domain can contribute to the possibility of durable political love in our fraught American society.

NATIONAL SELF-UNDERSTANDING AFTER "REFLECTING BACK" ON THE DOMAIN OF PLAY

While playing is a ubiquitous aspect of human life for Winnicott, it will be easiest to understand what he means by the discovery of a new sense of self if we look at how he describes it in the therapeutic context. Psychotherapy, according to Winnicott, happens in the overlapping play of the therapist and patient.[3] Playing is crucial to the therapeutic process because "it is in playing that the patient is being creative."[4] And it is only through this creativity that "the individual discovers the self."[5] Winnicott describes the process of discovery as following a sequence: "(a) relaxation in conditions of trust based on experience; (b) creative, physical, and mental activity manifested in play; (c) the summation of these experiences forming the basis for a sense of self."[6]

The first stage in this sequence involves achieving "relaxation" as a result of trust that has developed over time in the relationship between the therapist and the patient. This involves creating an environment where the patient can freely associate words, ideas, and whatever else, even when this seems to flow nonsensically and chaotically. Therefore, it is particularly important for the therapist to avoid shutting down the nonsensical flow with "explanations" that try to bring order to the chaos. Winnicott is extremely protective of the patient's free-flowing formlessness and condemns any therapist who would interrupt it out of her own desire to be or seem perspicuous or authoritative.[7] A presumptuous explanation asserted at the wrong moment will only provoke the patient to organize his thoughts around a "defensible" personality, at which point his creative capacity is lost to his anxiety and defenses and he is no longer susceptible to self-discovery.[8]

Once relaxation is achieved—relaxation of a particularly fecund variety, not comatose disassociation—then play can ensue: with sounds, poems, toys, string, and gestures. The possibilities are endless, if only formlessness is allowed to find its own way to creative expression. A few features of this kind of play are worth keeping in mind. First and foremost, (especially when we remember Fanon's prayer and Nussbaum's political conception of the person), Winnicott specifies that "playing involves the body."[9] What he means, here, is that infant playing is a way of coping with the infant's early failure to satiate his own urges—urges that, at this early phase, inextricably link physical hunger with the idea of the breast. Playing thrives most, in Winnicott's sense, when it connects back to and copes with this root failure by involving the body that hungers and defecates every bit as much as the mind that desires.

He also writes that playing happens when we are "enjoying ourselves."[10] Playing is not just a complicated negotiation between the internal and the external world—it is a source of pleasure. In fact, it is the most sophisticated pleasure, as far as Winnicott is concerned. It is a pleasure that endures for its own sake, not like pleasure that is directed toward a climax. Furthermore, with respect to playing as the source of creativity, Winnicott clarifies that creative expression per se is not yet the emergence of a new "sense of self." Winnicott reports that while artists sometimes go through a process like play when creating their works, some are disappointed to find that the finished work, even when it is an aesthetic achievement, bears no relation to self-discovery.[11]

The third stage in Winnicott's sequence requires "summation" or "reverberation" produced by the right sort of intervention. Something new emerges in the "unintegrated state of personality" that characterizes play, and this novelty "if reflected back, *but only if reflected back*, becomes part of the organized individual personality, and eventually this in summation makes the individual to be, to be found; and eventually enables himself or herself to postulate the existence of the self."[12] The novelty that emerges may be a new perspective on oneself, a new combination of ideas, a new way of connecting disparate concerns, a new motion, a new song, a new feeling. The patient cannot see it, of course, because he is *in* it. But a trusted therapist or friend, who is well placed and has just the right timing, can point to this novelty: "look at what you're doing." "Look at what this says about who *we are* playing together, and who *you* can be."

The tone must be appropriate to the moment, of course. The trusted person must "justify the trust" by intervening in a way that fully acknowledges the vulnerability of the one playing. But, with the right kind of "look" from a trusted person, the player can be drawn out of play to see

himself in light of the novelty that he has produced. And under these conditions he can respond to the intervener in this light—that is, without
replacing his achievement with a defensive "false self." A new nonplaying
"sense of self" has then emerged out of the "unmitigated" state of play
without being preemptively swallowed up by anxiety. As Winnicott writes,
it emerges "not as a defence against anxiety but as an expression of I AM,
I am alive, I am myself"![13]

Winnicott thus offers an account of how self-understanding is transformed through play. The value of the novelty produced in creative play,
which is reflected back by the trusted person appropriately, is affirmed
independently as a full-throated expression of self-understanding *outside of the play space*. The new self-understanding is not a final reconciliation of the materials that are at play. It is not "closure." For instance, it
would not entail a final reconciliation between selfness and groupness or a
subordination of one to the other: selfness and groupness, or whatever else
one might need to play with, will remain indeterminate in the latent state
of play to which one will surely return again in therapy or elsewhere.

For my purposes, it is a key element of Winnicott's account that playing must be protected from the intervention of any Medusa-like gaze and
only warrants a "look" of a very special kind from a trusted observer when
it becomes creative in a particular way. The indeterminacy of play is delicate and must be carefully guarded. It is so important to Winnicott that
he formulates the basis of something like a moral duty: "*Of the transitional
object it can be said that it is a matter of agreement between us and the
baby that we will never ask the question: 'Did you conceive of this or was it
presented to you from without?' The important point is that no decision on
this point is expected. The question is not to be formulated.*"[14]

One should not say to the child: "you created this tattered cloth lamb
or puppy blanket as a meaningful object, you founded it, and it is meaningless without you, so I can just throw it in the trash before your very
eyes." That is a horrifying prospect. No less horrifying is the claim about
objects and activities associated with groupness that "this is just your illusion, it is created by you, meaningful to you, just for your own subjective
reasons, let me destroy it before your very eyes."[15] It is equally horrifying,
however, to resolve the ambiguity on the other side: to demand that the
child complies with *our* expectations of how a sacred object, in this case
a stuffed animal or blanket, should be treated when the child wants to bite

it, pick out its eyes, or throw it in the bathtub. And it is likewise horrify-ing to compel adults to subjugate themselves to their groupness. We should not say, for instance, "you have a duty to your group, which we will define and police." Accepting Winnicott's morality of play means that at play "a paradox is involved which needs to be accepted, tolerated, and not resolved."[16]

Consider, again, the description I gave of my compulsion to eat mat-zah on Passover. The meaning of this practice has varied for me over the years: sometimes it connects me deeply to the history of the Jewish people, sometimes I associate it closely with ethical ideals about what it means to be a "stranger" or "in exile," themes associated with Passover, sometimes it is theologically interesting, sometimes it is unremarkable and perfunc-tory, and sometimes it is just a complete pain in the ass. Inevitably, my lack of any good reason for continuing this activity becomes conspicu-ous, and I start to wonder in the recesses of my mind why I should con-tinue doing it at all. But I do not want to say that this is just something I have invested with importance early in my life, and, now that I have no good reason to do it, I should stop.

At the same time, I do not actually *believe* the claims that others might assume are implicit in the act: that I am obliged, for instance, to comply with a divine order to eat crackers in springtime. To say that I will con-tinue to do it "for its own sake" begs the question, at best, and asserts a "reason," in bad faith, at worst. It seems appropriate just to allow myself *to play it out*, to let myself proceed as a godless Jew as far is it takes me. In Winnicott's words, it seems best to allow that no decision on this point is expected. Others, likewise, should let me play this out. To demand that I give a reason for my action, or demand that I comply with its implicit logic of divine command, would breach Winnicott's morality of play. What emerges is the idea of the time/space of play as protected: we agree not to decide who or what motivates the activity or what the activity means (playing with its meaning may be an exciting form of play).

Now let's turn back to the fact of fraught societies. We might want to approach it by requiring that people resolve the indeterminacy of their selfness/groupness: given the legacies of historic injustice that we all carry, we can only become a genuine political "we" if either selfness or group-ness is allowed to take precedence. Groupist arguments of this sort go like this: you are, in the end, a member of your group, and we will remove the obstacles to your political inclusion as such by recognizing, celebrating, or deferring to authorized representatives and representations of your group. The assumption here is that what is good is to thrive as a member of your group. You want to live a life that is good for people like you. And you want to be appreciated, respected, and recognized for it. This response dials up groupness.

Antigroupist arguments go like this: you are, in the end, a self who is burdened by an entirely constructed categorical attribute that is stigmatized or implicated in historical oppression, and we will remove the obstacles to your political inclusion by repudiating this attribution and treating you like a truly independent self." Here the assumption is that what is good for you is to thrive unencumbered by your alleged membership in a group. You want to rid yourself of the intrusive attribution and thrive as an individual without any of its remnants. And you want to be treated as a dignified individual by others and not reminded of the groupist identification that you have left behind. This response hopes to dial up selfness while dialing down groupness.

Winnicott's story about transformed self-understanding helps me to paint an alternative picture of how genuinely to invite everyone in our fraught society to join the pursuit of political love and justice in America. Protecting the indeterminacy of play means not unilaterally deciding the question of groupness/selfness. This means that we should take a decidedly *non*groupist position and leave people to work out their own dynamics of identification in a background culture protected from inappropriate intervention. Winnicott's account of "self-discovery" at play suggests that one can take a perspective on—even somehow *above*—one's groupness and one's selfness, simultaneously, and this can transform self-understanding, without requiring us to repudiate the ways that we are driven/drawn to play.

I propose that we view the public cultural critic as the "trusted observer" whose task it is to "reflect back" just at the right moment of "creativity" on the domain of play and thereby cultivate new *national* self-understanding. This means searching for and identifying extraordinary moments of play and making interpretive arguments in public on behalf of including snapshots of these moments in the public political culture that we are all meant to share. In the process of this reflecting back, people who live in the United States are invited to take a metaperspective on the interminable conflicts between groups (and *within* varieties of groupness and selfness) that characterize American society. The ongoing inclusion of these snapshots as part of the public political culture can bolster the possibility of political love. In order to see how, it will be helpful to explain how and why Rawls thought that comprehensive views from the background culture could sometimes be included within the domain of the political.

According to Rawls, there are positive reasons to introduce comprehensive views into the public political forum "provided that in due course proper political reasons—and not reasons given solely by comprehensive doctrines—are presented that are sufficient to support whatever the comprehensive doctrines introduced are said to support"; Rawls refers to this as "the proviso."[17] Rawls thought that when people introduce their comprehensive doctrines into public debate, as long as this is done in accordance with the proviso, they increase the public sense that using distinctly "political" reasons is a good way to make arguments from a variety of perspectives. It offers evidence for all to see that people holding diverse comprehensive views can genuinely overlap on a political conception of justice.[18]

Showing acceptance of the proviso when arguing about politics is also a performance of citizenship—it makes a person recognizable, tangible, as someone who sees herself according to a political conception of the person as a citizen (like the modified capabilities conception that I have promoted). By increasing the salience of this way of seeing oneself and others, such "public manifestation," in and of itself, moves us closer to our ideal of a just society.[19] Insofar as progress toward the goal serves to justify the goal, publicly manifesting oneself as a citizen also contributes to the justification of the political conception of justice.

Rawls also mentions two additional ways for people to make themselves publicly recognizable to each other as citizens: declaration and conjecture. In the former case, you try to explain how it is that you are able to endorse a political conception of justice given your particular comprehensive view.[20] For instance, you might say, "I'm an Orthodox Jew [devout Muslim, Marxist, Millian liberal] and I endorse the capabilities conception of political justice for these reasons . . ." This helps reassure other people that overlapping on a general idea of justice is possible despite our diversity. With respect to conjecture, you try to make the case that others, who do not share your particular comprehensive view, might be able to endorse a political conception of justice too. So, I could try to make the case, perhaps drawing on canonical texts and historical precedents, that an Orthodox Jew (devout Muslim, Marxist, Millian liberal) can indeed endorse the capabilities conception.[21]

The effect of using the proviso, declaration, and conjecture is to make it possible to see that other people can share a political conception of justice with you even if they do not share your comprehensive view. The work of public cultural criticism can have the same effect. It can make it possible to see that other people are open to widely shareable political love even if they maintain grudges and antipathies in the domain of play that ostensibly contradict the political conception of justice (and the ways that *you* like to play).

The contribution of public cultural criticism follows the structure laid out by Winnicott in his description of the therapist's delicate intrusion into the patient's play. Recall that for Winnicott play functions creatively when, under the right free-flowing, formless, and relaxed conditions, it involves doing something new with transitional phenomena. In Winnicott's account, this something new emerges in an area of overlap where both the patient and the therapist are engaged. In my political adaptation of Winnicott, I imagine the relevant novelty emerging where the public cultural critic has identified—and "joined"—an instance of playing that, on her interpretation, implicitly or explicitly invites public cultural criticism.

The relevant instances of play invite public cultural criticism by including an implied or explicit sense of "us" or "we." This is playing that invites its participants to conjure a sense of "we Americans"—"this is what *we* are like," "this is what *we* have been through," "this is what *we* do." And this sense of we should include, or gesture in some way toward, the idea that *we* are vulnerable, dependent, human animals who carry legacies of injustice and long to live a life in common characterized by political justice. I assume that the more the basic structure of American society guarantees exercise of the central human capabilities above the threshold level to everyone in America, the more of this sort of playing will bubble up in the background culture. Institutions of the basic structure must provide some hope that justice is possible and worth striving for if the "trust" and "relaxation' required for the right sort of creative play is to emerge.

Paradigmatically, as we shall see in the next chapter, Jews in America produced more aggressive, resentful, divisive comedy as they became more secure in American society after World War II. But this comedy was also distinct because it was both explicitly antagonistic toward gentiles *and* invited Jews and gentiles alike to play together in ways that evoked a new shared American we. How much justice is enough for the relevant kind of play to emerge? There is no clear-cut answer. But the work of public cultural criticism will give us some idea.

Like Winnicott's therapist, the public cultural critic should be on the lookout for a certain kind of creativity: specifically, the emergence of a new perspective on dynamics of selfness and groupness, which others are invited to take as a common perspective. Creativity, here, does not necessarily imply aesthetic, intellectual, or any other kind of excellence. It is only a matter of provoking a new perspective on fraught dynamics of selfness and groupness, from which one sees oneself and others as equal members of a new American we. When the public cultural critic "reflects back" on this sort of play by offering a public interpretation of it, she may incite new collective self-understanding. If she can convince others that a snapshot of this instance of playing ought to be established as part of the public political culture, she can thereby solidify a collective self-understanding that ephemerally transcends, without repudiating or purging, interminable legacies of conflict and injustice.

The sort of playing she's looking for will in some way *involve the body*: it will affirm human animality. It will often also share the characteristics of formlessness, free association, and nonpurposiveness that Winnicott assumes are necessary for creative play. Among the clearest indicators of play is the inversion, jumbling, or breakdown of seemingly stable social categories. Comedy, as we will see, is often an apt medium for this sort of playing with conventions and commonsense. Finally, the kind of playing that the public cultural critic is looking for is "pleasurable" in the sense that participants take a kind of pleasure in it, even if it is rough, scary, or disorienting. It is activity that a person is moved to do without the hope of any consequence other than the state of doing that activity.

If at just the right moment a deft and trusted public cultural critic "reflects back" on the right kind of creative play, the ultimate result can be the production of new national self-understanding. Through the mediating institutions of society (in a book or newspaper, on TV or social media), the public cultural critic promotes an interpretation of a particular snapshot of playing in the background culture that, she claims, illustrates the possibility of political love despite the fact of fraught societies. If it is a particularly extraordinary example, she argues for it to be established as an enduring point in the public political culture of American society. This means that everyone in America is invited to engage with this snapshot of play in schools, public events, publicly funded publications, and so on. It means that seeing oneself as an American should mean, among other things, having the emotions that come with engaging this snapshot of play. (To be sure, however, emotional and interpretive responses will always be unpredictable, and this may be a source of future interpretative contestation.) This is how Americanness comes to be animated by political love that can persist despite persistent Jewish contempt for the goyim, persistent black anger toward whites, persistent Chicano distrust of gringos, and even despite persistent white Christian resentment toward all of those who have displaced the white Christian core group from national centrality.

Every American should be brought up and sustained by fixed points in the public political culture that function as touchstones of American political morality: the Declaration of Independence, Lincoln's Gettysburg Address, Martin Luther King's "I Have a Dream" speech, Baldwin's *The Fire Next Time,* and so on. But we should also be raised and sustained by playful engagement with Emma Lazarus's "The New Colossus," Allen Ginsberg's "America," Philip Roth's *Portnoy's Complaint,* Norman Lear's *All in the Family,* Spike Lee's *Do the Right Thing,* and so much more that should also be established as enduring points in the public political culture. *These* snapshots of play would thus be recognized as ways that *we* need to play as a society. They expose and publicize the complex emotions of our fraught society, which we must be able to abide as a precondition for genuinely inclusive political love. Because it is only if these complex and conflicting emotions are welcomed into what it means to be an American, and to love America, that historically oppressed people will be truly welcomed in an American future. And this is likewise true for those who will justifiably lose power as America becomes more just. They will only feel that they have a place in the America that we are striving to become if they are allowed to love that America despite their enduring resentment.

In my vision, the domain of play and the public political culture mutually transform each other through the mediating effect of the public cultural critic and her interpretations. As new enduring points are established, new citizens will be cultivated from birth with an ever-enriched sense of complex, emotionally fraught Americanness. Whatever their backgrounds, everyone in America will be invited to play with Jewish contempt, black rage, white resentment, and innumerable other emotions. In each case, the playing will register interminable conflicts *and* gesture toward political love at the same time. As the diverse multiplicity of conflicts and grievances are fastened through exemplary instances of play to the public political culture, people in America will increasingly share in the experience of political love despite the fact of fraught societies.

Then, I imagine, the ways that people want to play in the background culture will change, riffing on historical injustice in unexpected ways, reflecting new, unanticipated injustices and sorrows. This energy should also be cycled into the public political culture through the interpretive work of public cultural critics. And on and on. The long-term ideal is a society characterized by broadly shared political love that reckons continuously with its own history of injustice through dynamic relations between the background culture and the public political culture that are mediated through the role of the public cultural critic. I will illustrate this process by taking on the role of the public cultural critic in the next chapter. Before moving on, I suspect that it will be helpful for me to spell out more concretely what it means to use normative social theory to differentiate between play and politics in everyday American life.

DIFFERENTIATING BETWEEN PLAY AND POLITICS IN EVERYDAY LIFE

I have introduced a variety of terms and concepts that now give us a shared vocabulary: political love, the fact of fraught societies, selfness, groupness, and self-understanding, the domain of the background culture, the capability of play, the domain of play, etc. With these tools in hand, I can now return to the core proposition that motivates this book: despite the fact of fraught societies, broadly shared political love is still worth striving for in America since the impact of the fact of fraught societies can be absorbed into the domain of play. I can now describe even more precisely how this works. But first I want to reiterate and enhance what I have already suggested about what *else* needs to be going on for this idea to work.

Most important, we need to make profound changes to the basic structure of American society. Until we can look at every single person living in the United States of America and say that each one genuinely faces a lifetime of opportunities to exercise the central human capabilities at a threshold level, our society is unjust, unacceptable, and demands constant, strenuous, critical political action. As part of a critical response to this injustice, I have also suggested that we take on a certain posture. We shouldn't see ourselves the way that liberals usually see themselves: as bestowing high-minded political dignity onto others. Instead, we should immerse ourselves in the muck of our own animality, as vulnerable and dependent beings, who are morally frail and marked by historic injustice, and then reach out to others to join with us in shared political love. An important practice for cultivating this way of seeing ourselves and others is by promoting a public political culture that ritually returns to tragic narratives about those who have historically suffered under injustice in America. Museums on the mall in Washington, D.C., and months dedicated to historically marginalized groups can contribute to this. But I believe something more is needed.

We need a truly profound public reckoning on a national scale, as robust and all-consuming as Thanksgiving and Christmas, that ritually returns us year after year to the atrocities at the heart of the American story: massacres of Native Americans and the usurpation of their lands, slavery, Jim Crowe, and mass incarceration, colonial expansion into "the West," systematic deprivation of women's combined capabilities, the exploitation of workers dragooned in lives that are overwhelmed by stultifying work, a permanent class of "the poor" that is required to persist in misery in order for the unjustly rich to brand themselves "philanthropists"— the list goes on and on. As Nussbaum has suggested, we need to affix detailed, textured, compelling, very particular stories into the public political culture in order to cultivate ever-rejuvenated political compassion for those that have suffered and continue to suffer injustice in American society. The work of crafting such a public political culture is as crucial as the work of legal and policy innovation meant to promote institutions of the basic structure that genuinely guarantee the exercise of the central human capabilities at a threshold level.

In the context of these profound changes to American society, I believe it is equally crucial for us to cultivate a widespread propensity to differentiate appropriately between what belongs in the domain of the political and what belongs in the domain of play: the special ingredient that will allow us to endure the fact of fraught societies. There will be cultural legacies of historical injustice that *do not* belong in the public political culture. But if we know how to toggle between play and politics, we can "switch the tracks," if you will, and rerail these elements into the domain of play. Now that I have clarified my conception of play, I can elaborate on what is involved in this shift.

For instance, recall my description of play as noninstrumental activity. In our actual society, nasty epithets, caricatures, tropes, and hierarchies that conflict with how we *should* see each other as citizens float throughout all aspects of life. Using the tools that I have developed, we should be able to posit sites of American life as "within the domain of the political," where we are meant to see each other as equal citizens involved in pursuing the shared goal of a just society—and where nasty legacies of historical injustice like epithets, caricatures, and stereotypical tropes should be *repudiated and eradicated*. We should, likewise, be able to posit other sites of American life as "within the domain of play," where we can play with *the same materials* denuded of their instrumentality.

This only works if we sincerely believe that play is possible—that it is possible for someone to play with hierarchy, aggression, disgust, and revenge, for instance, without enacting what these structures, motivations, and emotions would effect outside the domain of play. And this, in turn, requires that we strive for more clarity about where and when we are stepping into a play frame and about how to egress if we find that it is not the kind of playing we want to do. If we are doing our job to make sure that the basic structure of society genuinely affirms each person's sense of herself as a citizen, then egress from an unwanted domain of play will always land you in a place where you feel seen as a person who is *owed* a lifetime of opportunities to exercise the central human capabilities at a threshold level.

So when is it appropriate to say that this is OK because it is happening within the domain of play? The easiest cases are recognizably bounded sites like stand-up comedy clubs and live theaters. We must allow that regardless of what happens during the show, *inside the activity of play between the performer and the audience* nothing is transpiring that has a set meaning or necessary consequence outside of that time/space of play. After the show, critics should certainly be expected to interpret it in the background culture, showing how it thwarts or promotes comprehensive goals that they care about. And a *public cultural* critic might take a snapshot of this instance of playing and make an interpretive judgment about what it means about who we are as a nation, or even mount a case for its inclusion as an enduring point in the public political culture. But the stand-up comedy show per se, as a time and space of humorous play, will have been *worth it* or *not worth it* after the show for reasons that have nothing to do with anything outside the play frame. For instance, *was it funny?*

A set of objections to my view may now arise. How can play, which seems to include art, games, festivals, and entertainment, be free of politics? Isn't the border allegedly circumscribing the domain of play really a pretense distracting from the unjust ideological and commercial structures and forces that actually dominate this territory? In the case of art, don't artists often express political viewpoints through their art? Can't art, games, festivals, and entertainment be countercultural, utopian, progressive, regressive, or otherwise "political"?

In order to answer these questions, let me first reiterate precisely what we are supposed to do with the ideas that I am offering here (the domain of play, the capability of play). Describing an activity, instance, time, or space as play will always be a contestable act of interpretation. Nothing out in the world is obviously, naturally, or necessarily play. Upon closing this book and setting it aside, a reader informed by its ideas might find himself confronted with a person making jokes on a stage using nasty stereotypes and interpret (or simply *enjoy*) the experience as occurring in the domain of play. But another reader might interpret the same experience as an instance of an individual instrumentally promoting a nonpublic project using ridicule as a rhetorical strategy.[22] The perspective that I am offering can thus provide reasons to protect, promote, criticize, or simply enjoy a person making jokes on a stage using nasty stereotypes. It is a perspective that offers tools with which to argue about meanings in the world. It does not offer an absolute stamp of approval, explanation, or condemnation to be wielded with an expectation of immediate assent from others.

At the same time, since it includes Winnicott's "morality of play" my view does demand a bias on behalf of maximal permissiveness regarding the ways in which people want to play. Obviously, there are limits. For example, with great care, people should be able to employ basic structural institutions to regulate aspects of the domain of play on behalf of public health.[23] But if you are convinced of my view, you will take great care to avoid ruining other people's play unless it is absolutely necessary. The fact of fraught societies means that people will want to play in perverse and disturbing ways, even in the best America we can realistically imagine. Enduring the perversity of play for the long-term will involve a collective process of converging perception, one through which we conjure the borders of play together while making difficult, murky, provisional claims about what is play and what is not. The more we can converge on our perception of the boundaries of play, the more we can trap the ugly legacies of historical injustice that we carry within it.

I do not, therefore, assume that everything called art, or otherwise with features commanding aesthetic attention, is best described in terms of play. There are presumably instrumental goals that are best served, or served in distinct and important ways, through aesthetic means. That is, sometimes in pursuit of a goal you might want to provoke perceptual attention to formal relationships of unity, complexity, and symmetry or to qualitative properties like an "arresting impression of massiveness," an unnerving sense of disorder, or the shock of irreverent juxtaposition.[24] I assume that provoking aesthetic attention will pervade the domain of the political and the nonplay domains of the background culture as much as it pervades the domain of play.

In the nonplay domains of the background culture, it is easy to think of performances, styles of dress, and music that provoke aesthetic attention in the service of "religious" or "spiritual" goals. Artworks can function similarly. Following Noël Carroll, I consider something to be an artwork if it has a purpose, and this purpose is constitutively embodied by provoking perceptual attention to aesthetic properties (namely, the formal and qualitative properties that I referred to in the previous paragraph).[25] Thus an artwork may be the product of an artist's nonpublic project to provoke particular ideas and emotions, or to interrupt conventional thoughts and feelings, or to accomplish something else. And a person who gives his attention to the artwork might do so in order to be instructed about how best to think, feel, or be.

Given that the production and the activity of attending to artworks can be instrumental in these ways, it will be appropriate to interpret some of what happens under the rubric "art" as happening in the nonplay domains of the background culture, where people pursue nonpublic goals instrumentally and sometimes through aesthetic means. However, it will also be possible to interpret a great deal of the production and attention to art that happens in the background culture as happening within the domain of play. When time or space is set aside for the activity of attending to artworks *just for the sake of doing that activity—of being in the state of perceptual attention that the artworks provoke*, then we are solidly within the domain of play.

I expect that there will be ongoing and unresolvable disagreements about when and how to interpret art as play. Those who think that art is by definition *for its own sake* might see all art as play. Those who view art in largely consequentialist terms, asking only how artworks promote or thwart political justice or certain comprehensive goals, are less likely to interpret art as play. These are matters about which reasonable and compassionate people can disagree.[26] With my view, citizens are given tools that should enrich this disagreement and make it possible for them to render an interpretive judgment: "this is play" or "this is the pursuit of a comprehensive goal." As I will explain, how we subsequently relate to the activity in question will be significantly impacted by this interpretive judgment.

Is there an aesthetic dimension to the domain of the political? Consider a courthouse, a crucial site of the basic structure. It will need an architectural design. What will be on its walls? How will the judge be dressed? Similarly, the president will use narrative, metaphor, and humor in her speeches. Symbols, heroes, images, monuments, installations, are all essential to the public political culture. The approach that I am advocating asks only that we make a judgment about where a particular act or expression fits and then treat it appropriately. Courthouse architecture and decoration should promote the political conception of justice—it should, for instance, make all those who enter feel they are owed equal respect as vulnerable, dependent, human animals who carry legacies of historical injustice and want to share in a common life with others. It should also include very specific symbols, narratives, and other materials that highlight our particular national successes and failures at realizing this conception.

When it comes to play, I expect that there will be interpretive disagreements about many particular cases even among those who are generally persuaded of my view. How should we interpret gambling, pornography, hunting, and professional sports, for example? What I offer is the opportunity to say, "this is an exercise of the capability of play within the domain of play and we should relate to it as such." Or, one might decide, "this is the pursuit of a nonpublic project within the (nonplay) domain of the background culture and we should relate to it as such." I will elaborate on the consequences of this latter decision in a moment.

If we make the interpretive judgment that this is play, then we should accept in it words, actions, ideas, and emotions that we would never accept in the domain of the political. Though, as I have explained, we can still offer interpretations of these instances of play from our comprehensive perspectives or as public cultural critics. Indeed, the background culture should be characterized by an ongoing interpretive struggle between diverse critics to define the *meaning* of how we play. For, once the preliminary decision has been made that this is play, only the question of its meaning remains—at play, all things are permissible.[27]

Let's look at some more of the worries that confront this decision to be so hands off with perversity. What about the fact that the basic structure of society is not sufficiently just to assure egress from play into the security of genuine political respect? What about the influence of market forces that are not sufficiently regulated by the institutions of the basic structure? First and foremost, these concerns should push us to hurry up and make the basic structure of society more just. They are not necessarily reasons to intrude on the unconventional or perverse ways that people want to play. We cannot demand that everyone in America cease and desist from making choices and expressing themselves until we have made the basic structure of society sufficiently just and reformed all of our pathological preferences. This is precisely the sort of desire for purity that will arise because of the missing link problem. The best thing to do with this desire, in my view, is to redirect it into the domain of play and then keep working on the basic structure.

Likewise, it should come as no surprise that what happens in the domain of play is utterly saturated with cultural legacies of racism, misogyny, economic exploitation, and anti-Semitism. That's the whole point! The fact of fraught societies means that this stuff never really goes away and that we will always want to exercise our lingering grudges and aversions, along with our longings for wholeness and rupture. The domain of play is where all of this can thrive. In fact, I assume that while comprehensive views that directly conflict with the political conception of justice will diminish under an increasingly just basic structure, the ways that we play will become *more perverse* and *more outrageous* the more just our society becomes. This requires further explanation.

Some of what is not appropriate for the public political culture will persist in the parts of the background culture that are not the domain of play, where people work, engage in interpersonal relationships, and pursue the goals of their nonpublic projects. A lot of this stuff will be pretty nasty too. For instance, I assume that some of my neighbors will persist in thinking that I have damned my children to burn in hell for eternity because they are not baptized and I will persist in thinking that these neighbors suffer from the inanity that is characteristic of a *goyishe kop.*

How precisely it is best to navigate the friction of our divisive affirmations and aversions in the nonplay domains of the background culture is a question that goes beyond the scope of my argument. But I do assume that a lively and inclusive domain of play, amidst a basic structure that is increasingly just, will impact life in the nonplay domains of the background culture. Furthermore, as people come increasingly to see each other as citizens within the domain of the political, it should also become "common sense" to see oneself and others in this way *as a starting point* in situations of potential conflict in the nonplay domains of the background culture. When it is necessary to communicate across differences in the background culture, it will seem increasingly obvious to show your willingness to expose yourself as a flawed, vulnerable, dependent human animal who carries legacies of historical injustice and wants to live well with others that are different from you.

Nevertheless, there will always be nonpublic projects that directly conflict with the political conception of justice that we are trying to actualize through the basic structure. The people pursuing these projects will find an increasingly just society increasingly inhospitable. As Rawls consistently reiterated, a political conception of justice is not a neutral conception. It is a *moral* conception. When it is embedded in the basic structure of a society, it will favor people who are committed to a good life with others of diverse comprehensive views. In an increasingly just society, then, people who pursue nonpublic projects that directly oppose political justice will either take legitimate political action to promote their projects and endure the frustration of continuous failure, abide begrudgingly within the dominant political norms as a countercultural minority whose rights are protected as such, or take illegitimate action (for instance, using violence) against the political order and be justifiably thwarted by the coercive force of the state.

But there is another option too. Those pursuing nonpublic projects that ostensibly conflict with the political conception of justice can embrace the political conception of justice as the political aspect of their noninstitutional moral self-conception.[28] This can mean a few different things. They can, for instance, reinterpret their comprehensive view so that it is compatible with the political conception of justice. They can maintain the two views in a way that is incoherent and unresolved but nevertheless always prioritizes the values of the political within the domain of the political. Or they can shift their comprehensive longings and drives into the domain of play. In the domain of play, it is possible, permissible, and indeed encouraged to play out your wildest perverse, exclusionary, totalizing, or utopian fantasies.

All nonpublic projects are welcome in the vision of America that I am advocating, even if some will only be welcome within the domain of play. The domain of play should be the ultimate trajectory of human urges toward cruelty, domination, purity, wretchedness, and all manner of perversion. I assume that these urges are naturally occurring in human beings and that they will be reproduced in ways marked by particular historic conflicts and injustices as a result of the fact of fraught societies. Since there is a lot of this nastiness circulating throughout our actual society, I assume that the domain of play will become nastier and more outrageous as it absorbs these elements in the process of our society becoming more just. I will return to this point in the epilogue.

MITIGATING THE PROBLEM OF REMAINDERS

Let us now return to the key problems that make up the fact of fraught societies to see how these problems are mitigated once we acknowledge a distinct domain of play within the background culture. The problem of remainders, we recall, is that any effort to eradicate or police nasty epithets, caricatures, symbols, and other legacies of historic oppression threatens to extend the power of the liberal state too far and infringe upon the right to expressive capabilities of some of its citizens. Liberal states are therefore unable to prevent demeaning content from lurking in the background culture. Let's consider some of the real-world questions raised by the problem of remainders. What about television commercials that use stereotypes? What about the use of caricatures for sports mascots? What about Confederate flags? What about misogynistic lyrics? What about the white bourgeois fantasylands that dominate movie screens?

Am I saying that this is all merely play and we ought not to say anything else about it? Hopefully it is clear that this is not what I am saying. Each of these cases is different, and answering each question requires several steps of interpretation. First, we decide where to locate the concerning material within our normative social theory. Do we want to frame this as within the domain of the political, within the nonplay domain of the background culture, or within the domain of play? In some of these cases, we are concerned about something that appears on the massive screen of the mediating institutions of society, which can host the domain of the political *or* the domains of the background culture (including the domain of play).

Second, we decide if the material is appropriate to its domain. If there is a Confederate flag flying over a state capital, we can decide, first, that it is attached to an institution of the basic structure of society and, second, that this is inappropriate insofar as this flag promotes a comprehensive view that is incompatible with political justice. After deciding where the material is located and whether or not it belongs there, the third step in our interpretive process is to decide what we think ought to be the fate of this material.

So, we can make a case against Confederate flags on capital buildings, but then argue that Confederate flags are entirely appropriate for reenactments of Gettysburg in the domain of play. We can make a case against discriminating between Jews and gentiles in the workplace, while being entirely permissive when it comes to jokes about the Jews vs. the goyim at a comedy show. If we can circumscribe professional sports fandom as play, then we might want to accept caricatured mascots like the "Redskins." I find this difficult to stomach, given the reality of ongoing capability deprivation among Native Americans. If we're going to come to this conclusion, it must immediately trigger a concomitant, forceful, and urgent demand that the basic structure of American society do a better job of acknowledging the atrocities and ongoing injustice endured by Native Americans in the U.S.

If we're going to play Cowboys and Indians, then we'd better be damned sure that Native Americans are treated by the basic structure of society and seen outside the domain of play as owed the equal respect befitting vulnerable, dependent human animals who carry a legacy of historical injustice and long to flourish in a common life with others. The hope is to promote a future where legacies of conflict and oppression are as meaningful to the employment of caricatures in American professional sports as they now are to the emotions that animate sports rivalries between Western European national teams representing countries that once slaughtered each other by the millions.

With respect to material carried by the mediating institutions of society (on TV, at the movies), careful curating and regulation are essential. It is appropriate for the government to regulate what any seven-year-old can find inadvertently on television, the radio, or public billboards. The political conception of justice that I have advocated here, and its attendant political conception of the person, can be a guide for producing and evaluating such content. It also provides a justification for assuring that adults are able to pay for access to the *Howard Stern Show,* pornographic online video games, rated R movies, and other invitations to play that are not appropriate for children.

We might interpret television commercials as instances of nonpublic projects pursued in the background culture through a mediating institution of society. The nonpublic project is almost always somebody's effort *to get rich.* But people might sincerely want to promote their art or the use of some technology for reasons other than mere greed. If we interpret television commercials in this way, we should expect some unpopular cases. And we should expect people who have opposing nonpublic projects to respond using the tools of protest and persuasion that should characterize ongoing struggle in the background culture. What is more, television commercials that represent the pursuit of nonpublic projects in the background culture will be subject to the constraints that apply to all nonpublic projects. As society becomes more just, these pursuits will find it increasingly inhospitable to the extent that they directly contradict the political conception of justice. By contrast to commercials, if we interpret

TV sitcoms as invitations to play then we will see them as standing in a very different relation to the nonpublic projects pursued in the background culture and to the domain of the political. An increasingly just society is not an inhospitable place for even the most outrageous forms of play.

MITIGATING THE PROBLEM OF REPRODUCTION

The problem of reproduction is the fact that the groupness of many individuals in American society will include grudges and antipathies toward other groups, which will be reproduced even in the most just society that we can realistically imagine. Without the domain of play we would have to assume that, if our society is becoming increasingly just, groupness of this sort will be faced with the inhospitable conditions faced by all nonpublic projects that directly contradict the political conception of justice. This would mean that individuals who carry groupness that is marked by historical oppression—Jewish resentment toward the goyim, black resentment toward whites, Mexican American resentment toward gringos, Native American resentment toward the U.S. government—would find an increasingly just America increasingly inhospitable. But this is hardly a vision of American society that the historically oppressed can be expected to accept. It asks people to affirm and pursue an America in which they are not really welcome.

However, as we acknowledge a domain of play in the background culture, we make the inclusion of fraught groupness easily imaginable. The lingering grudges and antipathies of those who are empowered by a more just basic structure, and the lingering grudges and antipathies of those who justifiably lose power as a result of a more just basic structure, can all be performed, ritualized, or otherwise represented in the domain of play. And this should be especially imaginable given the story about moral psychological development that I have told with Winnicott and Rawls.

Recall that transitional phenomena develop within the earliest "intermediate" spaces of play, where the border between oneself and others is rendered ambiguous. Groupness is ultimately produced or maintained through playing with transitional phenomena. When we are playing as adults, we are very often intensifying our groupness just for the sake of experiencing that intensified groupness. When groupness is connected to the primordially important stuff of childhood, this intensification amplifies both our sense of being part of a group *and* our earliest, most formative relationships and experiences. Since playing with the primordially important stuff of childhood is always among the activities that we most want to do, we can expect that people who carry fraught groupness attached to the primordially important stuff of their childhood will want to play with this stuff.

Without a political conception of play, we will have to assume that this drive is always necessarily *instrumental*. That is, we will have to assume it motivates the pursuit of comprehensive or political goals. Making this assumption has the effect of encouraging people to think about their groupness instrumentally when this need not be their only option. It interrupts play and demands a resolution to the restless ambiguity of selfness and groupness. With a political conception of play, however, it is possible to understand how we can luxuriate in divisive groupness within the domain of play and nevertheless see everyone in American society as entitled to equal respect in the domain of the political. The problem of reproduction is mitigated when we acknowledge that the drive to heighten divisive groupness is often better interpreted as a drive to *play with* heightened divisive groupness. Often better interpreted, that is, as a drive to experience heightened divisive groupness just for the sake of having that experience. A vision of society that welcomes this kind of playing is hospitable whether or not your groupness is marked by historical victimization, the perpetration of injustice, or both.

And yet, while the political conception of play clarifies how we can be expected to endure the problem of reproduction, many practical judgments will always need to be made about what this entails in everyday life. Let me suggest the following. If you want to play with divisive groupness in a way that others might abhor, you should carve out some time and space in the background culture and hang the biggest and brightest possible sign on the entrance that reads, THIS IS PLAY. Arguably, some sites—like comedy clubs, live theaters, and museums—should be given the benefit of the doubt as hanging these signs implicitly. The more subtle the frame that distinguishes your activity of play, the more you will court umbrage and misunderstanding.

In the nonplay domains of the background culture, knowing when it is possible to break into play with others requires honed interpersonal judgment and a clear understanding of communal, associational, and professional norms. It may not be appropriate to invite *this* friend to play in the way that you invite *that* friend to play, and playing at your office or at your church or at your kid's school will be limited by local norms. The best way to build the trust, indeed the *political love*, that is necessary to play with others who are different from you is to leave no doubt whatsoever that you see them, and yourself, as owed equal respect befitting vulnerable, dependent human animals who carry legacies of historic injustice and long to live well in a common life characterized by political justice.

At the same time, within the space and time of play, you should feel welcome to be as uninhibited as possible. Be nasty, be gross, be whimsical, be strange—play with your historical grudges, exclusionary fantasylands, and the primordially important stuff of your childhood as you must. And, if you come upon others playing in a way that would offend you outside of the domain of play, do not interrupt. Remember, we are—*every single one of us*—morally frail animals who are the products of a grotesquely unjust world. Whether as part of our selfness or groupness, we all have tendencies toward domination, disgust, revenge, aggrandizement, and ressentiment. Likewise, we all have an idiosyncratic assortment of preoccupations and desires that we will have more or less courage to explore.

No one should be denied political love for having perverse elements of selfness and groupness that they want to exercise in the domain of play, because then all of us should be denied political love. If the basic structure of society does not guarantee egress from the domain of play *for everyone* into a society where they feel respected as an equal citizen, then we should all be inflamed by justified indignation and strive to correct the injustice of the basic structure of society. The fact of fraught societies means that there will be play with fraught and inflammatory groupness even in the best society we can realistically imagine. So we shouldn't go after the perverse ways that people want to play. We should go after the basic structure of society, which should make it possible to live well with others who want to play that way.

MITIGATING THE MISSING LINK PROBLEM

This brings me, finally, to the missing link problem: the fact that we will inevitably be tempted by the thought that we can somehow eventually cross a threshold into a society unmarred by perversity. The problem, we may recall, is that our incorrigible desire for the "perfect justice" of angels will always inevitably clash with our interminable status as products of historical injustice. We can now imagine a vision in which utopian longings for wholeness are redirected toward the domain of play and away from the domain of the political, where we must settle for merely political justice instead of "perfect justice." Remember, this is not a purgation theory. The idea is not that we must purge the frustration produced by merely political justice or that the domain of play is the receptacle where the purged material is contained. Instead, the idea is that flourishing is bifurcated through cognitive and social processes of framing: what is exercised in the domain of play is not "waste"; it is constitutive of a thriving life for the person playing. It is differentiated not by its level of importance, but by the frame that distinguishes it from the instrumental domains of the political and the background culture.

In fact, the play with wholeness, totality, purity, and transgressive action that happens in the domain of play will often feel *more* important to an individual in everyday life than does his political participation. Playing has a personalized quality and is more immediate. Given the political conception of the person that I advocate, I obviously assume that every member of society will consider it a great and gratifying good to thrive together in a common political life. But thriving in the domain of the political can never be entirely satisfying.

However much human beings long for a common life together, characterized by justice, they will also yearn to feel their grudges and aversions without inhibition, and to exercise their tendencies to domination, disgust, revenge, aggrandizement, and ressentiment. Thus thriving in political life will not be quite as gratifying—or gratifying in the same way—as thriving in the games, fantasies, joking, and aesthetic experiences that we enter in the domain of play. After all, the primordially important stuff of childhood is often implicated in play, and this gives playing very great importance indeed. Far from feeling frivolous or trivial, playing can be utterly immersive, and a person can reach the heights of intense human experience while playing.[29] It is precisely because play thriving can be as immersive and intense as political thriving, *if not more so*, that the missing link problem can be "absorbed" into the domain of play.

In the context of the missing link problem, it is worth mentioning a feature of play that I did not include in my formal definition. Huizinga thought that play tends to produce "play-communities" that maintain the tradition of play when the play has ended.[30] He wrote, "the feeling of being 'apart together' in an exceptional situation, of sharing something important, of mutually withdrawing from the rest of the world and rejecting the usual norms, retains its magic beyond the duration of the individual game."[31] The clubs, societies, and realms of fandom that help to maintain particular contemporary spaces and times for play are clear examples of this. Play communities can thus be understood as collectives in the background culture that are organized around the pursuit of a comprehensive goal, which includes maintaining a particular space/time for play. Huizinga thought that these play communities are inclined to secrecy, exclusivity, and dress-up.[32]

Caillois basically dismisses this feature of Huizinga's definition of play.[33] But I think it captures something important that relates to the missing link problem. We can imagine utopian or messianic responses to the missing link problem that involve organizing secretive, exclusive communities of people who see themselves as a vanguard proleptically evoking a utopian or messianic order. As long as they resist the temptation to "force the End," as the Rabbis used to say, they are perfectly suited to abide as a play community in precisely the manner that Huizinga imagined. When we start to consider what these communities actually look like, we will find that they are very much predisposed to costuming, or dress-up, just as Huizinga presumed. I will reflect on these groups in the epilogue. Before that, however, I will don the hat of the public cultural critic and interpret some opportunities for play produced after World War II in the U.S. In the process, I will show how the domain of play is also a place where Fanon's desire for bodily transgressive outburst can be absorbed. But first let me explain some of the distinctive features of "humorous" play, since the playing that I will interpret in the next three chapters has these features.

HUMOROUS PLAY

While all of what happens in the domain of play might be interpreted by a public cultural critic and thereby brought into dynamic relation with the domain of the political, in the concluding chapters I explore contributions of humorous play in particular. Humorous play, I will show, can be a particularly rich source of enduring points to attach to the public political culture and register our capacity for political love despite the fact of fraught societies.

What characterizes humorous play? Philosophers who write about humor tend to follow three general approaches: the superiority theory, the relief theory, and the incongruity theory.[34] The superiority theory has been identified with Thomas Hobbes, who wrote in *Human Nature*: "men laugh at the infirmities of others, by comparison wherewith their own abilities are set off and illustrated."[35] The relief theory is identified with Sigmund Freud, who wrote in *Jokes and Their Relation to the Unconscious*: "A joke will allow us to exploit something ridiculous in our enemy which we could not, on account of obstacles in the way, bring forward openly or consciously; once again, then, the joke *will evade restrictions and open sources of pleasure that have become inaccessible*."[36]

The incongruity theory is different from the other two in that it describes what makes humor funny, rather than how and why people engage in humor. According to John Morreall, this theory states that "what amuses us is some object of perception or thought that clashes with what we would have expected in a particular set of circumstances."[37] While elements of superiority, relief, and incongruity will likely always hover around attempts to describe humor, I think that Noël Carroll makes a strong case for the incongruity theory as the most promising overall theory. He offers the following account: "someone is comically amused if and only if (i) the object of her mental state is a perceived incongruity, (ii) which she regards as neither threatening or anxiety producing, and (iii) which she does not approach with a genuine, puzzle-solving attitude, but (iv) which, rather, she enjoys. Humour is the response-dependent property that affords comic amusement."[38]

It is helpful to place Carroll's account of humor in the broader context of play that I have presented.[39] The play frame is what allows a person to regard the incongruity "as neither threatening or anxiety producing." And it is the noninstrumental feature of playing that assures the humorous player does not approach the incongruity with "a genuine, puzzle-solving attitude." Further, humorous play is indeterminate and ambiguous activity *that one "enjoys"*—it is something that one wants to participate in when participation is in no way necessary or required.[40] It is also worth noting that "comic amusement," for Carroll, is an emotion, construed according to a cognitive theory of emotions.[41] In his book on mass art, which is a key basis for my own thinking on that subject, Carroll lists comic amusement with other "garden-variety emotions"—like fear, anger, horror, and suspense—that are "the cement that keeps audiences connected to the mass artworks that they consume."[42] It will be important, moving forward, to remember that humor is a property, cognition of which entails a specific emotion: comic amusement. Recalling Nussbaum's analysis of compassion, we can say that Carroll's definition, which I have quoted, provides the constitutive judgments involved in having that emotion.

Before moving on, I want to note a distinct moral psychological function of humor: it can involve a process by which a person elastically sees herself from a distance.[43] If a person succeeds at making an aspect of her own self-understanding the object of humorous play, then she has, even if only ephemerally, staked out a new perspective on herself and perhaps even stretched toward an altogether new self-understanding. If this new perspective is a point of convergence with others who are comically amused in the same way, then the fundament of a new "we" may be forged. And with just the right look from a trusted observer—just the right reflecting back—this we can become *us*.

But enough with all this highfalutin theoretical talk. Let's turn to the funny business.

6

LENNY BRUCE AND THE INTIMACY OF PLAY

JEWISHNESS IN AMERICA IN THE FIRST HALF OF THE TWENTIETH CENTURY

In order to appreciate what Lenny Bruce, Philip Roth, and Norman Lear invite us to play with in their comedy, it is important first to set more of the cultural context. These virtuosos of play were part of a boom in Jewish American creativity. But this boom followed immediately after the height of anti-Semitism in American history. At the turn of the twentieth century, as I noted in chapter 1, the large wave of Eastern European Jewish immigration corresponded with a rise in the stigmatization of Jews. Already at the end of the nineteenth century, in a "mood of evangelism," popular Christian novels featured grim, legalistic, deicidal Jewish Pharisees.[1] This period also saw the rise of that American political populism that sought to defend "real America" from the malevolent, global, conspiratorial House of Rothschild (playing off of the long-standing Shylock character).[2] By the first decade of the twentieth century, there were incidents in New York, Chicago, Philadelphia, Boston, and other cities of Jews subjected to increased violence at the hands of Irish gangs and the corruption of Irish police.[3]

The Jewish immigrants who were eking out new lives for themselves and their families on the Lower East Side of Manhattan were depicted in popular culture as a filthy animal swarm.[4] The growing popularity of pseudoscience in this period featured Jews as racial degenerates, an alarming mongrelizing threat—one taken very seriously by those in the bourgeoning eugenics movement.[5] Jews in this period were also stigmatized as dangerous Bolshevik radicals.[6] And they were stigmatized as sexually menacing: as pimps, prostitutes, and pedophiles who sold gentile women into "white slavery."[7]

More generally, Jewish men were depicted both in populist propaganda and in popular and high-brow literature as harboring "intense, uncontrollable sexual desires."[8] When a thirteen-year-old girl named Mary Phagan was found murdered in the factory where she worked in Atlanta in 1913, anti-Semitic accusations that the Jewish factory manager, Leo Frank, was driven by uncontrollable lust to rape and murder her were part of what got him falsely convicted and then lynched by a mob after he was freed by the governor.[9]

One historian has called the period between the 1920s and the 1940s "the peak years of American anti-Semitism."[10] The 1920s saw Jews restricted from resort hotels, Masonic lodges, real estate in Upper Manhattan and other desirable neighborhoods around the country where Jews sought upward mobility. Quotas at Ivy League and other prestigious colleges and universities proliferated, along with quotas at medical schools and law schools. An unbreakable ceiling separating Jewish workers from executive positions in business (and discrimination in white-collar employment in general) was widespread.[11]

This is the period that I referred to in chapter 1 as a time when fears about unfolding processes of modernization gripped the country and many whites responded by clinging ever more tightly to the stable, comforting persistence of the black-white racial hierarchy—to white supremacy. Jewish racial ambiguity exerted newly intolerable pressure on whites, given their increased desire for racial clarity at this time.[12] Jews emerged in the public imagination as an unassimilable group distinguished, in particular, by their role as the quintessential carriers and beneficiaries of the very processes of modernization that so many whites feared.[13] Father Charles Coughlin ranted against "world Jewish domination," extending further the Shylock, House of Rothschild, Elders of Zion mythology. Explicitly anti-Jewish organizations gained in popularity: the Christian Front, the Silver Shirts, and the American Christian Defenders, for instance.[14] In the 1930s, historian Hasia Diner writes, "increasingly,

Gentiles in America voiced the opinion that Jews took care of their own, and in the process everyone else suffered, reflecting the common belief in Jewish clannishness and self-centeredness."[15]

In this period, too, those who opposed President Roosevelt would sometimes publicly blame his policies on the cadre of Jews in his administration.[16] In fact, Roosevelt claimed before the Second World War, "If there was a demagogue around here of the type of Huey Long to take up anti-Semitism there could be more blood running in the streets of New York than in Berlin."[17] Nevertheless, there was actually only limited real violence against Jews in America, even at the height of American anti-Semitism, and Jews were able to take advantage of all sorts of opportunities that were open to them.[18] Despite discriminatory government policies, workplace discrimination, negative stereotyping in the media, the sheer uncontrollable breadth and variety of American life (and of the American economy) allowed Jews to thrive in out-of-the-way places.

Jews found opportunities to thrive in industries that were not heavily guarded by unambiguously "white" Christian establishment elites: the garment industry, scrap metal, tobacco distribution, liquor, real estate in undeveloped areas, cosmetics, and entertainment.[19] Moreover, Hasia Diner explains that by the 1920s,

> Jews had enough excess income to fuel a building boom in synagogues, community centers, schools, resorts, summer camps, and philanthropic ventures for others less fortunate than they. Their coffers bulged enough to allow them to send millions of dollars overseas to relieve Jews in distress in Eastern Europe and Palestine. In fact, by the end of this period, American Jews made up the richest and most powerful Jewish community in the world, and they ranked among the most affluent ethnic groups in America.[20]

The key point, for our purposes, is that the very Jews who will contribute so much to American popular culture from the mid-1950s to the mid-1970s, and whose access to these institutions resulted in part from the general economic prosperity of their parents, would have grown up steeped in the psychological impact of the heightened anti-Semitism that characterized the period between the 1920s and the 1940s. They might, for instance, have witnessed or absorbed some of the fear and shame about

Jewishness that led many Jews at the time to repress their Jewishness and avoid being "exposed" in public as a Jew at all costs. Many Jews tried to pass as gentiles by changing their names or getting nose jobs.[21] Diner writes, "Although anti-Semitism in these years may have seemed tame when set against the cataclysm engulfing Europe, it continued to mold Jewish political consciousness. On a personal level it caused Jews discomfort and even anguish as they negotiated their path into the middle class."[22] Thus anti-Semitism and Jewish anxiety about being Jewish were at their height in America precisely when the primordially important stuff of the mid-century Jewish virtuosos of play was being forged.

After World War II, circumstances changed dramatically for Jewish Americans. Bess Meyerson, a Jewish girl from a poor family in New York, was selected to be Miss America in 1945. That same year, Hank Greenberg hit a celebrated ninth-inning grand slam home run, winning the American League pennant for the Detroit Tigers.[23] In 1947, *Gentlemen's Agreement*, a film about a non-Jewish journalist who goes undercover as a Jew to expose anti-Semitism, won the Academy Award for best picture. Jeffrey Alexander writes of this period: "Members of American core groups became interested not so much in allowing Jewish persons to separate from Jewishness as in recognizing the civil legitimacy of Jewishness as such."[24]

According to Irving Howe, after the Second World War "a benign philo-Semitism, the consequence of some shudders over the Holocaust, settled over the culture for a decade or two."[25] Of course, Jews could only be so sanguine about this abrupt shift in their reputation. Diner recounts, "American Jews walked a tightrope from the end of the 1940s through the 1960s. They remembered the anti-Semitism that had flourished through World War II. They had seen from a distance where hatred of Jews could lead. They knew that many individuals in the [Jewish] community had been involved with causes and organizations deemed questionable by large numbers of Americans. They perceived anti-Semitism as sleeping but not dead."[26]

Will Herberg's book *Protestant-Catholic-Jew*, which I referred to in chapter 1, is a key text for understanding the shift in the meaning of Jewishness that took place after the war. It is considered a landmark in the sociology of religion and presented a very influential picture of America at this time.[27] Herberg's book describes and exemplifies the emerging idea of a "tri-faith America." By mid-century, going to a suburban "house of worship," sending your children to religious school on Sunday, charitable work through your religious institution—all meant signaling one's rightful place as an upstanding member of American society; it meant making oneself visible as a citizen. According to Herberg, postwar pressure to be Jewish *by religion* resulted in the dissolution of Jewish nationalism, Jewish socialism, and a range of other "secular" Jewish ideologies.[28] "It is incontrovertible," he wrote, "that the Jewish community in the United States has become a religious community in its own understanding, as well as in the understanding of the non-Jew. Old-line secular Judaism is obsolescent."[29] Since Jews were still stigmatized as communist radicals in this period, the incentive to disavow that particular secular ideology was probably very great.[30]

Unmistakably, Herberg's book was as constructive as it was dispassionately sociological. After all, it set Judaism as a fundamental axis of Americanness alongside Protestantism and Catholicism despite the fact that Jews only amounted to a tiny percentage of the actual population.[31] Herberg promised Judaism and its adherents an equal and integral part in the triune conscience of American society.[32] Sociologists have found all sorts of problems with Herberg's analysis over the decades since the publication of *Protestant-Catholic-Jew*, but it seems right for him to have noted the "religionization" of Jewishness in those years. It seems right to say that at the time Jews increasingly identified themselves in terms of the categorical attribute "religion" and its subcategory, "Judaism." And it seems right to say that this kind of identification functioned as a convention of civility in American society. Of course, if this religionization increased in the late 1950s, and the decades that followed, it was in no small part because of the influence of Herberg's book. Herberg's theological and sociological works were themselves representations of Jews as adherents to the religion of Judaism and solidified the appearance of Jews in society as one of the three important religious groups.

So Jews presented themselves to their non-Jewish neighbors as adherents of "Judaism," a vaguely Hebraic version of American Protestantism, hoping henceforth to be seen as "real Americans." They knew that they were *not* invited to the American mainstream if they were going to be cosmopolitan, atheistic, communistic, or sexually liberated. The Jew as carrier of modern godlessness and sexual deviancy (increasingly associated by anti-Semites with psychoanalysis and the bourgeoning "sexual revolution") was still seen as a problem by many gentiles after the war. The feeling of being penned in by the dominant American convention of civility—the Protestant picture of what it looks like to be an upstanding citizen—must have chafed.

On the other hand, if Jews mostly pretended at "religion" in temples and synagogues, they exercised their Jewishness without inhibition at mountain resorts like Grossinger's in the Catskills. There, Jews could be together at leisure, entertained by a pantheon of Jewish comedians ready with material just for them. Thus, Sig Altman could write in 1971,

> the essentially religious identity prescribed by the American milieu also became the only "natural" one for the Jew: no alternative self-definition, whether racial, national, or cultural, seemed quite so viable. And so the synagogues have increased and the membership figures have swelled. Yet religion is now much more a matter of social organization than of inner conviction. Herberg shows that of all religious groups in America, Jews *believe* the least. And the deadly earnest of old is no longer present even in the synagogue. In those mountain retreats, on the other hand, where vacationing American Jews may be said to have been most "genuinely" themselves, it is not the rabbi but the comedian who officiates, and the daily liturgy is not the Hebrew prayer but the comic monologue. Although religion, then, is the official tag of the Jew in American society, his consciousness cannot be characterized as religious. It might more justly be characterized as ironic-about-itself.[33]

Joyce Antler confirms that Jews found in these sites of leisure an opportunity to exercise their bourgeoning middle-class credentials as consumers and vacationers while, at the same time, exercising their Jewishness without inhibition. In keeping with the atmosphere of uninhibited Jewishness, some of the famous comedians who played the Catskills would do Jewish shtick, which they would never do on radio, on television, or in the movies, where "Jewishness was communicated through gestures, allusions, accents, and inflections that non-Jews had difficulty recognizing."[34]

Henry Popkin observed in 1952 that explicitly Jewish characters and themes had all but disappeared from American popular culture since the early 1930s as a result of fears among producers that their representations of Jews might inadvertently fuel the rising anti-Semitism.[35] Popkin also thought that film producers presumed, no doubt in part because of rising anti-Semitism, that Jewish elements in movies would feel like an ugly intrusion to gentile audiences: "their presence is suppressed just as other odd, unsightly things are suppressed."[36] But at the Jewish mountain resorts, comedians were free of these constraints. Many of the comedians who would saturate American popular culture in the 1940s and 1950s were nurtured there. Comics and comedy writers who got their start in those venues include Milton Berle, Fanny Brice, Mel Brooks, Lenny Bruce, George Burns, Myron Cohen, George Jessel, Sam Levenson, Carl Reiner, Neil Simon, Sid Caesar, Danny Kaye, Buddy Hackett, Henny Youngman, Joan Rivers, Jerry Lewis, and Woody Allen.[37]

By the late 1950s and early 1960s, some of the comedians in this tradition began to do more explicitly Jewish material in their acts beyond the Borscht Belt, including widely available comedy albums. At the same time, more explicitly Jewish fiction emerged from literary writers like Bernard Malamud, Saul Bellow, and Philip Roth, and from popular writers like Herman Wouk and Leon Uris. By the period of 1967 to 1973—a key moment in Jewish American cultural history that J. Hoberman and Jeffrey Shandler rightly note fits almost perfectly between Barbara Streisand's *Funny Girl* (1968) and her *The Way We Were* (1973)—Jews were all over American popular culture *as* Jews, with their distinctive Jewish anxieties, grievances, longings, hair, names, and noses.[38]

A "Jewish new wave" in American movies emerged, featuring, along with Streisand, Dustin Hoffman, Elliot Gould, Woody Allen, Jeannie Berlin, George Segal, Richard Benjamin, and Mel Brooks.[39] Hoberman recounts, "Anticipating the so-called Blaxploitation and Italian-American films of the 1970s, the movies of this kind thrived on the sort of ethnic stereotyping that had largely disappeared from Hollywood films thirty years before. The image, however, was something new."[40] The image was not of a cartoonish stock character. But it was also not anything like the image of the "religious" Jew that Herberg and the rabbis from their pulpits hoped to promote as dignified contributors of the "Judeo" to Judeo-Christian America.

The Jewishness that emerged in American popular culture between the 1950s and the 1970s had nothing to do with piety or any other norms of American religion. Nor did it acquiesce to whiteness. The characters in these films, novels, and plays and the comic personae on stages and comedy records were decidedly *Jewish,* and their Jewishness was fraught with anger, fear, distrust, and resentment toward the goyim (which includes both white and black America). These characters (and their creators) presented themselves to the American public *as the Jewish problem* that they and their parents were accused of being between the 1920s and the 1940s. They presented themselves as urban, atheistic, intellectual, socialist, loudmouthed, hypersexualized, brimming with infectious modern anxieties, showbiz infatuated, hilarious, fully embodied (one might even say *racial*) Jews. But the best of these didn't just mirror old stereotypes.[41] They *played* with these elements of American Jewishness in new ways, adding distinct nuances and texture from lived Jewish experience.

Since Jews could now be largely uninhibited and creative *as Jews* in American popular culture, American popular culture came to function for many Jews in the same way that the old mountain resorts had functioned. Jews would continue to meet in temples and synagogues in order to spend time together and have familiar experiences, but they would really feel uninhibited Jewish satisfaction when watching Barbra Streisand, Dustin Hoffman, Mel Brooks or Woody Allen, reading Saul Bellow, Philip Roth or Cynthia Ozick, listening to Lenny Bruce, Allan Sherman, or Joan Rivers, or talking about them with their Jewish friends and family. The Jewish sitcom boom in the 1990s eventually added television to the virtual Borscht Belt and *Seinfeld, Will & Grace, Curb Your Enthusiasm*, and many other shows came to function similarly.[42]

But there is a crucial difference. The Catskills resorts were exclusively Jewish environments. The films, novels, comedy albums, and television shows that I've just referred to were created and mass produced for anyone in America to enjoy, Jew or gentile. Some of them have thus seemed to introduce an element of Jewishness into the collective way that Americans imagine what it's like to be an American. But now we are ready to dig in. We are ready to see how Jewish virtuosos of play invited Jews and gentiles to play together with the legacy of Jewish stigmatization in a way that illustrates our capacity for political love despite the fact of fraught societies.

THE INTIMACY OF LENNY BRUCE

In the 1950s and early 1960s a new practice of humorous play emerged in the background culture of American society.[43] It started among the relatively small self-selective population of people who were already experimenting with the jazz aesthetic and the countercultural Beat sensibility. The hungry i in San Francisco, the Crescendo in Los Angeles, and the Bitter End and Café Wha? in New York City drew small crowds in the 1950s to hear jazz, folk music, and poetry. These were the first venues to offer a stage for a new breed of stand-up comedians.[44] These comics didn't want to perform shtick—canned material that anyone could do, like campy rapid-fire one-liners or the old Borsht Belt acts. Instead, their material was more personalized: they stood on stage and started a timely conversation with the audience, expressing their own distinct points of view.

The groundbreaking innovator of this type of comedy was Mort Sahl, who was known to get onstage and read through the day's newspaper offering funny satirical remarks.[45] Sahl was part of a cohort of performers who shared in common "Jewish ethnic backgrounds, left-liberal political upbringing, affinity for Popular Front political theater, and . . . relatively high levels of education"; they also "evinced strong desires to escape the slick, artificial conventions of their craft and instead present themselves as informally, authentically, and spontaneously as possible."[46] Mort Sahl's early success at the hungry i, dressed casually in a sweater like a graduate student (rather than in a suit like the older generation of comics) encouraged similar venues, like the Greenwich Village coffeehouses, to book others in this cohort.[47] Among them was Lenny Bruce.

Lenny Bruce helped to establish mainstream stand-up comedy as a space where the comic and the audience could engage in distinctly intimate humorous play with perverse stereotypes, epithets, and emotions *as humorous objects*.[48] He is a comedy legend: a celebrated influence on the major comics who came after him in the 1970s and 1980s, including George Carlin, Richard Pryor, and Joan Rivers. He is likewise remembered for his daring refusal to bend to censorious moralists who stalked him to the end of his short life with obscenity charges. And he is lauded as a "liberal satirist," already promoting the left-liberal project of social transformation from the comedy stage in the late 1950s.[49] Wearing the hat of the public cultural critic, I suggest that we interpret Lenny Bruce's stand-up comedy as an instance of play that illustrates *our* capacity—as equal participants in the American endeavor to be a just nation—to cultivate political love despite the fact of fraught societies. By introducing a kind of playful intimacy that coexists with fraught divisive words and emotions, Bruce lays the groundwork for invitations to play, offered by Phillip Roth and Norman Lear, that I will argue should be established as enduring points in the public political culture of American society.

The distinctive intimacy that Bruce developed can be appreciated if we recall the routine I described in the introduction called "How to Relax Your Colored Friends at Parties." Recall that in this routine Bruce takes on the role of the "well-intentioned white guy" who is interacting with a "black guy" at a party (the latter role is played by Bruce's friend Eric Miller, the jazz musician, who is black). This is the bit where the white guy introduces himself to the black guy by barking, "That Joe Louis's a hellavu fighter!," and then toasting, "Here's to Bo Jangles!"[50] I noted that the humor in this routine comes from the incongruity between the white guy's polite intentions and his insulting bungled actions.

The routine also produces an unmasking effect that is funny. Something that is meant to be hidden is revealed. The racist ideas and manners that the white guy is desperate to suppress are abruptly exposed in his gaffes, taking the audience by surprise and producing a jolt of comic amusement. Given the way that Bruce has set up the routine, there is added humor to be derived from white audience members' identification with the white guy. The well-intentioned white audience members may perceive something like the following: "We do this, *I do this*, I stumble awkwardly when trying to make good-faith conversation across the fraught racial divide." If they are so perceptive, then these audience members are well situated for mirthful self-reflexivity over the course of the rest of the routine: they have started to laugh at themselves. The white audience member who refuses to identify with the white guy and is willing only to laugh *at* him derisively is not really getting the joke.

Notably, much hinges in this routine on the white guy's language: he is trapped in words, symbols, and ideas associated with stigmatized blackness, and this just compounds his absurd inability to see the man behind "the black guy" with whom he is interacting. If the white guy can be imagined as not so different from "the well-intentioned white liberal," then Bruce has his audience imagine that this type of person will carry implicit biases and perverse emotions that lag even as he strives to see nonwhites as truly equal citizens.[51] As we know, the problem of reproduction and the problem of remainders will leave blind spots that are invisible to the well-intentioned white liberal. Bruce makes these blind spots hilarious.

And instead of holding out hope for the white guy to "get it right," to eradicate his blind spots, there is a sense in this routine that genuinely "relaxed" interracial interaction comes precisely from the ability to play with all of the fraught language over which the quintessential white guy stumbles. While the audience laughs at the white guy and the black guy failing to communicate well, they are also watching Lenny Bruce and Eric Miller *playing together very well indeed*. Bruce and Miller's bit about *mis*communication between blacks and whites also performs subtle, comfortable, even artful *communication* between friends *across* the color divide.

At the end of the routine, Miller's character, who has been gracious throughout, agrees to go back to the white guy's house. He accepts the well-intentioned white guy's comically flawed effort to communicate respect and a desire for friendship. He is forgiving and acknowledges the good intention behind the buffoonery. But, on his way out, Miller's character toasts, "Here's to the Mau Maus!" which has a rich ambivalence in it. He is mocking the ridiculous toasts made earlier—to Bo Jangles, for instance—and hinting at rebellion: the Mau Maus were notoriously violent black insurgents who rebelled against their white oppressors. In effect, the black guy is saying, "I forgive your inability to communicate respect, I accept your intention, the whole thing is a little ridiculous, and by the way I still harbor some *less forgiving* emotions too, but what the hell, let's have another drink at your place—let's try to be friends, such as we can." The black audience member for Bruce's routine, then, is allowed, more than a mere straight man, to identify with in Miller's character.[52] Miller's concluding ambivalence is crucial to the routine.

If the audience experiences this routine in the way I imagine, then they share jolts of comic amusement resulting from hidden prejudices exposed and a newly rich perception of the tense interaction in their society. The narrow view of a white audience member who fancies himself an integrationist pure of heart is, in the playful context of the routine, layered with the view that the legacy of stigmatization will haunt every effort at comfortable interracial interaction, which is in turn layered with the emotion of comic amusement as a response to this contradiction—an emotion that can be shared by both blacks and whites who must endure the failed interactions together. I claim that this layered perception, compounded by the shared emotion of comic amusement, amounts to a type of intimacy: *metaperspectival intimacy*. This is a feeling of closeness that comes from sharing a contrived, detached viewpoint in relation to the same object. Taking this perspective brings the participants closer to each other. In this case, they take the same viewpoint and feel the same emotion about a version of themselves from which they are artificially detached through the playful dynamics of the routine.[53]

But nothing is resolved. This is play, after all. The well-intentioned white guy is not ultimately condemned for his boorishness, nor is he forgiven without lingering ambivalence. The metaperspectival intimacy that can emerge in humorous play is ad hoc and fleeting. I do not claim that shared comic amusement is just a funny type of compassion: it does not bind you emotionally to the good of others. Neither does metaperspectival intimacy, as I have described it, necessarily imply any common normative commitments. Sharing perception of the subtleties and ambivalence of social interaction does not entail endorsing a morality of equal respect, for instance. I am making a more modest claim. When metaperspectival intimacy emerges, it reinforces a moral intuition about sociability that is foundational for the capabilities approach to political justice: human life is fundamentally *with others* in a shared social world.[54] The intuition of sociability is not, properly speaking, endorsed or justified as a result of this feeling of intimacy. What Bruce provokes is the feeling of an American life truly *with others* that will involve carrying unresolved legacies of historical injustice, an American life with others *despite* the fact of fraught societies.

"AND MY MOTHER WAS SWEATING AND JEWISH AND YELLING"

Bruce's *attitude* was very important: he was informal, irreverent but sweet (before he sank into immobilizing bitterness at the end of his career), disarmingly personal and sincere, prepared to embarrass himself, youthful and hip and cool and charming, but still a little nerdy and intellectual.[55] His whole presence, as I perceive it, anyway, from a historical distance, seemed to carry a message: "let's cut through the bullshit and really talk, have a little fun." A lot of the surprise in his act comes from moments when he abruptly cuts through bullshit and unmasks hypocrisy, or exposes something bodily or sexual that is usually concealed, or says something that is usually whispered behind someone else's back. At the same time, the substance and structure of what is masked and unmasked is itself always a contrivance, performed by Bruce for comic effect.[56] So, Bruce is always playing with authenticity, sincerity, and cutting through the bullshit while he is also modeling it.[57] The overall result was to make viable an alternative to the conventions of civility popular on television shows like *The Dick Van Dyke Show*, *Leave It to Beaver*, and *The Adventures of Ozzie and Harriet*. For instance, he did a bit about the Andy Hardy series of movies that appeared from 1937 to 1958. Although there seems to be some confusion, because it was Fay Holden, not Faye Bainter, who played Andy Hardy's mother in these films. Anyway, here's the bit:

> Faye Bainter, Andy Hardy's mother, screwed up every other mother in the world. Because what mother can be like Faye Bainter, Faye Bainter was in the kitchen with a crisp apron, a sweet up-turned nose, and my mother was sweating and Jewish and yelling.
>
> "Why can't ya be like Faye Bainter, ma?" Faye Bainter never calls any of Andy Hardy's friends bums. Andy Hardy can bring fifty guys home at two in the morning and she don't care, not only that, but she gives'em all a glass of milk and a peanut butter sandwich. Not chicken fat on rye bread. Faye Bainter [grumbles].
>
> And no salesman ever pinched Faye Bainter on the ass in the kitchen. And best of all, Faye Bainter was a virgin. With all those kids. Cause that's what everyone wants their mother to be. You don't want to see your mother even getting kissed. . . . Nothing horny, man, you don't wanna see that."[58]

In the *Essential Lenny Bruce* version he concludes, "So that's some heavy propaganda, man."[59] These television shows and movies, where people were depicted as polite and appropriate, virginal and clean, where sons are happily deferential to their fathers and wives to their husbands, seemed to mask the fraught reality of everyday life. In Bruce's everyday life as a kid, according to the conceit of this bit, people were instead loud, sweaty,

Jewish, rude, and sexual. On the one hand, he seems to decry his mother and his childhood, wishing he could have milk and peanut butter sandwiches for his friends, wishing that his mother was not at all sexualized or dirty. But, at the same time, he is decrying the propagation of the image of Andy Hardy and Andy Hardy's mother because it has compelled him unnecessarily to denigrate his childhood; it has put an unfair burden on his mother—an image she could never live up to. He resents the goyish Faye Bainter for making his own mother seem like a Jewish slob, but he also resents his mother for seeming to be a Jewish slob.

The contrast between Faye Bainter and his mother is funny in and of itself, but the routine also invites the audience to experience a feeling that is performed as Bruce's personal unresolved ambivalence and resentment. He is not ultimately condemning or excusing the cause of this resentment; he is playing with it in such a way that the audience is allowed to participate. A society where people are at pains to prove themselves civil on the model of "Faye Bainter" is very different from one where people are at pains to communicate, "let's cut through the bullshit and really talk." Bruce's attitude, his willingness to expose his dirty world in the space of play, can be viewed as a way of thrusting forth his animality. Bruce puts his secreting human body on display. This is one of the hallmarks of his comedy.[60] I suspect it is among the reasons he was called a "sick" comedian.[61] It is also why he was arrested so many times on obscenity charges.[62]

And his frequent references to sex and bodily secretions are related to the work he does with perverse stereotypes, epithets, and emotions. It is not a coincidence that the dichotomies clean/dirty, virginal/sexual, good/bad track with the dichotomy gentile/Jewish in his "Faye Bainter" routine. The bit is equally about exposing the dirty under the veneer of the clean *and* exposing the Jewish under the veneer of a gentile society, among other things. Here Bruce echoes elemental features of modern Jewish comedy that are evident in its earliest formations at the turn of the twentieth century. It is worth taking a quick detour to hear the sound that Bruce echoes in his distinct American context.

German Jews at the turn of the twentieth century produced the first collections of jokes saturated with anxiety about modernization, stigmatization, heightened Jewish embodiment, and social incorporation.[63] Established German Jews at that time were particularly concerned to distinguish themselves from the stigmatized *Ostjuden* (Eastern European

Jews). They worried that behind the polite smiles their non-Jewish neighbors were really thinking: "The 'Eternal Jew,' the evil Jew, the parasitic Jew is the Eastern European Yiddish-speaking Jew now rapidly infesting the West, who is also hidden behind the pseudo-civilized mask of the assimilated German Jew." The jokes that assimilated German Jews collected and told in the first years of the twentieth century record both their identification with and repulsion from the Ostjuden. These jokes show a particular preoccupation with Yiddish language as the quasi-biological taint of the Ostjuden.[64] Quintessential is a joke that Sigmund Freud collected in his book on jokes from this period:

> The doctor who has been requested to attend the Baroness at her confinement declares that the moment has not yet arrived, and suggests to the Baron that meantime they play a game of cards in the next room. After a while the Frau Baronin's cry of pain reaches the ears of the two men: "*Ah mon Dieu, que je souffre.*" The husband leaps up, but the doctor detains him. "It's nothing. Let's carry on playing." A while later they hear her crying out in labour: "*Mein Gott, mein Gott, was für Schmerzen!*" [lit. "My God, my God, how it hurts!"]—"Won't you go in, professor?" asks the Baron. "No, no, it's still not time."—Finally, from the next room they hear an unmistakable cry of "*Ai, waih, waih*" [equivs. "O weh!" "Oy veh!"]; then the doctor throws away his cards and says: "It's time."[65]

Freud interpreted this joke as a universal example of primal nature breaking through the pretenses of civilization (and of the importance of sensitivity to trivial phenomena for decision-making). But this universal interpretation itself betrays mere pretense. The primal cry is unmistakably that of deep *Jewishness*, here identified with Yiddish, breaking through the *civil* French and German. John Murray Cuddihy interpreted this joke as paradigmatic of Freud's response to the "ordeal of civility," his insistence on revealing what is suppressed in polite *gentile* society: "The French layer is peeled away, then the German layer, finally laying bare the '*mama-loshen*' [mother tongue] of primary socialization 'underneath.' Freud's 'primitive nature' that breaks through the cultural restraints of a Westernized superego is the premodern Jew of the preemancipated *shtetl* [the *Ostjude*]. Freud turns it into a quasi-biological 'id.'"[66] The final cry in

Yiddish reveals the "hidden language" of the Jews and thereby disrupts the rhetoric of civility, which Freud himself tries to suppress with his universal interpretation in his "scientific" joke book.[67]

In Freud's defense, the joke probably also works if the woman proceeds from refined exclamations of pain to a final inarticulate scream, without incorporating a hierarchy of languages. Told this way it would be a joke about the extreme pain of childbirth. But that's not really the same joke. With the Yiddish ending, the joke suggests a kind of primordial embodied Jewishness from which there is no escape. The setting, childbirth, contributes to this sense of primordial significance. What cannot be civilized in Freud's joke is the taint of "oriental" Jewishness that flows from the root of the Yiddish language, which he wanted both to liberate in universal terms with the new language of psychoanalysis and suppress out of personal shame.[68]

Lenny Bruce sets up the same structure of sterile gentile civility vs. suppressed animalistic Jewishness that is central to Freud's joke. But Bruce can do something new with it. He is on stage with an audience that he can presume includes both Jews and gentiles. He invites this audience to an interaction where messy human bodies and nasty ideas, emotions, and words are exposed—where he evokes the feeling of "no bullshit." And this includes thrusting fraught Jewishness into the play frame. In this interaction, a special intimacy is possible—we can *really talk* and *play* together. In this interaction we together are allowed to be vulnerable, dependent, human animals who carry legacies of historical injustice.[69] However, like the metaperspectival intimacy that he provokes in the "How to Relax Your Colored Friends at Parties" routine, the intimacy that he provokes in the "Faye Bainter" bit entails no necessary consequence.

To be sure, Bruce does sometimes make more resolute claims in his routines about dirtiness and dirty Jewish bodies (including his own body). In one famous bit he says, "If you believe that there is a god, a god that made your body, and yet you think that you can do anything with that body that's dirty, then the fault lies with the manufacturer. *Emmis.*"[70] There is certainly a provocative idea in this bit. In fact, when he performed it at the Jazz Workshop in San Francisco on October 4, 1961, he prefaced it with, "Now, if the bedroom is dirty to you, then you are a true atheist."[71] On Bruce's reasoning, you can't believe that god is perfect, that god created human beings, *and* that god's creation is fundamentally dirty. He is offering his audience the chance to have the thought your rabbi, priest, or nun, who claims to be a paragon of piety, is really an atheist.[72] The reveal, the deflation of authority, the exciting energy in the rebellious and plausible claim of hypocrisy—all these elements are part of what make it a good bit.

This routine does not exactly disclose undiscovered hypocrisy among the clergy. Criticizing the absurdity of self-righteous clerics was not a new invention in 1961. Voltaire had Bruce beat by a couple of centuries. Nor does Bruce really offer anything particularly original about how we ought to relate to our bodies. Bruce's affirmation of the human body, human sexuality, and whatever is conventionally labeled disgusting reflects the broader influence of Freudian psychoanalysis and Wilhelm Reich's anti-fascist sexology on the arts in the postwar period.[73] He acknowledges as much in the lead-up to his "The Fault Is with the Manufacturer" routine.[74]

Bruce's routines about dirtiness, which frequently connect dirtiness with Jewishness in a way that affirms both, are important because of how they contribute to the intimacy that Bruce strives to forge in his comedy.[75] What is important is not this or that "Truth" that he may propagate on stage, but the evocation of *truthfulness* in his comedy. He cultivates an enjoyable sense of closeness that is facilitated by his posture of uninhibited, raw, often free-associated, and formless expression. Bruce invites his audience to have an intimate experience, one that they are meant to enjoy, with the hip, funny, sexual, lefty, intellectual Jew that he *is*, and *is playing*, on stage—hang-ups, grievances, fraught embodiment, and all. He highlights the distance between himself and the audience by sharing his idiosyncratic or distinctly Jewish fixations, but he simultaneously forges intimacy as a result of his willingness to be so exposed.[76]

The dynamic elasticity of distance and proximity that he accomplishes in his routines, underwritten by a shared expectation with the audience of nothing more than time well spent, is what makes Bruce's stand-up comedy exemplary play. The fact that he is able to play this way with fraught Jewish embodiment, with the "dirty Jew" and the "ordeal of civility," shows how the fact of fraught societies can be absorbed into new sites of play. With Bruce, audiences can experience intimacy and divisive resentment at the same time in a moment that is set apart from everyday life and from the hard, deliberative work of political action.

"JEWISH AND GOYISH"

Let's look at another example of dynamic elasticity in one of Bruce's best and most famous routines. It is entitled "Jewish and Goyish." It goes like this:

> Dig: I'm Jewish. Count Basie's Jewish. Ray Charles is Jewish. Eddie Cantor's goyish. B'nai B'rith is goyish; Hadassah, Jewish.
>
> If you live in New York or any other big city, you are Jewish. It doesn't matter even if you're Catholic; if you live in New York, you're Jewish. If you live in Butte, Montana, you're going to be goyish even if you're Jewish.
>
> Kool-aid is goyish. Evaporated milk is goyish even if the Jews invented it. Chocolate is Jewish and fudge is goyish. Fruit salad is Jewish. Lime jello is goyish. Lime soda is very goyish.
>
> Negroes are all Jews. Italians are Jews. Irishmen who have rejected their religion are Jews. Mouths are very Jewish. And bosoms. Baton-twirling is very goyish.
>
> Underwear is definitely goyish. Balls are goyish. Titties are Jewish.
>
> Celebrate is a goyish word. Observe is a Jewish word. Mr. and Mrs. Walsh are celebrating Christmas with Major Thomas Moreland, USAF (ret.), while Mr. and Mrs. Bromberg observed Hanukkah with Goldie and Arthur Schindler from Kiamesha, New York.[77]

Bruce starts by identifying with a categorical attribute: "Dig: I'm Jewish." The pretense is that he will delineate the differences between Jews like himself and goyim—non-Jews, people who are different from him. But immediately the audience is taken by surprise as he mixes up the usual associations and shifts group membership across racial, geographical, and cultural lines. "Count Basie's Jewish. Ray Charles is Jewish. . . . B'nai B'rith is goyish." But the humorous effect is not, at least at first, derived from mere arbitrariness. He relies on commonplaces about Jewishness versus gentileness in order to maintain the pretense that this is still a good-faith analysis: Jews live in big cities, so if you live in a big city you are ostensibly Jewish, but "if you live in Butte, Montana, you're going to be goyish even if you're Jewish." These commonplaces could, of course, be negatively or positively construed.

There is also the sense that Bruce means purposely to construct Jewishness as hip and urban: associated with jazz and New York. He seems also to hint at some idea of Jewishness as "secular": "Irishmen who have rejected their religion are Jews." Constructively, then, the routine may pretend to build a universal category of Jewishness that includes anyone who is hip, urban, secular, and historically stigmatized.[78] By contrast, the universal category described by the appellation *goyish* includes anyone who is square, provincial, religious, and a member of a historically dominant group. This is certainly a relevant distinction to make in the 1960s. And it tracks closely with the "red state" vs. "blue state" distinction that is still often used to describe American politics.

But then the routine plummets into total absurdity, mocking the very idea of difference—like this list of assertions: "Underwear is definitely goyish. Balls are goyish. Titties are Jewish." The ultimate effect of the routine is to start the audience off with a naive intonation of a difference, then to muddle the differentiated conception immediately, and to "transvaluate" it by contrasting it to new and counterintuitive opposites, only then to mock the very idea of differences by making the whole process of differentiation seem absurd. And after the routine is over, what has changed?

The audience can still presumably distinguish between what is conventionally Jewish and non-Jewish with the same confidence as when they started. They may now have a sense that for people like Lenny Bruce "Jewish" has a broader cultural meaning than they realized (this is not Herberg's American Judaism). At the height of its absurdity, they would have perceived that there might be something silly altogether about differentiating people according to these kinds of categorical attributes. If they laughed, though—if the audience of Jews and gentiles were jolted into an outbreak of comic amusement together by Bruce's surprising reversals, then I hypothesize that they shared an important experience of metaperspectival intimacy. Bruce's routine does not leave them with platitudinous universalism: "Jews and gentiles are really all the same." Neither does he leave them with some exaggerated self-aggrandizement of what makes Jews different from others: "Jews are totally different from gentiles, and you gentiles can't really understand us Jews." Nor are they just left with "Jews are hip, gentiles are square." All the relevant categories of differentiation have been so jumbled by the routine that no clear message about their meaning can be deduced.

The audience is left with their brief experience of having felt the same positive emotions and having perceived divisive categories in a new way, ambiguously, together. They will leave the club still divided between Jews and gentiles (at a time in American history when, as I explained earlier, these groups still rarely shared leisure time and space). They will leave with a touchstone of intimacy that makes no claims, even as it experientially reinforces the sense that they are deeply connected to one another every bit as much as they will remain separate and sometimes opposed.

"ARE THERE ANY NIGGERS HERE TONIGHT?"

Humorous play can involve relating to others in ways that would justifiably cause explosive friction were it not acknowledged by all involved to be *play*. Lenny Bruce was able to play with extremely flammable language because the line separating the comedy stage from "serious" social life was so explicit. As I explained in the previous chapter, by agreeing to step into a space of play together, the participants in the interaction agree that when the expression of Y communicates Z outside of the play frame, and the expression of X communicates Y inside of the play frame, nevertheless X does not communicate Z inside of the play frame.[79] If Z is disrespectful or cruel, then this shift in meaning from outside to inside of the play frame must be accepted in order for X to communicate Y without also communicating disrespect or cruelty. I suspect that Bruce was able to invite his audience to make this shift successfully in part because of his success at exposing his own vulnerability and cultivating intimacy with the audience in the process.

Consider the routine that begins, "Are there any niggers here tonight?" Outside of the framework of play, to ask such a question communicates acceptance of morally repugnant language and categories. Nevertheless, when Lenny Bruce performs this routine he must hope that the audience is prepared to hear it as *not* communicating acceptance of such language or categories. With the play structure in place, Bruce can express the full range of ugly terms that linger in his society. He can then exploit this material for the work of his routine, which goes like this:

> By the way, are there any niggers here tonight?
>
> [*Outraged whisper*] "*What did he say? 'Are there any niggers here tonight?'* Jesus Christ! Is that *cruel*. Does he have to get that low for laughs? Wow!
>
> Have I ever talked about the *schwarzes* when the *schwarzes* had gone home? Or spoken about the Moulonjohns when they'd left? Or placated some Southerner by absence of voice when he ranted and raved about nigger nigger nigger?"
>
> Are there any niggers here tonight? I know that one nigger who works here, I see him back there. Oh, there's two niggers, customers, and, ah, *aha!* Between those two niggers sits one kike—man, thank God for the kike!
>
> Uh, two kikes. That's two kikes, and three niggers, and one spic. One spic—two, three spics. One Mick. One mick, one spic, one hick, thick, funky, spunky boogey. And there's another kike. Three kikes. Three kikes, one guinea, one greaseball. Three greaseballs, two guineas. Two guineas, one hunky funky lace-curtain Irish mick. That mick spic hunky funky boogey.
>
> Two guineas plus three greaseballs and four boogies makes usually three spics. Minus two Yid spic Polack funky spunky Polacks.
>
> Auctioneer: "Five more niggers! Five more niggers!"
>
> Gambler: "I pass with six niggers and eight micks and four spics."[80]

Immediately before doing this routine, we can imagine the audience waiting with anticipation for his next bit with an overall sense of self-congratulation. They are confident in their open-mindedness. After all, they chose to attend a show performed by a very controversial comedian—Bruce, remember, was banned from several cities. Then their prejudices are put smack in front of their faces: "Are there any niggers here tonight?" Should they laugh? Should they try to appear skeptical? They all know the meaning of the word *nigger*. And they all know that, however much they might disdain the word, some prejudices associated with the word still linger among their own ideas and emotions. Bruce encourages this self-reflection when he performs it himself: "have I ever used these cruel terms?" He wants the audience to ask themselves this question and, more broadly, "have I ever had the cruel thoughts associated with such terms?"

Then he puts the dangerous slur back on the table: "Are there any niggers here tonight?" Just as the audience is starting to get nervous—where's he going with this?—they are caught in a deluge of slurs. Everyone in the audience is subject to the offense. The whole audience is degraded and broken down into derogated versions of the various groups with which they might identify. They are forced into empathy. Each of them is now on the receiving end of an offensive epithet. At this point they may be both empathetic, as victims of some derogatory slur, and divided along group lines: they are kikes, micks, spics, guineas, or Polacks.

As in "Jewish and Goyish," Bruce then slips quickly into absurdity, throwing in words that make no sense in this context like "hick, thick, funky, spunky," implying that all of the words he is using (including, of course, the slurs) are nonsense. By the end of the bit, the audience has gone through a three-step transformation: from 1. starting the show with the shared open-mindedness that brought them to see Lenny Bruce, to 2. being confronted by their implicit prejudices and divided along group lines, and finally 3. being reunified as an ad hoc "community" in and of themselves: laughing together about the absurdity of prejudice, groupness, and stigmatization in their shared society. Bruce was a sincere advocate of civil rights. But rather than try to erase words like *kike* and *nigger* from our vocabulary, he sought to proliferate them into absurdity. This is how he often explained the use of profanity and epithets in his comedy: proliferation to achieve meaninglessness through absurdity. However, I think he failed as his own critic to perceive the virtuosity of play he in fact achieved: during the fleeting moments of the routine his entire audience is simultaneously separated and bound together in categorical ambiguity and formlessness.

The metaperspectival intimacy stimulated by this routine is especially interesting. This is humorous play in which nasty epithets are on flagrant display and aimed directly at the audience, while they laugh together with comic amusement. Again, nothing is claimed or agreed upon in this interaction. But while the legacy of stigmatization persists, putting these materials in a play frame, and playing with them like this in a limited way, reinforces the sense of common social experience upon which political justice depends. And, in the context of play, these terms lose their plausibility as tools for instrumental reasoning—they are, instead, the butt of a joke. Of course, this kind of play is dangerous: in the wrong hands, in the wrong spirit, efforts to initiate humorous interaction using the language of stigmatization can end in disaster. Lenny Bruce was, after all, a master of his art. After seeing this routine, Dick Gregory reportedly told his friend, the cultural critic Grover Sales, "This man is the eighth wonder of the world and if they don't kill him or throw him in jail he's liable to shake up this whole fuckin' country."[81]

In Bruce's stand-up, the fact of fraught societies is absorbed into a special site of play where perverse material is allowed to persist reframed. This material is thus denuded of its instrumental function and becomes fodder for the creativity of future virtuosos of play. Arguably, Lenny Bruce significantly facilitated the shift of such materials from predominantly instrumental use to predominantly playful use in the bourgeoning domains of play in mid-century American society. Richard Pryor was equally important, as Bruce's heir. He took up Bruce's legacy. But he is not the heir to Bruce because he talked about politically controversial issues or because he used racial epithets on stage and on his albums—like the 1974 landmark LP *That Nigger's Crazy*. Pryor is the great heir and contributor to the Bruce tradition in stand-up because he so fearlessly invited his mixed audiences into a moment of intimacy where his personal experience as a black man in America—hang-ups, grievances, fraught embodiment, and all—is not bracketed or repressed, but amplified and exacerbated.[82]

While Lenny Bruce pioneered a metaperspectival intimacy that reinforces the possibility of political love despite the fact of fraught societies, his shows were attended by a demographically limited audience, and his records became treasures for only a small subculture of enthusiasts. By contrast, Philip Roth's *Portnoy's Complaint* was number 1 on the *New York Times* fiction best sellers list in 1969. Roth's invitation to play was widely accepted. Let's explore why that matters.

7

PHILLIP ROTH TELLS THE GREATEST
JEWISH JOKE EVER TOLD

Apatient sits down on the couch of his therapist's office. He begins to rant about the parochial Jewish community of his childhood, his absurdly obtuse and repressive parents, and he starts lavishly to reveal sordid secrets of obsessive adolescent masturbation—now he's really worked up!—he confesses his abuses of women and his all-consuming sexual desire and his contempt for almost everyone around him and for *himself*, but he's just as frenzied about his debt to his parents and his desire to be a good, respectable, admirable person. He goes on and on like this, relishing every detail of travesty and desire. Finally, bursting with fury, he screams, he howls! And then, exhausted, he falls silent. Therapist: "So, now vee may perhaps to begin. Yes?"[1]

This is the humorous play frame that circumscribes Philip Roth's *Portnoy's Complaint*. It is often and easily noticed that *Portnoy's Complaint* unfolds like a Lenny Bruce spritz: it is brisk, articulate, intimate, funny, brimming with lament, aspiration, criticism, ire, and Jewish self-consciousness.[2] Everything humiliating is exposed, utterly hilariously exposed: "'Come, Big Boy, come,' screamed the maddened piece of liver that, in my own insanity, I bought one afternoon at a butcher shop and, believe it or not, violated behind a billboard on the way to a bar mitzvah lesson."[3] As we will see, such bits are not simply meant to shock the reader. There is complex ambivalence in Alex's reflections about his sexuality, even though there is also bravado and aggression in it too (to which, by the way, *he* draws our attention and thereby takes a metaperspective on his own perverse accounting of his perversity).[4] I will show how *Portnoy's Complaint* invites a kind of intimacy that is similar in structure to the metaperspectival intimacy that Lenny Bruce's routines were structured to produce.

But *Portnoy's Complaint* is not a joke in a Jewish joke anthology or a stand-up routine. It is a work of literature.[5] It is, in a sense, the full artistic flourishing of male, Ashkenazi, Jewish American humor: uncensored, aggressively Jewish, aggressive toward everything Jewish, contemptuous and admiring of the goyim, showcasing indeterminate selfness that is *both* self-transcending *and* interminably groupist—it's all there. But "Jewish humor" is also among the aspects of Jewishness that Roth plays with in *Portnoy's Complaint*. It is itself a central aspect of what is at play in the book. It is, in this sense, Jewish humor *about Jewish humor.*

In the analysis that follows, Alexander Portnoy will not emerge as a moral exemplar. He is not a character narrated to "humanize" Jewish people and present the dignity and respectability of Jewish life (much to the dismay of Jewish critics). Alexander Portnoy is a character whose primordially important stuff is constituted by profoundly fraught Jewish groupness. The *ur*-facts of his moral psychology, his pictures of health and love and goodness, his desires and what he desires to desire, are refracted through primordially important experiences of "Jews vs. goyim," *Jewish* guilt, *Jewish* moral outrage, outrage about being *Jewish*. And there's no escape. Except that the entire book is structured in order to bump the reader up to a metaperspective on Alex's moral psychology, which is itself an escape.[6] The virtuosity of play with fraught Jewishness and Americanness in Roth's book is perhaps the pinnacle of its exercise. I will argue that it ought to be set as an enduring point in the public culture of American society.

BEFORE WHOM HE STANDS

Synagogues often have the words *Da lifneh mi atah omed!* engraved above the ark that holds the Torah: "Know before whom you stand!" The opening pages of *Portnoy's Complaint* establish before whom Alex Portnoy stands: "She was so deeply imbedded in my consciousness that for the first year of school I seem to have believed that each of my teachers was my mother in disguise."[7] Alex's mother is powerful. And though he doesn't fully understand her mysterious powers of ubiquity, he knows that "it had to do with finding out the kind of little boy I was when I thought she wasn't around."[8] Far from the denigrated "Jewish mother" stereotype that she is sometimes said to represent, Mrs. Portnoy evinces all of the power, jealousy, wrath, and founding imperatives of the God of Israel.[9] She is the source of infinite demands that Alex cannot shake from his consciousness. She is the beginning of responsibility, of *ought*. Indeed, his primordial sense of her omniscience provokes his earliest moral anxiety: knowing somehow she was watching, he was compelled to be honest.[10]

The structure and terms of Alex's relationship with his mother resonantly echo the structure and terms of the relationship between God and Israel; this cannot be ignored.[11] The analogical reference to divine omniscience, which replaces the demanding eyes of God with the demanding eyes of Sophie Portnoy is similar to a process of "secularization." In *Portnoy's Complaint,* the conceptual legacy of the God-Israel relationship is perceptible in Alex's mother always watching.[12] Divine authority lurks in the background as the analogical referent that makes Sophie Portnoy's "authority" thinkable at all. When Alex sets out to describe his earliest memories of his mother, he cannot help but do so in a way that evokes a Jewish sense of authority: a powerful, demanding being who watches and judges everything that *you* do. That is our first glimpse of Alex's idiosyncratic primordially important stuff, which is shot through with Jewish anxiety about being judged and his mother's particularly forceful presence as the judge.[13]

Let's dig deeper into Alex's founding relationship with his mother. He seems to recount a primal scene as he describes the period of his youth when he refused to eat. His mother, lavishing praise on his many accomplishments and genius, as usual, challenges him to be a man: "am I to be allowed to think I can just starve myself to death for no good reason in the world?. . . Which do I want to be when I grow up, weak or strong, a success or a failure, a man or a mouse?"[14] It is, first of all, worth noting that his mother, not his father, adjures him to be a man. But I will come to his father in a moment. Second, and most important, Alex feels that throughout his life he has been stuck in a minefield of taboos that were continuously reinforced by his parent's fearful attitude toward life, which kept them locked up in their parochial world. So it is galling that his mother would have challenged *him* to be strong and undaunted by meaningless hang-ups.

He connects the local family taboos that hobble his parents to the seemingly infinite little rules piled on top of each other in Jewish law that set the standard by which one's status in "the book of life" is determined every Yom Kippur.[15] This image is engraved on his imagination. Here is how he imagines God and his annual bookkeeping: "It's the breaking alone that gets His goat—it's the simple fact of waywardness, and that alone, that He absolutely cannot stand, and which He does not forget either, when He sits angrily down (fuming probably, and surely with a smashing miserable headache, like my father at the height of his constipation) and begins to leave names out of that book."[16] It is transgression that Alex is taught to fear and foreswear. And it's not just shellfish, but any chazerai!

He recounts that his mother would say the word *hamburger* with such contempt that you'd think she was saying the word *Hitler*—but she was no less appalled by the prospect of French fries.[17] If we return for a moment to the passage about the goyim in the introduction, it will now be possible to see how a few things hang together for Alex: his primordial fixation on transgression, the demanding God of Israel lurking in the background of his mother's demands, the lingering anger, fear, and resentment toward non-Jews that is implicit in his Jewish groupness, distinct elements of his Jewish masculinity, and the profound primordial importance of his parents and their idiosyncratic little world. "They will eat *anything*," Alex reflects, "anything they can get their big *goy* hands on! And the terrifying corollary, *they will do anything as well.* . . . Thus saith the kosher laws, at least to the child I was, growing up under the tutelage of Sophie and Jack P., and in a school district of Newark where in my entire class there are only two little Christian children, and they live in houses I do not enter, on the far fringes of our neighborhood."[18]

It is all knotted together for Alex. The danger of the goyim—the fear that Alex has imbibed, which he will want to overcome in his pursuit of non-Jewish girls—has to do with their association with transgression. And this is related to their violence and their ideas of manliness (this is the passage where he describes the dead animal strapped to each fender as a boast of goyish manliness). But none of this is a halachic matter. It is a matter of beer-breath and pick-up trucks (which, by the way, seems a mere figment of the Newark Jewish imagination given the lack of actual non-Jews in the area). The "Kosher laws," here, are only what they are for Alex as a result of growing up with *his* parents, in *his* neighborhood: they are entirely structured around the very idiosyncratic categorical distinctions between Jews and gentiles that are forever vivid in his mind.[19]

But in a household so gripped with the fear of transgression, how odd for his mother to wonder with outrage, when Alex refuses to eat, why he should starve for no good reason in the world? How odd for her to adjure him to be a man, to eat and be strong. Like the goyim? And, after all, this should be *Alex*'s rebellious motto, not his mother's: throughout the entire book he wonders aloud in desperation why he should starve sexually, why he should deny himself just because of his congenital fear of transgression, which is *no good reason at all*. When he fasts, he is told to eat. At the very idea of him actually satiating himself, however, he is condemned. This sense of bewildering and painfully frustrating contradiction pervades his reflections on his mother. At another important moment, which haunts him, she actually pulls a knife on him because he won't eat.

It would be one thing if she were just abusive and crazy. But she's not. She loves him and he knows it. She is intelligent and really engages him. They would pass the hours after he came home from school talking about everything in the world, and she would be effusive in her pride.[20] But "how can she rise with me on the crest of my genius during those dusky beautiful hours after school, and then at night, because I will not eat some string beans and a baked potato, point a bread knife at my heart? And why doesn't my father stop her?"[21]

One more bit about Alex's reflections on his mother is crucial for us to review. Amidst one of his torrential rants, Alex notes that in his youth his mother was forever ranting to him about her life: "As other children hear the story of Scrooge every year, or are read to nightly from some favorite book, I am continually *shtupped* full of the suspense-filled chapters of her perilous life. This in fact is the literature of my childhood, these stories of my mother's . . ."[22] And how does he describe what runs through the entirety of her work (which he entitles *You Know Me, I'll Try Anything Once*): "that she is some sort of daredevil who goes exuberantly out into life in search of the new and the thrilling, only to be slapped down for her pioneering spirit. She actually seems to think of herself as a woman at the very frontiers of experience, some doomed dazzling combination of Marie Curie, Anna Karenina, and Amelia Earhart."[23]

In his idiosyncratic and testosterone-driven way, Alex ranting is a repetition of Sophie ranting—even when he is ranting about his mother on behalf of his own spirit of sexual adventure.[24] Just as his mother was shtupping him full of the chapters of her life, this is precisely how Alex is shtupping us. And what a contradiction: to be inundated with stories of daring by a mother who seems otherwise to have constructed barriers of fear in front of every possible line of transgression. It is an elegant depiction of the primordially important stuff of childhood: Alex's mother presents the medium for criticism (ranting and storytelling), the thing criticized (her), and the ideal for the purpose of which criticism is leveled (adventure). *Imitatio Dei!*

ISRAEL, PROSTRATE ON THE TOILET

If Alex stood beneath his mother's sovereign watchful eyes, he stood in solidarity with his father.[25] Or at least he wanted to, desperately. His father was the sufferer. "He suffered—did he suffer!—from constipation."[26] Alex's father is stopped-up with humiliation. His wife has attention only for her prodigious son. Compounding this, respect is never forthcoming from the non-Jews who run the insurance company for which he slaves thanklessly. He is a man holding tight, throughout his suffering in this world, whose singular solace is his messianic aspiration for a good bowel movement. "As a little boy I sometimes sat in the kitchen and waited with him. But the miracle never came, not at least as we imagined and prayed it would, as a lifting of the sentence, a total deliverance from the plague."[27] Alex's father waits for redemption, usually in the bathroom, like Israel in exile.

His father's experience of stigmatization is particularly salient for Alex. This is evident in the way he describes his father's ambivalence about "the Company" (the insurance company he works for). He takes great pride in the Company. But he also curses it because of his limited upward mobility, which he assumes results from being stigmatized as a Jew. Alex recounts his father's appreciation for getting a wage during the depression and for having his own stationary with his name under a picture of the Mayflower, the company's insignia "and by extension his, ha, ha."[28] The Company seemed to Alex to represent *America itself* for his father. He served it dutifully and resented it continuously.

His father's professional motto is "a man has got to have an umbrella for a rainy day. You don't leave a wife and child out in the rain without an umbrella!"[29] As Alex describes it, his father would deliver this speech to "the callow Poles, and violent Irishmen, and illiterate Negroes who lived in the impoverished districts that had been given him to canvass by The Most Benevolent Financial Institution in America."[30] There had never been a Jewish manager at the Company, and Jack Portnoy (and his son Alex) knew that he would not be the first. This is why, as loyal as he was, Alex's father despised the Company.[31] He was forever "doomed to be obstructed by this Holy Protestant Empire!"[32]

Obstructed, of course, in the sense of constipated as much as in any professional sense. The play on words is crucial. Alex's earliest exposure to stigmatization, which is palpable in the way he views his father's professional life, is inextricably linked to his father's constipation, which is inextricably linked, as well, to his emasculation at the hands of his wife (who pushes him aside in her adoration of Alex). It's all intertwined. There is no such thing as "discrimination against Jews in America," per se, for Alex Portnoy growing up; this is just one constituent part of what is at stake for his father prostrate on the toilet. Furthermore, given that Alex's reflections are so often tongue-in-cheek, it is difficult to know the extent to which he might think of his father as actually "oppressed" in any real way. He seems more often to think of him as trapped in his sense of his own oppression: "The self-confidence and the cunning, the imperiousness and the contacts, all that enabled the blond and blue-eyed of his generation to lead, to inspire, to command, if need be to oppress—he could not summon a hundredth part of it. How could he oppress?—he *was* the oppressed. How could he wield power?—he *was* the powerless. How could he enjoy triumph, when he so despised the triumphant—and probably the very idea."[33]

Here we begin to see Roth's critique of the schlemiel tradition in modern Jewish literature.[34] This is crucial to the context of *Portnoy's Complaint*, so it will require some explanation. Irving Howe helped to make this tradition salient when he published an edited anthology in 1953 entitled *A Treasury of Yiddish Stories*.[35] In the words of one of his biographers, Howe set about to construct a Yiddish literary tradition that would comprise "the sacred texts of secular Jewishness."[36] In Howe's long introduction to this volume lies the "kernel" of "a moral code for secular Jews who either no longer believed in, or considered themselves morally superior to, the Torah."[37] This moral code refused despair despite the catastrophes of modern history, reveled in the ordinary and the domestic, and saw a kind of inverted heroism among the most humble.[38] The hero of Howe's Yiddish literary tradition is *dos kleine mentshele*—"the little man."[39]

"*Dos kleine menschele*," Howe writes, "appears again and again at the center of Yiddish fiction: it is he, long-suffering, persistent, lovingly ironic, whom the Yiddish writers celebrate; it is the poor but proud householder trying to maintain his status in the Jewish world even as he grows poorer and poorer who appeals to their imagination far more than might an Aeneas or an Ahab. Anyone, they seem to say, can learn to conquer the world, but only a Tevye or a literary descendent of Tevye can learn to live in it."[40] The hero of Yiddish literature, of Howe's sacred canon of secular Jewishness, is passive. He endures his suffering patiently. He does not rebel. But he is also highly motivated. He pursues something doggedly, even if his pursuits necessarily end in folly. At the same time, unlike Ahab, he is not driven by some personal conquest-obsession: he is a householder. His goals are domestic, familial, community goals. His personal goals do not put him at odds with his family, though his bumbling incompetence might.

Power in the Yiddish tradition, according to Howe, is the power that radiates in a loving home, that connects loving parents to their children, and that reaches out compassionately to the vulnerable and abused. "For whatever the deficiencies of Yiddish culture, the power of love remains: for the child, the poor, the weak, for the insulted and injured everywhere. It is the power at the heart of the Yiddish tradition."[41] This is the Yiddish value of *heymishkeyt*.[42]

The little man is powerless in the gentile world, but he has an alternative kind of power. And, further complicating his "passivity," he does not really accept the world as it is given: he plays with the meaning of his suffering ironically. But his is not a cold, disinterested, satirical, or merely parasitic irony. He remains ever-strongly rooted in loving relationships and plays with meaning on their behalf. By contrasting him to Aeneas, Howe opposes his Yiddish hero directly to virtues associated with violence and conquest. He sees heroism in restraint, irony, and endurance, not in the quest to dominate the world.

On Howe's reading, the Yiddish literary tradition is a critique of Western civilization. His sources of secular Jewishness reject "the whole ethos of historical aggrandizement as it has come to us from the Greek drama and been colored by the era of Christian expansion."[43] Through the theme of "antiheroism," Yiddish writers express "their contempt for what the outer world takes to be greatness but which they often feel is no more than an appetite for blood."[44] Howe's Yiddish ethos does not admire but is instead profoundly suspicious of the powerful: the achievement of greatness is presumptively the result of a dominative will.

And this suspicion is often couched within the broad humorous sensibility that also characterizes Yiddish literature, in which folk humor is prominently represented.[45] Howe describes it as the "first and last line of defense, though in a sense an impregnable defense" for a burdened and beleaguered people.[46] On Howe's reading, the thickness of humor in Yiddish fiction functions as a weapon of the weak and an opportunity for readers in solidarity to acknowledge their distinctive form of life. The humor serves to invigorate an idealization of Old World *Gemeinschaft* in Yiddish.[47] This is also accomplished through the predisposition in Yiddish literature to use archetypal characters, rather than characters with complex individual psychologies.

On Howe's account, only "a culture that has bitten into the apple of power and success, is likely to indulge itself in the luxury of individual self-examination."[48] The subject in Yiddish fiction is, instead, seen as "the agent and embodiment of the community, who must be prevented, if he shows any such inclinations, from tumbling into the pits of Western egotism."[49] Yiddish literature thus aspires "toward cultural expressions of a collective type."[50]

In the American postwar climate, where Jews saw enough tokens of acceptance to feel optimistic and free to be more publicly Jewish, Howe's anthology offered an alternative convention of civility to that of the dominant "Western egotist" he distrusted and resented.[51] Clumped around the dominant convention were the heroism of conquest, rebellion, violence, might, greatness, historic aggrandizement, coldness, Christianity, the West, indulgent self-examination, and disconnection from community. Clumped around dos kleine mentshele were refusal of despair, the ordinary and domestic, long-suffering, persistence, loving irony, humor, imagination, passivity, patience, family, community, solidarity with the poor, weak, insulted, and injured, heymishkeyt, *edelkeyt,* Jewishness, restraint, tolerance, and cohesive community.[52]

Howe had drawn his own political conception of citizenship to counter the mainstream American picture. Citizens, he seems to suggest, ought not to valorize confidence, willfulness, strength, control, empowerment, or basking in the admiration of others. Citizenship should hold a different bundle of virtues altogether: "*The virtue of powerlessness, the power of helplessness, the company of the dispossessed, the sanctity of the insulted and the injured.*"[53] It would be better, he seems to say, to live among people who respect antiheroic endurance in themselves and others than among those who respect heroism in themselves and others. I will call this the value of schlemielkeyt.

Compelled by the trauma of the Holocaust, and the simultaneous appearance of unprecedented opportunities for Jews in the United States, Howe looked back at Yiddish fiction in 1953 and saw the tradition of "the little man" and the value of schlemielkeyt juxtaposed against the tradition of the Western, Christian, self-aggrandizing, violent individual. By the end of the 1960s, this alternative picture clearly dominated Jewish literature, film, theater, and other media. Saul Bellow's translation of Isaac Bashevis Singer's "Gimpel the Fool," which appeared in Howe's anthology, was popular. Bellow's *Herzog* appeared in 1964, Bernard Malamud's *The Fixer* in 1966. These works would later be considered canonical Jewish American fiction and important works of American fiction more broadly. Of course, Woody Allen's characters began to gain visibility in the late 1960s as well, with *Play It Again, Sam* appearing on Broadway in 1969 and a series of iconic movies to follow: *Bananas, Sleeper, Love and Death.*[54] The cover story of *Life* magazine on July 11, 1969, was "Dusty and the Duke: A Choice of Heroes," and featured a graphic with Dustin Hoffman (at the time of *Graduate* fame) slouching, standing on the hat of John Wayne.[55] Such was the extent of the visibility and plausibility of this alternative picture.

The primordially important stuff of Alex Portnoy's childhood includes the value of schlemielkeyt, which he experiences as stifling. He has contempt for his father's self-destructive rejection of confidence, power, and triumph. But he loves his father and he has also imbibed some of his father's schlemielkeyt, along with his contempt for the goyim and their self-sovereignty. So Alex ends up sometimes reeling with contempt for his own contempt.

When he is in a mood to be critical of schlemielkeyt, he admires the self-respect of the non-Jews that his father despises. For instance, consider this description of Alex's college girlfriend Kay Campbell engaging in political discussion: "Unencumbered by the garbled syntax of the apocalypse or the ill-mannered vocabulary of desperation, without the perspiring upper lip, the constricted and air-hungry throat, the flush of loathing on the forehead."[56] She demonstrated: "Authority without the temper. Virtue without the self-congratulation. Confidence sans swagger or condescension. Come on, let's be fair and give the *goyim* their due, Doctor: when they are impressive, they are very impressive."[57] Here is a self-respecting person that we can really *respect*—someone not satisfied to embrace schlemielkeyt in order to serve a deeper ressentiment.

On the other hand, lest we think that Alex unambiguously takes the side of his father's presumed enemies, it is worth noting his behavior in relation to Sarah Maulsby (nickname: "the Pilgrim").[58] This is a nasty bit in the book (one among many), and it shows the deep and perverse legacy of stigmatization that haunts Alexander Portnoy. Sarah Maulsby is from an elite family. She is from the very triumphant "blond and blue-eyed" WASPs that have kept his father on a steady diet of All-Bran and prunes.[59] When she refuses to accede to his request for oral sex, he stops seeing her abruptly, leaving her humiliated. "Sally Maulsby was just something nice a son once did for his dad. A little vengeance on Mr. Lindabury for all those nights and Saturdays Jack Portnoy spent collecting down in the colored district. A little bonus extracted from Boston & Northeastern, for all those years of service, and exploitation."[60]

Here Alex seems entirely to have absorbed his father's resentment. The difference, though, is that he does not respond with resignation as he imagines his father to have responded all those years. He responds with vengeance. But his "vengeance" is not a corrective to past injustice of the sort Kay Campbell would inspire. It is not a moral reckoning undertaken with confidence and virtue. It is, instead, a cheap and degrading act undertaken on an innocent and vulnerable young woman. This is the legacy of stigmatization that he carries. And it is perhaps corroboration of a point about schlemielkeyt made by the historian Paul Breines. In his book *Tough Jews: Political Fantasies and the Moral Dilemma of American Jewry*, Breines describes a disturbing process by which the picture of the Jew as essentially a weak victim has produced an agitated response from Jewish men living in macho societies who are humiliated by such a picture.[61] These men, he thinks, are likely to be attracted to a particular version of Zionism—which goes back to Sholem Asch's "Kola Street" and perhaps most notoriously to Max Nordau's famous 1903 essay on "muscle Jews"[62]—that specifically repudiates this picture.

Breines sees schlemielkeyt as, ironically, integral to this version of Zionism, which purports to overcome the "little man." In Breines's view, "Zionism needs its weak and gentle Jewish counterparts to give moral justification to Jewish participation in the world of bodies, specifically, of physical violence, including killing or even sadism. To put the matter most starkly: the image of Jewish victimization vindicates the image of the Jewish victimizer."[63] Breines sees a danger in the perpetuation of the "little man" as a picture of Jewish political subjectivity because it represses the kinds of aggressive fantasies that Jews have—like everybody else—and leaves Jewish men prone to exaggerated exhilaration in response to the possibility of toughness and violence. Ultimately it functions as a ready justification for violence on behalf of Jews.[64]

Breines claims that when American Jews—especially American Jewish *men*—are talking about Middle East politics or Israel or the Holocaust or anti-Semitism or terrorism, "they are also speaking with the passions aroused by images of tough and weak Jewish bodies that come into play in the primal, tough Jew experience. They are not, in other words, speaking only on the basis of rational political interests and aims."[65] The "primal tough Jew experience" is the moment of exhilaration felt by a Jew who has been raised on images of weakness and gentleness when presented with images of Jewish power and violence. In his treatment of Sarah Maulsby, Alex Portnoy is arguably reacting pathologically to his father's self-indulgent valorization of weakness and resignation exactly like a "tough Jew"—he seizes his opportunity for physical empowerment, preemptively justified no matter the extent of its violence or even sadism.

AFFIRMING ANIMALITY AT THE *SHVITZ*

Alex is entirely confused about how to be a "full-blooded" American, about how to be different from his father, who has remained anemic and resentful on the margins. In effect, this is how he explains his frantic sexual obsession with non-Jewish women: "What I'm saying, Doctor, is that I don't seem to stick my dick up these girls, as much as I stick it up their backgrounds—as though through fucking I will discover America. *Conquer* America—maybe that's more like it."[66] Alex seems to have tasked his penis with overcoming the legacy of stigmatization. While this is sometimes shocking, sometimes funny, sometimes morally objectionable, and sometimes just cringe-inducing in the book, it is also very obviously pathological (from our perspective as readers and from Alex's perspective). It looks like the kind of "distortion" of self-understanding that Fanon claimed to identify in the psychology of the wretched of the earth.[67]

But Alex gives us a clue about nonpathological Jewish male bodies, too. His "member," he understands, need not be a weapon wielded in the quixotic conquest of shikse-America. I am thinking of Alex's account of his childhood trips with his father to the steambath, the *shvitz*. On these trips Alex would descend into the lair of the Jewish man-beast: "If it were not for the abrupt thunderclap of a fart, or the snores sporadically shooting up around me like machine-gun fire, I would believe we were in a morgue, and for some strange reason undressing in front of the dead."[68]

In the shvitz Alex dances around without shame. He describes it as something like a prehistoric landscape:

> I lose touch instantaneously with that ass-licking little boy who runs home after school with his *A*'s in his hand, the little over-earnest innocent endlessly in search of the key to that unfathomable mystery, his mother's approbation, and am back in some sloppy watery time, before there were families such as we know them, before there were toilets and tragedies such as we know them, a time of amphibious creatures, plunging brainless hulking things, with wet meaty flanks and steaming torsos. . . . It is as though they have ridden the time machine back to an age when they existed as some herd of Jewish animals, whose only utterance is *oy, oy* . . . They appear, at long last, my father and his fellow sufferers, to have returned to the habitat in which they can be natural. A place without *goyim* and women.[69]

It is unfortunate that freedom from shame for these men entails separation from non-Jews and women. The better shvitz time machine, one would like to imagine, would somehow go even farther back into prehistory where proto-amphibious creatures predate even these antagonisms. This, though, is not imaginable for these Jewish men, whose Jewishness and masculinity are steeped in the legacy of stigmatization. But I think it is very important that the shvitz is where Alex feels "natural" and sees the men in his little world of primordially important stuff as "natural." After all, I can easily imagine a Jewish character positing the synagogue as such a place, conforming to Will Herberg's postwar picture of self-respecting Jewishness as definitively "religious." But in *Portnoy's Complaint* this site is rejected as a place where a Jew (really a Jewish *man*) can be free of pretense, unguarded, and vulnerable. Instead, the shvitz.

The shvitz is a cavern of animality, a steaming farty cave of Jewish man-beasts. This is where these men can *be* what is disgusting about them to the rest of world: where they can be threateningly mortal animals. There is no shame in the company of the resting herd. In fact, it is where primordial shame (in Nussbaum's sense) and Jewish shame (which has been produced in part by non-Jewish stigmatizers who have not acknowledged *their own* primordial shame) can find relief. If only the Jew-beasts in the shvitz could reevolve under better conditions—who knows how they could flourish? If they could reevolve *not* under conditions of stigmatization, could they, perhaps, avoid the adaptive preferences that so distort and confuse their efforts to live well?

This is what we are left to wonder about in the case of Alexander Portnoy. Let me explain. In the shvitz, Alex remembers actually feeling admiration for his father: for his father's penis, his *shlong*. "*Shlong*," he reflects, "the word somehow catches exactly the brutishness, the *meatishness*, that I admire so, the sheer mindless, weighty, and unselfconscious dangle of that living piece of hose through which he passes streams of water as thick and strong as rope—while I deliver forth slender yellow threads that my euphemistic mother calls 'a sis.' A sis, I think, is undoubtedly what my sister makes."[70]

The one thing about his father that provokes effusive even extravagant admiration is his father's shlong, which can dangle mightily in the shvitz: "Oh, thank God! Thank God! At least *he* had the cock and the balls! Pregnable (putting it mildly) as his masculinity was in this world of *goyim* with golden hair and silver tongues, between his legs (God bless my father!) he was constructed like a man of consequence, two big healthy balls such as a king would be proud to put on display, and a *shlong* of magisterial length and girth."[71] At home, on the other hand, Alex's mother screams at his father to shut the door when he pees because of "the example he might set" for young Alex. "If only I could have nourished myself upon the depths of his vulgarity," Alex recalls resentfully, "instead of that too becoming a source of shame. Shame and shame and shame and shame—every place I turn something else to be ashamed of."[72]

I'm not sure what it would really mean for Alex to have nourished himself upon the depths of his father's vulgarity, as opposed to being compelled to view it as a source of shame. We are meant to think, in part, that this may have allowed Alex to pursue his desires without inhibition. But I think that Alex's aggressive triumphalist sexuality may also be read as a pathologization of his respect for his father's penis, which is itself already pathologically exaggerated as a result of Alex's tough Jew response to his father's pitiful schlemielkeyt. I mean that Jack's penis would not have been so important to Alex if the two of them were not sweltering in the legacy of stigmatization. But that's precisely where they were stuck.

Fixated on the size of his father's penis, the only claim his father had to his respect, full of resentment toward the non-Jewish world, turned on by the sexual taboo of non-Jewish women, and turned on by the transgression of taboos altogether—Alex's primordially important stuff is a recipe for disaster.[73] On my reading, his magnified admiration for his father's lumbering and beleaguered shlong, which is already a result of his father's otherwise unadmirable masculinity, is distorted *into* the maniacal will driving his own unappeasable prick. In the shvitz, though, penises need not be differentiated from the "wet meaty flanks and steaming torsos" and other hulking parts. Alex's father's penis stands out to Alex because he is on the lookout for any sign of potency. I can't help but think that the better outcome for Alex was not uninhibited sexual desire—the outcome that he expects would have followed had his mother not shamed his father, among other things.

The better outcome was a reevolution of the prehistoric Jewish animal upon emergence from the shvitz, one not adapted to the weight of stigmatization. The shvitz was the right place to go, given the circumstances. It was a better place to go than the institutions of groupist ideologies (the synagogue and the State of Israel, for example). But the shvitz can only do so much when one emerges from it back into stigmatization. The book knows these limits. After all, *Portnoy's Complaint* functions a bit like a shvitz in itself: Roth takes us into the utterly exposed, unprotected, physical world of a certain male Jewishness. In this he is not unlike Lenny

Bruce, as I have described him in the previous chapter. Both Bruce and Roth play at a deep vulnerable stratum of human animality with the fraught materials of their social life. For both, however, there is no imaginable primordiality that takes us beyond the legacy of historical conflict and oppression they both carry with their Jewish groupness.

To recap, here is a snapshot of just the few elements of Alexander Portnoy's primordially important stuff that I have covered: "it had to do with finding out the kind of little boy I was when I thought she wasn't around," "am I to be allowed to think I can just starve myself for no good reason in the world?", "the book of life," "they will eat *anything*, anything they can get their big *goy* hands on! And the terrifying corollary, *they will do anything as well*," *You Know Me, I'll try Anything Once*, constipation, the Company, "How could he enjoy triumph, when he so despised the triumphant—and probably the very idea," shvitz, shlong. Indeed, this is just how we should imagine a person carrying his or her primordially important stuff: in heuristic fragments like this, jumbles of shorthand, hyperlinks that access the deepest thoughts, cares, and motivations of the soul.

Before moving on, I want to make clear that Alex's monologue, which constitutes the book *Portnoy's Complaint*, is not just a hateful rant against his parents—against his overbearing "Jewish mother" and pathetic schmuck of a "Jewish father." For instance, at one point he doubles back on himself, putting his lamentations about his father into perspective. He asks, how unusual is it, after all, to not at all relish what one's father has to offer? "Why must it continue to cause such pain? At this late date! Doctor, what should I rid myself of, tell me, the hatred . . . or the love? Because I haven't even begun to mention everything I remember with pleasure—I mean with a rapturous, biting sense of loss!"[74] His confused ambivalence is palpable. And then he is moving. He reflects with deep sincerity on "memories of practically nothing—and yet they seem moments of history as crucial to my being as the moment of my conception . . . so piercing is my gratitude—yes, *my* gratitude!—so sweeping and unqualified is my love. Yes, me, with sweeping and unqualified love!"[75]

This is truly an account of the primordially important stuff of childhood. This is the *good* stuff, the pictures of goodness that one carries around like Polaroids in the back pocket to shuffle through nostalgically, the stuff that one is always looking somehow to recapture: his mother pointing to the purple in the sky, his sister counting the supports on the bridge as they drive by on a road trip, his father walking with him in the "good winter piney air" (a poetic phrase he adores: "I couldn't be more thrilled if I were Wordsworth's kid!"), his father's routine of putting his watch in his shoe before going into the water to swim (which he himself repeats to this day).[76]

At one point, taking a metaperspective on everything that's come before, he reflects: "Is this truth I'm delivering up, or is it just plain *kvetching*? Or is *kvetching* for people like me a *form* of truth? Regardless, my conscience wishes to make it known, before the beefing begins anew, that *at the time* my boyhood was not this thing I feel so estranged from and resentful of now. . . . I don't remember that I was one of those kids who went around wishing he lived in another house with other people, whatever my unconscious yearnings may have been in that direction."[77] From this metaperspective, it is hard to take any of the preceding indictment of his parents seriously. One begins to wonder if Alex is in on the joke about the Jewish guy who walks into the therapist's office and starts ranting about his parents that frames the book.

ALEX'S ORDEAL OF CIVILITY

I will return to this suspicion, that Alex is on the joke, in a moment. First, I need to say more about the function of stigmatization in Alex's reflections and the personal experiences of stigma that he recalls (beyond what he has imbibed from his parents' experiences). The ice skating scene at Irvington Park is paradigmatic. This is where he has his first opportunity to interact with non-Jewish girls, and he is, predictably, in a panic. "'Portnoy, yes, it's an old French name, a corruption of *porte noir*, meaning black door or gate. Apparently in the Middle Ages in France the door to our family manor house was painted . . .' et cetera and so forth. No, no, they will hear the *oy* at the end and the jig will be up."[78] Alex is terrified to be found out, to have his secret revealed, to find that his fly is open and his Jewishness is exposed for all to see.

His *nose* puts him in a particular panic. "It actually seems that this sprouting of my beak dates exactly from the time that I discovered the *shikses* skating in Irvington Park—as though my own nose bone has taken it upon itself to act as my parents' agent! Skating with *shikses?* Just you try it, wise guy. Remember Pinocchio? Well, that is nothing compared with what is going to happen to you. They'll laugh and laugh, howl and hoot—and worse, calling you Goldberg in the bargain, send you on your way roasting with fury and resentment."[79] Without question "the nose" is the primary appendage of Jewish stigmatization. And the burden on Alex to somehow hide or justify his nose—a weight presumably unlike anything being carried by the other kids skating on the ice—is the legacy of stigmatization that he must endure.

If Jack Portnoy experienced stigmatization primarily in relation to the Company, or to Mr. Lindabury, Alex felt it primarily in relation to the girls at Irvington Park. Of course, Jack could point to his stifled upward mobility as a justification for his resentment (whereas Alex gives us reason to believe that he may also have been stifled by his own rejection of the idea of triumph). We have no idea whether or not the ice skating girls were even capable of the thoughts Alex attributed to them. As readers, we are given no reason to believe that they in fact intended to ridicule any Jew that would dare step on the ice. Actually, Alex discovers that many of the non-Jewish girls he longs for *long in their own right for a nice Jewish boy.*[80]

None of this matters, though. The only thing that is important is Alex's palpable anxiety about the stigma he carries. This is what it means to have fraught groupness as an integral part of one's primordially important stuff. It means being haunted by anxiety, by a feeling that one needs to hide or, otherwise, to mount some justification for oneself. It means always wondering if one knows the true picture of one's situation. Alex's anxiety about his nose is a result of the historical stigma attached to the "Jewish nose" that is woven into his Jewish groupness. This is an anxiety that is constitutive of identification as Jewish in his world.

A look at the fate of Kay Campbell, "the Pumpkin," will further illustrate the impact of Alex's fraught Jewish groupness on his life. I have already quoted Alex's description of her intelligence, reasonableness, and virtue. So what happened to her? How did their relationship turn out? Alex goes home from college one year with Kay to spend Thanksgiving (a painful phone call to his parents, of course, which he describes as his "Emancipation Proclamation").[81] While there he cannot rid himself of the feeling that he will be exposed and humiliated as a Jew, regardless of the fact that her parents are, in actuality, impeccably hospitable. It's the Irvington Park skating rink all over again. In this "pressure-cooker" (as far as he is concerned), his primordially important stuff is piping hot and all-consuming; the world quickly breaks down to its most fundamental elements: "Everything I see, taste, touch, I think, 'Goyish!'"[82] In spite of himself, though, Alex seems to survive Thanksgiving at the Campbells' without any incident to validate his frantic paranoia and manic differentiation of everything into Jewish and goyish.

What, then, finally undoes Alex's healthy relationship with someone who doesn't let him down, who is every bit as smart as he is, whom he truly admires? They are contemplating marriage, after Kay misses her period, and Alex says, off the cuff and ironically, "And you'll convert, right?" She responds, "Why would I want to do a thing like that?," and this "put our Portnoy in a rage."[83] Alex and Kay had bonded over their shared rejection of religion. They were devotees of Bertrand Russell and Dylan Thomas. "How could I be feeling a wound," Alex wonders, "in a place where I was not even vulnerable?"[84] As readers, we know perfectly well that this is one of the places where he is *most* vulnerable. The "religion" of his family is, of course, no more the essence of Jewishness for Alex than is his nose. But both are irritated and extremely sensitive and no salve (atheism, poetry, or even a nose job, one suspects) could reduce the embarrassingly uncomfortable redness. The end of his relationship with Kay Campbell is quite sad, actually. As he remembers, "it would seem that I never forgave her: in the weeks following our false alarm, she came to seem to me boringly predictable in conversation, and about as desirable as blubber in bed."[85]

It seems clear that Alex's behavior is self-destructive. He gets in his own way. And this makes his choice to work with a therapist particularly admirable and wise. For our purposes, though, it is better to say: his stigmatized groupness is, in this case, a disruptive or limiting constituent part of his overall self-understanding.[86] Be careful, though: *Portnoy's Complaint* is not an autobiography written by Alexander Portnoy. There is no such person. This is a novel written by Philip Roth. Given the metaperspective on identification produced by framing the entire book as one big Jewish joke at the end, it is implausible to assume that the book earnestly takes a position against Jewishness, as though it were a congenital misfortune.[87] It is not a book earnestly claiming that Jewishness is a fundamentally self-destructive groupness. It cannot be a book *of* such self-hatred directed against Jewishness. It is a book precisely *about* this kind of "Jewish self-hatred" (among other things)—it *plays* *with* "Jewish self-hatred."[88]

There are many passages that clearly complicate any account of Alex Portnoy as simply a pitiable patient suffering from his Jewishness. The primordially important stuff of his childhood—*including his Jewishness*—is every bit as much the basis for his aspirations to health, flourishing, and goodness as it is the basis for the failure of his aspirations. Perhaps Kay Campbell seemed good to Alex because she appeared to be the very opposite of everything that was bad about the mother he remembers tortuously. But not all his pictures of health, flourishing, and goodness are *negations* of his primordially important stuff.

SWEET DISTORTED JEWISHNESS FOR "FOUL-MOUTHED SWEETHEARTS"

To be sure, sexual liberation is the aspiration that Alex beats us over the head with.[89] But Alex's penis is such a weapon of revenge, so tightly gripped and wielded angrily, that it is difficult to see it as liberatory.[90] On the other hand, he does offer us glimpses of far more plausible ideals, some of which are deeply rooted in the same Jewish world that he seems so completely to contemn. Recall the importance of his sense of ownership over his penis for understanding his penis-obsession—"My wang was all I really had that I could call my own."[91] Masturbation and sexual escapades function, in lieu of this, as rare exercises of self-determination. But he was also able to feel self-determining while playing center field in baseball as a kid, "where no one will appropriate to himself anything that I say is *mine!*"[92] Playing center field, he feels an "ease, the self-assurance, the simple and essential affiliation with what is going on," not because he was such a great player, but because "one knew exactly, and down to the smallest particular, how a center fielder should conduct himself."[93]

He imagines that there are people who live their whole lives feeling this way and he is desperate to be one of them. He is describing something like "self-respect": confidence and conviction in pursuit of one's ends.

Self-respect is part of this story. It is contrasted to what he experiences in most of his everyday life: friction, anxiety, complexity, and estrangement from himself and everything around him—it is contrasted to his bewilderment about how best, in the end, to conduct himself. But he knows self-respect. He knows it to be good and laments its absence.

One passage where he laments this absence is particularly telling. He does a funny bit about a band of "nice Jewish boys" like himself—fellows whose primordially stigmatized Jewish groupness is experienced like his own—all stacked in bunks on some tottering ship: "the stories we tell, as the big ship pitches and rolls, the vying we do—who had the most castrating mother, who the most benighted father, I can match you, you bastard, humiliation for humiliation, shame for shame. . . . Oh, my Jewish men friends! My dirty-mouthed guilt-ridden brethren! My sweethearts! My mates! Will this fucking ship ever stop pitching? When? *When*, so that we can leave off complaining how sick we are—and go out into the air, and live!"[94]

Would Alex really prefer to be "free"? Would he really prefer to live an unestranged life of self-respecting action with no distorted, convoluted, painful, hilarious rants and no solidarity with his foulmouthed sweethearts? This is vintage Alex: his prophetic call for liberation is pronounced in a style that unabashedly luxuriates in the very "oppression" and "sickness" from which he calls to be liberated and healed. Sometimes I think Alex feels most guilty of all about how much he loves everything he hates about his parents, Jewishness, and himself.[95]

His most expansive vision of goodness in the book also happens to be about his "foul-mouthed sweethearts." He remembers watching the men in his neighborhood play softball on Sunday mornings (he remembers this on a plane to Israel—he thinks maybe he'll be "natural" in the Jewish state; it becomes very clear at the end of the episode that he should have taken a trip to the shvitz instead). The men ridicule each other hilariously in the field:

I'll tell you, they are an endearing lot! I sit in the wooden stands alongside first base . . . laughing my head off. I cannot imagine myself living out my life any other place but here. Why leave, why go, when there is everything here that I will ever want? The ridiculing, the joking, the acting-up, the pretending—anything for a laugh! I love it! And yet underneath it all, *they mean it, they are in dead earnest.* . . . Losing and winning is not a joke . . . and yet it is! And that's what charms me most of all. Fierce as the competition is, they cannot resist clowning and kibitzing around. Putting on a show! How I am going to love growing up to be a Jewish man! Living forever in the Weequahic section, and playing softball on Chancellor Avenue from nine to one on Sundays, a perfect joining of clown and competition, kibitzing wiseguy and dangerous long-ball hitter.[96]

Alex sees something to aspire to in these men that is entirely continuous with his primordial Jewishness. And when he lands in Israel he's weeping as he remembers the games he would watch as a nine-year-old. He doesn't weep because of "a first glimpse of the national homeland, the ingathering of an exile," but because of his memory of himself at nine: "a back-talker and a *kvetch* . . . but a laugher and a kidder too, don't forget that, an enthusiast! a romantic! a mimic! a nine-year-old lover of life! fiery with such simple, neighborhoody dreams!"[97] He would call out to his mom that he's off to the field "-*to watch the men!*," and that's the phrase that gets him crying: "Because I love those men! I want to grow up to *be* one of those men!"[98] These Jewish men he admires are not sober and dignified. They're jokers. And they *really play*: they play softball, which offers the joys of straightforward center-fieldership, but they also ransack the game with trash talk and joking around.

These games must have burned a deep imprint in Alex's primordially important stuff because what "charms" him most of all is how for these guys "Losing and winning is not a joke . . . and yet it is!" Alex wants to win. He wants to be a winner. He doesn't want to be a schlemiel like his father, who seems to take opposition to winning as an important value. He wants to fulfill his desires and be a great moral hero like Abraham Lincoln.[99] This is not a joke, folks. And yet manifestly it is! Doesn't Alex seem to love *his own* ability to whip us from grinning to cringing and back and forth and on and on? When "the doctor" at the end of the book drops the punch line, "So, now vee may perhaps to begin. Yes?"—doesn't some of the humor come from the doctor meaning something like: "Well, I'm glad to see you're enjoying yourself. Can we start the serious therapy now?"[100]

METAPERSPECTIVAL INTIMACY AND PRAXIS
IN *PORTNOY'S COMPLAINT*

Let me try to explain the metaperspectival play that Roth offers the reader of *Portnoy's Complaint* by using a kind of "state of nature" reconstruction. Here's what I mean. Imagine Moishe. Let's say he lives in his world naively, without ever taking a metaperspective. Now here comes Shmule visiting from a few towns away. He's got some jokes to tell, and he tells them to Moishe. When Moishe hears the jokes, he laughs his *tukhes* off. He laughs so hard because the jokes seem to capture all sorts of aspects of his own personal world, which had never come into focus quite like they do in Shmule's jokes: stuff about his parents, his everyday life, his friends, and so on. Shmule's jokes use stock characters, commonplaces, themes, etc., that seem to "sum up" Moishe's world in a funny way. Moishe has that familiar feeling: "that is *sooo* true!!" It is the feeling that one has when hearing humor of the it's funny because it's true variety. Moishe is, of course, excited to go off and tell his friends all his new jokes, since his friends occupy a similar world and will laugh their tukheses off too. Moishe has graduated from naïveté to a metaperspective on his own experiences and relationships.

But ever since Shmule came along with his jokes, Moishe sees everything in his world as an example of one of the stock characters, commonplaces, themes, in a good "Shmule joke." Now people, events, things in Moishe's everyday life are funny because "hey, it's like that joke!" Before the jokes were funny because they resembled his world, now his world is funny because it resembles the jokes. But Moishe is now a jokester himself. His friends so enjoyed hearing him tell Shmule's jokes that Moishe has started coming up with new jokes—modeled on Shmule's jokes. His friends like the new jokes, and they start coming up with their own jokes. They become a regular band of jokesters. Only now everything in their shared world is an opportunity for a joke or an example of something captured by a joke.

Soon one of the gang, Yitze, feels that the jokes are getting a bit stale. They are all about the naive world that Moishe captured with the first jokes he told, which he learned from Shmule. That "first world" has, by now, been totally pilfered for jokes and is at this point impossible to look at without constantly thinking in the back of one's mind, "hey, it's like that joke!" Well, Yitze, that smart-ass, he starts telling jokes that are funny because they capture the new world of this band of jokesters. Because now everyday life includes telling jokes about everyday life. Yitze starts telling jokes about how they're all telling jokes. His jokes are about a "second world." And this catches on too. So now they're a band of jokesters who joke about being jokesters. They joke in a "third world" about the "second world." Uh oh. Here comes Mendele!

Somehow Mendele is able to craft a joke about joking about being a jokester. Somehow Mendele sets up a "fourth world," from which to joke about the "third world" that Yitze had set up. Philip Roth writes *Portnoy's Complaint* from the perspective of this "fourth world." Alexander Portnoy humorously fantasizing aloud about his "nice Jewish boy" comrades on the proverbial tottering ship, joking about their "castrating Jewish mothers" and "benighted Jewish fathers," is Yitze. Alex is joking about his world of "foul-mouthed sweethearts" who joke about their childhoods. Structurally speaking, then, Philip Roth is Mendele joking about the "third world" that Alex (Yitze) sets up in order to joke about the "second world" of his foulmouthed sweethearts. Well, sort of. Because here's the twist: Alex isn't one of a band of jokesters laughing about the aptness of some stock character from a metaperspective. He *is* the stock character! And—hopefully you're sitting down because Philip Roth is about to blow your mind—he knows it!!

"Spring me from this role I play of the smothered son in the Jewish joke!" He cries.

> Because it's beginning to pall a little, at thirty-three! And also it *hoits*, you know, there is *pain* involved, a little human suffering is being felt, if I may take it upon myself to say so—only that's the part that Sam Levenson leaves *out!* . . . Help, help, my son the doctor is drowning! [the old joke goes]—ha ha *ha*, ha ha *ha*, only what about the *pain*, Myron Cohen! What about the guy who is actually drowning! Actually sinking beneath an ocean of parental relentlessness! What about him—who happens, Myron Cohen, to be *me!* Doctor, *please*, I can't live anymore in a world given its meaning and dimension by some vulgar nightclub clown.[101]

When we think about Alex's inability to maintain any confidence, conviction, or actual success in his pursuit of a good life (whatever a "good life" might mean for him), we have to remember that his condition may result largely from the fact that he is, literally, a stereotype—he *is* a stock character represented in a book.[102] He has the extraordinary self-awareness to know that he is, in fact, the Jewish son in one very long Jewish joke. But think about this for a moment: in my state of nature reconstruction of ever-higher levels of metaperspectival joking, I said that after a while the world may start to look like the jokes, rather than the other way around. I think that this is one of the things we worry about when we worry about the psychological impact of stigmatization.

We worry, as a result of "misrecognition" or "internalization" or some such, people will get trapped in the stereotypes, commonplaces, stock characters, and themes that circulate in the culture of a society not yet just. Especially because there are some really nasty stereotypes out there, and the problem of remainders means they will persist, even in the best society that we can realistically imagine. This is why we worry with Fanon about the impact of fraught groupness on the primordially important stuff of childhood. Anyone in this condition will be like Alex, stuck from the very beginning in some tense differentiation—"The very first distinction I learned . . . was not night and day, or hot and cold, but *goyische* and Jewish!"—and haunted by all the anger, fear, distrust, resentment, ambivalence, confusion, aggression, lack of confidence, lack of conviction, and so on that comes with it.

Roth's answer to this problem is to invite readers to have an intimate experience with Alexander Portnoy, but also with the "implied author" and "flesh-and-blood author" of *Portnoy's Complaint*.[103] In fact, the book invites its readers into an experience of intimacy that shares much in common with what Lenny Bruce fostered in his stand-up. Entering a relationship with *Portnoy's Complaint,* the reader will entertain Alex's varied judgments about his parents, himself, and others. In the process, the reader is exposed to the most intimate and embarrassing parts of Alex's life, which prominently includes the grievances, obsessions, and perversions that emanate from his primordially important, fraught Jewish groupness. But however intimate the relationship with Alex might be, the more profound relationship on offer is with the implied author of *Portnoy's Complaint*.

The structure of the book demands that we posit a "joke teller" to tell the joke: this posited joke teller, who gets the jokes in the book but also gets the joke that *is* the book (and has actually written that joke) is the implied author. I will refer to the implied author simply as *Portnoy's Complaint*. We are invited into an intimate relationship with *Portnoy's Complaint* not as people with serious religions, gods, cultures, races, traditions, or nations to serve. We are invited as people with parents and primordially important stuff to serve—parents and primordially important stuff that we are always living against and for.[104] We are invited to appear fully exposed with our dirty little secrets about our coming of age, bare in the open for all to see. And when our primordial relationships with our parents are full of religious, ethnic, racial, and other qualities of groupness, then these idiosyncrasies and absurdities of our groupness too should be exposed.[105]

Within this intimate, playful relationship lies Roth's response to Fanon. Alex Portnoy's penis is Fanon's instrument of transgressive bodily praxis.[106] Alex is desperate to recreate himself through self-determining acts of fucking. Masturbation and having sex with non-Jewish women are, in Alex's mind, a liberatory praxis. But we, as readers, know that Alex is trapped in a "vicious circle" of self-assertion and self-doubt and that he is mistaking what (he thinks) is powerful in him for what is good for him, even as this distracts him from what he really cares about, what is really *good*, to him.[107] Then again, as in the case of Fanon, we have no good reason to conclude, finally, that "Alex *really* aspires to the life of the baseball playing Jewish men of Newark" or "Alex *really* cares mostly about sexually conquering *shikse*-America."

And yet, if Alex is lost, *Portnoy's Complaint* is not. And if we are willing to relax and play with *Portnoy's Complaint* as its readers, we can pass through the metaperspectival process that I described in my state of nature parable and take a metaperspective (the perspective of the book) on Alex's ostensibly self-determining penis. And if the reader identifies a little bit with Alex—because the reader is a Jewish American man in 1969, or a Jewish American man after 1969, or just a person who carries fraught groupness as part of her primordially important stuff, or anyone who is willing to accept the book's invitation to intimacy—then any yearning for a liberatory praxis that is organized around sexual conquest as it is for Alex can never again seem unselfconsciously plausible.[108] And that goes for everything else that *Portnoy's Complaint* exposes and plays with, including distinctions like Jewish and goyish, the kind of ethnic panic that is forever on the lookout for slights and insults, and even the efficacy of humor.

If the reader goes through this process with the book, I suggest that a process of metaperspectival praxis is achieved. The reader is engulfed in Alex's propulsive desire for triumphalist sexual liberation and perhaps even excited by the graphic recounting of his exploits. The reader is caught up in Alex's transgressive bodily outbursts. But the reader does not become Alex. The reader is equally intimate with the implied author, who presents Alex as a painfully self-aware pathological "type." The reader and *Portnoy's Complaint* undergo Alex's outbursts together while knowingly glancing at each other from a metaperspective that sees Alex's propulsion for what it is: the legacy of fraught primordially important stuff. The punch line at the end—"So [*said the doctor*]. Now vee may perhaps to begin. Yes?"—provokes a laugh, but it also projects a possible convergence between the metaperspective the reader has shared with *Portnoy's Complaint* and the future self-understanding of Alexander Portnoy.

The implicit hope behind the punch line is that once the serious conversation begins with Dr. Spielvogel, Alex, presumably collapsed and exhausted on the couch speaking in a more sober tone, will be able to take a metaperspective on himself ranting and howling earlier. The punch line is Dr. Spielvogel's "reflecting back" on Alex playing with his fraught selfness and groupness. The hope is that a self-understanding will emerge for Alex after the punch line that perceives a difference between itself and the mess of fraught selfness and groupness that preceded the punch line. If Alex can *be* this new self-understanding in everyday life outside of the therapist's domain of play, then the time with Dr. Spielvogel was well spent. Undoubtedly, were this the case, Alex may still need to play with his fraught primordially important stuff from time to time. But he would know the difference between how he needs to play and what it means to make sober judgments about his life outside the play frame.

Regardless of whatever happens to Alexander Portnoy after the book ends, as readers we join Alex in the heat of the "vicious circle" produced by his fraught primordially important Jewishness, we experience the transgression of his lewd bodily outbursts, and we come out on the other side with new self-understanding—through our relationship with the implied author—that is less bound by the historical legacy of stigmatized Jewishness. This is the metaperspectival praxis that is accomplished by

Portnoy's Complaint, which breaks the binds of stigmatized groupness (in this case, Jewishness) precisely as Fanon had hoped would occur through actual physical outburst.[109] But I want to take another step. I think that the book *Portnoy's Complaint* should be established as an enduring point in the public political culture of American society. It should be part of what it means to be an American to experience the metaperspectives provoked by *Portnoy's Complaint*.

Curated with a caption providing the interpretation that I have just offered, the book contributes compelling substantive and formal elements to our public political culture. On substantive grounds, *Portnoy's Complaint* heightens our sense of human embodiment and animality by drawing us into Alex's sexual life, and into his fragile, flawed, sometimes sadistic motivations, as well as by taking us to the shvitz. This heightened bodily experience is special because it is also saturated with the legacy of historical anti-Semitism in America and the divisive emotions that still fester among Jews about the goyim. The book also contains subtle and hilarious insights into Jewish American life, which capture many unresolved tensions (like the schlemiel/tough Jew dynamic and the Jewishness repressed by the demand that Jews appear in public as a religious minority) that are likely to persist as a result of the problem of reproduction.

Finally, through the achievement of metaperspectival praxis, readers are able to experience intimacy with a Jewish consciousness—the implied author and the flesh-and-blood author Philip Roth—who knows that there is a difference between all that this book plays with and the kind of thinking and perceiving appropriate to nonplay life. Interpreted as a popular American novel, a novel presented to the American public to be read in the tradition of novels about who "we" are as a nation, *Portnoy's Complaint* invites readers to share this distinct Jewish metaperspective *as Americans*.

If it were established as an enduring point in the public political culture, it would thereby incorporate this distinct Jewishness *into* Americanness. The metaperspective of *Portnoy's Complaint* would become a feature of new national self-understanding that knows how some Jews may want to play, given the fact of fraught societies, but likewise knows the difference between playing this way and the kind of intimacy and earnest communication that Americans are capable of despite the fact of fraught societies. Indeed, it demonstrates that even someone who likes to play as rough as Philip Roth can be just as ready to invite others—even to invite *all Americans*—to join him in sharing an intimate metaperspective on this playing.

Formally, the experience of reflecting back with the implied author of *Portnoy's Complaint* on the metaperspectival praxis that the book achieves, if established as an enduring point in the public political culture, can serve to reinforce the general sense that we are not so tainted by the fact of fraught societies that we are unable to share a common perspective as Americans. It likewise illustrates an absolutely crucial aspect of the moral psychology of citizenship, as I have advocated, which is *the capacity to know the difference between what belongs in the domain of play and what belongs in the domain of the political.* And it models a way of offering yourself to the public—a way to admit, expose, and reveal your vulnerability, a way to give up your dignified pretensions in order to meet others in the muck of our common indignity—that I have advocated throughout this book.

Philip Roth offers a model of how to expose yourself in the domain of play as a solicitous citizen carrying a heavy load of fraught primordially important stuff. As an enduring point in the public political culture, *Portnoy's Complaint* can be a source from which future virtuosos of play, coming from different backgrounds and carrying diverse kinds of fraught primordially important stuff, can draw inspiration. And from their contributions the public political culture can expand, including in our national self-understanding an ever-deeper sense of the fact of fraught societies that we must endure together, thereby making America increasingly worth loving.

8

ALL IN THE FAMILY IN THE MORAL
HISTORY OF AMERICA

The television sitcom *All in the Family* has long been celebrated as a national treasure. In 1978, Archie and Edith Bunker's chairs were unveiled behind a glass enclosure as part of the permanent exhibition at the National Museum of American History in Washington, D.C. Democratic House Majority Whip John Brademas, who was chairman of the House subcommittee on supervising the Smithsonian Institution, argued for acquiring the chairs: "*All in the Family* programs reflect with accuracy, sensitivity and humor many important dimensions of American life. I think it would be most appropriate if two symbols of the series were to be preserved as part of the cultural legacy of our country."[1] A plaque next to the chairs reads,

> Archie and Edith Bunker's chairs symbolize the conflict between bigotry and tolerance that is central to *All in the Family*, the groundbreaking TV comedy series that premiered in 1971. Archie and Edith sat in these chairs discussing social and political issues, with Archie's outbursts of prejudice tempered by Edith's pleas for tolerance. Syndicated columnist "Dear Abbey" commented that "*All in the Family* has accomplished more about understanding America and what it's all about than any other show that's ever been done on television."

In 1999 the show was honored with a thirty-three-cent stamp.

In chapter 8 I will make an original case for the pilot episode of *All in the Family* to be set as an enduring point in the public political culture of the United States. I interpret *All in the Family* as play in the tradition of Lenny Bruce with whiteness, class, the American "patriarch," political antagonism, the ideal of liberal progress, generational dissonance, blackness, and Jewishness. Norman Lear, who wrote and produced the show, made this connection explicitly:

> If you're looking for where *All in the Family* began in American life . . . it began with Lenny Bruce. He really was a prophet. Of course, I saw him practically everywhere he played; I was devoted to him. And I think he would have adored the success of the show, because it proves a lot of what he said. When I was in New York recently, I saw the Tom O'Horgan production of *Lenny*, and I said to myself: 'Oh my god, that's the man who started it all!' I never realized what a strong influence he was on my thinking—particularly in these television series.[2]

I will show how *All in the Family* illustrates our capacity for political love despite the fact of fraught societies.

Since *All in the Family* is already celebrated as a product of popular culture that promotes "understanding America and what it's all about," it will be helpful to review some of the reception of the show. This will prove particularly worthwhile given that responses to the show have not been universally positive. Once the full range of arguments about the show are laid out, I introduce my own interpretation and explain how it helps to clarify what is important about *All in the Family* in the moral history of America. First, though, some background. The 1970s is a decade that was characterized at the time, and is still characterized in retrospect, as a period when many Americans felt adrift. According to David Farber, "Ritualistically, one public voice after another intoned that Americans had lost all faith in their leaders and, maybe, in themselves."[3] Along with this distrust and generalized malaise, the Nixon administration in the early 1970s also contributed directly to the development of a politics of white resentment.

Eric Porter explains that while Nixon oversaw the first attempts to apply affirmative-action programs to projects funded by the federal government, Nixon also "played a large role in galvanizing resistance to such programs. His emphasis on 'law and order' and his appeal to the 'silent majority' during the 1968 presidential campaign—both of which implicitly defined law-abiding whites as the moral center of the nation, put in harm's way by political radicals and by the changes wrought as people of color made legal and political gains during the 1950s and 1960s—helped create animosity toward programs intended to end white supremacy."[4] Nixon and his allies promoted the idea that the *real Americans*, the good "law-abiding whites" who make up the majority of the country, had been ignored and victimized as a result of excessive attention paid to the demands minorities and radical elites.

When white working-class activists and voters in the Midwest and Northeast started to claim the mantle of Nixon's beleaguered white core group, the white middle-class professionals who dominated the political conversation in the mediating institutions of society appeared openly shocked to "discover" their existence. As Barbara Ehrenreich reports, the white working class "showed scattered signs of discontent that became, in the media, a full-scale backlash: against the civil rights movement, the antiwar movement, and apparently against middle-class liberalism in general. More specifically, *some* members of the traditionally Democratic, white working class, in some parts of the country, were suddenly rallying to public figures who appealed to racist sentiments."[5] Ehrenreich describes the precise moment of "discovery" coming soon after the violence at the Democratic convention held in Chicago in late August of 1968.

Media figures expressed shock after finding out that, according to widely publicized polls taken after the convention, most Americans seemed to sympathize with the Chicago police and not the bludgeoned demonstrators or the roughed-up press. She writes, "Media leaders moved quickly to correct what they now came to see as their 'bias.' They now felt they had been too sympathetic to militant minorities (a judgment the minorities might well have contested). Henceforth they would focus on the enigmatic—and in Richard Nixon's famous phrase—silent, majority."[6] For instance, award-winning NBC News documentarian Fred Freed was quoted by the conservative writer Edith Efron in a September 1969 *TV Guide* article entitled, "The 'Silent Majority' Comes into Focus," saying, "The blue- and white-collar people who are in revolt now do have a cause for complaint against us. We've ignored their point of view. . . . It's bad to pretend they don't exist. We did this because we tend to be upper-middle-class liberals."[7]

Between the summer of 1968 and 1971, Ehrenreich identifies a genuine cultural obsession emerging. Nixon started a taskforce on the Problem of the Blue-Collar Worker, the mayor of New York City started looking for new ways to benefit white neighborhoods, the Ford Foundation had a conference on "the blue-collar problem," books were published including *The White Majority, Middle Class Rage, The Radical Center,* and *The Troubled American*—"and in the fall and winter of 1969, every major news-magazine ran a cover story on the 'middle Americans,' the 'troubled Americans,' or the 'forgotten Americans.'"[8] According to Ehrenreich, the profile of the white working class that ultimately emerged from all of this attention was a distortion. It was a projection contrived by white middle-class professionals who were themselves growing more conservative.[9] Most obviously, the emerging picture of "the working class" did not include men and women of color, who made up a significant number of low wage laborers. White laborers who understood their own interests *as workers* to ally them with the struggles of oppressed minorities were also left out of the picture. The "blue-collar worker" of the public imagination was necessarily white, male, and politically reactionary.[10]

Ehrenreich writes, "in turning to the working class, middle-class observers tended to seek legitimation for their own more conservative impulses. They did not discover the working class that was—in the late sixties and early seventies—caught up in the greatest wave of labor militancy since World War II. They discovered a working class more suited to their mood: dumb, reactionary, and bigoted."[11] Notably, the contempt went in the other direction too. There was, in fact, growing hostility among the white working class at this time, but it was directed as much toward a newly constructed image of the white middle class as it was directed toward minority groups.

Members of the white working class resented the exemptions that had allowed white middle-class students to avoid going to Vietnam. They felt that they had to "bear the brunt" of programs like busing and workplace diversification while the white middle-class liberals who engineered these programs looked on sanctimoniously from their protected suburbs and "executive suites or faculty lounges," which were not the focus of workplace integration at that time.[12] They had disdain for white student activists who they viewed as the spoiled self-righteous children of the very white middle-class professionals that had targeted them for contempt. And they sneered with disbelief about the white middle-class critics of consumer culture, who championed "tasteful," "authentic," and "organic" products and ridiculed the "Budweiser, tuna casserole, and TV dinners" that were often all that working-class families could afford.[13]

Ehrenreich suggests that white middle-class professionals promoted the centrality of the "forgotten" white working class, in part, as a self-loathing attempt to deflate the high-minded values of their own class, which they increasingly viewed as stifling, shameful, and weak. It was as if they wanted to convey: look at these simple, law-abiding, hard-working, salt-of-the-earth Americans who we've left behind. They're frustrated, frustrating, maybe crude, and certainly seething with resentment—but maybe they're on to something![14] The historian Jefferson Cowie reinforces this point, suggesting that films in the 1970s about white working-class men "lend credence to Barbara Ehrenreich's conviction that professional middle-class creators of popular culture in the decade were using working-class subjects as a vehicle for their own macho anti-liberal impulses."[15]

With politicians, journalists, and academics doing their part since 1968 to centralize and distort the character of "the blue-collar worker," by 1971 television and film producers were ready to add their own caricature to the mediating institutions of society.[16] As Cowie has written about this period, "A multifaceted resurrection of blue-collar America appeared in commercial culture from Nashville to Hollywood, echoing the issues in the factories and the voting booths."[17] The first episode of *All in the Family* aired on Tuesday night January 12, 1971, introducing America to a bigoted white working-class man who has remained a fixture in the American public imagination ever since: Archie Bunker. The ultimate effect of *All in the Family*, according to Ehrenreich, "was to impress the blue-collar stereotype onto a generation of viewers. Well into the eighties, literate and quite liberal people would use *All in the Family* as a major sociological reference point, and refer to white working-class males conveniently as 'Archie Bunker types.'"[18]

Arguably, Archie Bunker represented the completion of a cultural process that transformed the image of "the worker" in American society.

Cowie notes that "Archie is an inversion of the noble and suffering prole-tariat; he has only scant economic identity but an enormous racial one."[19] Archie, he explains, "was one of the most prominent fictional figures in the postwar drift of the idea of 'worker' from a materially based to a cul-turally based concept, from the vanguard to the rearguard of history."[20]

Archie Bunker was a pop culture icon in the 1970s. In *Archie Bunker's America*, Josh Ozersky observes,

> a kind of Archiemania broke across the landscape in the early to mid-1970s, a time (1972–1976) when *All in the Family* was the number one show in television for five straight years, a feat not equaled before or since. T-shirts, buttons, bumper stickers, and other merchandise capitalized on the show's currency. Archie's favorite expressions—"Meathead," "Ding-bat," "stifle yourself," and so on entered the popular lexicon. Facetious "Archie Bunker for President" campaigns were even held in 1972 and 1976, with the silver-haired patriarch actually receiving a vote at the 1972 Dem-ocratic nominating convention.[21]

Advocates for the show thought it was refreshing that a television pro-gram was willing to be realistic about the ugliness that is really out there in the country.[22] The American Civil Liberties Union gave Norman Lear the Freedom of Press Award in 1973, saying that the show was a television "breakthrough . . . in terms of presenting life as it really is. In attacking controversial subject matters, in dramatizing the attitudes of the far right as well as the left, and doing this in terms of warm human comedy and drama, *All in the Family* has opened wide the boundaries of the small screen."[23] Nat Hentoff wrote in the *Village Voice*, "Yes, there are times when one feels warmly toward the man [Archie], hive of prejudices though he be. In thereby opening 'situation comedy' to the human condition—it is possible to like certain people despite all kinds of principled reasons not to—'All in the Family' is almost equivalent, in television, to the invention of the wheel."[24]

But the show was not universally beloved. Some people asked: why do we need to see this sort of ugliness—Archie's use of offensive epithets and his bigoted attitude—when we turn on the TV to watch a sitcom?[25] And some saw it as a throwback to the racial stereotyping that had dominated American entertainment in the age of *Amos 'n' Andy* and *Abie's Irish Rose*.[26] Some thought that the show would unnecessarily exacerbate and prolong festering social wounds, while others thought it would provoke helpful conversations about topics that were usually swept under the rug.[27] A Christian campaign against "indecency" and "permissiveness" was launched against the show by groups like Morality in Media and Stop Immorality on TV, which awarded Lear their Shield of Shame.[28] Indeed, some critics thought that Lear tried to evade criticism by seeking moral cover, while his real desire was simply to be obscene.[29]

William F. Buckley Jr didn't like the way that conservatism was depicted on the show, writing: "Conservatives, in the eyes of conservatives, came off on the show as crude, primitive, know-nothing fools. Their beliefs were presented as 'intrinsically loony, prejudiced and anti-intellectual.'"[30] But there were also complaints from the left about how workers were depicted. In a speech to the Sixteenth Constitutional Convention of the United Steelworkers of America, National Urban League executive director Vernon E. Jordan Jr. argued, "The Archie Bunker-ization of the American working man is a myth fed by the media, by the enemies of both working people and black people, and by those who would roll the clock back to the good old days when blacks knew their place and unions weren't recognized. . . . And to the degree that the general public is convinced that labor is selfish and bigoted, the labor movement will lose the moral standing and public goodwill it needs to succeed in its aims."[31]

In a cover article for *Ebony* entitled "Is Archie Bunker the Real White America?" Charles L. Sanders wrote powerfully,

> Black people must be reminded that they ought always [to] hold in contempt Archie Bunker and his kind. They, above all others, ought to do so not because of "paranoid touchiness" but because of their special intimacy with a history they have bought with such a high price in suffering and struggle and murdered black heroes. Black people know the Archie Bunkers—well. Thus they must know that he, no matter how "lovable," symbolizes the very real flesh and blood white man who, for centuries, has crushed black hope and stifled every black dream; the "decent" racist who refused to punish the killer of Medgar Evers and who dealt far too kindly with the murderer of Martin Luther King. This Archie—he represents every barrier that blacks still face; he's "the man" every black

man still rightly blames. Thus, how could any black person laugh at his wickedness. Who he is and what that means isn't funny at all.[32]

Sanders went on to quote psychiatrist Alvin Poussaint, who responded to the suggestion that black viewers should be able to laugh along with everyone else: "They want to put the burden of *their* racism on *your* shoulders."[33] On the other hand, Pamela Haynes wrote in the *Los Angeles Sentinel*, an influential African American newspaper,

> The paramount thing about "All in the Family" is that for the first time, instead of trying to pass off an expensively groomed and immaculately coiffed Doris Day as "the typical American housewife" and a distinguished, suave and ever so tolerant Robert as everyone's father, they have presented a fat, ignorant, angry middle aged pig who swears at his wife, belches at the table and gets choked up over sugary tributes on greeting cards. In other words, Archie Bunker is real. Far from protesting, members of minorities slandered by Archie should rejoice at this non-cosmetized portrait of the "master race." . . . What is hoped is that the show will be given a chance to go on doing its outrageous thing and not be strangled by the outrage of some narrow, uptight people. Archie Bunker lives in millions of American homes, and it's about time that we saw him in all of his white-sock-wearing glory.[34]

In the 1980s, media studies scholar Mark Crispin Miller argued that Archie Bunker and his many television iterations are, in the end, merely objects of ridicule devised to build a reliable audience for advertisements.[35] Situation comedies with white working-class "buffoons," he explained, are meant to depoliticize television viewers in order further to cultivate a passive, cynical audience preoccupied with product consumption alone. The point is to make sure that nothing is taken seriously. Every political opinion or challenge is met with a sense of knowing distance, unifying viewers in a blasé attitude. Once pigeonholed and politically neutered, the audience can be targeted by advertisers—like fish in a barrel.

"Seemingly progressive," warns Miller, "the televisual animus against the Dad of old is, in fact, a device that works not to enlighten but to paralyze us."[36] According to Miller, we laugh at the buffoonish dads on television and feel ourselves emancipated from the traditional white patriarch even as we passively abide the same old distribution of power and wealth. "In turning against the early TV Dad," he writes, "we merely turn against a superannuated figurehead, and only to the benefit of the very forces that invented him and that encourage us to keep on laughing at his memory. Once purified of Dad's stern image, TV was perfectly resolved to carry on the advertisers' long campaign for our absolute surrender, their effort to induce an incapacity far more profound than that of any bullied wife or son."[37] What is more, comedy for Miller is an essential ingredient in the pacification that TV induces. Comic derision of tension and uptightness serves to cut off "the possibility of waywardness, resistance, of a self impenetrable by TV."[38] If subversive irony may have once functioned as a critical challenge to the powerful, in the age of the buffoonish TV dad "irony consists in nothing but an easy jeering gaze that TV uses not to question the exalted, but to perpetuate its own hegemony."[39]

Todd Gitlin has also examined the values of capitalism that lay at the foundation of all television, whatever its content: "This is television's fundamental politics. Whatever the shifts in program emphasis to left or right, Maude's living room and that of Farrah Fawcett's fictional Angel don't look all that different. In other words, if television is unkind to businessmen, it is scarcely unkind to the values of a business civilization. Capitalism and the consumer society come out largely uncontested."[40] More recently, media scholar Richard Butsch has argued that "the male working-class buffoon" in particular, who is reiterated in shows like *The Honeymooners*, *The Flintstones*, *All in the Family*, *The Simpsons*, and *King of Queens* serves, more than anything else, to "justify class relations of modern capitalism."[41]

Other more recent critics have viewed Norman Lear's presumed liberal intentions in producing *All in the Family* and other groundbreaking shows like *The Jeffersons* as fundamentally unfulfilled or misguided. Ozersky adjudges that "despite Lear's liberalism, the show was essentially conservative. . . . *All in the Family* did trivialize serious issues. Once the novelty of dinner-table discussions of war and Watergate wore off, *All in the Family* came more and more to use topical issues merely as springboards for character-driven humor."[42] Television critic Saul Austerlitz writes,

The parallels between Archie and George [Jefferson] are indicative of Lear's 1970s-progressive strain of liberalism, which stubbornly insists, against all evidence to the contrary, that black and white racists, and racism, are precisely identical. . . . In Lear's world, there appear to be just as many Georges as Archies, with equally pernicious results stemming from their bigotry. This nonsensical false equality was perhaps the only way that Lear could create characters as outspokenly politically incorrect as he did, but gives both *All in the Family* and *The Jeffersons* a strange never-never land quality.[43]

Austerlitz concludes, "Archie in particular is a challenge for contemporary viewers, for whom he will likely have crossed over from provocative to unacceptable. . . . In 1971 Archie hugged the boundary of what was shocking; more than forty years later, much of the humor of *All in the Family* has curdled."[44]

For their part, Norman Lear and his coproducer Bud Yorkin were fairly clear from the beginning that they were motivated, above all, by the desire to make great television. In the late 1960s, Lear and Yorkin perceived an immense distance between potential television viewers among the youth and what was on television at the time. It was a distance also perceived anxiously by Robert Wood, the president of CBS who eventually put *All in the Family* on the air. Lear and Yorkin wanted to find something that would have the appeal of *honesty*. Yorkin explained, "Coming out of the sixties, the climate was right, the kids were letting it all hang out, the kids didn't want to see Doris Day: 'quit jerking us off and give us something real.'"[45]

Lear's theory of comedy set him up perfectly to meet this challenge. As he put it, "I've always considered that an audience laughs hardest when they're concerned most."[46] Without explicitly articulating a sophisticated theoretical conception of play, Lear clearly intuited the noninstrumental value of what he offered his audiences. He reflected, "I've never heard that anybody conducted his or her life differently after seeing an episode of *All in the Family*. If two thousand years of the Judeo-Christian ethic hadn't eradicated bigotry and intolerance, I didn't think a half-hour sitcom was going to do it."[47] But, in order to appreciate all that is at play in *All in the Family*, it is worth analyzing one particular debate about the show that transpired on the pages of the *New York Times* in 1971.

IS ARCHIE BUNKER BIGOTED ENOUGH?
THE HOBSON-LEAR EXCHANGE

In September of 1971, Laura Z. Hobson, author of the antiprejudice novel *Gentleman's Agreement* (whose film adaptation was awarded the 1947 Academy Award for best picture) wrote an editorial complaining to the *New York Times* about the controversial television show that everyone was talking about. The show had just started its second season. "I have a most peculiar complaint about the bigotry in the hit comedy," she wrote. "There's not enough of it."[48] She continued, "Hebe, spade, spic, coon, Polack—these are the words that its central character Archie Bunker is forever using, plus endless variations, like jungle bunnies, black beauties, the chosen people, yenta, gook, chink, spook and so on. Quite a splashing display of bigotry, but I repeat, nowhere near enough of it."[49] What was she getting at?

Something disturbed Hobson when she read reviewers calling it an "honest show" with "honest laughter" about a "lovable bigot."[50] What bothered her finally coalesced after *All in the Family* took home the best comedy award at the twenty-third annual Emmy Awards. Master of ceremonies Johnny Carson quipped about the show's creator, "Norman Lear—a nice guy for a Hebe."[51] Hobson reflected, "The audience roared with laughter. I suppose Norman Lear laughed too. Would he have laughed, I suddenly wondered, if Johnny Carson had said, 'Norman Lear, a nice guy for a kike?'"[52] Hobson wondered, "Had Norman Lear never realized that what bigots really called Jews was kike or Sheeny?... Then why did Norman Lear, in this honest portrayal of the bigot next door, never say either? And that other word. Where was that one, among the spades and coons and jungle bunnies and black beauties?... You know the word they use. The one word, the hideous word. Unthinkable too. Don't even print it. Nigger."[53]

This is the word that real bigots use. So why, Hobson asked, "doesn't this honest show use the real words that real bigots always use?"[54] She thought perhaps Lear kept a list of "forbidden words" he has committed not to use. She concluded that, even if it might be unconscious, the producers of the show and the network were making bigotry more acceptable: cleaning it up, deodorizing it, making people more comfortable hearing it and indulging in it.[55] The trick, she claimed, was to maximize audience share by attracting the bigots and the targets of bigotry. She also noted that some targets were more targeted than others on the show: not a lot of harsh anti-Catholicism or epithets for Irish or Italian Americans.[56] She pondered whether including these would be too much, in the minds of the producers, to garner the needed Nielsen ratings.[57]

By sanitizing Archie Bunker's language, Hobson viewed the show as meant to present "a lovable bigot that everybody except a few pinko atheistic bleedin' hearts will love. Well, I differ. I don't think you can be a bigot and be lovable, nor an anti-Semite and lovable. And I don't think the millions who watch this show ought to be conned into thinking that you can."[58] It is hypocritical, she suggested, to accept accolades for daring honesty about social issues and intergroup antagonism when the show purposefully fabricates a sanitized image of bigotry. Hobson understood that it is supposed to be a comedy, but she calls on the network to consider its charge to care about the public interest. She worries in particular about the announcement that the show will soon air on Saturday nights at 8 PM—"a time when even the kindergarten set can be in on the laughable business of bigotry."[59]

She wrote,

> To be among the first to teach impressionable children that they're not wanted in certain neighborhoods, that there's something that makes people laugh at them and look down on them and call them names, seems to me callous, even cruel. Indeed, to teach other children that it's quite all right to go around saying spade and Hebe and coon and spic—for of course kids always imitate what they see on tv—that seems to me pretty cruel too.[60]

When she addressed the "comedy defense" directly, she marshaled Henri Bergson on "the absence of feeling which usually accompanies laughter" and the "momentary anesthesia of the heart," considering how "comedy can only begin at the point where our neighbor's personality ceases to affect us. It begins, in fact, with a growing callousness. . . . In laughter we always find an unavowed intention to humiliate."[61]

When Norman Lear responded to Hobson in the *Times* a few weeks later, he rebutted her claim that Archie is not given the words that real bigots use by reporting that he had been provoked into fistfights several times as a youngster after being called "dirty Jew," "Christ-killer," and

"Hebe." He also suggested that Hobson, in attacking the show, may be protecting her turf as an antibigotry innovator. Lear defended Archie's choice of words as follows:

> The important thing about bigots and their choice of expression, however, is that unless they are conversing with other known bigots, they will always tread very carefully, testing, before coming out directly. For example, I have heard a man laughingly wonder how many of the "chosen people" were at a cocktail party one night. Had he not learned immediately that I was Jewish, he would have felt free to go much further thereafter, I am sure. Archie Bunker does that. A bigot motivated not by hate, but by fear—fear of change, fear of anything he doesn't understand—he knows that Mike and Gloria will jump his every bigoted remark, which indeed they do, so he tries forever to sneak them by.[62]

Notably, Lear did not address the possibility of a scene that depicts Archie with other bigots or grumbling to himself in the terms that Hobson demanded. And that is lamentable. But Lear's point is extremely important. Archie Bunker is not a clear-thinking, conscientious white supremacist activist who maintains a coherent, racist view. Nor does he seem actively driven in any way by a desire to see others suffer harm or disadvantage because they are Jewish, black, female, and so on. Archie feels overwhelmed by social changes that make it difficult for him to imagine how he will fit in—even how he will survive. So he settles on his prerogative to belittle, mock, and derogate others at home—usually in a rather sly manner—as a way of building himself up. This presumably makes him feel that he is above the overwhelming tide of people and ideas that are displacing him from his status (in his own mind) as the "quintessential American."

The key point for Lear was this: Archie quietly resigns himself to the fact that real political changes have made American laws and institutions more just in his lifetime. But he is still Archie Bunker, and he is not going to take on the affect and lifestyle of Mike and Gloria. Nor is he going to give up his resentment about having to cope with such changes. Lear explained, "We mustn't expect Mike to convince Archie of anything. A liberal will not change the mind of a bigot that way, not on television and not in real life, so week after week, Mike the liberal doesn't defeat Archie."[63]

There is nothing really to defeat. Archie barely has arguments. He only has perverse words, ideas, and emotions, which are always vague and which he can't give up without ceasing to be himself (this is the fact of fraught societies). Most important, the show itself does not make an argument. It provokes emotions for the sake of *having those emotions*. It *plays with* liberal outrage, white resentment, intergenerational conflict, and more.

With respect to Hobson's claim that when it was aired in prime time on Sundays it would have the effect of inflicting alienation and fear on some children, Lear had a telling response. He replied, "Life teaches children that 'they aren't wanted in certain neighborhoods,' and that 'there's something that makes people call them names.' 'All In The Family' simply airs it, brings it out in the open, has people talking about it."[64] This, then, is the effect that we should anticipate from *All in the Family*, according to Lear. "They will ask questions about the bigotry they see on 'All in the Family' and parents will have to answer. Conversation in the home; how bad can that be?"[65]

But Lear was even more engaging when he took a different tack. He suspected that none of his arguments on behalf of the show would satisfy Hobson. And that is because she would only accept one kind of portrayal of bigotry. He also suggested that she shared this criterion of representation with others in her generation who have produced the "stereotypes" of bigotry that were popular in the media.[66] Hobson and her generation asserted that "a bigot is a white man who says 'nigger!' to a black man's face, forcing him to move aside so that he may pass, and spitting as he does. A bigot is a vigilante who lynches a black man, sometimes castrating him first."[67] Lear lamented, "We've had these bigots through the years—one-dimensional, stereotypes—ad nauseam."[68] As far as Lear is concerned, this bigot fantasy kept the bigot at such a distance from Hobson that she never had to be troubled by the possibility of relating to him, seeing herself in him, or caring about him.

"On the other hand," he wrote, "most of us have known people who drop words like spade; and people who with a sly smile have tossed a yenta into the conversational waters to see if it would float. And I have also known people to use that word. The hideous one. Don't print it again. Schwartze."[69] This is where Lear got *really* interesting. He was clearly mocking Hobson by repeating her "that word. The hideous one. Don't print it." He used this rhetorical jab already at the beginning of the piece in a passage he left dangling without explanation: "Now, I have a most peculiar complaint about Mrs. Hobson's complaint. Nigger, kike and sheeny were the words she found missing in 'All in the Family,' which, according to her, made the show dishonest. But there is another word bigots use—some liberal bigots. You know the word they use. The one word, the hideous word. Don't even print it. No, Mrs. Hobson, not nigger. Schwartze. Mrs. Hobson didn't mind our not using that word."[70] What was he on about?

Shvartze is a derogatory epithet for black people in Yiddish. Lear wondered, "In the publishing world, at a literary dinner, at a cocktail party, sometime in your lifetime, dear lady, have you never heard the word schwartze pass through the lips of an otherwise respectable, outstanding, humane and even lovable person?"[71] Hobson, he explained, "doesn't associate the highly educated, very sophisticated, upper-class individual who uses the word schwartze with a common, lower-class bigot like Archie Bunker."[72] Lear, on the other hand, associated them completely.[73] In fact, he wondered if the lower-class bigot who might insult many people over his lifetime was far more benign than the upper-class sophisticate who only says shvartze privately, but takes no responsibility for his economic exploitation of black people.

It was in this moment of the exchange that Lear signaled the distinct Jewish background of *All in the Family.* While Lear got the bare bones idea of the show from reading a blurb about the successful BBC-TV series *Till Death Us Do Part* in *Variety* magazine, his model for the dynamics between Archie and Mike came from his own relationship with his father, Herman Lear.[74] Jeffrey Shandler has gone so far as to call Archie Bunker a "crypto-Jew" on these grounds.[75] In his exchange with Hobson, Lear revealed the extent to which he was playing in *All in the Family* with the fraught relationship between Jewishness and whiteness in America in the early 1970s. Having recounted some of the story of this relationship in chapter 1, and elsewhere in this book, I can now shine a light on its crucial contribution to *All in the Family.*

Born in 1922, three years before Lenny Bruce and eleven years before Philip Roth, Lear grew up in an America simmering with racial anti-Semitism. Even if as an adult he would see America become a place where

Jews prospered and were indeed celebrated, Norman Lear's primordially important sense of Jewishness was saturated with early experiences of stigmatization. He reflects in his memoir *Even This I Get to Experience*, "The news that to be a Jew in America was to be 'different' had come to me shockingly when I was nine years old."[76] Lear had received a crystal radio kit as a gift from his father and when listening to it alone in his bedroom one night happened upon Father Charles Coughlin. Young Norman Lear was affected deeply by Coughlin, who "despised Franklin Roosevelt, fulminated endlessly about the New Deal as a betrayal of American values, and attached prominent Jews to everything he was railing against. . . . This was my introduction to the fact that there were people who disliked, mistrusted, even hated me because I was born a Jew. If I didn't have a nose for the slightest whiff of anti-Semitism before, I had it from that moment on."[77]

As a senior in high school, Lear managed to get a much-needed scholarship to Emerson College by winning first prize at the county level in the National Oratorical Contest. Providing further insight into the contours of his primordially important Jewishness and Americanness, his speech was about the special significance of the U.S. Constitution to him as a Jew. As he remembers it, he was "fueled by the idea of a quota for Jews seeking admission to certain colleges, my memory of Father Coughlin, and now the word out of Europe—where Hitler had marched into Austria, and Benito Mussolini, emulating Hitler, began enacting the first anti-Jewish legislation in Italy."[78] The impact of these constitutive elements of his Jewishness stayed with him. Once he arrived at Emerson College, he reports feeling conspicuous as the only person in his rooming house who was not a Christian.

He reflects, "despite my lack of direct connection to my religion, I couldn't have been more conscious of myself as a Jew if Hitler had been in the room pointing at me. Not that my being Jewish mattered to anyone else—I never got a hint of that."[79] That is, of course, the classic experience of the person who carries stigmatized Jewishness as part of his primordially important stuff, which is so well captured in the character of Alexander Portnoy.[80] Lear had the potent feeling of "Jewish vs. goyish," which is all-consuming, even when no one else is actually calling attention to the distinction. He even describes avoiding the shower when others might be there, out of fear that his circumcised penis would be exposed, and the huge relief when his efforts failed and he noticed that one of his Christian housemates was also circumcised.[81]

In another telling instance, Lear's uncle, who was doing marketing for the war effort, sought to help his nephew Norman start selling defense stamps and bonds for the treasury department. Lear's uncle told his boss about the idea, and the boss phoned Norman from Washington, D.C. Lear was astonished to be called long distance by such a powerful gentile. Writing about the telephone call half a century later, he sums up this aspect of his Jewishness: "Millburn McCarthy, Jr. Holy shit! Talk about your stirring, rock-ribbed American names. This was a name that suggested real class and power, and a family history that didn't begin within a thousand miles of a shtetl. Such thoughts occurred to me then, and do to this day, because that kid poking around on his crystal [radio] set, spooked by a Jew hater, still lives in me."[82]

Lear's adult life as a television producer and political activist demonstrates his sense of identification *as a Jew* with those who feel different, who are targets of stigmatization, and who suffer injustice in America. But the boldness and virtuosity of play in *All in the Family* comes from the fact that he simultaneously acknowledged the capacity of Jews, and others, tacitly to accept and actively to exploit the psychological and material advantages of whiteness. Now we can return to Lear's response to Hobson: "But there is another word bigots use—some liberal bigots. You know the word they use. The one word, the hideous word. Don't even print it. No, Mrs. Hobson, not nigger. Schwartze."[83]

It's a strange charge, since Archie Bunker obviously would never use this word. *Shvartza*, in the sense that Lear is referring to, is a word used exclusively by Ashkenazi Jewish people when they want to assert distinctly *Jewish* racial superiority and contempt for black people. A Jewish person who imagines himself to be unambiguously white in America presumably uses the word *nigger*. In my entire life, I have never personally witnessed a Jewish person using that word. But growing up, I heard the word *shvartze* used plenty of times—by *alte kackers* coming out of the shvitz at the Jewish country club where my friends belonged, by older kids telling racist jokes, and even once by some guy sitting with me in the ready-room behind the bimah at our liberal Reform temple, where I was waiting to participate in the Shabbat service, who I vividly remember responding to me spilling my Coke with, "Don't worry, the shvartze will clean it up."

When Lear reminded Hobson that there was a horrible word that "some liberal bigots" use, he meant Jews. He meant that there are plenty of Jews tossing the word shvartze around at the shvitz even if when they emerge they vote for Democrats. It was among prosperous Jews where you would find "the highly educated, very sophisticated, upper-class individual who uses the word schwartze." Lear was not merely pointing out to Hobson that victims of prejudice, like Jews, can also have prejudices. Nor was he merely suggesting that white liberals like to make it easy on themselves by imagining racism as the exclusive purview of inbred Southern Christian maniacs. Lear was also, and what is more important, making this point: there is someone that you love who is profoundly morally flawed! If it's not a parent or grandparent, a friend or colleague, a mentor or idol, *then it is America itself.* If Jewish liberals like Hobson loved the America that enabled Jews to prosper only a couple of decades after the high tide of American anti-Semitism, then they loved a nation that was forged through horrifying oppression, where the cultural legacies of oppression will linger interminably.

Archie Bunker was Norman Lear's bigoted Jewish father, who used to call him "the laziest white kid he ever met"—a line that Archie uses on Mike in the first episode of the show.[84] But Archie is also the liberal Jew who mischievously uses the word *shvartze* with his buddies over a cocktail at a fancy event or on the golf course. Archie is even Norman Lear, who recognizes that he too carries the privileges and prejudices that come with counting as a white man in America.[85] But if Archie contains these Jewish multitudes, he is a Jew in *goy*face. Because Archie is the politically reactionary, white, Christian, working-class man who had been anointed to represent "the silent majority" by 1971, as we have seen. Archie is the American patriarch, who loses power and centrality as America becomes more just. If Archie is a "lovable bigot," it is not because *All in the Family* invites its audience to take bigotry less seriously. It is not because Norman Lear is soft on racism. It is because *All in the Family* is about the possibility of political love despite the fact of fraught societies. But, in order to see this, we need to dig into the show itself.

MEETING THE BUNKERS

At 9:30 PM on a Tuesday night in January in 1971, just before the first episode of *All in the Family* was about to air, a solemn voice pronounced: "The program you are about to see is *All in the Family*. It seeks to throw a humorous spotlight on our frailties, prejudices and concerns. By making them a source of laughter, we hope to show—in a mature fashion—just how absurd they are."[86] CBS clearly recognized that the show would be controversial. The network's preface suggests to viewers that what they are about to see is meant to build an audience that views some of its own propensities as unfounded and ridiculous. But the inaugural episode— "Meet the Bunkers"—does a lot more than this.

It is Archie and Edith Bunker's twenty-second anniversary. Gloria, their daughter, and her husband Mike, have plotted to celebrate it with a festive brunch. They know that Archie will not recognize the day. They even go so far as buying a gift and card for Edith and signing it with a poem from Archie.[87] Over the course of the brunch, the audience meets Archie Bunker and hears him using ethnic and racial epithets, decrying progressive politics, and so on. The brunch is generally strained by incessant eruptions into political conflict between Mike and Archie.

Before they even come to the table, Archie is clearly unnerved by the overt sexual intimacy shared by Mike and Gloria as well as by the way Gloria is dressed. Archie complains from his den chair: "What the hell is it nowadays? Will ya tell me? Girls with skirts up to here, guys with hair down to there. I stopped in a gents' room the other day. So help me, there was a guy in there with a ponytail. My heart nearly turned over in me. I thought I was in the wrong 'terlet.'" It is important that Archie's discomfort with overt sexuality and changing gender norms is part of his overall feeling of being overwhelmed by social change. And it is also important that Gloria and Mike, unable to keep their hands off each other, are juxtaposed with the lack of any overt intimacy between Archie and Edith. Archie's problem with a changing world, which confronts him with people who do things differently than he does, is connected to his deeper problem with intimacy. He can barely show affection for his own wife and daughter, so it is difficult to imagine him expanding his affection to the people who populate the new world that encroaches upon him.

After Archie's "What the hell is it nowadays?" rant, Mike asks him what viewers are presumably meant to ask of him in most episodes of the show: "Why fight it? The world's changing." When Edith indicates that this was the topic of the reverend's sermon at the church service from which they had just returned, Archie shifts to a defensive position: "I ain't sittin' still for no preacher tellin' me that I'm to blame for all this breakdown in law and order that's goin' on." Mike asks, "Why not? We're all to blame for not paying attention to the cause of it." Then Archie reverses the accusation: "I'll tell you the cause of it—these sob sisters like your reverend Feltcher and the bleedin' hearts and weepin' nellies like yous two."

Interestingly, this exchange also hinges on Archie's emotions. Archie feels personally attacked by the reverend (and Mike) who claim that he is complicit in some way or even to blame for a "breakdown in law and order." Archie's defense is to argue that the reverend, Mike, and Gloria have the wrong emotions: they are "sob sisters," "bleedin' hearts," and "weepin' nellies." They care too much and too ostentatiously about others. The proper way to care, presumably from Archie's perspective, would look more like his own relationship with his family: never-admitted love and support buried under overt indifference and bullying. We will see that Archie himself ends up acknowledging, albeit indirectly, the limits of his own emotional repression.

Notice also Archie's sense of blamelessness. He feels that he is innocent. He cannot imagine that he is in any way complicit in injustice or social ills. I am reminded of James Baldwin writing to his nephew about white people who do not want to know about their complicity in historic oppression: "It is the innocence which constitutes the crime."[88] In the same essay he writes, "The really terrible thing, old buddy, is that *you* must accept *them*. And I mean that very seriously. You must accept them and accept them with love. For these innocent people have no other hope. They are, in effect, still trapped in a history which they do not understand; and until they understand it, they cannot be released from it."[89]

Carroll O'Connor, the actor who played Archie, seems to have shaped his performance to some degree by this very passage. He explained in an interview with *Playboy* in 1986 that it was in this spirit that he managed to find something that he could love in the character of Archie Bunker: "I have a great deal of sympathy for him. As James Baldwin wrote: the white man here is trapped by his own history, a history he himself cannot comprehend. And, therefore, what can I do but love him?"[90] Without this particular kind of sympathy, O'Connor felt, he would be playing a monster, not a human being.

It is easy to understand why viewers like Hobson might perceive Archie as monstrous. Consider this typical exchange. Mike finally unloads on Archie about the "law and order" problem.

MIKE: "You know why we got a breakdown in law and order in this country, Archie? Because we got poverty. Real poverty. You know why we got that? Because guys like you are unwilling to give the black man, the Mexican-American, and all the other minorities their just and hard-earned share of the American dream."

ARCHIE: "Now let me tell you somethin'. If your spicks and your spades want their rightful share of the American dream, let 'em get out there and hustle for it just like I done."

MIKE: "Yeah, but Archie you're forgetting one thing. You didn't have to hustle with black skin."

ARCHIE: "I didn't have to hustle with one arm and one leg neither."

MIKE: "So what? So you're admitting that the black man is handicapped."

ARCHIE: "Oh, no, no more than me. He's just as good as me."

MIKE: "Now I suppose you're gonna tell me that the black man has had the same opportunity in this country as you."

ARCHIE: "More. He's had more. I didn't have no million people marchin' and protestin' to get me my job."

EDITH: "No, his uncle got it for him."

Already in this exchange, early in the first episode, we hear Archie using the derogatory epithets "spicks and spades" to describe Mexican Americans and black Americans. Later he explains that he learned a Yiddish word, because "we got a couple of Hebes workin' down at the building." There is a lot going on in this exchange. On the one hand, Archie expresses what may be reducible to a "color-blind," principled political position about each citizen's responsibility for his own economic productivity. On the other hand, as with most expressions of views like this, the degree to which it is a "principled position" is belied by facts about the speaker—in this case by Archie's snide, self-satisfied use of derogatory epithets.

But it is significant that Archie feels he must argue with recourse to an idea of "fairness." He wants Mike to know that he thinks black and Mexican Americans are "just as good as me"—their problems, he purports to believe, come from their own lack of initiative and the handout policies of liberal "sob sisters," "bleedin' hearts," and "weepin' nellies." He does not simply exclaim that they are racial inferiors and do not deserve the same considerations of fairness that are owed white people.[91] Along these same lines, note that Archie makes the same kind of "black privilege" argument Matthew Frye Jacobson identified in *Rocky* (which came out about four years later). Minorities, according to Archie, have had unfair *advantages* by contrast to working-class whites like himself. This self-justifying notion is, of course, deflated by Edith's closing aside, to which I will return shortly.

The interactions presented by the show are not offered to viewers as a point-counterpoint enactment of opposing political views represented by Mike and Archie, from which the audience is meant to choose. To be sure, the plausibility and immediacy of such characters making such arguments (in 1971 and today) adds significantly to the tension and humor the show is meant to provoke. But one ought not to look for serious political or historical analysis on a TV sitcom. As an invitation to play, the show is circumscribed by a banner readsing that the thoughts and emotions expressed and provoked by this show do not mean what these same thoughts and emotions would mean outside of the play frame. The point is just to have these thoughts and emotions, to feel the tension, to be amused. Norman Lear once told Todd Gitlin, "This was a comedy, and I wanted to make an audience laugh."[92]

At the same time, even if a television comedy—as *play*—serves no instrumental purpose, it can nevertheless show us something about how *we* want to play, and how we *can* play. As public cultural critics, we might see in *All in the Family* something about *us as a nation* that can enrich our capacity for broadly share political love amidst the fact of fraught societies. Let's look, for instance, at the concluding scenes of the first episode, when Edith finally opens and reads the card "from Archie." Predictably, when she reads the card she is moved. *But so is Archie.* Mike sees this and calls attention to it, "the card kinda got to you, huh?" Archie gets very defensive and, referring to the card, accuses Mike of not "appreciatin' the finer things in life." Mike responds somewhat apologetically, but also a bit bewildered as to why Archie is so upset. Mike is exasperated: "All right! All right! What are you gettin' so excited about? It's a stinkin' little greeting card. It's not like you wrote the thing." Then Archie explicitly "owns" the gift and the card that were given to Edith in his name: "No, I didn't write it. But who had the good taste to pick it out?" Mike smiles and shakes his thumb toward his chest to indicate that, of course, *he* was the one. Delivering the last line of the episode, Archie smirks with exasperation and, swiping his arm dismissively, walks away, puffing on his cigar: "Aw, go on, will ya, meathead."

Archie doesn't concede the point, nor does he walk off in a rage. He knows that Mike knows that he is lying when he takes credit for the card. But there is something else important under the surface too. He knows that Mike knows that the reason behind the lie is his actual love for Edith. He really does love her in the tender way suggested by the card. But Archie will never acknowledge this softness directly; he is more likely to further harden his shell if he thinks that the softness might be exposed. Mike knows this too. This is why he doesn't seize the opportunity to shout the truth in Archie's face and instead gestures silently, smiling. At this point, Archie *must* walk away—he must leave the situation in a stalemate of inarticulate emotions rather than risk the possibility of being refuted outright in words.

Gloria and Mike have "spoken for" Archie, in a sense. They have represented him as, in the end, loving his beleaguered wife. Even though Archie had nothing to do with it, he finds himself moved and tempted to embody the "Archie" that has been represented, the Archie who would buy a gift and card for Edith on their anniversary. The show ends unresolved. There is only a glimmer of tenderness in Archie. But the viewer of this first episode is initiated into the kind of playing that *All in the Family* is going to offer throughout much of the series.

It is not just a matter of inviting viewers to make light of their own absurdities, as the CBS preface suggested. Archie Bunker is going to be projected onto television screens across the nation, and white, Christian, working-class fathers are going to be invited to identify with him. This invitation is just like Mike and Gloria's invitation to Archie to accept responsibility for Edith's gift. When these viewers identify with Archie, they will feel a range of emotions and think a variety of ideas. Sometimes they will indulge in emotions and ideas that may be perverse (namely, emotions and ideas that are not defensible as *political* emotions and ideas). They might savor Archie's dismissive aggravation toward his daughter's generation, his bullying, macho, indifferent attitude toward Edith, and his willingness to challenge burgeoning norms of ethnic and racial sensitivity.

But, in the process of identifying with Archie, television viewers will also find themselves opened to suggestive moments of self-awareness. Even as they get caught up in Archie's fuming about alleged "black privilege," they will soon have to endure Edith's deflationary reminder that Archie's uncle got him his job—he did not "pull himself up by his bootstraps." They will have to watch Archie placated mockingly by Mike and Gloria's friend Lionel Jefferson, who is black. Lionel humors Archie, while Archie remains oblivious to the fact that he is being mocked. Viewers identifying with Archie in the scenes with Lionel may perhaps wonder if some of their own interactions and relationships are not what they thought they were. Most important, those who identify with Archie will be invited to share with him in occasional moments of tenderness that break down his hardened shell—for example, when he slips up and shows a glimpse of his love for Edith on their anniversary.

Viewers who identify with Mike and Gloria will have a chance to savor their indignation about Archie. They'll get the chance to vicariously unload on the self-proclaimed "patriarchs" in their own lives. But they too will have to endure some challenging moments. Archie reminds Mike at one point that he would not be able to pursue his academic degree without Archie's support, and this is certainly an inconvenient truth. In a later episode, Mike shows that despite all his liberal rhetoric he is still not really prepared to see Gloria as entirely his equal.[93]

Of course, there are limits to the range of identifications available through characters in the show. Lionel is actually a pretty rich character, but he is still only a secondary cast member.[94] There are guest stars representing various kinds of people in almost every episode, but these characters are fundamentally peripheral. Lear only introduced new substantial opportunities for identification with *The Jeffersons* (which is a spinoff about Lionel's family) and *Good Times*. At the same time, we should not presume that the show works entirely through one-to-one audience-character identification. If there is creative apperception while watching television, and not mere dissociation, it is not necessarily because the viewer identifies with any of the characters. Watching the show can mean hovering over and through all of its characters, taking on their contradictory perspectives and moods, laughing at the quips coming from their perspectives even when they are not one's own.

In fact, the most important identification that can happen while watching the show may be with Archie, Edith, Mike, and Gloria *as a family*. In the first couple of seasons, Mike and Gloria don't move out of the house. Archie doesn't disown them. They stay together. They just keep living together, and even supporting each other, while none of their fundamental grievances are resolved. The reassurance that they endure as a family, episode after episode, despite their irreconcilable ideas and emotions, is likely a feeling that some audience members looked forward to having for its own sake week after week. Perhaps this is what Todd Gitlin was pointing to when he suggested, "Lear might have had a point in believing it was healthier for the society to flush out its rancor than to evade it. Giving vent to the various grievances of class, race, sex, and generation, Lear's formula did indeed help to keep wrenching conflicts 'all in the family.'"[95]

So it is not as a satire of bigoted, white, Christian, working-class fathers that I want to highlight *All in the Family*. Though the show includes ample such satire, and I enjoy that aspect of it. Neither is it the "political incorrectness" in the show that I wish to spotlight. Archie definitely transgresses liberal taboos with the terms that he uses to describe blacks, Jews, women, Latinos and Latinas, and others. But that, in and of itself, is not interesting or important. What I wish to capture in this snapshot is a massively popular instance of *play* with potent ideas and emotions that will haunt even the best future America that we can imagine.

I have already suggested that *as a nation* we ought to feel Alexander Portnoy's anger, fear, distrust, and pathological erotic pull toward the goyim in order to share an intimate perspective on the fact of fraught societies that we must endure together. Obviously, I do not make this suggestion because I think Alex is an admirable character who has emotions that are worth emulating in nonplay life. I make this suggestion because Alex's perverse emotions are part of the interminable legacy of historical American injustice. I suspect that a similar argument could be made on behalf of establishing Richard Wright's *Native Son* as an enduring point in the public political culture and inviting the nation forevermore to revisit the emotional life of Bigger Thomas. And there are undoubtedly as many more worthy snapshots of play out there for the public culture critic to find as there have been experiences of stigmatization, exploitation, and domination in America.

But the more difficult challenge posed by *All in the Family* for those who are already sympathetic to the historically oppressed is to recognize that the problem of remainders, the problem of reproduction, and the missing link problem also apply to Archie Bunker and those who identify with him. We do not genuinely invite the white Christian man into a just American future if we demand that his perverse emotions, his lingering anger, fear, distrust, and resentment, must first be eradicated. This does not mean that we have to tolerate the ideas, vocabulary, or emotions that cluster in the Archie Bunker caricature within the domain of the political. Like Alexander Portnoy, much of what Archie thinks, feels, and says is directly at odds with the political conception of justice that I have advocated in this book. If Archie's sensibility *in fact* circulates throughout institutions and interactions that we think should be designated as within the domain of the political, then my view gives us a powerful justification to point to it and decry its presence as unjust.[96]

But if Archie Bunker's epithets and aversions are not welcome in the domain of the political, they can nevertheless live on in the domain of play. And if Archie Bunker, like Alex Portnoy, is not worthy of our admiration, the metaperspectival intimacy offered by *All in the Family*, like the metaperspectival intimacy offered by *Portnoy's Complaint*, is nevertheless worthwhile for everyone in America to accept. On my reading, *All in the Family* is not so much a show about a "lovable bigot" as it is an invitation to America's bigoted, resentful white men to allow themselves to be loved as equal, rather than privileged, members of American society.

If America's "patriarchs" are willing to redirect their longing for Archie Bunker's satisfying political incorrectness into the domain of play—into the time and space where they watch shows like *All in the Family*—then they can participate as equals in the project of making America more just. *All in the Family* is an invitation from Norman Lear to white America. Over the course of his life, Lear felt both stigmatized as a nonwhite Jew and implicated as a member of an elite white subculture where racist derogation persists. It is from this complex and compromised position that

Lear sends his invitation to America's "founding fathers," one that neither demands unconditional surrender nor the guillotine. Like Mike and Gloria writing the anniversary poem from Archie to Edith, Lear has written the script for the "*real* America." You can be lovable in the domain of the political, he seems to say, if you are willing to displace your bigotry entirely onto the domain of play.

To those who have been targets of stigmatization and suffered injustice as a result of the actions, or feigned "innocence," of white Christian America, Lear offers a similar invitation. You can have the bigoted, buffoonish, white, working-class man—the product of a confluence of contingent cultural and political forces that converged between 1968 and 1971, as Barbara Ehrenreich has explained—to ridicule, despise, and condemn. But only in the domain of play. In the domain of the political it is incumbent upon everyone in America to see themselves and each other as vulnerable, dependent human animals who carry legacies of historic injustice and who long to live well together, however else we might want to see ourselves and each other. It is not appropriate in the domain of the political to dismiss others, or make arguments to or about others, on the premise that they are Archie Bunker types.

To be clear, I am not suggesting the false equivalence according to which white men are presumed to be just as much victims of stereotyping and prejudice as women and minorities. That idea is preposterous. As I have argued throughout this book, progress toward justice in America will involve a dramatic incorporation of ritual and symbolic reckoning with the injustices perpetrated by U.S. governmental and social institutions and the white Christian men who have dominated them. And I have likewise claimed that those who are empowered by white supremacy, Christian hegemony, patriarchy, heteronormativity, economic exploitation, and other structures of injustice in American society will lose power as American society becomes more just. It is in the context of our commitment to these unfolding processes that I likewise suggest that the historically oppressed must defy the temptation to target any particular population as fundamentally retrograde and therefore necessary to purge. It is a temptation that arises predictably as a result of the missing link problem, and it must be resisted.

Norman Lear's *All in the Family* exhibited a desire and capacity to have feelings of love, anger, and resentment *all at the same time* about America's original core group—its white "fathers." It facilitated these feelings by absorbing perverse words, ideas, and emotions into its play frame. Reflecting back on it now, we can build from it a collective self-awareness that *we*, Americans, desire and are capable of having these feelings, all at the same time. And this is an important part of the story that we should tell about our national endeavor to cultivate political love that can endure despite the fact of fraught societies.

EPILOGUE

Losing Our "Religion" in the Domain of Play

I have offered a vision of America in this book, and I invite you to strive with me to realize it.

In this vision every person living within the United States—regardless of race, gender, national origin, sexuality, form of work or lack thereof—genuinely faces a lifetime of opportunities to exercise the central human capabilities at a threshold level. Everyone feels seen by the basic structure of society as a vulnerable, dependent, human animal who carries a legacy of historic injustice and longs to live well in a collective life characterized by justice. Within the domain of the political, everyone sees herself this way too, sees everyone else this way, and feels seen by everyone else this way.

The basic structure of American society radiates vigilant opposition to ideologies of oppression that have historically saturated all spheres of American life: white supremacy, patriarchy, economic exploitation, Christian hegemony, heteronormativity, and so on. Diverse, particular stories of American suffering and hope are broadcasted throughout the public political culture so that everyone is ritually invited to feel political compassion in response to the injustice that has been the norm in American history.

Profound disagreements and irreconcilable differences nevertheless abide. In the domain of the background culture, people pursue nonpublic projects and promote comprehensive views that others reject as perverse, silly, unappealing, or false. But most of these projects and views are compatible with the capabilities conception of political justice, even if each relates to it differently.

In the domain of play within the background culture, people play in all sorts of ways, and this includes *rough play*, with the legacies of historic injustice they carry. Deep antagonisms between groups, nasty epithets and caricatures, interminable grudges, and self-indulgent fantasies are all able to thrive in the domain of play. People generally make convincing interpretive judgments about what should count as political and what should count as play, and they value the capacity to make this distinction well. Public cultural critics take snapshots of playing when it illustrates a capacity for political love, despite the fact of fraught societies, and they post these snapshots as enduring points onto the public political culture.

Since everyone in America ritually experiences a common reckoning with the injustice that has dominated American history, and each person feels respected by the basic structure of society, and by their neighbors, as entitled to a lifetime of opportunities to exercise the central human capabilities, and all this obtains *despite* the perverse ways that people play with the legacies of historic injustice that they carry—and indeed some of this playing is publicly celebrated!—most people would say, "This is *my* nation, and its flourishing as a *just* nation is essential to *my own* flourishing." Thus is my vision characterized by shared political love.

An aspect of this vision, which I have alluded to throughout this book, is that *there is no religion in it*. What is conventionally labeled religious, like the Eucharist, *salat, torah lishmah*, and *puja*, will certainly be able to thrive. But it will not be distinguished as religion from nonreligion. This is a subtle point, but it is important. Ridding ourselves of the assumption that there are special ideas, objects, groups, or activities that should be privileged or penalized because they are religious is a crucial step toward living well together despite the fact of fraught societies.

When we take a political perspective, in the vision that I propose, we see no obvious categorical difference between the range of activities that might be underway in the background culture: playing online video games, hiking trails, participating in Passover seders, shooting hoops, shooting guns, shooting craps, reading fiction, dressing up like your favorite superhero, taking Communion, reenacting wars, participating in BDSM, gardening, fasting on Ramadan, going to the movies, collecting rarities, dancing at nightclubs, or meditating. When we take a political perspective, we ask the following: Which is the pursuit of a nonpublic project and which is play? Making this distinction is never a clear-cut matter. It requires us to make an imperfect, contestable, and always provisional interpretive judgment. But there are consequences to our judgments, which I explained in chapter 5: the pursuit of a nonpublic project in tension with our guiding political conception of justice should result in friction that even the most perverse kinds of play should not have to experience at all.

What I want to reinforce in this epilogue is that the conventional distinction between religion and nonreligion should not track in any predictable way with the distinction between nonpublic projects and play. Some of what is conventionally deemed religious will count as the pursuit of a nonpublic project and some of it will count as play. Nothing will be the object of special reverence, fear, or contempt as a result of being deemed religious.

Why is this important? Scholars involved in the academic study of religion have long recognized that the distinction between religion and nonreligion, the idea that there could be a list of World Religions, and the idea that every person has some private "faith" which must be respected, are contingent products of early modern European history and conceptually problematic.[1] Already in 1962, Wilfred Cantwell Smith famously opined, "I suggest that the term 'religion' is confusing, unnecessary, and distorting."[2]

More recently, scholars focusing on the use of religion as a category in law and policy have shown that trying to protect "religious freedom" is either impossible or results in injustice. We might simply try to protect freedom of thought, freedom of expression, and freedom of assembly and assume that we will catch whatever we need to protect—including what is conventionally designated as religious—in our net. "What is arguably impossible," Winnifred Sullivan has explained, "is justly enforcing laws granting persons rights that are defined with respect to their religious beliefs or practices."[3]

Granting privileges or legal exemptions to religion requires a paradigm case that can be used do decide what should count as religion at all. I pointed to this problem in the introduction, where I referred to the IRS and its charge to determine what ought to be exempt from taxes because it is religious. In America, Christianity is inevitably the paradigmatic case of religion. Whatever looks like conscientious commitment to a private faith or obedience to the dictates of a holy scripture (like Protestantism) and whatever looks like deference to an institutional hierarchy with clearly defined dogmas and representatives of theological authority (like Catholicism) will be privileged when America privileges religion.[4]

These privileges are often denied, however, when requested on the basis of indigenous claims to "sacred land," or by New Religious Movements (which are often stigmatized as "cults"), or on behalf of popular beliefs and practices that claim to be religious but are denigrated by established "religious authorities" as merely "cultural" or "folk" beliefs and practices. Laws and policies that single out religion for special privileges and protection ultimately promote orthodoxy within long-established churches and the elites who govern them. These are promoted over the heterodox, syncretic, idiosyncratic beliefs and practices of most people in America. As Sullivan explains, "Ordinary religion, that is, the disestablished religion of ordinary people, fits uneasily into the spaces allowed for religion in the public square and in the courtroom."[5] And, of course, there are myriad activities, places, relationships, objects, commitments, and other things that people care deeply about that are not even considered for special privileges or protection because they are conventionally presumed *not* to be religious at all.

The religion clauses of the First Amendment are gravely incoherent: whenever we protect the free exercise of religion, we thereby reinforce the establishment of the paradigmatic religion that sets the criteria for all claims to status *as* religion. This paradigm of religion is unjustly privileged over all others and religion per se is privileged over nonreligion. But the incoherence goes in the other direction too. Whenever we try to prevent the explicit establishment of religion, we end up unjustly saddling the paradigmatic religion (and everything like it) with special burdens and restrictions. A dance group committed to transcending the atomized self through communal dancing might be allowed space to dance after hours in a public school building without any trouble, while a New Testament reading group might be denied the same space or provoke a lawsuit.

How legislators, policy makers, and judges ought to deal with the absurdity of the First Amendment's religion clauses and the general impossibility of religious freedom is an incredibly complicated matter that I cannot address here.[6] What I can say is that in my ideal vision of America I do not want to duplicate the problems that arise with the religion vs. nonreligion distinction.[7] The pervasive sense in America that distinctly *religious* freedom is very important, while sometimes aiding the protection of minorities, is also responsible for the coercive processes of "religionization" that I have referred to throughout this book. For instance, the emergence of national pride in "religious tolerance" may have seemed like a hospitable gesture in mid-twentieth-century America, but it also conveyed the menacing demand that Jews disappear, be religious, or be a problem.

The result is a twenty-first-century landscape of temples and synagogues offering a kind of Hebraic liberal American Protestantism, with members who mostly show up a few times a year, and a massive proportion of Jews who are tongue-tied and bewildered when they have to explain why they feel so Jewish when they don't consider themselves religious at all. When it is common sense that a good American has a religion (beliefs and practices that resemble Christianity), which serves in his private life and buoys his moral participation in public life, then vulnerable minority populations who want to be seen as good Americans will feel a powerful incentive to fit this mold. What I am offering is an alternative to this common sense.

In the America that I envision, the public political culture is brimming with enduring reminders of how people with diverse and otherwise conflicting nonpublic projects can nevertheless overlap in their support for a political conception of justice. Some of these nonpublic projects will be individualistic, idiosyncratic, or eccentric. Some will be communal, institutional, and ancient. But none will get special treatment for being deemed religious. You might pursue a life well lived as a sexual libertine, Presbyterian, or Big Foot hunter. All that matters from the perspective of the public political culture is whether or not at the same time you can endorse the idea that everyone in America is entitled to a lifetime of opportunities to exercise the central human capabilities at a threshold level. You shouldn't feel enticed to set up a Church of Sex or a Church of Big Foot in order to garner special benefits and public appreciation.

Under the regime of common sense that distinguishes between religion and nonreligion, devout members of long-established churches and the elites who govern them will always serve as the dominant archetypes of "people pursuing projects that we ought to take seriously." They will be the paradigms of "people with profound concerns" or "people with unequivocal commitments." Dissolving the distinction between religion and nonreligion when we take a political perspective, as I propose, would level the playing field for the majority of Americans who pursue heterodox, syncretic, ambiguous, idiosyncratic projects eclectically over the course of their lives. This may be particularly important with respect to new immigrants to the United States.

Recall Olivier Roy's point that new immigrants quickly get the message, "it is better to be Hindu than Indian, Buddhist than Asian, Greek Orthodox than Arab."[8] We might add, "Catholic than Mexican." But who knows how people would choose to identify themselves if they were not immediately compelled to evade racial stigmatization by finding a place on the list of venerable World Religions? Tribe, subregional language group, football club affiliation, national origin, intellectual style might be more important to a person than her identification as Hindu, Buddhist, Greek Orthodox, or Catholic—and she might want to combine, disentangle, or otherwise change her relationship to any of these over the course of her life. In the America that I envision, she has greater opportunity to do so because she is not constantly faced with the hovering question "But what is your *religion*?" Nor does she feel compelled to answer the equally artificial and constricting question "Are you religious or not?"[9]

The religionization of immigrants and refugees from certain places is particularly cruel. People from Sudan, Somalia, Syria, Iraq, and elsewhere are preemptively religionized as *essentially* Muslim in the rhetoric and policies of the Trump administration, which stigmatizes Islam as fundamentally threatening to the United States. If people from these countries are able to make it to America, and they identify as Muslims, their new neighbors will undoubtedly tend to see them, and encourage them to see themselves, as *essentially* Muslims.

They are not craftsmen, football fans, Nubian or Beja, musicians, doctors, al-Fartous or al-Bu Ali, Francophiles, fashion-obsessed teenagers, cantankerous elders, or mothers who worry about their children—they are *only* Muslims. But in this case they will not get the usual boost that otherwise accrues in an environment that privileges people who identify with a venerable world religion. Instead they are targeted for suspicion: religionization is also stigmatization. To be sure, opposing the stigmatization of Islam in America will require more than just working against the American propensity to religionization. But religionization is part of the problem.

Part of an effort to avoid duplicating the problems that arise with the religion/nonreligion dichotomy is to fastidiously refuse to make this distinction among nonpublic projects when taking a political perspective. But in the vision that I have conjured, people are not imagined to spend their lives only ever pursing the goal of political justice and pursuing their nonpublic projects. They are also imagined to play. And playing is viewed as a part of a person's life that is presumptively *equal in importance* to her nonpublic projects.

Recognizing the importance of play encourages opportunities for human flourishing that are otherwise stifled, distorted, and demoralized in a society that is predisposed to carve up what people care about into religion and nonreligion. At play there may be an omnipotent God, angels, powerful icons of Mary, wizards and warlocks, spiritual forces, obligatory matzah, UFOs, divine words revealed by a holy prophet, magic, telepathy, or self-transcendence through bodily exercises. Because it is play, we do not ask, "is this stuff *real*?" "Do you really *believe in it*?" We absolutely refuse to demand an explanation or a declaration of faith. We just let you play. And saying that it is play does not mean that we are winking at each other, surreptitiously acknowledging that it's not *really* real. Think instead of a shockingly vivid dream that makes you feel genuinely unsure if you are in fact dreaming, or if you are only just waking up from what has been a dream all along. In an America that recognizes a domain of play, we agree *not to decide* which is the dream and which the reality. The justice that we pursue together outside the domain of play is meant to make this ambiguity tolerable.

It is crucial that the domain of play is a place where you are not compelled to explain yourself, justify what you care about, make sense out of what you're doing, or put yourself into a recognizable category. I think we should lament, with Saul Bellow's character Artur Sammler, the "liberal spirit of explanation" that demands in every sphere of human life a justification, a good reason.[10] Here is the ever-contemplative Sammler, in the stunning first paragraph of the book:

> You had to be a crank to insist on being right. Being right was largely
> a matter of explanations. Intellectual man had become an explaining

creature. Fathers to children, wives to husbands, lecturers to listeners, experts to laymen, colleagues to colleagues, doctors to patients, man to his own soul, explained. The roots of this, the causes of the other, the source of events, the history, the structure, the reasons why. For the most part, in one ear and out the other. The soul wanted what it wanted. It had its own natural knowledge. It sat unhappily on superstructures of explanation, poor bird, not knowing which way to fly.[11]

Recognizing a domain of play is a constraint on the incorrigible modern will to explain, which, unchecked, melts everything into a mire of skepticism.[12] The poor bird doesn't know which way to fly because, perched as it is stratospherically high atop a heap of unmasked ideologies, it has no incontestably *right* reason to go anywhere. But bring the bird back to earth and it will fly. If the domain of play is acknowledged, then we will not make people feel that in every sphere of life they must be able to explain the beings that impact their lives, which groups they are in, why they always do this ritual or relish that bit of nastiness. We welcome them back to earth, to push off from the primordially important stuff of childhood toward what they *have to do*. Recognizing a domain of play should make people feel that they can, from time to time, *turn/be turned* toward inexplicable realms about which we must remain silent.

Of course, I am not suggesting that in the domain of play it is possible to extricate oneself from the categories, affects, and relational dynamics that have been forged by historic oppression. That's the whole point of the fact of fraught societies. So I disagree with Sammler if he's suggesting that we have access to a "natural knowledge" that is somehow pristine and will guide us if only we will let it. Instead, I assume that we are products of an unjust world all the way down. And this means that the ways we want to play will not be free from legacies of white supremacy, patriarchy, economic exploitation, and so on. In fact, this is often precisely the stuff that we most want to play with. But if we really are capable of playing, then we can strip these forces of their harmful instrumentality by framing them within the domain of play. Recognizing a domain of play means making *noninstrumental life* imaginable and supporting it. And this, too, is a stark contrast to the reigning regime of common sense.

Karl Marx warned almost two hundred years ago that modern states, which take on a secular posture and relegate religion to the private sphere of civil society, diminish human beings into crass egoists who can't help but boil everything down to the instrumental pursuit of individual interests. Under these circumstances, religion is "only an abstract avowal of an individual folly, a private whim or caprice."[13] He even pointed specifically to North America, where "the infinite fragmentation of religion already gives it the *external* form of a strictly private affair. It has been relegated among the numerous private interests and exiled from the life of the community as such."[14] From Marx's perspective, political emancipation from state-sponsored religion, and the norm of religious freedom that comes with it, is an essential part of how modern states dragoon human beings into atomized selves who only know how to own and exchange fungible things and pursue fungible ends.

Marx identified something important. Even today, the special treatment given to religion in America reinforces the assumption that everything important to a person will involve individual striving toward a goal. This is especially evident among "religious liberals" who measure their piety in terms of their individual contributions to environmental sustainability, social justice, and "interfaith" peacemaking. But the same goes for "religious conservatives" who measure their piety in terms of their individual contributions to humanity's salvation, redemption, submission, or whatever. And this fits right in with the all-pervasive pressure in America *to succeed*—whether it is at happiness, mindfulness, business, social justice, or merit in the eyes of God. While religion is set aside for special treatment in America, it is not because it is at odds with the hegemonic *neo*liberal principle of success. The conventional distinction between religion and nonreligion reinforces the reigning common sense that everyone is only ever striving toward a personal goal or resting in order to strive later. Recognizing a domain of play leaves open possibilities of unselfconscious purposelessness, communitas, and intrinsic value that are preemptively reduced to individual interests by current conventions.[15]

Dissolving the religion/nonreligion dichotomy would also open to interpretation *as play* a massive amount of activity that would otherwise be hidden behind the category of religion. It could then be exposed to the interpretive judgment of public cultural critics who might see in it illustrations of how we are able to share political love despite the fact of fraught societies. I suspect, for instance, that it would be fruitful to interpret some observances of Passover and Purim as play. I can easily imagine an interpretation of an American Haggadah or Purim shpiel that would show Jews playing with their ambivalent Jewishness and fraught American-ness, which might be worth establishing as an enduring point in our public political culture.

I suspect that demolishing the sign that reads "This is religion" when we take a political perspective would be particularly revealing where people cannot (and may not want to) participate in play that currently requires access to elite social networks and disposable income. It may be especially illuminating to look for playing that might be hidden by the category of religion among other minoritized and economically disadvantaged populations. Black, Latino/a, Native American, and poor white populations, for instance, have been subjected to processes of religionization in America as much as Jews, if not more. Indeed, according to the reigning regime of common sense, these are generally "highly religious" populations.

But how often, for example, are people playing with Christian ideas, symbols, stories, and rituals, and how often are these features of nonpublic projects that they pursue? Drawing this distinction will always be a matter of provisional, contestable interpretive judgment, but I suspect that there is plenty of both. And I'd be willing to bet that there are extraordinary Sioux analogues to Purim, Black analogues to Passover, and so on, that can—with just the right "reflecting back" of a trusted public cultural critic—help all of us imagine how it is possible to share political love despite the fact of fraught societies.

So the political perspective that I'm promoting should reveal important playing that is hidden behind the category of religion. But it should also serve to elevate important playing that is conventionally dismissed as trivial by contrast to whatever counts as religion. I have a strong suspicion, for instance, that some instances of Civil War reenactment can be interpreted as a ritualization of Southern white resentment that redirects this emotion from instrumental pursuits in the domain of the political or the background culture to noninstrumentality in the domain of play. If this is true, then we might be willing to say that Civil War reenactment could continue even in the best American society that we can realistically imagine. It might exemplify the possibility of Southern whites holding onto their grudges in the domain of play, even as they simultaneously come to view *everyone* in America as a vulnerable, dependent human animal who carries a legacy of historic injustice and longs to live a collective life characterized by political justice.[16]

I have a similar suspicion about sexual play with hierarchy and violence among participants in BDSM (bondage and discipline, sadomasochism). It seems possible that in some cases people participating in these activities are shifting dynamics of patriarchy, misogyny, and heteronormativity from the instrumental domains of the basic structure of society and the background culture to the noninstrumental domain of play. If this is the case, then we might be willing to say that BDSM could continue even in the best America that we can realistically imagine. It might exemplify the possibility of women and men performing their interminable and erotically entangled rage and resentment, across all possible combinations of gender and sexual identification, even as they simultaneously come to see each other and themselves as truly entitled to a lifetime of opportunities to exercise the central human capabilities at a threshold level.[17]

Civil War reenactment and BDSM are extremely fraught activities. In the America that we actually live in, it seems appropriate to assume that instrumental racial and gender power dynamics circulate from the battlefield and the dungeon to, for instance, party politics and workplace dynamics. And, notably, we shouldn't assume that Civil War reenactment is just about race, while BDSM is just about gender. Both activities often involve innumerable dynamics related to race and gender, but also class, sexuality, regional identity, language, and much else.[18] What I'm suggesting is that we strive not to eradicate troubling and provocative activities, but instead to cultivate our capacity to frame them as play— and to prevent the perverse dynamics they carry from being instrumentalized in the domain of the political.

But there are other activities, which are not quite as fraught, that should also be elevated by the breakdown of the religion/nonreligion divide when it accompanies acknowledgment of the importance of play. Following the Grateful Dead (back in the day), or Phish, or Insane Clown Posse, participating in live action role-playing, where you dress up as a knight or sorceress or some such for battles and adventures, going to *Star Trek* conventions, having an elaborate life as an avatar in a virtual environment online like *Second Life*, and the list could go on and on. These activities, like war reenactment and BDSM, deserve the same respect as everything that has conventionally been called religion.[19] And who knows what we will find if we reflect back on these varieties of play as public cultural critics?

In conclusion, let me state explicitly: what I have presented here is not a secular vision of America, a vision that pretends to be neutral with respect to religion, or a vision that is morally relativist. On my view, we refuse to acknowledge that anything can be appropriately distinguished as religion or religious from anything else (when taking a political perspective). Since secularity (as a political conception) means having a normative definition of religion, which is used to keep religion out, my view cannot be considered secular. The ideal America that I have conjured derives from *substantive* moral values and concepts: central human capabilities, compassion, justice, political love, and so on. I have tried to cobble these values and concepts together with the explicit intention of inviting anyone who lives in America to join me in pursuit of an ideal that we can share despite our interminable conflicts.

A perhaps surprising consequence of not distinguishing between religion and nonreligion in the domain of the political is that, presumably, quite a bit of what we now conventionally label religious will likely end up incorporated into the public political culture. For instance, since so much of American life is saturated with Christian elements, we can assume that a lot of the stories of suffering and hope, exemplary nonpublic projects that endorse the political conception of justice, and snapshots of play that we will want to highlight in the public political culture will include Christian elements. Christian words, stories, symbols, and the like cannot be excluded from the domain of the political in the way that they would be excluded from a secular regime or a public sphere that tries to maintain a "wall of separation" between religion and the state. Bluntly, given the background culture that we're starting with, the American ideal that I'm advocating may end up *more* publicly Christian than the America of today.

The choice to highlight particular nonpublic projects or snapshots of play in the public political culture should have nothing to do with whether or not these projects or instances of play include gods, holy scriptures, magical incantations, or anything else that we conventionally associate with "religion." The only relevant question is how they relate to the political conception of justice. If they support the political conception of justice, then they support an ideal that we can all share—that we can all support *without* accepting the gods, scriptures, incantations, etc.

As you can imagine, I am not particularly thrilled to promote an idea that could lead us toward an America that is *even more* saturated with Christianity. At the same time, I take it as a good indication that what I'm offering is not simply my own nonpublic project passed off as a political ideal. If the public political culture in America is more saturated with Christian elements *for the right reasons*, then I have no good reason to complain. And if it is for the right reasons, then there will be plenty else in the public political culture to assure me that this is *my* country as much as anyone else's who lives here.

To be sure, I will struggle in the background culture to promote my own nonpublic projects, as is my prerogative. And I suspect that my nonpublic projects are at odds with a lot of nonpublic projects that have Christian elements. In the background culture, I will most certainly promote an atheistic worldview; I will advocate an account of human virtue that ranks interpersonal tenderness, introspective courage, intellectual profundity, and artistic excellence as admirable above all else; I will celebrate sexual thriving and comic amusement as among the greatest human goods; I will deride the absurd attention given to sports, express contempt for people who spend their lives pursuing wealth, and generally condemn all of the stuff in our world that I consider to be bullshit.

You don't have to agree with the value of any of this to endorse the conception of justice that I have offered as a *political* ideal in this book. And I am obviously just as committed to pursuing this political ideal as I am to pursuing my own nonpublic views. After all, the more people accept the political ideal, the more I can be assured a lifetime of opportunities to exercise my capabilities according to my own sense of what constitutes a good life. But I do not assume that the success of the political ideal will produce more adherents to my particular nonpublic projects in the background culture. The point is that the ultimate "look and feel" of America—how people choose to exercise their central human capabilities *above* the basic threshold level—is not predetermined by the political conception of justice. Much is left to be determined by the vicissitudes of struggle among nonpublic projects in the background culture. Even if most people in America came to accept the same political conception of justice, America will still look very different depending on which nonpublic projects populate the background culture and their relative popularity.

Many questions remain. How can people argue for exemptions from generally applicable laws without the category of religion? Should there be such exemptions? What about "claims of conscience"? Will a breakdown of the distinction between religion and nonreligion ultimately result in discrimination against minorities who might be better protected by the explicit guarantee of "religious freedom"?[20] What about the idea that we *can* define religion, and identify religions, and that they are distinctly beneficial to society or distinctly harmful to society? These are questions that I will grapple with in my ongoing research.

I have offered this book to you as a gesture of political love. I have invited you to sit and imagine with me a distinct vision of a more playful, more just America. There are still many questions left to confront in order to make this vision increasingly attractive and inclusive. There are undoubtedly suppressed assumptions or motivations that I have not yet sufficiently admitted to, blind spots that must be revealed, problems that should be exposed. Nevertheless, I hope I have made it a little easier to imagine that America can be a more just society, despite the fact of fraught societies, and that it is still worthwhile to strive to make it so.

NOTES

INTRODUCTION

1. Hermann Cohen, "The German and the Jewish Ethos II" [1916], in Eva Jospe, ed., *Reason and Hope: Selections from the Jewish Writings of Hermann Cohen* (Cincinnati: Hebrew Union College Press, 1993), 187–88. Robert Erlewine has recently offered a compelling revision of Cohen's reputation as a "tragic or hopelessly deluded figure" in *Judaism and the West: From Hermann Cohen to Joseph Soloveitchik* (Bloomington: Indiana University Press, 2016), 15. According to Erlewine, Cohen was more assertive about Judaism in relation to Germanism than apologetic. For Cohen, he writes, "Germanism is only Germanism to the degree it is *Jewish* in its Christianity" (Erlewine, 32; my emphasis). Nevertheless, I met Cohen as a cautionary figure in graduate school, and this Cohen still lingers in my historical imagination.
2. The French National Assembly, "Debate on the Eligibility of Jews for Citizenship (December 23, 1789)," in Paul Mendes-Flohr and Jehudah Reinharz, eds., *The Jew in the Modern World: A Documentary History*, 2d ed. (New York: Oxford University Press, 1995), 115.
3. French National Assembly, 115.
4. Leora Batnitzky has written an introduction to modern Jewish thought that focuses on Jewish responses to this demand. Leora Batnitzky, *How Judaism Became a Religion: An Introduction to Modern Jewish Thought* (Princeton: Princeton University Press, 2011).
5. Samson Raphael Hirsch, "Religion Allied to Progress," in Mendes-Flohr and Reinharz, *The Jew in the Modern World*, 201.
6. David Meyers writes, "In 1924 Rosenzweig observed, with Hermann Cohen uppermost in mind, that 'all modern Jews, and German Jews more than any others, are Protestants.'" David N. Meyers, "Hermann Cohen and the Quest for Protestant Judaism," *Leo Baeck Institute Year Book XLVI* (2001): 199.

7. Franz Rosenzweig, "Towards a Renaissance of Jewish Learning," in *On Jewish Learning* (New York: Schocken, 1965), 57. He also wrote, "All recipes, whether Zionist, orthodox, or liberal, produce caricatures of men, that become more ridiculous the more closely the recipe is followed" (66).

8. Along with Cohen, Hirsch, Rosenzweig and the like, I also absorbed the work of contemporary scholars, like Jonathan Z. Smith, Talal Asad, and Winnifred Sullivan, who are critical of the way that the category of religion works in modern liberal states. For instance, Jonathan Z. Smith, "Religion, Religions, Religious," in Mark C. Taylor, ed., *Critical Terms for Religious Studies* (Chicago: University of Chicago Press, 1998); Talal Asad, "Religion as an Anthropological Category," in *Genealogies of Religion: Discipline and Reasons of Power in Christianity and Islam* (Baltimore: Johns Hopkins University Press, 1993), and Winnifred Fallers Sullivan, *The Impossibility of Religious Freedom* (Princeton: Princeton University Press, 2005).

9. Jonathan Z. Smith, "God Save This Honorable Court: Religion and Civic Discourse," in *Relating Religion: Essays in the Study of Religion* (Chicago: University of Chicago Press, 2004), 377.

10. Max Nordau, "Speech to the First Zionist Congress (1897)," in Arthur Hertzberg, ed., *The Zionist Idea* (New York: Jewish Publication Society, 1959), 236.

11. Nordau, 239.

12. Nordau, 239.

13. Philip Roth, *The Plot Against America* (New York: Vintage International, 2004), 13.

14. Roth, 84.

15. Roth, 85.

16. Roth, 34.

17. For historical evidence of this plausibility, see Richard Frankel, "One Crisis Behind? Rethinking Antisemitic Exceptionalism in the United States and Germany," *American Jewish History* 97, no. 3 (July 2013): 235–58.

18. Roth, by the way, was not the only person who felt compelled to write about anti-Semitism in the mid-2000s. A blitz of books appeared about "the new anti-Semitism," though they focused mostly on Arabs, Muslims, and left-wing anti-Israel activists on college campuses. I read as many of these as I could find and wrote a one-hundred-page seminar paper about them in graduate school. Here are just a few of the more prominent titles: Phyllis Chesler, *The New Anti-Semitism: The Current Crisis and What We Must Do About It* (San Francisco: Jossey-Bass, 2003), Abraham H. Foxman, *Never Again? The Threat of the New Anti-Semitism* (San Francisco: Harper Collins, 2003), Gabriel Schoenfeld, *The Return of Anti-Semitism* (San Francisco: Encounter, 2004), and Ron Rosenbaum, ed., *Those Who Forget The Past: The Question of Anti-Semitism* (New York: Random House, 2004).

19. Roth, *The Plot Against America*, 114.

20. Martin Luther King Jr., "I Have a Dream," in James M. Washington, ed., *A Testament of Hope: The Essential Writings and Speeches of Martin Luther King, Jr.* (New York, HarperCollins, 1991), 219.

21. My approach to political love will rely heavily on Martha C. Nussbaum's account in Martha Nussbaum, *Political Emotions: Why Love Matters for Justice* (Cambridge: Belknap, 2013), which I will explain in the next chapter.

22. Well, it's written for those scholars, intellectuals, and other people who live in the United States of America at the beginning of the twenty-first century who are willing to read an academic book of this sort.

23. Wendy Brown explains, "what liberal democracy has provided over the past two centuries is a modest ethical gap between economy and polity. . . . It is this gap that neoliberal political rationality closes as it submits every aspect of political and social life to economic calculation: asking not, for example, what liberal constitutionalism stands for, what moral and political values it protects and preserves, but rather what efficacy or profitability constitutionalism promotes . . . or interdicts." Wendy Brown, "Neoliberalism and the End of Liberal Democracy," in *Edgework: Critical Essays on Knowledge and Politics* (Princeton: Princeton University Press, 2005), 46.

24. Writing during the George W. Bush presidency, Wendy Brown asked, "if we are slipping from liberalism to fascism, and if radical democracy or socialism is nowhere on the political horizon, don't we have to defend liberal democratic institutions and values? Isn't this the lesson of Weimar?" Brown, "Neoliberalism and the End of Liberal Democracy," 56. Brown claimed that these questions presuppose a false diagnosis, in part because "neoliberal governmentality . . . is not fascism" (Brown, 56). In 2018, slipping into fascism is a far greater concern. I think that these questions are now entirely appropriate. My hope is to help make imaginable a vision of liberal democratic institutions and values that left critics of liberalism might be willing to defend under these circumstances.

25. If, reader, you are an avowed supporter of white Christian nationalism and/or an economy that is not regulated to guarantee a life of human dignity to everyone within the United States, then we find ourselves in an irreconcilable conflict over the future of the country. I hope we can conduct ourselves respectfully in this conflict. For my part, I have tried to conjure a vision in this book that genuinely includes you, that genuinely offers you opportunities to flourish in your own way, albeit in the status of political loser. I hope you will do the same for me.

26. Mills uses the phrase "occupy liberalism!" in Charles W. Mills, *Black Rights/White Wrongs: The Critique of Racial Liberalism* (New York: Oxford University Press, 2017). For instance, it is the title of chapter 2 of that book. I have similarly taken to heart what Wendy Brown has suggested are prerequisites to "liberalism's prospects for renewal, even redemption, or at the very least for more modest and peaceful practices." Wendy Brown, *Regulating Aversion: Tolerance in the Age of Identity and Empire* (Princeton: Princeton University Press, 2008), 24. The liberal view that I propose does not pretend to be "norm-free," neutral, or "a-cultural." It is entirely upfront about the history of liberalism in the United States in which it is embedded and the power structures that reinforce its ongoing failures. And it is likewise upfront about carrying constitutive anxiety about a threatening "Other": totalitarianism (see chapter 3, this volume).

27. Ginsberg thought this way about Whitman:

> He pointed out the longing for closeness; erotic tenderness is of course implicit here, his own as well as in empathy, the spinster lady behind her curtains looking at the naked bathers. He pointed to that as basic to our bodies, basic to our minds, basic to our community, basic to our sociability, basic to our society, therefore basic to our politics. If that quality of compassion, erotic longing, tenderness, gentleness, was squelched, repressed, pushed back, denied, insulted, mocked, seen cynically, then the entire operation of democracy would be squelched, debased, mocked, seen cynically, made into a paranoid, mechanomegalopolis congregation of freaks afeard of each other.

Allen Ginsberg, "On Walt Whitman, Composed on the Tongue Taking a Walk Through Leaves of Grass," in *Deliberate Prose: Selected Essays 1952–1995* (New York: Harper Perennial, 2000), 297.

28. In his journal notes, a draft of the poem includes the line "I Allen Ginsberg Bard out of New Jersey take up the laurel tree cudgel from Whitman." Quoted in Michael Schumacher, *Dharma Lion: A Biography of Allen Ginsberg* (New York: St. Martin's, 1992), 219. Schumacher writes the following about the line, "It occurs to me that I am America": "Echoing sentiments expressed a century earlier by Walt Whitman, Ginsberg was proclaiming in public his acceptance of his own body and spirit" (Schumacher, 219). Thomas F. Merrill reads the first line, "America I've given you all and now I'm nothing," as expressing "the souring of Whitman's exuberant optimism toward America into a disillusionment that suggests the breaking of a covenant." Thomas F. Merrill, *Allen Ginsberg* (New York: Twayne, 1969), 102. He also reads "America when will you be angelic?/ When will you take off your clothes?" as an "appeal to America to shake off its hypocrisy and be equal to Whitman's challenge." Merrill, 103.

29. This is my transcription of the poem as it is read by Allen Ginsberg, *Holy Soul Jelly Roll: Poems and Songs, 1949–1993* (Lose Angeles: Rhino Records, 1994); the poem "America" is track 7 of vol. 1: *MOLOCH!*

30. Booklet to Ginsberg, 13.

31. Gerald Nachman, *Seriously Funny: The Rebel Comedians of the 1950s and 1960s* (New York: Back Stage, 2004), 57.

32. The 1956 draft that he reads has "America this is the impression I get from reading the newspaper." The published poem in *Howl* has: "America this is the impression I get from looking in the television set."

33. Defending Lenny Bruce in an argument with William F. Buckley on *Firing Line*, in an episode that appeared on May 7, 1968 (two years after Bruce's untimely death), Ginsberg said this about Bruce's performances of bigoted characters in his stand-up: "what you call scatological tirade was the language he was using [for] paraphrasing redneck southern sheriffs; he was doing old Swiftean satire, making use of the actual language of what he felt was the psychic enemy; he was presenting it in public, in front, and he was arrested for presenting that political evidence, so to speak."

34. On *Lenny Bruce: Let The Buyer Beware* (Los Angeles, Shout! Factory, 2004), disc 1, track 13.

35. Maimonides writes, "All the books of the Prophets and all the Holy Writings will be nullified in the Messianic era, with the exception of the Book of Esther. It will continue to exist, as will the five books of the Torah and the *halachot* of the Oral Law, which will never be nullified. Although all memories of the difficulties [endured by our people] will be nullified, as [Isaiah 65:16] states: 'For the former difficulties will be forgotten and for they will be hidden from My eye,' the [celebration of] the days of Purim will not be nullified, as [Esther 9:28] states: 'And these days of Purim will not pass from among the Jews, nor will their remembrance cease from their seed.'" Maimonides, *Mishneh Torah: Hilchot Ta'Aniot, Hilchot Megilah Vachanukah*, trans. Rabbi Eliyahu Touger (New York: Moznaim, 1991), 140. *Hilchot Megilah*, 2:18.

36. Maimonides, *Mishneh Torah: Sefer Shoftim*, trans. Rabbi Eliyahu Touger (New York: Moznaim, 2001), 622. *Hilchot Melachim U'Milchamoteihem*, 12:4–5.

37. Maimonides, 618. *Hilchot Melachim U'Milchamoteihem*, 12:2.

38. Maimonides, *Mishneh Torah: Hilchot Ta'Aniot, Hilchot Megilah Vachanukah*, trans. Rabbi Eliyahu Touger (New York: Moznaim, 1991), 140. *Hilchot Megilah*, 2:18.

39. Elliot Horowitz, *Reckless Rites: Purim and the Legacy of Jewish Violence* (Princeton: Princeton University Press, 2006), 17.

40. Horowitz, 12.

41. Philip Goodman, *The Purim Anthology* (New York: Jewish Publication Society, 1988), 327–28.

42. Quoted in Horowitz, *Reckless Rites*, 29–30.

43. Horowitz, 30.

44. Eviatar Zerubavel, *The Fine Line: Making Distinctions in Everyday Life* (Chicago: University of Chicago Press, 1991), 11.

45. Erving Goffman, *Frame Analysis: An Essay on the Organization of Experience* (Boston: Northeastern University Press, 1974), 45.

46. Goffman, 46.

47. As I will explain later, "perversity" has a special meaning in this book. It is the quality of not being justifiable to others and being most likely judged unfair or obscene by others. Perverse emotions are, in a sense, the opposite of what I call "political emotions" (drawing on Nussbaum). Political emotions—i.e., political compassion and political love—are judgments that we hope can be shared by people even as they maintain their respective perverse emotions.

48. Digby Diehl, "Q&A: Norman Lear," *Los Angeles Times*, July 30, 1972, W16.

1. JEWISHNESS, RACE, AND POLITICAL EMOTIONS

1. After all, we see in the film that Mookie has real affection for Pino's brother Vito.

2. Of course, *Do the Right Thing* ends tragically with very little register of hope. But even if it is not a hopeful film, it is a film that gestures toward political love—it plays the music of political love.

3. Carole Pateman reflects with Mills on "the difficulty of writing about sexual and racial power today, especially in the rich countries," where it "exists in a context of formal equality, codified civil freedoms, and antidiscrimination legislation. People are thus encouraged to see any problems as a matter of discrete remnants of older discrimination or the outcome of unfortunate, backward individual attitudes." Carole Pateman and Charles W. Mills, *Contract and Domination* (Malden, MA: Polity, 2007). This collaborative book followed Pateman's 1988 book *The Sexual Contract* and Mills's 1997 book *The Racial Contract*.

4. Charles W. Mills, *The Racial Contract* (Ithaca: Cornell University Press, 1997), 11.

5. Mills, 16.

6. Mills, 18.

7. James Baldwin, "Down at the Cross," in *The Fire Next Time*, in *Baldwin: Collected Essays* (New York: Library of America, 1998), 344.

8. Charles W. Mills, *Black Rights/White Wrongs: The Critique of Racial Liberalism* (New York: Oxford University Press, 2017), 49–71.

9. Mills, *The Racial Contract*, 18–19.

10. Mills, 18–19.

11. I am not the only Jew in America who feels this way about these sites in New York. On the Lower East Side of Manhattan as a "sacred space" for Jewish Americans, see Hasia Diner, *Lower East Side Memories: A Jewish Place in America* (Princeton: Princeton University Press, 2000).

12. Matthew Frye Jacobson, *Roots Too: White Ethnic Revival in Post-Civil Rights America* (Cambridge: Harvard University Press, 2006), 7.

13. Jacobson, 7.

14. Jacobson, 98.

15. Jacobson, 104.

16. Jacobson, 108.

17. Jacobson, 108.

18. Mills, *The Racial Contract*, 40.

19. Mills, 129. He has written more recently of his intention to recuperate Rawls: "What is the essence, the valuable core, of Rawls? It is, I would claim, the innovation of resurrecting social contract theory in the form of a thought-experiment involving veiled prudential choice within carefully stipulated parameters as a means of generating principles of justice. Despite the criticisms I have made throughout of Rawls, this core still seems to me to be a significant contribution to political philosophy." Mills, *Black Rights/White Wrongs*, 212.

20. Mills, *Black Rights/White Wrongs*, 10.

21. Mills, 214.

22. Racial liberalism is the historical liberalism that has been hegemonic up to now, "in which conceptions of personhood and resulting schedules of rights, duties, and government responsibilities have all been racialized. And the contract, correspondingly, has really been a *racial* one, an agreement among white contractors for white benefit." Mills, 29.

23. Frank B. Wilderson III, *Red, White and Black: Cinema and the Structure of U.S. Antagonisms* (Durham: Duke University Press, 2010), 58.

24. Wilderson, 20–21.

25. Wilderson, 19.

26. Wilderson, 37. The line, "simple enough, one has only not to be a nigger" is in Frantz Fanon, *Black Skin, White Masks*, trans. Charles Lam Markmann (New York: Grove, 1967), 115.

27. Wilderson, *Red, White and Black*, 37.

28. Wilderson, 45.

29. Wilderson, 10. Wilderson puts Indians in the category of "Savages," which is contrasted to "Masters" and "Slaves" in a very complex way. I will not be able to address this nuanced distinction here.

30. For Wilderson, it is Fanon who "lays the groundwork for a theory of antagonism over and above a theory of conflict." Wilderson, 75.

31. Wilderson, 36, citing Fanon, *Black Skin, White Masks*, 115.

32. Indeed, he concludes, with respect to Marxism, white feminism, and indigenism, "the world they seek to clarify and deconstruct is the world they ultimately mystify and renew." Wilderson, *Red, White and Black*, 338.

33. Wilderson, 337. As Wilderson indicates, Fanon is quoting Aimé Césaire.

34. Wilderson, 338.

35. Kimberlé Williams Crenshaw, "Demarginalizing the Intersection of Race and Sex: A Black Feminist Critique of Antidiscrimination Doctrine, Feminist Theory and Antiracist Politics," *University of Chicago Legal Forum*, no. 1 (1989): 139–67, article 8; Kimberlé Williams Crenshaw, "Mapping the Margins: Intersectionality, Identity Politics, and Violence Against Women of Color," *Stanford Law Review* 43 (July 1991): 1241–99.

36. Crenshaw, "Mapping the Margins," 1269.

37. Indeed, intersectionality studies may itself suffer from persistent blind spots. Jasbir Puar has argued that the mainstream of intersectionality studies has served to reify unnecessarily rigid categories of representation and to re-establish "the centrality of the subject positioning of white women." Jasbir K. Puar, "'I would rather be a cyborg than a goddess': Becoming-Intersectional in Assemblage Theory," *philoSOPHIA* 2, no. 1 (2012): 52. According to Puar, "Despite decades of feminist theorizing on the question of difference, difference continues to be 'difference from,' that is, the difference from 'white woman.' Distinct from a frame that privileges 'difference within,' 'difference from' produces difference as a contradiction rather than recognizing it as a perpetual and continuous process of splitting" (53).

38. Mills is well aware of this complexity. See, in general, Pateman and Mills, *Contract and Domination*. He has also written more recently about the limits of the black/white paradigm in Mills, *Black Rights/White Wrongs*, 201–2.

39. Jonathan Freedman, *Klezmer America: Jewishness, Ethnicity, Modernity* (New York: Columbia University Press, 2008), 13.

40. Freedman mentions Los Tigres del Norte, Ricardo Arjona, and the Jornaleros del Norte. Freedman, 13.

41. Freedman,14.

42. Freedman, 14.

43. Freedman, 15.

44. Freedman, 34. Some key early works that tell the story of Jewish accession to whiteness are Michael Rogin, *Blackface, White Noise: Jewish Immigrants in the Hollywood Age* (Los Angeles: University of California Press, 1996); and Karen Brodkin, *How Jews Became White Folks and What That Says About Race in America* (New Brunswick, NJ: Rutgers University Press, 2000).

45. Freedman, *Klezmer America*, 34.

46. Freedman, 34.

47. Eric L. Goldstein, *The Price of Whiteness: Jews, Race, and American Identity* (Princeton: Princeton University Press, 2006).

48. Susan Glenn argues, relatedly, that

> Jews have been deeply invested in the idea of their own physical difference, but the terms of that engagement have shifted over time in response to both external and internal pressures. Whether trying to prove to racists and xenophobes that Jews would eventually cease to look stereotypically "Jewish," or seeking plastic surgery to normalize their appearance, or playing the game of visual connoisseurship, American Jews have acknowledged and even embraced physical difference as an aspect of what makes Jews "Jewish."

Susan A. Glenn, "'Funny, You Don't Look Jewish': Visual Stereotypes and the Making of Modern Jewish Identity," in Susan A. Glenn and Naomi B. Sokoloff, eds., *Boundaries of Jewish Identity* (Seattle: University of Washington Press, 2011), 83.

49. Goldstein, *The Price of Whiteness*, 6. The sense that Jewishness is somehow biological or ontological is not a modern invention. Premodern anti-Semitism is preoccupied with Jewish bodies. And premodern Jewish thinkers, perhaps most notably the early twelfth-century Jewish philosopher Yehudah Halevi, argued for ontological Jewishness in ways that are still controversial among Jews. For a review of recent approaches to Halevi, see Lawrence J. Kaplan, "'The Starling's Caw': Judah Halevi as Philosopher, Poet, and Pilgrim," *Jewish Quarterly Review* 101, no. 1 (Winter 2011): 97–132, especially 121–23.

50. Goldstein, 18.

51. Goldstein.

52. Goldstein, 29–30.

53. Goldstein, 37.

54. Goldstein, 40–41.

55. Goldstein, 76–82.

56. Quoted in Goldstein, 96.

57. Goldstein, 96.

58. Laura Levitt, "Impossible Assimilations, American Liberalism, and Jewish Difference: Revisiting Jewish Secularism," *American Quarterly* 59, no. 3 (2007): 814.

59. Levitt has identified a troubling irony here:

> The idea that Jewish difference must be defined in religious terms, as a matter of private faith, challenges the promise of liberal inclusion by helping us see the connections between liberalism, secularization, and the lingering power of the Protestant imaginary in shaping this peculiar version of American secular culture. These secular forms of social acceptance ended up denying the explicitly secular forms of Jewish identification favored by large numbers of immigrant Jews because it construed religious pluralism as the relevant form of containing and expressing Jewish difference. . . . Secular American culture rejected the possibility of secular forms of Jewishness.

Laura Levitt, "Shedding Liberalism, All Over Again," *Scholar and Feminist Online: Religion and the Body* 9, no. 3 (Summer 2011). The groundwork for this critique is in Laura Levitt, *Jews and Feminism: The Ambivalent Search for Home* (New York: Routledge, 1997). Whereas Levitt makes a compelling case "that we stop imagining ourselves as always already within this liberal horizon," I hope to incorporate a strong critique of classical liberalism into a new plausible vision that remains within the liberal horizon. Levitt, *Jews and Feminism*, 5.

60. Goldstein, *The Price of Whiteness*, 119.

61. Goldstein, 127.

62. Goldstein, 128.

63. Kevin Schultz, *Tri-Faith America: How Catholics and Jews Held Postwar America to Its Protestant Promise* (New York: Oxford University Press, 2011).

64. Schultz, 96.

65. Hasia R. Diner, *The Jews of the United States: 1654–2000* (Berkeley: University of California Press, 2004), 289.

66. Levitt, "Impossible Assimilations," 819.

67. Diner, *The Jews of the United States*, 292–93.

68. Diner, 206–7.

69. Diner, 212.

70. Quoted in Michael Staub, *Torn at the Roots: The Crisis of Jewish Liberalism in Postwar America* (New York: Columbia University Press, 2002), 95.

71. See Staub, chapter 3, "'Artificial Altruism Sows Only Seeds of Error and Chaos': Desegregation and Jewish Survival," in *Torn at the Roots*, 76–111.

72. Goldstein, *The Price of Whiteness*, 215.

73. James Baldwin, "Negroes Are Anti-Semitic Because They're Anti-White" (New York: Library of America, 1998), 746; originally published in the *New York Times Magazine*, April 9, 1967.

74. Baldwin, 744.

75. Goldstein, *The Price of Whiteness*, 218.

76. David A. Hollinger, *After Cloven Tongues of Fire: Protestant Liberalism in Modern American History* (Princeton: Princeton University Press, 2013), 152.

77. Hollinger, 154.

78. Hollinger, 154.

79. David Biale, Michael Galchinsky, and Susannah Heschel, *Insider/Outsider: American Jews and Multiculturalism* (Los Angeles: University of California Press, 1998), 4.

80. Irving Howe, "Introduction," in Irving Howe and Eliezer Greenberg, eds., *A Treasury of Yiddish Stories* (New York: Penguin, 1953), 38.

81. This Jewish way of seeing others is captured well in a cartoon from a Yiddish humor magazine, published in 1908, reproduced by Goldstein. It shows a white man attacking a black man with a knife, annotated in Yiddish with the word "civilization;" below it is the same black man attacking the same white man with a knife, annotated in Yiddish with the word "barbarism." Goldstein's caption reads, "This cartoon satirizing white Americans' notions of civilization and barbarism appeared in the Yiddish humor magazine *Der kibetser*." Goldstein, *The Price of Whiteness*, 80.

82. The Talmud and Midrash contain a set of oaths that long served as axioms of Jewish political theory. Aviezer Ravitzky paraphrases them as follows: "'that Israel not ascend the wall' from the exile, 'that they not rebel against the nations of the world,' and that 'they not force the End' (although another version has 'that they not postpone the End'—*yirhaku* rather than *yidhaku!*) (Cant. R. 2:7; BT Ketubbot 111a). The Talmudic midrash goes on to tell of a parallel oath imposed upon the nations of the world: 'that they not oppress Israel overly much.'" Aviezer Ravitzky, *Messianism, Zionism, and Jewish Religious Radicalism* (Chicago: University of Chicago Press, 1996), 22. See, more generally, David Biale, *Power and Powerlessness in Jewish History* (New York: Schocken, 1987), especially 34–57.

83. Philip Roth, *Portnoy's Complaint* (New York: Vintage, 1994 [1969]), 81–82.

84. Roth, 75–76.

85. Hillel Halkin made the case in 1977 in *Letters to an American Jewish Friend: A Zionist's Polemic* (New York: Gefen, 2013).

86. "The Vanishing American Jew" is the title of a cover story in *Look*, May 5, 1964, which frightened Jews in America with statistics about increasing assimilation. Alan Dershowitz published a book on the same subject in 1997, titled *The Vanishing American Jew: In Search of Jewish Identity for the Next Century*.

87. And this belief emboldens me to believe that the foreign policy of the United States should be to promote institutions that guarantee political justice for Jews, Palestinians, Druze, migrant workers from Africa and Asia, and everyone else who lives in the historical land of Israel. I don't know exactly what a viable, just arrangement would look like. But I assume that it will require an end to the Israeli occupation of territories seized in 1967, accommodations for Palestinian refugees, and equal rights for everyone who lives within the current borders of the State of Israel regardless of their kind of Jewishness or lack thereof.

88. John Rawls, *Political Liberalism* (New York: Columbia University Press, 1996), 37.

89. This statement raises complex philosophical questions that I cannot take up here. An exploration of these questions might begin with R. Jay Wallace, *The View from Here:*

On Affirmation, Attachment, and the Limits of Regret (New York: Oxford University Press, 2013). He writes, for instance,

> If the attitude of unconditional affirmation commits us to affirming the historical conditions of the things that give meaning to our lives, then for all we know we might be committed by our attachments to affirming the most obscene atrocities and disasters. Our fate, in other words, might well be that we are committed to affirming things that cannot possibly be regarded as worthy of affirmation, and only our ignorance of the ways in which we are causally implicated in the past would seem to save us from having to face up to this unsettling nihilistic thought.

(13–14)

90.   John Rawls, *Justice as Fairness: A Restatement* (Cambridge: Harvard University Press, 2001), 9.

91.   Thanks to Susan Pensak for suggesting that I include the prevalent experience of women being treated dismissively by male doctors.

92.   Nussbaum has done significant work to distinguish political liberalism from other versions of liberalism. See, for instance, Martha C. Nussbaum, "Perfectionist Liberalism and Political Liberalism," *Philosophy and Public Affairs* 39, no. 1 (Winter 2011): 3–45.

93.   Martha C. Nussbaum, "Constitutions and Capabilities: 'Perception' Against Lofty Formalism," 121 *Harvard Law Review* 4 (2007): 10.

94.   Nussbaum, 10.

95.   Nussbaum, 11.

96.   Martha C. Nussbaum, *Frontiers of Justice: Disability, Nationality, Species Membership* (Cambridge: Harvard University Press, 2006), 70. The complete list is provided on pp. 76–78. A change of the wording within the capability of "Emotions" from "and justified anger" to "and emotions of justified protest" is indicated in Martha C. Nussbaum, "Philosophy in the Service of Humanity," *Know: A Journal on the Formation of Knowledge* 1, no. 2 (Fall 2017): 234n2. On the application of political liberalism beyond the U.S., see Martha C. Nussbaum, "Political Liberalism and Global Justice," *Journal of Global Justice* 11, no. 1 (2015): 68–79.

97.   Nussbaum, *Frontiers of Justice*, 158.

98.   Nussbaum, 85–86.

99.   Martha C. Nussbaum, *Upheavals of Thought: The Intelligence of Emotions* (Cambridge: Cambridge University Press, 2001), 418.

100. Nussbaum, *Frontiers of Justice*, 87–88.

101. Nussbaum, 88–89.

102. Nussbaum, 88.

103. Nussbaum, 88.

104. Martha Nussbaum, *Political Emotions: Why Love Matters for Justice* (Cambridge: Belknap, 2013), 384.

105. Martha C. Nussbaum, "Compassion: Human and Animal," in N. Ann Davis, Richard Keshen, Jeff McMahan, eds., *Ethics and Humanity: Themes from the Philosophy of Jonathan Glover* (New York: Oxford University Press, 2010), 205.

106. Nussbaum, "Compassion," 203. The term *anthropodenial* is borrowed from primatologist Frans de Waal, according to whom it "denotes willful blindness to the human-like characteristics of animals or the animal-like characteristics of ourselves." Frans de Waal, *Primates and Philosophers: How Morality Evolved* (Princeton: Princeton University Press, 2006), 65.

107. With respect to the object-relations tradition, Nussbaum explains that she treats these figures "as humanistic interpretive thinkers, very closely related to Proust and Plato, whose work gains texture and depth through having a clinical dimension." Nussbaum, *Upheavals of Thought*, 181.

108. Nussbaum, "Compassion," 214–15.

109. Nussbaum, 216.

110. Nussbaum, 216.

111. Nussbaum, 216.

112. Nussbaum, 216. See also Nussbaum, *Upheavals of Thought*, 200–6.

113. Nussbaum, "Compassion," 216.

114. Nussbaum, 217. The construction of what counts as "normal" is also important in this process:

> I believe the use of the category "normal" to stigmatize deviant behavior should be understood as the outgrowth of the primitive shame that to some degree affects us all. Because we are all aware that there are many ways in which we fail to measure up to the exorbitant demand of infancy for complete control over the sources of good, because we retain our nostalgic longing for the bliss of infantile oneness with the womb or the breast, we need a surrogate kind of safety or completeness. And those who call themselves "normals" find this safety in the idea of a group that is both widespread, surrounding them on all sides, and good, lacking in nothing. By defining a certain sort of person as complete and good, and by surrounding themselves with such people, normals gain comfort and the illusion of safety. The idea of normalcy is like a surrogate womb, blotting out intrusive stimuli from the world of difference.

Martha C. Nussbaum, *Hiding from Humanity: Disgust, Shame, and the Law* (Princeton: Princeton University Press, 2004), 219.

115. See especially, Nussbaum, *Hiding from Humanity*, 71–123.

116. Nussbaum, *Upheavals of Thought*, 426.

117. Nussbaum, 426. The arts and humanities, she writes, "make a vital and irreplaceable contribution to citizenship, without which we will very likely have an obtuse and emotionally dead citizenry, prey to the aggressive wishes that so often accompany an inner world dead to the images of others. Cutting the arts is a recipe for pathological narcissism, of citizens who have difficulty connecting to other human beings with a sense of

the human significance of the issues at stake" (426). See also Martha C. Nussbaum, *Not for Profit: Why Democracy Needs the Humanities* (Princeton: Princeton University Press, 2010).

118.   Nussbaum, *Upheavals of Thought*, 429.

119.   Nussbaum, 238.

120.   Nussbaum, *Hiding from Humanity*, 224.

121.   Nussbaum, *Upheavals of Thought*, 431–432.

122.   Nussbaum, *Hiding from Humanity*, 36.

123.   Nussbaum, 35.

124.   Nussbaum, 209.

125.   Nussbaum, *Political Emotions*, 210–11.

126.   Nussbaum, 211.

127.   Nussbaum, especially 225–49.

128.   Nussbaum, *Hiding from Humanity*, 120.

129.   Martha C. Nussbaum, *Anger and Forgiveness: Resentment, Generosity, Justice* (Oxford: Oxford University Press, 2016), 5.

130.   Nussbaum, 31.

131.   Nussbaum, 172.

132.   Nussbaum, 218.

133.   As always, Nussbaum is not at all naive about her bold aspirations. In the conclusion of *Anger and Forgiveness* she reveals that the essential goal of the argument is to help readers "to see clearly the irrationality and stupidity of anger." But she admits, "I don't always take my own medicine. . . . It's hard not to be stupid." Nevertheless, she is quick to remind us that being difficult doesn't make something unworthy of effort. She recognizes that we will fall into stupidity, and this is part of the reason why she wants us to focus on institutions: "Our institutions should model our best selves, not our worst. They should exemplify adulthood, even if we are often children" (249). I agree with this focus on institutions. The difference is that I think there is far more to anger and other perverse emotions than mere stupidity. For instance, sometimes feeling and expressing anger is part of thriving as the kind of person that you take yourself to be.

134.   In the worldview of ancient Hebrew texts, the Amalekites were descendants of Esau who lived in the Negev and Sinai deserts. When the Israelites were on their way from Egypt to the Land of Israel, the Amalekites attacked the stragglers at the back of the caravan by surprise and slaughtered them (Deuteronomy 17–18). The Amalekites were presumed to want to wipe out Israel as a nation, making it so the name Israel would be forgotten forever (Psalm 83:4–7). God tells Moses to relay that He will "surely wipe out the name of Amalek from under the heavens" (Exodus 17:14) and adjures Israel to do its part by blotting out their memory as well (Deuteronomy 25:19). But Moses also relays that God will be at war with Amalek "for all time" (Exodus 17:16). Later in the saga of Israel, King Saul is called upon by God to slaughter the Amalekites and specifies that this include women, children, and animals (1 Samuel 15:1–3). I have used Robert Alter's translations from Alter, *The Five Books of Moses* (New York: Norton, 2004), 414, 415. With respect to Amalek, Maimonides affirms the positive commandment

298 1. JEWISHNESS, RACE, AND POLITICAL EMOTIONS

"to constantly remember their evil deeds and their ambush [of Israel] to arouse our hatred of them. . . . For it is forbidden to forget our hatred and enmity for them." Maimonides, *Mishneh Torah: Sefer Shoftim*, trans. Rabbi Eliyahu Touger (New York: Moznaim, 2001), 538. *Hilchot Melachim U'Milchamoteihem*, 5:5. He also suggests that Amalek still exists in his time and will presumably exist until the messianic era (note 29). The passage from Deuteronomy that mentions Amalek is traditionally read before Purim, highlighting that Haman is said to be a descendant of the Amalekites (note 33). On the modern Jewish practice of testing a pen by writing "Amalek" and then crossing it out, as a way of fulfilling the commandment to blot out the name of Amalek, see Elliot Horowitz, *Reckless Rites: Purim and the Legacy of Jewish Violence* (Princeton: Princeton University Press, 2006), 107–10.

135.   Leon Wieseltier, "Against Ethnic Panic: *Hitler Is Dead*," in Ron Rosenbaum, ed., *Those Who Forget the Past: The Question of Anti-Semitism* (New York: Random House, 2004), 181; originally published in the *New Republic* (May 27, 2002).

136.   Wieseltier, 186.

137.   Wieseltier, 186–87.

138.   In his book *Racial Paranoia*, anthropologist John Jackson explores similar forces. He writes, "after the social changes of the 1960s, African Americans have become more secure in their legal citizenship but concomitantly less sure about other things, such as when they're being victimized by silent and undeclared racisms. This uncertainty can make people all the more paranoid about the smallest slights, the subtlest glances, the tiniest inconveniences. Any of those can be telltale signs of 'two-faced racism,' of hidden racial animus dressed up to look politically correct, racial conspiracies cloaked in public niceties and social graces." John L. Jackson, *Racial Paranoia: The Unintended Consequences of Political Correctness* (New York: Basic Books, 2008), 9.

139.   Kenneth Warren has shown how a profound sensitivity to this paradox has, in fact, haunted the political aspirations of African American literature since Jim Crow: "One was facing the paradox that the condition one was fighting to overcome was the very condition that gave one's own existence meaning. As an instrument for pursuing social justice, this literature was forced at least to contemplate its own wished-for obsolescence." Kenneth W. Warren, *What Was African American Literature* (Cambridge: Harvard University Press, 2011), 18.

140.   Horowitz, *Reckless Rites*, 1–10.

141.   On the medieval censorship of the *Aleinu*, which resulted in the excising of this passage for centuries, and the more recent return of the passage in Israeli and American Orthodox prayer books, see Ruth Langer, "The Censorship of Aleinu in Ashkenaz and Its Aftermath," in Debra Reed Blank, ed., *The Experience of Jewish Liturgy: Studies Dedicated to Menahem Schmelzer* (Boston: Brill, 2011), especially 161. The morning blessings for a Jewish man include thanking God "for not having made me a gentile," "for not having made me a slave," and "for not having made me a woman"—in that order. *The Complete Artscroll Siddur—Nusach Ashkenaz*, pocket ed. (Brooklyn: Mesorah, 1984), 19.

142. Aztlán is the mythical Aztec place of origin. On the utopian yearning for Aztlán that persists in the scriptural practices of the Chicanx movement, see Jacqueline M. Hidalgo, *Revelation in Aztlán: Scriptures, Utopias, and the Chicano Movement* (New York: Palgrave Macmillan, 2016).

2. THE FACT OF FRAUGHT SOCIETIES I

1. John Jackson explains that the target of racial paranoia is "*de cardio* racism": "a kind of hidden or cloaked racism, a racism of euphemism and innuendo, not heels-dug-in pronouncements of innate black inferiority." John L. Jackson, *Racial Paranoia: The Unintended Consequences of Political Correctness* (New York: Basic Books, 2008), 78. He writes,

    > *De cardio* racism is about what the law can't touch, what won't be easily proved or disproved, what can't be simply criminalized and deemed unconstitutional. It is racism that is most terrifying because it is hidden, secret, papered over with public niceties and politically correct jargon. It is a very powerful way that many Americans think about race today, as a subtle by-product of the ineluctably human fact that people feel things they'll never admit (sometimes, not even to themselves), particularly when the topic of discussion is race.

    (87)

2. David Graham, "The Stubborn Persistence of Confederate Monuments," on the *Atlantic* website, April 26, 2016.
3. Eugene R. Sheppard, *Leo Strauss and the Politics of Exile: The Making of a Political Philosopher* (Waltham, MA: Brandeis University Press, 2006), 9.
4. See, for instance, selections from Hermann Cohen written in 1915 and 1916, compiled and translated as "German Humanism and Jewish Messianism," in Eva Jospe, ed., *Reason and Hope: Selections from the Jewish Writings of Hermann Cohen* (Cincinnati: Hebrew Union College Press, 1993), 174–93. See, in general, Paul Mendes-Flohr, *German Jews: A Dual Identity* (New Haven: Yale University Press, 1999).
5. Kenneth Hart Green, "Editor's Introduction: Leo Strauss as a Modern Jewish Thinker," in Leo Strauss, *Jewish Philosophy and the Crisis of Modernity: Essays in Modern Jewish Thought,* ed. Kenneth Hart Green (Albany: State University of New York Press, 1997), 4.
6. Lucy S. Dawidowicz, *The War Against the Jews: 1933–1945* (New York: Bantam, 1986), 403.
7. Leo Strauss, "Preface to *Spinoza's Critique of Religion*" [1965], in Strauss, *Jewish Philosophy and the Crisis of Modernity,* 137–38.
8. Strauss, 142.
9. Strauss, 140. For more on this passage, see Ritchie Robertson, "The Limits of Toleration in Enlightenment Germany: Lessing, Goethe and the Jews," in Tony Kushner and Nadia Valman, eds., *Philosemitism, Antisemitism, and the Jews: Perspectives from the*

Middle Ages to the Twentieth Century (Burlington, VT: Ashgate, 2004), 213–14. Saul Bellow was also impacted by this passage. See his 1988 lecture "A Jewish Writer in America" in *There Is Simply Too Much to Think About*, ed. Benjamin Taylor (New York: Viking, 2015), 361.

10. Strauss, "Preface to *Spinoza's Critique of Religion*," 140.

11. Strauss's critique, in this case, actually has some structural elements in common with feminist critiques of the public/private divide. Mark Warner recounts, "Feminists such as [Carole] Pateman and [Catharine] MacKinnon, for example, point out that the liberal protection of the private from public interference simply blocked from view those kinds of domination that structure private life through the institutions of the family, the household, gender, and sexuality." Michael Warner, *Publics and Counterpublics* (New York: Zone, 2005), 43. Nancy Fraser has written:

> The official bourgeois public sphere is the institutional vehicle for a major historical transformation in the nature of political domination. This is the shift from a repressive mode of domination to a hegemonic one, from rule based primarily on acquiescence to superior force to rule based primarily on consent supplemented with some measure of repression. The important point is that this new mode of political domination, like the older one, secures the ability of one stratum of society to rule the rest.

Nancy Fraser, "Rethinking the Public Sphere: A Contribution to the Critique of Actually Existing Democracy," *Social Text*, nos. 25/26 (1990): 62.

12. Strauss, "Preface to *Spinoza's Critique of Religion*," 143–44. Eugene Sheppard describes this aspect of Strauss's argument as "a truncated form of Marx's critique of liberalism in his 1843 essay 'On the Jewish Question.'" Sheppard, *Leo Strauss and the Politics of Exile*, 122. This is an important insight and may explain some of why I see Strauss and Fanon as responding to similar concerns.

13. Strauss, "Preface to *Spinoza's Critique of Religion*," 141.

14. It should be noted that, given the choice between liberalism and communism, Strauss endorsed liberalism as the least bad option: "the uneasy 'solution of the Jewish problem' offered by the liberal state is superior to the communist 'solution'" (144).

15. Leo Strauss, "Why We Remain Jews: Can Jewish Faith and History Still Speak to Us?" in Strauss, *Jewish Philosophy and the Crisis of Modernity*, 313. In fact, Heine had a far more complex relationship to his Jewishness. See S. S. Prawer, *Heine's Jewish Comedy* (Oxford: Oxford University Press, 1986).

16. Strauss, "Why We Remain Jews," 315.

17. Strauss, 317.

18. Strauss, "Preface to *Spinoza's Critique of Religion*," 142.

19. Strauss, "Why We Remain Jews," 319.

20. Strauss, 319.

21. Strauss, "Preface to *Spinoza's Critique of Religion*," 143.

22. Strauss, 143.

23. Strauss, 143.

24. Strauss, 143.

25. Strauss, 143.

26. Strauss, "Why We Remain Jews," 315.

27. Strauss, 321.

28. Strauss, "Preface to Spinoza's Critique of Religion," 141.

29. Leo Strauss, "Jerusalem and Athens," in Strauss, Jewish Philosophy and the Crisis of Modernity, 380.

30. Leo Strauss, Philosophy and Law: Contributions to the Understanding of Maimonides and His Predecessors (Albany: State University of New York Press, 1995), 132.

31. Strauss, 36–38.

32. Haym Soloveitchik, "Rupture and Reconstruction: The Transformation of Contemporary Orthodoxy," Tradition 28, no. 4 (Summer 1994).

33. Strauss, "Preface to Spinoza's Critique of Religion," 144.

34. Strauss, "Jerusalem and Athens," 380.

35. Strauss, "Why We Remain Jews," 317.

36. Straus, 317. After all, Straus is pointing to a deep problem of politics that extends far beyond modern liberal states: he also describes as "extralegal but not illegal" the late fifteenth-century Spanish practice of differentiating between Spaniards of pure blood and Spaniards of impure blood (i.e., Jews who converted to Christianity at the time of the Inquisition; 314). These conversos, as they were called, "were forced to remain Jews, in a manner" (314).

37. Leo Strauss, "Progress or Return?" in Strauss, Jewish Philosophy and the Crisis of Modernity, 116.

38. As Leora Batnitzky has written, "Even if Strauss were shown to be a critic of various aspects of liberal democracy, this would in no way automatically remove him from the parameters of debates about and defenses of liberal democracy." Leora Batnitzky, Leo Strauss and Emmanuel Levinas: Philosophy and the Politics of Revelation (New York: Cambridge University Press, 2006), 209.

39. Charles Taylor, "The Politics of Recognition," in Multiculturalism: Examining the Politics of Recognition, ed. Amy Gutmann (Princeton: Princeton University Press, 1994), 25; see also pp. 36, 64.

40. Taylor, 64. By fundamental harm I mean a harm that is bad in and of itself, not because it produces some worse harm (for example, inequality or infringement upon a person's liberty).

41. Taylor, 65.

42. Emmanuel Hansen, Frantz Fanon: Social and Political Thought (Columbus: Ohio State University Press, 1977), 23; Lewis R. Gordon, What Fanon Said: A Philosophical Introduction to His Life and Thought (New York: Fordham University Press, 2015), 9–11.

43. David Macey, Frantz Fanon: A Biography (New York: Picador USA, 2000), 91. See also Gordon, What Fanon Said, 11.

44. Gordon, What Fanon Said, 12.

45. Hansen, Frantz Fanon, 27.

46. Macey, *Frantz Fanon*, 63, 71.

47. Hansen, *Frantz Fanon*, 41.

48. Hansen, 43–45.

49. A few days after Fanon's death, French police seized the publisher's copies of *The Wretched of the Earth* under the pretense that they were a threat to national security. Macey, *Frantz Fanon*, 6.

50. Lewis R. Gordon, *Fanon and the Crisis of European Man: An Essay on Philosophy and the Human Sciences* (New York: Routledge, 1995), 69.

51. Macey, *Frantz Fanon*, 2.

52. Frantz Fanon, *The Wretched of the Earth*, trans. Richard Philcox (New York: Grove, 2004), 6.

53. Fanon, 2.

54. Fanon states his agreement on this point explicitly, citing this very sentence, in Frantz Fanon, *Black Skin, White Masks*, trans. Richard Philcox (New York: Grove, 2008), 73. The quotation is from Sartre, Jean-Paul Sartre, *Anti-Semite and Jew: An Exploration of the Etiology of Hate* (New York: Schocken, 1995), 69.

55. Fanon, *The Wretched of the Earth*, 2.

56. Fanon, 178.

57. Fanon, 239.

58. Fanon, 50.

59. Fanon, 44. I take Fanon to be using the term *mediation* in the sense of *Vermittlung*, as in Hegel's *Phenomenology*: "Jedes ist dem andern die Mitte, durch welche jedes sich mit sich selbst *vermittelt* und zusammenschliesst, und jedes sich und dem andern unmittelbares für sich seiendes Wesen, welches zugleich nur durch diese *Vermittlung* so für sich ist. Sie anerkennen sich, als gegenseitig sich anerkennend" (my emphasis). G. W. F. Hegel, *Phaenomenologie des Geistes* (Hamburg: Felix Meiner, 2006), 129. Or, "Each is for the other the middle term, through which each mediates itself with itself and unites with itself; and each is for itself, and for the other, and immediate being on its own account, which at the same time is such only through mediation. They *recognize* themselves as *mutually recognizing* one another." G. W. F. Hegel, *Hegel's Phenomenology of Spirit*, trans. A. V. Miller (Oxford: Oxford University Press, 1977), 112. Robert Williams comments on this passage as follows: "This is the 'syllogism of recognition'; each term is both extreme and mean. Each self must serve as mediator for the other, while receiving in turn mediation—that is, recognition—from the other. Only through such reciprocal action can the self 'return' to itself out of its 'othered' state, by gaining itself in the other's recognition." Robert R. Williams, *Hegel's Ethics of Recognition* (Berkeley: University of California Press, 1997), 59. On this reading, we might say that, for Fanon, violence has taken the place of recognition.

60. Michael W. Sonnleitner, "Of Logic and Liberation: Frantz Fanon on Terrorism," *Journal of Black Studies* 17, no. 3 (March, 1987): 289, 297–98. Anita Chari interprets Fanon as a philosopher of action in "Exceeding Recognition," *Sartre Studies International* 10, no. 2 (2004): 110–22. She writes, "Fanon argues that action, which exceeds, transforms, and transvaluates identity, holds out a greater promise for liberation" (121). A greater promise, that is, than "recognition."

61. Fanon, *The Wretched of the Earth*, 51. Messay Kebede explains this well: Fanon "sees violence as a necessary therapy for a cultural disease brought about by colonial subjugation. The mere departure of the colonizer is not enough; liberation and dignity cannot be recovered unless the colonized get involved in violent performances." Messay Kebede, "The Rehabilitation of Violence and the Violence of Rehabilitation: Fanon and Colonialism," *Journal of Black Studies* 31, no. 5 (May 2001): 539.

62. Fanon, *The Wretched of the Earth*, 96.

63. Hannah Arendt wrote a well-known denunciation of Fanon's violence as the fuel for unruly student rebels in the 1960s and early 1970s. She writes, "Not many authors of rank glorified violence for violence's sake; but these few—Sorel, Pareto, Fanon—were motivated by a much deeper hatred of bourgeois society and were led to a much more radical break with its moral standards than the conventional Left, which was chiefly inspired by compassion and a burning desire for justice." Hannah Arendt, "On Violence," in *Crises of the Republic* (New York: Harcourt Brace, 1972), 162. In On p. 116n19 she, like Simon de Beauvoir, describes Fanon as personally having a great distaste for violence.

64. Neil Roberts, "Fanon, Sartre, Violence, and Freedom," *Sartre Studies International* 10, no. 2 (2004): 146.

65. Fanon, *The Wretched of the Earth*, 159.

66. Fanon, 160.

67. Kwame Anthony Appiah, *In My Father's House: Africa in the Philosophy of Culture* (Oxford: Oxford University Press, 1992), 61.

68. Fanon, *The Wretched of the Earth*, 148.

69. Fanon, *The Wretched of the Earth*, lv.

70. Fanon, xlviii.

71. Fanon, *Black Skin, White Masks*, 89. It is interesting to compare this incident to Moses Mendelssohn's experience, about which he wrote two centuries earlier: "Sometimes in the evening I go for a stroll with my wife and children. 'Father,' asks a child in his innocence, 'what is that boy calling after us? What have we done to them? 'Yes, father,' says another, 'they always run after us in the street and call us: Jews! Jews! Is it such a disgrace among these people to be a Jew?' Alas, I cast down my eyes and I sigh within myself: 'Oh mankind, how could you have let it come to this?'" Quoted in Howard M. Sachar, *A History of the Jews in the Modern World* (New York: Vintage, 2005), 31.

72. Fanon, *Black Skin, White Masks*, 93. Robert Gooding-Williams describes Fanon's repetition of "Look, a Negro!" in chapter 5 of *Black Skin, White Masks* as Fanon's attempt to spotlight

> the racializing identifications that puncture day-to-day life in [negrophobic] societies. Fanon interprets these identifications as performative utterances that assail the Negro, destroying her "corporeal schema" and imposing on her a "racial epidermal schema." . . . Fanon describes the feeling of being subjected to a racial epidermal schema as a sense of being physically fastened or affixed to an image of oneself: one feels as if one had acquired a second epidermis (hence the concept of a racial epidermal schema) that had been superimposed on one's

body and then come to haunt it like a shadow. The verbal performances that effect this kind of enslavement to an image, because they also shatter one's corporeal schema, leave one feeling literally and utterly dislocated in physical space.

Robert Gooding-Williams, *Look, a Negro! Philosophical Essays on Race, Culture, and Politics* (New York: Routledge, 2006), 8.

73. Lest you are tempted to imagine that this is merely of historical interest, consider Hilton Als's more recent reflections on seeing lynching photographs. He writes:

Of course, one big difference between the people documented in these pictures and me is that I am not dead, have not been lynched or scalded or burned or whipped or stoned. But I have been looked at, watched, and seen the harm in people's eyes—fear that can lead to becoming a dead nigger, like those seen here. And it's those photographs that have made me understand, finally, what the word *nigger* means, and why people have used it, and the way I use it here, now: as a metaphorical lynching before the real one. *Nigger* is a slow death. And that's the slow death I feel all the time now, as a colored man.

Hilton Als, "GWTW," in *White Girls* (San Francisco: McSweeny's, 2014), 137.

74. Fanon, *Black Skin, White Masks*, 95.

75. At the same time, Fanon does recognize the ideational content of the white supremacist mythology that is responsible for the stigma attached to blackness: "The black man is unaware of it as long as he lives among his own people; but at the first white gaze, he feels the weight of his melanin." Fanon, *Black Skin, White Masks*, 128. Here, too, he refers to Sartre's analysis of anti-Semitism. Only in this case he seems to use the example of the Jewish experience as illustrative of the black experience, rather than as a contrasting experience. On p. 128*n*10, he reproduces the following passage from *Anti-Semite and Jew*:

Some children, at the age of five or six, have already had fights with schoolmates who call them "Yids." Others may remain in ignorance for a long time. A young Jewish girl in a family I am acquainted with did not even know the meaning of the word *Jew* until she was fifteen. During the Occupation there was a Jewish doctor who lived shut up in his home in Fontainebleau and raised his children without saying a word to them of their origin. But however it comes about, some day they must learn the truth: sometimes from the smiles of those around them, sometimes from rumor or insult. The later the discovery the more violent the shock. Suddenly they perceive that others know something about them that they do not know, that people apply to them an ugly and upsetting term that is not used in their own families.

(Sartre, *Anti-Semite and Jew*, 75)

76. Fanon, *Black Skin, White Masks*,158.

77. Fanon, 158–59*n*45; Sartre, *Anti-Semite and Jew*, 135–36. There is a crucial difference between Fanon's view and that of Sartre in *Anti-Semite and Jew*. In *Anti-Semite and*

Jew, Sartre seems to describe Jewishness as a condition that is superlatively or quintessentially human. As Sarah Hammerschlag explains, "for Sartre, being Jewish represents an intensification of the experience of *being human*." Sarah Hammerschlag, *The Figural Jew: Politics and Identity in Postwar French Thought* (Chicago: University of Chicago Press, 2010), 88. I do not think that Fanon would say this about the experience of being black or Jewish.

78. Fanon, *Black Skin, White Masks*, 159n45; Sartre, *Anti-Semite and Jew*, 136.

79. Fanon, *Black Skin, White Masks*, 73.

80. Fanon, 160. For "what others have said" he quotes psychoanalyst and princess Marie Bonaparte: "The anti-Semite projects onto the Jew, attributes to the Jew all his own more or less unconscious bad instincts. . . . Thus, by shifting them onto the shoulders of the Jew, he has purged himself of them in his own eyes and sees himself in shining purity. The Jew thus lends himself magnificently as a projection of the Devil. . . . The black man in the United States also assumes the same function of fixation." Quoting *Mythes de guerre*, 145n1; Fanon, 160.

81. Gordon, *What Fanon Said*, 24.

82. Gordon, 25.

83. Fanon, *Black Skin, White Masks*, 119. He also writes, for instance, "For me bourgeois society is a closed society where it's not good to be alive, where the air is rotten and ideas and people are putrefying. And I believe that a man who takes a stand against this living death is in a way a revolutionary" (199).

84. Fanon, 196.

85. Fanon, 197.

86. Fanon, 197.

87. Fanon, 204.

88. Fanon, 205.

89. A Kierkegaardian leap seems appropriate given the "paradox of failure" that Fanon constructs. Lewis Gordon writes, "Fanon examines not only failure but also, as we saw, the failure of failure. His work is, in effect, akin to the Kierkegaardian notion of an existential paradox." Gordon, *What Fanon Said*, 72.

90. Judith Butler, "Violence, Non-Violence: Sartre on Fanon," *Graduate Faculty Philosophy Journal* 27, no. 1 (2006): 18–19.

91. Fanon, *Black Skin, White Masks*, 206.

92. Fanon, 206.

93. Fanon, 206.

94. I can imagine a compelling reading of Allen Ginsberg's "Howl" along these lines. But there are other liberatory views of sado-masochist sexuality that would laud what I have described. For instance, Michael Hardt and Antonio Negri, *Empire* (Cambridge: Harvard University Press, 2000):

> Those who are against, while escaping from the local and particular constraints of their human condition, must also continually attempt to construct a new body and a new life. This is necessarily a violent, barbaric passage. . . . The new barbarians destroy with an affirmative violence and trace new paths of life through

their own material existence. These barbaric deployments work on human relations in general, but we can recognize them today first and foremost in corporeal relations and configurations of gender and sexuality.

(214–15)

95. On the other hand, Fanon understood that violence did *not* actually function as a successful catharsis for many revolutionaries. And he did seem to think that questions of responsibility could apply within the revolutionary framework. For instance, Fanon reflects on a patient living in an African country who had fought as a militant to win independence. In the fight for independence he had planted a bomb that exploded a café frequented by colonists. After independence he befriended nationals from the formerly colonizing nation, who lauded the revolution and supported the newly independent nation. He was wracked with guilt and "vertigo" because he wondered if such people might have been at the café that he blew-up. Fanon concludes, "In other words, our actions never cease to haunt us." Fanon, *The Wretched of the Earth*, 185n23. He also writes, "Such borderline cases pose the question of responsibility in the context of the revolution" (183). I agree with Nigel Gibson and Roberto Beneduce that "this kind of questioning, self-reflective and radically humanist, informed by his work as a political theorist and as a doctor of psychiatry, indicates a nuanced thinker quite in contrast to the caricature of Fanon as the Manichean theorist who simply propounded the birthing of a new kind of human being through violence." Nigel C. Gibson and Roberto Beneduce, *Frantz Fanon, Psychiatry and Politics* (New York: Rowman and Littlefield, 2017), 6. It is partly because of the obvious nuances in Fanon's real expectations related to the efficacy of violence that I hope my approach might be acceptable from a Fanonian perspective.

96. Fanon's idea of violence in *The Wretched of the Earth*, writes Robert Bernasconi, will "not only destroy the old order, but produce a new one. Theoreticians should avoid trying to disarm it ahead of time by presuming that they always know where it will lead." Robert Bernasconi, "Casting the Slough: Fanon's New Humanism for a New Humanity," in *Fanon: A Critical Reader*, ed. Lewis R. Gordon, T. Denean Sharpley-Whiting, Renee T. White (Cambridge, MA: Blackwell, 1996), 121. At the same time, Fanon does appear to endorse more mainstream arguments for national self-determination throughout *The Wretched of the Earth* and throughout his career as an advocate for the FLN. In various passages he emphasizes sovereignty and distributive justice and he often seems to promote a form of populist socialism.

97. Saint Augustine, *Confessions* (New York: Oxford University Press, 1998), 151.

98. Saint Augustine, 152.

99. Saint Augustine, 153, quoting from Romans 13:13–14.

100. Saint Augustine, 153.

101. On such judgments about the prioritization of one book over the other, see Gordon, *What Fanon Said*, 16–18.

102. On the idea of a "festival of cruelty" in Nietzsche, see Jonathan Glover, *Humanity: A Moral History of the Twentieth Century* (New Haven: Yale University Press, 2000), 16–18.

103.   See Gordon, *What Fanon Said*, 22.

104.   Gordon, *What Fanon Said*, 48. This is also "the realm of the epidermal schema," which Fanon refers to in *Black Skin, White Masks*, 92.

105.   John Rawls, "The Idea of Public Reason Revisited," in *The Law of Peoples* (Cambridge: Harvard University Press, 1999), 161.

106.   John Rawls, *Justice as Fairness: A Restatement* (Cambridge: Harvard University Press, 2001), 164–68.

107.   Martha C. Nussbaum, *Frontiers of Justice: Disability, Nationality, Species Membership* (Cambridge: Harvard University Press, 2006), 310. She also specifies that this is not the old public/private divide and points to the idea of the family, which is quintessentially private in classical liberal theories, as part of the basic structure to prove her point (444n31).

108.   On the idea of "self-respect" in general, see John Rawls, *A Theory of Justice* (Cambridge: Harvard University Press, 1971), 440–46.

109.   Rawls, *Justice as Fairness*, 58–61.

110.   Rawls, 60.

111.   On "the black" as fundamentally biological in Fanon, see Gordon, *What Fanon Said*, 60.

112.   On Rawls's problematic "Kantian split" between moral personality and animality, see Nussbaum, *Frontiers of Justice*, 130–34.

113.   Here is Marx:

> None of the supposed rights of man, therefore, go beyond the egoistic man, man as he is, as a member of civil society; that is, an individual separated from the community, withdrawn into himself, wholly preoccupied with his private interest and acting in accordance with his private caprice. Man is far from being considered, in the rights of man, as a species-being; on the contrary, species-life itself—society—appears as a system which is external to the individual and as a limitation of his original independence. The only bond between men is natural necessity, need and private interest, the preservation of their property and their egoistic persons.

Karl Marx, "On the Jewish Question," in *The Marx-Engels Reader*, ed. Robert C. Tucker, 2d ed. (New York: Norton, 1978), 43.

3. THE FACT OF FRAUGHT SOCIETIES II

1.   Philip Roth, *Portnoy's Complaint* (New York: Vintage, 1994 [1969]), 235.

2.   Wendy Brown has asked, relatedly, "where do elements of politicized identity's investments in itself and especially in its own history of suffering come into conflict with the need to give up these investments in the pursuit of an emancipatory democratic project?" Wendy Brown, "Wounded Attachments," *Political Theory* 21, no. 3 (August 1993): 390–91. Brown is concerned about a troubling dynamic in which activism by

historically oppressed people, directed at the failures of inclusion perpetrated by the liberal political order (which she decries), only reinforces this political order and lamentably perpetuates identities that are constituted by the pain of exclusion. She suggests that what this pain might need above all is "the chance to be heard into a certain reprieve, recognized into self-overcoming, incited into possibilities for triumphing over, and hence losing, itself. Our challenge, then, would be to configure a radically democratic political culture that can sustain such a project in its midst without being overtaken by it" (407). My argument is also an attempt to meet this need. Though I want to make it possible to imagine that historical pain need not necessarily lose itself; it might instead take on new meaning and new, unpredictable life in the domain of play. And, of course, I retain the framework of liberalism, albeit significantly reconstructed.

3. I take the phrase "kinds of people" from Ian Hacking. According to his "dynamic nominalist" approach, "numerous kinds of human beings and human acts come into being hand in hand with our invention of the ways to name them." Ian Hacking, *Historical Ontology* (Cambridge: Harvard University Press, 2004), 113.

4. Rogers Brubaker, *Ethnicity Without Groups* (Cambridge: Harvard University Press, 2006), 8. See also Anne Phillips, *Multiculturalism Without Culture* (Princeton: Princeton University Press, 2009). Amartya Sen similarly opposes "a 'solitarist approach' to human identity, which sees human beings as members of exactly one group," in Amartya Sen, *Identity and Violence: The Illusion of Destiny* (New York: Norton, 2006), xii. Taking a position with which Brubaker would certainly agree, Sen also writes: "Violence is fomented by the imposition of singular and belligerent identities on gullible people, championed by proficient artisans of terror" (2). Though Brubaker might add that in many cases the "singular and belligerent identities" arise *from* the violence, rather than the other way around.

5. Brubaker, *Ethnicity Without Groups*, 10.

6. Brubaker, 11.

7. Brubaker, 44.

8. Brubaker, 47.

9. Brubaker, 45.

10. But sometimes body art is precisely an expression of heightened groupness: gang affiliation, punk affiliation, etc. On "totemic" tattooing, see Emil Durkheim, *The Elementary Forms of Religious Life*, trans. Karen E. Fields (New York: Free Press, 1995), 116–17.

11. Presumably, something (self-understanding) that has qualities admitting of degrees (selfness and groupness) is not changed into another thing entirely when these qualities are heightened or lowered in any particular combination.

12. Brubaker, *Ethnicity Without Groups*, 41.

13. Brubaker, 42.

14. Kwame Anthony Appiah, *The Ethics of Identity* (Princeton: Princeton University Press, 2005), 22. On "collective identities," see also Appiah, 69. An earlier account of the narrative dimension of "identity" is Margaret R. Somers, "The Narrative Constitution of Identity: A Relational and Network Approach," *Theory and Society* 23 (1994):605–49. See Brubaker, *Ethnicity Without Groups*, 38–39.

15. Appiah, *The Ethics of Identity*, 66.

16. Ibid., 110–13. Appiah borrows this sense of "Limitations and Parameters" from Ronald Dworkin, *Sovereign Virtue: The Theory and Practice of Equality* (Cambridge: Harvard University Press, 2000), 260–63.

17. Appiah, *The Ethics of Identity*, 234.

18. John Rawls, *Political Liberalism* (New York: Columbia University Press, 1996), 31*n*34.

19. Rawls, 30.

20. Rawls, 30–31.

21. The political aspect of a person's noninstitutional moral self-conception will also be a justification for entitlements that should be guaranteed to anyone within the boundaries of the state, regardless of whether or not they have a Social Security number or any other official status recognized by the state. And it will be a justification for entitlements that ought to be guaranteed to everyone beyond the borders of the state as well and should thus significantly guide foreign policy.

22. Rawls, *Political Liberalism*, 31.

23. Rawls, 59.

24. Rawls, 59.

25. Rawls, 59.

26. John Rawls, "The Idea of Public Reason Revisited," in *The Law of Peoples* (Cambridge: Harvard University Press, 1999), 177.

27. Rawls, 177.

28. Rawls, 177.

29. Jonathan Z. Smith, "Religion, Religions, Religious," in Mark C. Taylor, ed., *Critical Terms for Religious Studies* (Chicago: University of Chicago Press, 1998), 277–80.

30. Immanuel Kant, *Religion Within the Boundaries of Mere Reason: And Other Writings*, ed. and trans. Allen Wood (Cambridge: Cambridge University Press, 1998), 130.

31. Rawls, *Political Liberalism*, 56–57.

32. Rawls, 54.

33. I say, "even if he merely comports his comprehensive groupness reasonably," in order to signal that a reasonable person can have an unreasonable comprehensive doctrine but "have it" reasonably. I believe that Rawls has this possibility in mind when he asks rhetorically, "how far in practice does the allegiance to a principle of political justice actually depend on the knowledge of or the belief in its derivation from a comprehensive view rather than on seeming reasonable in itself?" (59–60). Most people who identify as Jewish or Muslim or liberal or conservative do not engage in elaborate processes of deducing logically valid conclusions from clearly stated premises. Most people are not theologians or philosophers. See Robert A. Orsi, "Is the Study of Lived Religion Irrelevant to the World We Live In?" *Journal for the Scientific Study of Religion* 42, no. 2 (June 2003): 169–74.

34. This is a good place to note that my view does not reiterate the essentializing effect that Wendy Brown portrays as a surreptitious feature of liberal "tolerance." For Brown, paradigmatically,

> When, for example, middle and high schoolers are urged to tolerate one another's race, ethnicity, culture, religion, or sexual orientation, there is no suggestion

that the differences at issue, or the identities through which these differences are negotiated, have been socially and historically constituted and are themselves the effect of power and hegemonic norms, or even of certain discourses about race, ethnicity, sexuality, and culture. Rather, difference itself is what students learn they must tolerate.

Wendy Brown, *Regulating Aversion: Tolerance in the Age of Identity and Empire* (Princeton: Princeton University Press, 2008), 16. The effect is to naturalize differences (which are the result of ideological discourses and continue to be marked as "other" by contrast to the hegemonic norm) and make them permanent, if "tolerated." My view certainly welcomes people to pursue an America that will allow them never to give up on their resentment or whatever else they want to reproduce interminably into the future. But it also warns, explicitly, that the unpredictability of play, and the dynamic relations between the domain of the political and the domain of play, make it possible that we might be surprised by what we happily become in a future that we cannot yet imagine.

35. Michael Walzer, *Exodus and Revolution* (New York: Basic Books, 1985), 54. He is quoting Moses Maimonides, *The Guide of the Perplexed,* 1:526–28.

36. Walzer, 54.

37. Walzer, 54.

38. Frank E. Manuel and Fritzie P. Manuel, *Utopian Thought in the Western World* (Cambridge: Belknap, 1979), 687.

39. Walzer, *Exodus and Revolution*, 59.

40. Walzer, 61.

41. Lincoln Steffens, *Moses in Red: The Revolt of Israel as a Typical Revolution* (Philadelphia: Dorrance, 1926), 124.

42. Walzer, *Exodus and Revolution,* 66.

43. Walzer, 69.

44. Walzer, 68.

45. An excellent example of this posture, especially as it relates to the New Left, is taken by Sean McCann and Michael Szalay in "Do You Believe in Magic? Literary Thinking After the New Left," *Yale Journal of Criticism* 18, no. 2 (2005): 435–68. Admittedly, the book you are now reading might be another example.

46. Walzer, *Exodus and Revolution,* 119.

47. Walzer, 118, quoting Jeremiah 31:32.

48. Walzer, 119.

49. Walzer, 135.

50. Walzer, 145.

51. Walzer revisits the theme of revolution in his recent book, *The Paradox of Liberation: Secular Revolutions and Religious Counterrevolutions* (New Haven: Yale University Press, 2015). Reflecting on the cases of modern India, Israel, and Algeria, he identifies a pattern of unsustainable secular revolutions overwhelmed by religious counterrevolution. The secular revolutionary vanguards in these cases sought to liberate their

people from the impoverished self-understanding that comes from colonial oppression and the benighted "old ways" of religious tradition. Walzer notes, however, "the old ways are cherished by many of the men and women whose ways they are. That is the paradox of liberation" (19). Walzer concludes, "Like the ancient Israelites, the modern militants thought they had reached the promised land, only to discover that they carried Egypt in their baggage" (33).

52. Leo Strauss, "Preface to *Spinoza's Critique of Religion*" [1965], in Leo Strauss, *Jewish Philosophy and the Crisis of Modernity: Essays in Modern Jewish Thought*, ed. Kenneth Hart Green (Albany: State University of New York Press, 1997), 170–71.

53. Strauss, 138.

54. Strauss, 139.

55. Mark Lilla, *The Stillborn God: Religion, Politics, and the Modern West* (New York: Vintage, 2008), 58. While I share some anxieties and aspirations with Lilla, there are important differences between my argument in this book and his argument for a renewed liberal vision in Mark Lilla, *The Once and Future Liberal: After Identity Politics* (New York: HarperCollins, 2017). Lilla portrays liberals as stuck in a mire of identity politics, capable only of purity tests and taking offense, having long since abandoned the serious political work of promoting a liberal vision. He tells liberals: "Children do not respond well to scolding and neither do nations. It just puts their backs up" (116). But Lilla is very much scolding the left in his book. And he should expect people to get their backs up in response. Comparing our approaches, there is no equivalent in Lilla's book to the serious reckoning with the fundamental problems of liberal political theory that I highlight in the work of Martha Nussbaum and Charles Mills, among others. For instance, Lilla's liberal vision calls on us to become a "we," but it does not ask us to acknowledge our profound human vulnerability, dependence, and animality, and it does not demand that we halt our grand theorizing to confront, first, and genuinely repudiate the racial contract that has underwritten the liberal social contract tradition. What is more, my view does not entail "putting the age of identity behind us" (17). It imagines stories of oppression and group struggles for justice increasingly incorporated into our national narrative while the basic structure of society increasingly guarantees the exercise of the central human capabilities at a threshold level for all, and a new age of thriving groupness in the domain of play.

56. Lilla, *The Stillborn God*, 7.

57. Lilla, 7–8. By contrast to Lilla, I will not present "political theology" as the natural or necessary way of describing what political institutions ought to be separated from. Political liberalism ought to offer substantive claims about how we should see ourselves and others within the domain of the political. However, as I will explain at length in later chapters, what happens outside of the domain of the political (but within the borders of the state) need only be differentiated formally from a political perspective as the pursuit of nonpublic projects and play.

58. Lilla, 7.

59. Lilla, 308–9.

60.   The unsatisfying limitedness of liberal political institutions has historically been unnecessarily exacerbated by an insistence on conceptualizing its limits in terms of a public
and private sphere. Michael Warner has written, for instance:

> In modern culture . . . the felt gap between public selves or roles and private ones
> has given rise to a Romantic longing for unity—at least among those with the
> privilege of being public. . . . That longing for unity can also be seen in modes
> of collective public intimacy such as ecstatic spirituality. Inevitably, identity poli-
> tics itself magnetizes such longings, affirming private identity through public
> politics and promising to heal divisions of the political world by anchoring them
> in the authentically personal realm and its solidarity. In the ideals of ethnic iden-
> tity, or sisterhood, or gay pride, to take the most common examples, an asser-
> tive and affirmative concept of identity seems to achieve a correspondence
> between public existence and private self. Identity politics in this sense seems
> to many people a way of overcoming both the denial of public existence that is
> so often the form of domination and the incoherence of the experience that dom-
> ination creates, an experience that often feels more like invisibility than the
> kind of privacy you value.

Michael Warner, *Publics and Counterpublics* (New York: Zone, 2005), 25–26.

61.   The first kernel to emerge of the ideas that became this book was a graduate school seminar paper that I wrote for Martha Nussbaum entitled, "A Schlemiel's Guide to Life in
Disappointing Societies." I will revisit the schlemiel later in chapter 5.

62.   John Rawls, *Justice as Fairness: A Restatement* (Cambridge: Harvard University Press,
2001), 34.

63.   Lilla, *The Stillborn God*, 300. It is important to recall, here, that Strauss was personally
attracted to "political theology." Or, at least, this is one way of describing his attraction to the medieval Jewish and Islamic rationalists. Carl Schmitt also theorized the
fate of political theology in this context, although Lilla does not make the connection.
See Carl Schmitt, *Political Theology: Four Chapters on the Concept of Sovereignty* (Chicago: University of Chicago Press, 2005 [1934]); Raphael Gross, *Carl Schmitt and the
Jews: The "Jewish Question," the Holocaust, and German Legal Theory* (Madison: University of Wisconsin Press, 2007). Assessing Strauss and Schmitt in the context of an
ongoing conversation about political theology in modern Jewish thought, see Randi
Rashkover and Martin Kavka, eds., *Judaism, Liberalism, and Political Theology* (Bloomington: Indiana University Press, 2014).

64.   Lilla, *The Stillborn God*, 255. For a deeper analysis of engagement with occult research
and other forms of enchantment by key scholars and intellectuals associated with modernization, establishing that they had never really resigned themselves to a soulless
modernity, see Jason Josephson-Storm, *The Myth of Disenchantment: Magic, Modernity, and the Birth of the Human Sciences* (Chicago: University of Chicago Press, 2017).

65.   Lilla, *The Stillborn God*, 302.

66.   Lilla, 278.

67. Lilla, 282.

68. Lilla, 285.

69. Ian Buruma and Avishai Margalit, *Occidentalism: The West in the Eyes of Its Enemies* (New York: Penguin, 2004). To be clear, Buruma and Margalit explicitly insist that they do not mean to label all criticism of the West as Occidentalism (Buruma and Margalit, 8, 10, 123, 125). Akeel Bilgrami has an interesting critique of Buruma and Margalit entitled "Occidentalism, the Very Idea: An Essay on the Enlightenment, Enchantment, and the Mentality of Democracy" in *Secularism, Identity, and Enchantment* (Cambridge: Harvard University Press, 2014), 279–327. Bilgrami agrees with Buruma and Margalit that there is a deep intra-European conflict paradigm informing current conflicts between "the West" and its antagonists. He simply locates the origin of the paradigm earlier, with the development of Newtonian metaphysics (in collusion with an Anglican establishment that had entrenched and rapidly expanding commercial interests) and those who dissented from it (296–300).

70. Buruma and Margalit, *Occidentalism*, 77–80.

71. Buruma and Margalit, 79.

72. Although, Buruma and Margalit explain, "outside Europe, it is the West or Americanism that is blamed for the metropolitan condition and the vanished rural idyll— Americanism and some local variation of the big-city Jews, such as the Chinese in Southeast Asia or the Indian merchants in Africa, who are believed to conspire with venal 'Westernized' native elites, to poison and undermine authentic, spiritual, or racial communities" (29).

73. Buruma and Margalit, 35.

74. Hannah Arendt, *The Origins of Totalitarianism* (New York: Harcourt, 1976), 313–14.

75. Arendt, 470–71.

76. Martha C. Nussbaum, *Hiding from Humanity: Disgust, Shame, and the Law* (Princeton: Princeton University Press, 2004), 108. Depictions of Jews as repulsively animalistic and of Jewish men as having disgusting female bodily characteristics do not, of course, exhaust the dimensions of anti-Semitic psychology and ideology. As an example, Jews have been stigmatized on the basis of their association with capitalism and cosmopolitanism. That is, precisely for their disembodied transcendence of the human and the natural. And perhaps the key text of modern anti-Semitism, *The Protocols of the Elders of Zion,* does not seem to include associations between Jews and the disgusting. See Stephen Eric Bronner, *A Rumor About the Jews: Antisemitism, Conspiracy, and the Protocols of Zion* (Oxford: Oxford University Press, 2000); and Norman Cohn, *Warrant for Genocide: The Myth of the Jewish World Conspiracy and the Protocols of the Elders of Zion* (London: Serif, 1996). Furthermore, "The Eternal Jew" (sometimes "the Wandering Jew," or Ahasuerus) can hardly be a representation of reviled mortality: to the contrary, The Eternal Jew is horrifying for his immortality (though, to be sure, his wandering will cease, it was thought, with the Second Coming of Jesus Christ). In the end, I think that careful analysis of the history of anti-Semitism does show that even these cases are inextricably linked to associations with disgusting animals, sexual perversion, bodily fluids, and other invocations of animality. "Blood Libels" against Jews,

for instance, have reappeared continuously since the twelfth century. And even when the Jews were ostensibly associated with forces that transcend nature like capitalism and cosmopolitanism, or with modernity in general, when they were depicted pictorially they were shown as excessively embodied: with excessive fat, excessively large noses, ears, lips. A cartoon depiction of a Jew fitting precisely this description can be found on the frontispiece of a Polish edition of *The Protocols* from 1937. Cohn, *Warrant for Genocide*, 267. More to the point, the cover of a popular French edition of *The Protocols* from 1934 is a cartoon depiction of a typically caricatured Jewish face on the head of a tarantula body with six fury spider legs wrapped around the Planet Earth. Cohn, *Warrant for Genocide*, 185. The spider is, of course, a classic "disgusting animal." What is more, in the Nazi propaganda film *Der ewige Jude*, "The Eternal Jew" (1940), directed by Fritz Hippler, Jews are depicted as a filthy animal pestilence. A scene that juxtaposes film of scurrying rats with film of Jews in a Polish ghetto is narrated as follows: "Wherever rats appear they bring ruin, by destroying mankind's goods and foodstuffs. They spread disease, and plague, such as leprosy, typhoid fever, cholera, and dysentery. They are cunning, cowardly, and cruel, and are found mostly in large packs. They represent craftiness and subterranean destruction—just like the Jews among other human beings." The full transcript in English translation is available in appendix B of Stig Hornshoj-Moller and David Culbert, "'Der ewige Jude' (1940): Joseph Goebbels' Unequaled Monument to Anti-Semitism," *Historical Journal of Film, Radio, and Television* 12, no. 3 (August 1992). I have never seen an anti-Semitic pictorial representation of Jews that goes in the other direction—that caricatures the Jew by exaggerating some feature that makes him less bodily or less animalistic.

77.   Nussbaum, *Hiding from Humanity*, 108.

78.   Nussbaum, 110–11.

79.   Importantly, German Christian theologians at the time similarly sought to cleanse Christianity of its "purported" Jewish origins and to protect Germany and Christianity from the ongoing threat of Jewish infection. The Institute for the Study and Eradication of Jewish Influence on German Religious Life, founded in 1939, "carried out its program of eradicating the Jewish within Christianity precisely while the Jews of Europe were being deported and murdered." Susannah Heschel, *The Aryan Jesus: Christian Theologians and the Bible in Nazi Germany* (Princeton: Princeton University Press, 2008), 16.

80.   There has been a resurgence of political theology in Europe over the past couple of decades. One popular line of thought suggests that, today, the reigning totalitarian order is actually the order of liberal sovereignty that dominates the West. Referring to elements of this thought in the work of Giorgio Agamben and Jacques Derrida, Zachary Braiterman writes,

> By allowing Schmitt to define all forms of sovereignty on the basis of a caricature of divine omnipotence and miracle in medieval Christian theology, Agamben and also Derrida stack the deck against liberal democracy and liberal religion. With an eye set upon the more radical project of a "democracy to come"

and "religion without religion" they seek to undo the rigid binaries and arbitrary violence that they reject and that Schmitt affirms as marking all forms of sovereign power. In the process, a new binary opposition is produced between absolute sovereignty and absolute (or a "certain absolute") renunciation of sovereignty. Depending upon a religion of miracle, gift, and grace, what theorists on either opposite extreme fail to consider is the dull, middle place subjecting sovereign form and even the power of God to the imperfect vicissitudes of law. In search of the ultimate, they neglect penultimate, quotidian places.

Zachary Braiterman, "The Patient Political Gesture: Law, Liberalism, and Talmud," in Rashkover and Kavka, *Judaism, Liberalism, and Political Theology*, 245–46. Braiterman offers as a compelling contrast the Babylonian Rabbis in the Talmud who "recognize God's authority without, however, absolutizing it as a political principle" (250). On dangerous anti-Jewish currents in the new political theology, see Sarah Hammerschlag, "Bad Jews, Authentic Jews, Figural Jews: Badiou and the Politics of Exemplarity," in Rashkover and Kavka, *Judaism, Liberalism, and Political Theology*, 221–40.

81. Olivier Roy, *Jihad and Death: The Global Appeal of Islamic State* (New York: Oxford University Press, 2017), 6. Roy puts radicalism into context this way: "'There are no innocent bourgeois,' the anarchist Émile Henry said while standing trial for having thrown a bomb into the Café Terminus in Paris in 1894. If you replace 'bourgeois' with "French person," you've got the Bataclan" (11).

82. Roy, 21–32.

83. Roy, 70–71.

84. "Generation Jihadi," interview with Olivier Roy in *Spiked Review*, July 2016.

85. Roy, *Jihad and Death*, 56.

86. Roy reports, "No matter what database is taken as a reference, the paucity of religious knowledge among jihadis is patent" (42).

87. Roy, 49.

88. "Generation Jihadi."

89. Roy, *Jihad and Death*, 26.

90. Olivier Roy, *Globalized Islam: The Search for a New Ummah* (New York: Columbia University Press, 2004) and *Holy Ignorance: When Religion and Culture Part Ways* (New York: Columbia University Press, 2010).

91. Roy, *Holy Ignorance*, 5–9.

92. Roy, 82.

93. Roy, 2.

94. On "pure religion," see Roy, *Holy Ignorance*, 9–11. On self-proclaimed community leaders, see pp. 83–84.

95. ISIS, in particular, represents the convergence between a "pure religion" idea of Islam (that is utterly detached from any actual Islamic culture) with an enticing youth culture fantasy: "It is important to look at the photos and videos," Roy suggests. "ISIS has opened up a new gaming space in the literal sense: the vast desert which one can ride through in four-wheel drive vehicles, hair and flags blowing in the wind, guns raised,

fraternity exhibited by the uniform, often similar to the ninja model. Young losers from destitute suburbs become handsome, and plenty of young girls on Facebook go into raptures over their look. The video game turns into an epic adventure in a huge playground." Roy, *Jihad and Death,* 51.

96. See, for instance, the episode of Vice News Tonight, "Charlottesville: Race and Terror," which aired on HBO on August 14, 2017.

97. Roy, *Holy Ignorance,* 110–11.

98. Roy, 111.

99. On the other hand, reterritorialized "pure religion" can also function as a pure space of transgression, which has been cleansed entirely of the boring, "normal," bourgeois life that the pure religion heroes leave behind. Once this space is secured, however, it is no longer a space that transgresses the norms of everyday life; it is everyday life.

4. THE CAPABILITY OF PLAY

1. See Steven Seidman and Jeffrey C. Alexander, *The New Social Theory Reader,* 2d ed. (New York: Routledge, 2008), 109–10.

2. Iris Marion Young, *Justice and the Politics of Difference* (Princeton: Princeton University Press, 1990), 37.

3. On the non-naturalness of the liberal public/private divide, Raymond Geuss concludes his historical assessment this way: "The public/private distinction, I am claiming, does not have the fundamental status of human finitude, mutual ignorance, or the urges for self-preservation and self-assertion." Raymond Geuss, *Public Goods, Private Goods* (Princeton: Princeton University Press, 2003), 112.

4. John Rawls, *Political Liberalism* (New York: Columbia University Press, 1996), 11.

5. On the family as part of the basic structure, see John Rawls, *Justice as Fairness: A Restatement* (Cambridge: Harvard University Press, 2001), 162–68.

6. Rawls, *Political Liberalism,* 13–14.

7. Rawls, 8.

8. Rawls, 68.

9. There have been a variety of efforts to promote a "canon" of American political thought. Each, of course, reflects the normative project driving the canonizer. See, for instance, Stephen Prothero, *The American Bible: How Our Words Unite, Divide, and Define a Nation* (New York: HarperOne, 2012). Canons are a complicated matter. The shaping of canons always facilitates distributions of power and authority. At the same time, strategies of interpretation and countercanons can intervene in these processes and transform them. My own sense of the capaciousness and transformability of canon-like structures (i.e., the public political culture) comes from reading Jewish feminists like Judith Plaskow, *Standing Again at Sinai: Judaism from a Feminist Perspective* (San Francisco: HarperSanFrancisco, 1991). More generally, see Denise Kimber Buell, "Canons Unbound," in Elisabeth Schüssler Fiorenza, ed., *Feminist Biblical Studies in the Twentieth Century: Scholarship and Movement* (Atlanta: Society of Biblical Literature, 2014), 293–306.

10. Rawls, *Political Liberalism*, 214.

11. There are important exceptions to this demand. Rawls added to his view a "proviso," according to which there are positive reasons to introduce comprehensive views into the public political forum "provided that in due course proper political rceasons—and not reasons given solely by comprehensive doctrines—are presented that are sufficient to support whatever the comprehensive doctrines introduced are said to support." John Rawls, "The Idea of Public Reason Revisited," in *The Law of Peoples* (Cambridge: Harvard University Press, 1999), 152. Thinking about the public political culture as open to the proviso and its positive effects means taking the "wide view of public political culture," which I do indeed take (152).

12. Recognizing the diverse and unpredictable ways that people might perform public reason should help us to avoid the inherent privileging of some people in the U.S. over others, which comes with privileging verbal argumentation over all other ways of participating in political life. The idea is to avoid "the ways in which social inequalities can infect deliberation, even in the absence of any formal exclusions," described in Nancy Fraser, "Rethinking the Public Sphere: A Contribution to the Critique of Actually Existing Democracy," *Social Text*, nos. 25/26 (1990): 64. My approach tries to do better than the deliberative liberalism that Fraser critiques in this essay and in other work, but in the end I do make the judgment to stick with liberal norms and structures that Fraser might have us abandon.

13. I came to appreciate the significant of Jastrow's picture for thinking about human perception through my study of the philosopher Ludwig Wittgenstein in graduate school. For a general explanation, see Hans-Johann Glock, "Aspect-perception," in *A Wittgenstein Dictionary* (Malden, MA: Blackwell, 1996), 36–40.

14. Rawls, *Political Liberalism*, lix. On opportunities for meaningful work, see Jeffrey Moriarty, "Rawls, Self-Respect, and the Opportunity for Meaningful Work," *Social Theory and Practice* 35, no. 3 (2009): 441–59. When Rawls describes the basic structure of society, he includes in it "the political constitution with an independent judiciary, the legally recognized forms of property, and the structure of the economy (for example, as a system of competitive markets with private property in the means of production), as well as the family in some form, all belong to the basic structure." Rawls, *Justice as Fairness*, 10. So "the structure of the economy" is part of the basic structure, and it is presumably a structure that allows opportunities for meaningful work. The actual work that emerges, whether it involves individual creativity or more anonymous tasks that are regulated to be dignified, will be animated by the diverse nonpublic projects that guide people's pursuits.

15. Martha C. Nussbaum, *Creating Capabilities: The Human Development Approach* (Cambridge: Harvard University Press, 2011), 34.

16. See Kathi Weeks, *The Problem with Work: Feminism, Marxism, Antiwork Politics, and Postwork Imaginaries* (Durham, NC: Duke University Press, 2011). Though I do identify with Bertrand Russell when he writes,

> It will be said that while a little leisure is pleasant, men would not know how to fill their days if they had only four hours of work out of the twenty-four. In so

far as this is true in the modern world, it is a condemnation of our civilization; it would not have been true at any earlier period. There was formerly a capacity for light-heartedness and play which has been to some extent inhibited by the cult of efficiency. The modern man thinks that everything ought to be done for the sake of something else, and never for its own sake.

Bertrand Russell, *In Praise of Idleness* (New York: Routledge, 2004 [1935]), 11.

17. Rawls, "The Idea of Public Reason Revisited," 134*n*13.
18. I assume that mass media are not inherently fascistic or inherently bad in any other way, following Noël Carroll in *A Philosophy of Mass Art* (Oxford: Clarendon, 1998).
19. Rawls, "The Idea of Public Reason Revisited," 133–34.
20. Rawls, *Political Liberalism*, 68.
21. Martha C. Nussbaum, *Women and Human Development: The Capabilities Approach* (Cambridge: Cambridge University Press, 2000), 84.
22. Martha C. Nussbaum, "Constitutions and Capabilities: 'Perception' Against Lofty Formalism," 121 *Harvard Law Review* 4 (2007): 11.
23. Nussbaum, *Women and Human Development*, 85.
24. Nussbaum, "Constitutions and Capabilities," 11–12. As another example, "citizens of repressive nondemocratic regimes have the internal but not the combined capability to exercise thought and speech in accordance with their consciences." Nussbaum, *Women and Human Development*, 85.
25. Nussbaum, "Constitutions and Capabilities," 12.
26. Nussbaum, 12.
27. Nussbaum, 12.
28. Martha C. Nussbaum, *Frontiers of Justice: Disability, Nationality, Species Membership* (Cambridge: Harvard University Press, 2006), 74.
29. Nussbaum, "Constitutions and Capabilities," 12.
30. Nussbaum, *Frontiers of Justice*, 77; Nussbaum, *Creating Capabilities*, 34.
31. Nussbaum, *Frontiers of Justice*, 78.
32. Nussbaum, 78.
33. Brian Sutton-Smith, *The Ambiguity of Play* (Cambridge: Harvard University Press, 2001).
34. Listen to almost any interview with a stand-up comedian on Marc Maron's outstanding podcast WTF.
35. Sutton-Smith offers good reasons to consider some forms of play genuinely passive. He refers to the work of Dorothy and Jerome Singer on the connection between play and dreams: "there is a connection between the passivity and involuntary character of dreams and the passivity and involuntariness of many kinds of play. The active forms of play rise, as it were, from the groundswell of incessant and relatively involuntary mental play." Sutton-Smith, *The Ambiguity of Play*, 61. He is referring to what he calls "neural fabulation," which suggests that the brain is always in some sense playing with itself, producing extra material that is not task oriented.
36. Johan Huizinga, *Homo Ludens: A Study of the Play Element in Culture* (Boston: Beacon, 1955), 13.

37. Bernard Suits, *The Grasshopper: Games, Life and Utopia* (Toronto: Broadview, 2005), 54–55.

38. The Grasshopper says, "I would define an open game generically as a system of reciprocally enabling moves whose purpose is the continued operation of the system" (Suits, 124).

39. Suits, 125.

40. Thomas Hurka argues that the admiration of achievement in games reflects a modern intuitive admiration for overcoming difficulty; he says that this makes Suits's ethical account quintessentially modern. See his introduction to *The Grasshopper* and his "Games and the Good," *Proceedings of the Aristotelian Society, Supplementary* vol. 80 (2006): 217–35.

41. Sutton-Smith, *The Ambiguity of Play,* 24–26.

42. These are controversial questions addressed in a vast philosophical literature about action. I cannot assess all of the relevant views here. See, for starters, Alfred R. Mele, ed., *The Philosophy of Action* (Oxford: Oxford University Press, 1997).

43. Harry G. Frankfurt, "The Problem of Action," in Mele, *The Philosophy of Action,* 48.

44. Frankfurt, 48.

45. Is sneezing playing then? Or, the dilation of the pupil of a person's eye when light fades? No. Frankfurt explains, "the occurrence of this movement does not mark the performance of an action by the person; his pupils dilate, but he does not dilate them. This is because the course of the movement is not under his guidance. The guidance in this case is attributable only to the operation of some mechanism with which he cannot be identified" (Frankfurt, 46).

46. I have not really veered too far from Johan Huizinga's definition of play:

> a free activity standing quite consciously outside "ordinary" life as being "not serious," but at the same time absorbing the player intensely and utterly. It is an activity connected with no material interest, and no profit can be gained by it. It proceeds within its own proper boundaries of time and space according to fixed rules and in an orderly manner. It promotes the formation of social groupings which tend to surround themselves with secrecy and to stress their difference from the common world by disguise or other means.
>
> (Huizinga, *Homo Ludens,* 13)

Further points of convergence and divergence will emerge as my argument progresses.

47. This list is drawn from Sutton-Smith, *The Ambiguity of Play.*

48. On the way out the sign reads: "This is no longer play."

49. Gregory Bateson, "A Theory of Play and Fantasy," in *Steps to an Ecology of Mind* (Chicago: University of Chicago Press, 2000), 178.

50. Bateson, 180. This means that the actions outside of the play frame (y) denote something (z), and while the actions inside the play frame (x) denote (y), paradoxically (x) does not denote (z). Erving Goffman explains this in terms of the idea of "the key" in frame analysis: "the set of conventions by which a given activity, one already meaningful in terms of some primary framework, is transformed into something patterned on this activity but seen by the participants to be something quite else. The process of

transcription can be called keying." Erving Goffman, *Frame Analysis: An Essay on the Organization of Experience* (Boston: Northeastern University Press, 1974), 43–44.

51. Stuart L. Brown, "Animals at Play," *National Geographic* 186, no. 6 (1994): 2–35.

52. Mikhail Bakhtin, *Rabelais and His World,* trans. Helene Iswolsky (Bloomington: Indiana University, 1984), 222–27.

53. Victor Turner, "Liminal to Liminoid, in Play, Flow, and Ritual: An Essay in Comparative Symbology," in *From Ritual to Theatre: The Human Seriousness of Play* (New York: PAJ, 1982), 55.

54. Turner, 24. See also Victor Turner, *The Ritual Process: Structure and Anti-Structure* (Chicago: Aldine Transaction, 1995).

55. Turner, "Liminal to Liminoid," 27.

56. Turner, 27. In this phase of the ritual process, "reversal underlines to the members of a community that chaos is the alternative to cosmos, so they'd better stick to cosmos, i.e., the traditional order of culture, though they can for a brief while have a whale of a good time being chaotic, in some saturnalian or lupercalian revelry, some charivari, or institutionalized orgy" (Turner, 41).

57. Turner, 24.

58. Turner, 29.

59. Turner associates "play" with liminoid phenomena, whereas liminal phenomena exist in a world not yet divided between "work" and "play." Turner, 33–36.

60. Turner, 43.

61. The relation between play and ritual is a matter of disagreement among theorists of play. Huizinga had an old-fashioned developmental view of civilizational history and saw ritual and festival as originating within the play sphere. Huizinga, *Homo Ludens,* 18, 31. Roger Caillois, on the other hand, sharply distinguishes sacred ritual from play in *Man and the Sacred* (Chicago: University of Illinois Press, 2001), 152–62. The contemporary scholar Thomas Henricks also distinguishes play from ritual. Thomas S. Henricks, *Play and the Human Condition* (Chicago: University of Illinois Press, 2015), 53–58. My own view is that rituals—performative scripts that incline to repetition—can be a part of play if they are noninstrumental. Some rituals are instrumental in a way that is not at all play.

62. One scholar that I know of has already used Turner's sense of liminoid phenomena when describing stand-up comedy: "The genre of stand-up comedy affords female comics the freedom to engage in rhetorically charged social critique cloaked in the trappings of entertainment; in so doing, they are exemplifying the liminoid because, as Turner notes, by virtue of its liminoid nature, entertainment is 'suffused with freedom.'" Joanne R. Gilbert, *Performing Marginality: Humor, Gender, and Cultural Critique* (Detroit: Wayne State University Press, 2004), 3.

63. Turner specifically invokes Emil Durkheim here. Turner, "Liminal to Liminoid," 32.

64. Prominent among them are Huizinga, *Homo Ludens,* 7; and Roger Caillois, *Man, Play, and Games* (Chicago: University of Illinois Press, 2001), 7.

65. Mihaly Csikszentmihalyi's sense of "flow" makes the same voluntaristic assumption about play activities made by Turner, Caillois, and others. But within flow there does

seem to be an important loss of self-consciousness or a "feeling of union with the environment." Mihaly Csikszentmihalyi, *Flow: The Psychology of Optimal Experience* (New York: Harper Perennial, 1991), 63, 62–66.

66. D. W. Winnicott, *Playing and Reality* (New York: Routledge, 2005), 18.

67. Winnicott, 15.

68. Winnicott, 14.

69. Winnicott, 15.

70. Winnicott, 1.

71. Winnicott, 3.

72. Winnicott, 3.

73. Winnicott, 3., 69.

74. Huizinga, *Homo Ludens*, 11.

75. Winnicott, *Playing and Reality*, 7.

76. Winnicott, 7.

77. Winnicott, 3–4. It is important that "illusion" here does not suggest "not real"; it signals that the question of reality should be bracketed.

78. Stanley Cavell uses the language of "finding as founding" in his discussion of Emerson's role as an American philosopher. The possibilities of comparison are tantalizing, but I cannot elaborate on them here. Stanley Cavell, *This New Yet Unapproachable America: Lectures After Emerson After Wittgenstein* (Albuquerque: Living Batch, 1989), 77–121.

79. D. W. Winnicott, *The Family and Individual Development* (New York: Routledge, 2006), 136–37.

80. Winnicott, 71.

5. PLAYING IN FRAUGHT SOCIETIES

1. On "styles of thought," see Karl Mannheim, "Conservative Thought," in Kurt H. Wolf, ed., *From Karl Mannheim* (New Brunswick, NJ: Transaction, 1993), especially 260–65.

2. Winnicott, *Playing and Reality*, 18.

3. Winnicott, 72.

4. Winnicott, 72.

5. Winnicott, 72–73.

6. Winnicott, 75.

7. Winnicott, 74.

8. Winnicott, 75.

9. Winnicott, 69.

10. Winnicott, 142.

11. Winnicott, 73.

12. Winnicott, 86.

13. Winnicott, 76.

14. Winnicott, 17, see also p. 119.

15. Winnicott, 18.
16. Winnicott, 71.
17. John Rawls, "The Idea of Public Reason Revisited," in *The Law of Peoples* (Cambridge: Harvard University Press, 1999), 152.
18. Rawls, 153.
19. Rawls, 154.
20. Rawls, 155.
21. Rawls, 155–56.
22. Noël Carroll makes an important distinction between joke-type and joke-token that will come in handy when making such an interpretive judgment. A joke-type is the joke abstracted from any particular instance of its telling. A joke-token is the particular instance of telling, which includes the context of its telling. When a Holocaust joke-type is told as a joke-token by a Jew among Jews we might say that this is an instance of humorous play. When the same joke-type is tokened by a neo-Nazi as an "ice-breaker" at the beginning of his speech about how to finish the job, we may decide that this is not humorous play. Noël Carroll, *Humour: A Very Short Introduction* (New York: Oxford University Press, 2014), 90–92.
23. Similarly, the institutions of the basic structure should be used to demand that minors are never inappropriately incorporated into or otherwise jeopardized by adult play.
24. Noël Carroll refers to "the arresting impression of massiveness" in his description of the qualitative properties to which one attends with understanding when having an "aesthetic experience." Noël Carroll, "Recent Approaches to Aesthetic Experience," *Journal of Aesthetics and Art Criticism* 70, no. 2 (Spring 2012): 173.
25. Noël Carroll, "Defending the Content Approach to Aesthetic Experience," *Metaphilosophy* 46, no. 2 (April 2015): 174.
26. Making analytical distinctions between art and politics and claims about how they do or should relate is an extremely complicated matter. Jacques Rancière has argued, for instance, that there is an "originary and persistent tension between the two great politics of aesthetics: the politics of the becoming-life of art and the politics of the resistant form." Jacques Rancière, *Aesthetics and Its Discontents* (Malden, MA: Polity, 2009), 43–44. The former imagines that art can invite those who give it their attention to experience alternative human relations that are not characterized by domination (which characterizes human relations outside of art). But the realization of this alternative would entail that these relations are no longer differentiated *as art*, paradoxically requiring politically transformative art to demand the end of art. The latter imagines that art can offer transformative experiences of jarring dissonance in relation to the order of domination, but only insofar as it paradoxically makes itself wholly other to and entirely impractical as "politics." My own approach to differentiating the domain of play from the domain of the political (and from the pursuit of nonpublic projects in the background culture) is not meant to resolve these tensions. However, it is meant to offer a path forward at the always only limitedly satisfying, highly general level of analysis that is appropriate to public reason.

27. Though, as I've said, we will want to regulate the background culture on behalf of public health and other concerns. After all, the background culture—including the domain of play—is still governed by and significantly a product of the basic structure of society.

28. See the section, "The Idea of Comprehensive Groupness," in chapter 3, this volume.

29. Csikszentmihalyi's idea of "flow" is related. Within flow there is a loss of self-consciousness or a "feeling of union with the environment" that captures the immersiveness and intensity that I am pointing to here. Though, to be clear, one can enter flow while engaged in an instrumental activity, so it is not always play. If we want to use Csikszentmihalyi's idea of flow, we can say that some of what happens when the capability of play is exercised in the domain of play is "in flow." Mihaly Csikszentmihalyi, *Flow: The Psychology of Optimal Experience* (New York: Harper Perennial, 1991), 63, 62–66.

30. Johan Huizinga, *Homo Ludens: A Study of the Play Element in Culture* (Boston: Beacon, 1955), 12.

31. Huizinga, 12. In this regard see, more recently, Robert N. Bellah, *Religion in Human Evolution: From the Paleolithic to the Axial Age* (Cambridge: Harvard University Press, 2011), 567–606.

32. Huizinga, *Homo Ludens*, 13.

33. Roger Caillois, *Man, Play, and Games* (Chicago: University of Illinois Press, 2001), 4.

34. John Morreall, ed., *The Philosophy of Laughter and Humor* (Albany: State University of New York Press, 1987), 5. Henri Bergson has a rather idiosyncratic, interesting but implausible, "mechanical rigidity" theory of laughter, humor, and the comic, which I will not treat here: Henri Bergson, "Laughter," in *Comedy* (New York: Doubleday Anchor, 1956), 61–190. In *Humour*, Carroll distinguishes in addition to these theories the "play theory," the "dispositional theory," and his own "incongruity theory revisited," 42–54.

35. Excerpted in Morreall, *The Philosophy of Laughter and Humor*, 19–20.

36. Sigmund Freud, *Jokes and Their Relation to the Unconscious* (New York: Norton, 1989), 122–23.

37. Morreall, *The Philosophy of Laughter and Humor*, 6.

38. Noël Carroll, "Humour," in *The Oxford Handbook of Aesthetics*, ed. Jerrold Levinson (Oxford: Oxford University Press, 2005), 351. Carroll's most recent formulation goes as follows:

> creatures like us are in a state of comic amusement just in case (i) the object of one's mental state is a perceived incongruity which (ii) one regards as non-threatening or otherwise anxiety producing, and (iii) not annoying and (iv) towards which one does not enlist genuine problem-solving attitudes (v) but which gives rise to enjoyment of precisely the pertinent incongruity and (vi) to an experience of levity. And humour then is the response-dependent object of comic amusement, characterized thus.
>
> (Carroll, *Humour*, 49–50)

39.   When Carroll address the "play theory" of humor, he refers to Aristotle and Thomas Aquinas, focusing on play as a form of relaxation that provides respite from serious activities. Carroll rightfully points out that play and humor are not identical, since there is so much play that is not humor or humorous. Likewise, he notes, not all humor is play. Satire, for instance, is not play (43). I agree with Carroll, and my account of play allows us to distinguish rather clearly between the humorous elements of instrumental rhetorics like satire and humorous play.

40.   Another theorist who incorporates an incongruity theory of humor into a broader conception of play is Elliot Oring. He writes:

> Humor is a species of play, and while play may sometime be aggressive, it is much else besides. Play is expressive. It is auto- and allo-communicative. What play communicates requires a consideration of context. These contexts include the experiences that an individual brings to the humor that he or she hears and performs; the social interaction in which humorous performances are embedded; the social and historical conditions under which jokes arise, proliferate, and disappear; the cultural knowledge upon which humor depends and with which it plays; and the range of expressions, both within and beyond a society's boundaries, with which localized humorous performances may be compared and contrasted. When context is ignored, analysts are left either to consider humor as a form of aggression or dismiss it as mere amusement devoid of import.

Elliot Oring, *Engaging Humor* (Chicago: University of Illinois Press, 2003), 145.

41.   Carroll, *Humour*, 55–75.

42.   Noël Carroll, *A Philosophy of Mass Art* (Oxford: Clarendon, 1998), 248. Rod Martin has identified "mirth" as the distinctive emotion that is elicited by the perception of humor. He accepts the definition of mirth in the OED: "pleasurable feeling . . . joy, happiness; gaiety of mind, as manifested in jest and laughter; merriment, hilarity." Rod A. Martin, *The Psychology of Humor: An Integrative Approach* (Burlington, MA: Elsevier Academic, 2007), 7–9.

43.   John Morreall, "Comic Vices and Comic Virtues," *Humor* 23, no. 1 (2010): 1–26.

6. LENNY BRUCE AND THE INTIMACY OF PLAY

1.   Howard M. Sachar, *A History of the Jews in America* (New York: Vintage, 1992), 276.

2.   Sachar, 276.

3.   Sachar, 275. This was not a distinctive experience of Jews. It was merely one example of widespread ethnic conflict in urban America at that time.

4.   Referring to this sensibility in the work of Henry James, Sachar writes: "The image of Jews as swarming foreign animals appeared in ten of Jame's twelve novels, in eighteen short stories, one critical essay, and several travel essays" (279). He brings the following quote from James's 1907 *The American Scene*:

[a] great swarming that had begun to thicken, infinitely, as soon as we had crossed to the East Side and long before we had got to Rutgers Street. There is no swarming like that of Israel when once Israel has got a start, and the scene here bristled, at every step, with the signs and sounds, inimitable, unmistakable, of a Jewry that had burst all bounds. It was as if we had been . . . at the bottom of some vast shallow aquarium in which innumerable fish, of overdeveloped proboscis, were to bump together, forever, amid heaped spoils of the sea.

(279)

5. Sachar, 282.

6. Howard M. Sachar, *A History of the Jews in the Modern World* (New York: Vintage, 2005), 382.

7. Josh Lambert, *Unclean Lips: Obscenity, Jews, and American Culture* (New York: New York University Press, 2014), 27.

8. Lambert, 29, 30.

9. Lambert, 29–30.

10. Hasia R. Diner, *The Jews of the United States: 1654–2000* (Berkeley: University of California Press, 2004), 208.

11. Sachar, *A History of the Jews in the Modern World*, 383–86.

12. Eric L. Goldstein, *The Price of Whiteness: Jews, Race and American Identity* (Princeton: Princeton University Press, 2006), 37.

13. The historian Gerald Sorin has reflected on this period: "The essential driving force behind these repressive activities was anti-modernism, a fear held by many that alien forces were corrupting their country. It is striking to note how frequently in the literature of the era, in popular parlance, in the media, and in political rhetoric, Jews in particular among 'aliens' were blamed for the 'ills' brought by modernization." Gerald Sorin, *Tradition Transformed: The Jewish Experience in America* (Baltimore: Johns Hopkins University Press, 1997), 181.

14. Sachar, *A History of the Jews in American*, 455.

15. Diner, *The Jews of the United States*, 210.

16. Diner, 212.

17. Michael R. Beschloss, *The Conquerors: Roosevelt, Truman, and the Destruction of Hitler's Germany* (New York: Simon and Schuster, 2003), 41.

18. Diner, *The Jews of the United States*, 215.

19. Sachar, *A History of the Jews in the Modern World*, 386–90.

20. Diner, *The Jews of the United States*, 229–30.

21. Diner, 223–24.

22. Diner, 214.

23. Edward S. Shapiro, *A Time for Healing: American Jewry Since World War II* (Baltimore: Johns Hopkins University Press, 1992), 10.

24. Jeffrey C. Alexander, *The Civil Sphere* (New York: Oxford University Press, 2006), 525.

25. Irving Howe, *World of Our Fathers: The Journey of the East European Jews to America and the Life They Found and Made* (New York: New York University Press, 2005 [1976]),

603. Albert Goldman saw this process flowering fully in the 1960s, which he called "the Jewish Decade." According to Goldman,

> Overnight, the Jew was raised from his traditional role of underdog or invisible man to the glory of being the most fascinating authority in America. Benefiting from universal guilt over the murders by the Nazis, stiffening into fresh pride over the achievements of the State of Israel, reaping the harvest in America of generations of hard work and sacrifice for the sake of the "children," the Jews burst suddenly into prominence in a dozen different areas of national life. They became the new heroes of commerce, art, and intellect.

Albert Goldman, "Laughtermakers," in Sarah Blacher Cohen, ed., *Jewish Wry: Essays on Jewish Humor* (Detroit: Wayne State University Press, 1987 [1976]), 85.

26.   Diner, *The Jews of the United States*, 280.

27.   For a critical reevaluation, see Edward Shapiro, "Will Herberg's *Protestant-Catholic-Jew*: A Critique" in Jack Kugelmass, ed., *Key Texts in American Jewish Culture* (New Brunswick: Rutgers University Press, 2003), 258–74.

28.   Herberg, *Protestant-Catholic-Jew*, 190.

29.   Herberg, 196.

30.   Schultz, *Tri-Faith America*, 93.

31.   This is an obvious point with respect to the idea of a "Judeo-Christian tradition" as well. See Arthur A. Cohen, "The Myth of the Judeo-Christian Tradition [1969]," in David Stern and Paul Mendes-Flohr, eds., *An Arthur A. Cohen Reader: Selected Fiction and Writings on Judaism, Theology, Literature, and Culture* (Detroit: Wayne State University Press, 1998), 203–12; Deborah Dash Moore, "Jewish GIs and the Creation of the Judeo-Christian Tradition," *Religion and American Culture: A Journal of Interpretation* 8, no. 1 (Winter 1998); Mark Silk, "Notes on the Judeo-Christian Tradition in America," *American Quarterly* 36, no. 1 (Spring 1984).

32.   At the same time, he worried about American religion and American Judaism in particular. Since American religion was primarily a way of being identifiable as a good American (a convention of civility) and otherwise merely provided a feeling of "belonging," it had become a simulacrum of authentic religiosity, in Herberg's view. Herberg was not content to settle for a Jewish religiosity that was fervent about nothing more than its fund-raising. This had led him, before his sociological book came out, to offer a Jewish theology entitled *Judaism and Modern Man: An Interpretation of Jewish Religion*. Will Herberg, *Judaism and Modern Man: An Interpretation of Jewish Religion* (Philadelphia: Jewish Publication Society, 1960 [1951]). In *Protestant-Catholic-Jew* he seems to note with satisfaction a proliferation of theological works responding to the same problem. Herberg, *Protestant-Catholic-Jew*, 205n48. He mentions Ludwig Lewisohn's *The American Jew: Character and Destiny*, Abraham Joshua Heschel's *Man Is Not Alone: A Philosophy of Religion, Man's Quest for God*, and *God in Search of Man: A Philosophy of Judaism*, his own book, and recent translations of works by Martin Buber and Franz Rosenzweig.

33. Sig Altman, *The Comic Image of the Jew: Explorations of a Pop Culture Phenomenon* (Teaneck, NJ: Fairleigh Dickenson University Press, 1971), 201–2.

34. Joyce Antler, *You Never Call! You Never Write! A History of the Jewish Mother* (New York: Oxford University Press, 2007), 110. She writes, "The Jewishness of this environment, extending to the extravagant ten-course dinners and to the headliners with their riot of staccato one-line gags, was an absolute given. Jewish mother jokes arose out of this 'insider' milieu in which topics that touched a chord with vacationing Jews could be raised as together audiences breathed out a collective sigh of release" (111).

35. Henry Popkin, "The Vanishing Jew of Our Popular Culture," *Commentary* (July 1952): 46–55. Popkin concluded with a plea: "Let the Jew come back, not as apologist or walking object lesson, not as generalized focus for sentiments of tolerance or as a public-relations representative of his people, but the man himself in all his concreteness—his strengths and his weaknesses—the human being he used to be" (55). The Jewish comedian Sam Levenson wrote a sanctimonious response to Popkin entitled "The Dialect Comedian Should Vanish," *Commentary* (August 1952): 168–70. In it, he claims, citing Molly Goldberg as a model, that "dialect may be permissible if the subject matter, the content in itself does not discredit the Jew. Unfortunately, most of the history of dialect humor proves that such has not been the case" (169). He also suggests that he would literally edit out sentences from Sholom Aleichem's *The Old Country* if he were publishing them.

36. Popkin, "The Vanishing Jew," 53.

37. Lawrence J. Epstein, *The Haunted Smile: The Story of Jewish Comedians in America* (New York: PublicAffairs, 2001), 111–25.

38. J. Hoberman and Jeffrey Shandler, *Entertaining America: Jews, Movies, and Broadcasting* (New York: Jewish Museum, 2003), 220. Hoberman and Shandler rightfully situate this cultural development within the context of similar trends among other groups: "Jewry's newfound self-assertion in the American public sphere coincides with that of other groups—African Americans, women, gays, and lesbians, in particular. Indeed, Jewish participation in the 'new ethnicity' of the 1960s and 1970s often resembled these concomitant developments in identity politics and culture, and sometimes coincided with them (especially in the work of some feminist and gay activists)" (205).

39. Hoberman and Shandler, 220.

40. Hoberman and Shandler, 220. Images of Jews in the Jewish "new wave" films are worth comparing to the Jews that appear in the crop of films dealing with Jews that were made at the end of the 1950s. *Marjorie Morningstar* (1958) centers on Jewish American family life and introduces some of the characterizations that will be amplified in the late 1960s. However, in many of the films dealing with Jews during this period, or drawing from source material about Jews, the characterizations are "de-Semitized." See Patricia Erens, *The Jew in American Cinema* (Bloomington: Indiana University Press, 1984), 204–15. The Jewish new wave films anticipated Blaxploitation by only a few years. Arguably, the key early titles of the Jewish new wave, which played unabashedly with Jewish stereotypes and Jewish humor, and prominently used actors that had Jewish public personas, are *Funny Girl* (Columbia, 1968), *The Producers* (Avco Embassy, 1968), *Bye,*

Bye Braverman (Warner Bros., 1968), *I Love You, Alice B. Toklas!* (Warner Bros.—Seven Arts, 1968), *Goodbye, Columbus* (Paramount, 1969), *Bob & Carol & Ted & Alice* (Columbia, 1969), and *Move* (Twentieth Century Fox, 1970). Blaxploitation is conventionally said to start with *Sweet Sweetback's Baadasssss Song* (Cinemation Industries) and *Shaft* (MGM), both released in 1971. The film version of *Goodbye, Columbus*, in particular, received criticism in the press for exploiting negative Jewish stereotypes, especially in the infamous wedding reception scene. Hoberman and Shandler, 233–35. It is interesting to note that *Fiddler on the Roof* (United Artists) was released in 1971. *Fiddler* presents a fascinating contrast to the new wave films because, instead of playing with historically stigmatized contemporary American Jewishness, it offers exaggeratedly "religious" Jews in a romanticized faraway shtetl. These are very different invitations to play with Jewishness, for both Jews and gentiles.

41. I am not suggesting that Jews simply embraced being what anti-Semites had accused them of being all along. There is a very complex relationship between the historical Jewish passion for modernity—reason, individuality, individual rights, capitalism, meritocracy, sexual freedom, aesthetic experimentalism, science, mass media, and so on—and anti-Semitic paranoia about Jews as the modern menace. These are dynamics that may go all the way back to Spinoza, passionately arguing for rationalist democratic freedom in the seventeenth century, and his horrified detractors, who labeled him "IUDAEUS ET ATHEISTA." In the American context, these dynamics are analyzed well in David A. Hollinger, *Science, Jews, and Secular Culture: Studies in Mid-Twentieth-Century American Intellectual History* (Princeton: Princeton University Press, 1996).

42. See Vincent Brook, *Something Ain't Kosher Here: The Rise of the "Jewish" Sitcom* (New Brunswick: Rutgers University Press, 2003).

43. The history of American comedy in the 1950s has served as evidence for the broader claim that it was a radical decade in its own right. See Alan Petigny, *The Permissive Society: America, 1941–1965* (New York: Cambridge University Press, 2009), Stephen E. Kercher, *Revel with a Cause: Liberal Satire in Postwar America* (Chicago: University of Chicago Press, 2006), and Ed Sikov, *Laughing Hysterically: American Screen Comedy of the 1950s* (New York: Columbia University Press, 1996).

44. Mort Sahl played a key role in developing popular jazz venues as sites for the new comedy. "Sahl literally blazed a trail by forging an informal comedy circuit out of jazz clubs through his tours with Kenton and Brubeck, long before there were 'comedy clubs.' Jazz room's like Mister Kelly's in Chicago, the Village Vanguard in New York, and the Crescendo in Los Angeles began booking comedians after Sahl played them. 'I had to build up my own network of places to play because the others weren't available to me.'" Gerald Nachman, *Seriously Funny: The Rebel Comedians of the 1950s and 1960s* (New York: Back Stage, 2004), 69.

45. "Pre-Sahl was a time in which comedians, clad like band leaders in spats and tuxes, sporting cap-and-bells names like Joey, Jackie, or Jerry, announced themselves by their brash, anything-for-a-laugh, charred-earth policy and by-the-jokebook gags." Nachman, 6–7.

46. Kercher, *Revel with a Cause*, 204.

47. Kliph Nesteroff, *The Comedians: Drunks, Thieves, Scoundrels and the History of American Comedy* (New York: Grove, 2015), 159–62.

48. Dick Gregory was also crucial to this shift. Kercher, *Revel with a Cause*, 285–98.

49. Kercher, 397–424.

50. On *Lenny Bruce: Let the Buyer Beware* (Los Angeles: Shout! Factory, 2004), disc 1, track 13.

51. This routine can also be read as an impersonation of a "redneck," as it is in David E. Kaufman, *Jewhooing the Sixties: American Celebrity and Jewish Identity* (Waltham, MA: Brandeis University Press, 2012), 125–26. Though I think that the title Bruce gave to this bit suggests that we connect the character to the kind of white person who would have "colored friends," invite them to parties, and want to make them feel "relaxed." While I can hear the "redneck" version too, I think the *edge* of the piece is in its implications for white liberal audience members.

52. Richard Pryor had this to say: "Lenny had a routine called 'How to Relax Your Colored Friends at Parties.' He taught me not to go for the jokes to be funny; just tell the truth. When I did that, I was funny. Telling the truth may get you hell, but it also gets you into heaven. Thank you, Lenny. I love you man." *Lenny Bruce: Let the Buyer Beware*, 49.

53. Ted Cohen has written,

> And just what is *intimacy*? It is the shared sense of those in a *community*. The members know that they are in this community, and they know that they are joined there by one another. When the community is focused on a joke, the intimacy has two constituents. The first constituent is a shared set of beliefs, dispositions, prejudices, preferences, et cetera—a shared outlook on the world, or at least part of an outlook. The second constituent is a shared feeling—a shared response to something. The first constituent can be cultivated and realized without jokes. So can the second constituent, but with jokes, the second constituent is amplified by the first, and this is a very curious and wonderful fact about jokes. I may overvalue the intimacy available through joke-telling; after all, I am one of those who love and need joke-telling. But I am confident that it is an intimacy that should not be underestimated. When we laugh at the same thing, that is a very special occasion. It is already noteworthy that we laugh at all, at anything, and that we laugh all alone. That we do it *together* is the satisfaction of a deep human longing, the realization of a desperate hope. It is the hope that we are enough like one another to sense one another, to be able to live together.

Ted Cohen, *Jokes: Philosophical Thoughts on Joking Matters* (Chicago: University of Chicago Press, 1999), 28–29.

54. I have in my head some sense that there is a connection between metaperspectival intimacy and the kind of nonmoral compassion that Nussbaum describes as "focusing on suffering without asking the question of fault." Martha C. Nussbaum, "Compassion: Human and Animal," in N. Ann Davis, Richard Keshen, Jeff McMahan, eds., *Ethics*

and Humanity: Themes from the Philosophy of Jonathan Glover (New York: Oxford University Press, 2010), 210.

55.   Lenny Bruce did not, of course, invent the "hipster" persona. But the way he imbued his hipster persona with explicit Jewishness in public was particularly distinctive. Kaufman, *Jewhooing the Sixties*, 101–2, 124. There is some question as to when and how Leonard Schneider (aka Lenny Bruce) adopted his distinct hipster affectation and what were his most decisive influences in this direction. Albert Goldman, Bruce's biographer, claims that Bruce derived the style for which he became known from Jewish Brooklyn (drawing his legendary spritzing, especially, from the insider legend Joe Ancis). Albert Goldman and Lawrence Schiller, *Ladies and Gentlemen—Lenny Bruce!* (New York: Random House, 1974), 117–26. The historian Stephen Kercher suggests that Bruce really took on the relevant affectation when he got to the West Coast after 1951 (and that the key influences were not Jewish at all: the saxophone player Joe Maini and the comedian Lord Richard Buckley). Kercher, *Revel with a Cause*, 398–99, 527n19.

56.   As David Kaufman explains, Bruce "played on the inherent problem of masking—the fear of being unmasked—a motif that applied all too well to assimilated Jews, and one that would reappear in many of his routines." Kaufman, *Jewooing the Sixties*, 114.

57.   Reflecting on Bruce's distinctive contribution to Jewish comedy, Jeremy Dauber writes:

> What set Bruce apart from the pack . . . is not what he says. Bruce's routines don't hold up well on recording. He would regularly play to the band. His almost pathological hatred of phoniness (even as he made a career of phony-style impersonations) can weary. But it's the rhythms and flows of the way that he says it. It's the voice, the language, and particularly the Jewish voice: his embrace of his inauthentically authentic self, or vice versa, which leads to an approach markedly different from the one set out by Sahl.

Jeremy Dauber, *Jewish Comedy: A Serious History* (New York: Norton, 2017), 87.

58.   *Lenny Bruce: Let the Buyer Beware*, disc 2, track 11.

59.   John Cohen, ed., *The Essential Lenny Bruce* (New York: Ballantine, 1967), 39.

60.   His sense of disgust-politics can be seen as a bridge to his views about free speech. In one bit, for instance, he imagines a dialogue among the pilgrims who decided to come to America, retelling this "founding narrative" as follows: "'I'm tired of this shit, let's get somewhere else, let's go to a different country where we can have our meetings and be Protestants. Let's go somewhere else so we can be disgusting. And do disgusting shows. No one can stop us—flaunt it in their faces.' '*How* disgusting?' 'Well, go in front of a synagogue and sing about pork.' '*That* disgusting?' What about the Moslems?' 'Fuck'em. The Jews too, and the vegetarians. Cause that's our right—to be disgusting" (Cohen, 286).

61.   Though, this is not the sense of *sick* used in the July 13, 1959, article in *Time* entitled "The Sickniks" that is probably responsible for popularizing the term (pp. 42 and 44). The article identifies Mort Sahl as "the original sicknik" and describes the "sickness" of the new comedians as their contempt for the world around them and their callous

intimations of violence. It points, for instance, to Bruce's defense of the murderers Leopold and Loeb (two Jewish boys, by the way), quipping about their victim: "Bobby Franks was snotty." The novelist Nelson Algren is quoted in the article, opining, "This is an age of genocide. . . . People nowadays would rather be hurt than bored." I hear in this the suggestion that "the sickniks" were in part a response to the missing link problem.

62. John Limon may take a similar approach to Bruce, though in a different intellectual idiom, in his *Stand-Up Comedy in Theory; or, Abjection in America* (Durham: Duke University Press, 2000). Limon explains, referring to a concept in the work of Julia Kristeva, "what is stood up in stand-up comedy is abjection"; by abjection he means "a psychic worrying of those aspects of oneself that one cannot be rid of, that seem, but are not quite, alienable—for example, blood, urine, feces, nails, and the corpse." Limon, 4.

63. Actually, the earliest round of Jewish joke collections meant to be read by Jews appeared in Germany following emancipation; Sander Gilman dates the first such text at 1812. These jokes were presented in very refined German and, as indicated in prefatory remarks, intended to highlight the rationality of the Jews (the use of humor presumably indicating rationality). At the same time, they aimed to illustrate the damage done to Jews by persecution: the jokes reflected a rationality *distorted* by weakness and persecution. Sander L. Gilman, *Jewish Self-Hatred: Anti-Semitism and the Secret Language of the Jews* (Baltimore: Johns Hopkins University Press, 1986), 256–59. In this respect, these earliest collections reflect an attitude to Jewish incorporation and modernization similar to that of Christian Wilhem Von Dohm in his treatise "Concerning the Amelioration of the Civil Status of the Jews" written in 1781: the incivility of the Jew is due to his historic persecution, but proper education and civic inclusion can correct this distortion. The treatise is in Paul Mendes-Flohr and Jehudah Reinharz, eds., *The Jew in the Modern World: A Documentary History*, 2d ed. (New York: Oxford University Press, 1995), 28–36.

64. Gilman, *Jewish Self-Hatred*, 255.

65. Sigmund Freud, *The Joke and Its Relation to the Unconscious*, Trans. Joyce Crick (London: Penguin, 2003 [1905]), 68. This translation is careful to point out the Yiddish inflection of the final cry; see xli. The joke is as relevant today as it was when Freud recorded it and appears in a more contemporary rendition in the very popular Leo Rosten, *The New Joys of Yiddish* (New York: Three Rivers, 2001), 125. In Rosten's version the final cry is just "*Ge-valt!*" Theodor Reik glossed this joke in his book on Jewish humor as follows: "The transition from the French to the Yiddish cries interests us here because the return to the mother-tongue or to the jargon once spoken restores the emotional atmosphere of childhood and sweeps away all superstructure." Theodor Reik, *Jewish Wit* (New York: Gamut, 1962), 34. Of course, it is not lost on me that this most quintessential Jewish joke evokes the primordially important stuff of childhood—or, as Reik calls it, "the emotional atmosphere of childhood." Elliott Oring describes the message of the joke as follows: "In certain circumstances, particularly those of physical or emotional crisis, the true identity will emerge. Despite wealth, social status, and education,

the Jew will out." Elliott Oring, *The Jokes of Sigmund Freud: A Study in Humor and Jewish Identity* (Philadelphia: University of Pennsylvania Press, 1984), 49–50.

66.   John Murray Cuddihy, *The Ordeal of Civility: Freud, Marx, Levi-Strauss, and the Struggle with Modernity* (Boston: Beacon, 1987), 24.

67.   This is Gilman's sense of the "hidden language" of the Jews. Gilman, *Jewish Self-Hatred*, 250–70.

68.   The story of *Judenwitz* in nineteenth-century Germany and its twentieth-century legacy is too complex for me to address here; it would take us too far beyond the American context that is my focus. See Jefferson S. Chase, *Inciting Laughter: The Development of "Jewish Humor" in Nineteenth-Century German Culture* (New York: de Gruyter, 2000).

69.   By contrast to this positive view, Irving Howe offered a very negative assessment of Lenny Bruce (and the Jewish comic style that he represents), which is worth serious consideration. According to Howe, "what the Marx Brothers had done as surreal fantasy, shrewdly keeping in the realm of play, Bruce came to do with deadly intent." Howe, *World of Our Fathers*, 572. Howe concludes on Bruce: "Having stored up a bellyful of Jewish humiliation, Bruce cast it back onto his audiences. The laughter he won was a nervous laughter, tingling with masochism; it was like the laughter of convicts caught in a scheme to escape. Humor of this kind bears a heavy weight of destruction; in Jewish hands, more likely self-destruction, for it proceeds from a brilliance that corrodes the world faster than, even in imagination, it can remake it" (573). Howe's appreciation of Jewish humor did not extend to those who embraced and amplified its vulgarity at the expense of its Yiddish folkloric roots. This is clear in his attack on *Portnoy's Complaint*. And, in another way, in his disdain for the Broadway production of *Fiddler on the Roof*. Irving Howe, "Tevye on Broadway," *Commentary* 38 (November 1964): 73–75. A similar rebuke of Bruce can be found in Sanford Pinsker, "Lenny Bruce: *Shpritzing the Goyim*/Shocking the Jews," in Cohen, *Jewish Wry*, 89–104.

70.   This is how the bit is transcribed in Cohen, *The Essential Lenny Bruce*, 287.

71.   *Lenny Bruce: Let the Buyer Beware*, disc 3, track 8.

72.   He lumps rabbis, nuns, and priests together in the very next bit, "What Should Be/What Is." All are described as promoting a harmful ideal that is not realistic about the kinds of creatures that human beings actually are. *Lenny Bruce: Let the Buyer Beware*, disc 3, track 9.

73.   Lambert, *Unclean Lips*, 43–45.

74.   *Lenny Bruce: Let the Buyer Beware*, disc 3, track 7. This sentiment is also recorded in Cohen, *The Essential Lenny Bruce*, 102.

75.   While Bruce lumps rabbis in with nuns and priests in "What Should Be/What Is" (cf. note 72, this chapter), he elsewhere distinguishes Judaism and Jewishness as less repressive than Christianity:

> Or is it that the Jew has no concept? To a Jew f-u-c-k and s-h-i-t have the same value on the dirty-word graph. A Jew has no concept that f-u-c-k is worth 90 points and s-h-i-t 10. And the reason for that is that—well, see, rabbis and priests

both s-h-i-t, but only one f-u-c-ks. You see, in the Jewish culture, there's no merit badge for not doing that. And Jewish attorneys better get hip to that. And since the leaders of my tribe, rabbis, are *schtuppers*, perhaps that's why words come freer to me.

(Cohen, The Essential Lenny Bruce, 44)

76.   Another way to think about this might be in terms of the kind of friendship that Wayne Booth has suggested can emerge between a reader and a story. Booth was interested in what keeps us reading when we sit down to read a novel (when we are not assigned to read it for a class or otherwise compelled to read it). He suggested that we think of our persistence as accepting an offer of friendship with the "implied author" of the text. This friendship can be evaluated qualitatively according to a variety of measures that include the degree of intimacy it allows, its intensity, and its distance or proximity to our own sensibilities. But the ultimate value of this friendship is the time well spent, the simple goodness of being together with a friend, despite the friend's troubles, complexes, or peculiarities. He writes, "some good friends, in life as in literature, are wonderfully beneficial to my soul, even though they are clearly immoral on many a scale." Wayne Booth, *The Company We Keep: An Ethics of Fiction* (Berkeley: University of California Press, 1988), 179.

77.   William Novak and Moshe Waldoks, eds., *The Big Book of Jewish Humor* (New York: HarperPerennial, 1981), 60. Another version with some variations appears in Cohen, *The Essential Lenny Bruce,* 41–42.

78.   David Biale writes, "Bruce idiosyncratically defined 'Jewish' as a kind of urban, ethnic, secular irreverence." David Biale, *Eros and the Jews: From Biblical Israel to Contemporary America* (New York: Basic Books, 1992), 216. According to Kaufman, Bruce "is attempting to suggest that *Jewish* is a sensibility, an ineffable quality, rather than something more concrete and observable, like religion or race. In Bruce's usage, Jewish became a stand-in for hip or cool—for what is socially desirable. In this, directly challenged a cultural norm of the time: the deeply engrained idea that Jewishness is uncool and undesirable." Kaufman, *Jewhooing the Sixties,* 124.

79.   Gregory Bateson explains that a sign always hangs on the play-frame that reads: "This is play." He called this sign a "metacommunication." The metacommunicative frame around play claims: "These actions in which we now engage do not denote what those actions *for which they stand* would denote [outside of the play-frame]." Bateson, "A Theory of Play and Fantasy," 180.

80.   Cohen, *The Essential Lenny Bruce,* 15–16.

81.   Here's the whole anecdote:

[Grover] Sales . . . recalls going with Dick Gregory to see him. They walked in during the middle of the show: . . . Spotting Greg, Lenny peered at the audience for an unnerving interval. *"Are there any niggers here tonight?"* Greg stiffened like a retriever, with the rest of the audience. In 1962 nobody had ever heard that word onstage, not in a white nightclub. Bruce then rattled off a string of ethnic insults, trying to defuse brutal hate words like *nigger, kike, dyke, wop, grease-ball, gook, frog, sheenie,* and *jigaboo.* Gregory told Sales: "This man is the eighth wonder of the world and if they don't kill him or throw him in jail he's liable to shake up this whole fuckin' country."

(Nachman, *Seriously Funny,* 407)

82. Hilton Als writes about Pryor, "Instead of adapting to the white perspective, he forced white audiences to follow him into his own experience. Pryor didn't manipulate his audiences' white guilt or their black moral outrage. If he played the race card, it was only to show how funny he looked when he tried to shuffle the deck." Hilton Als, "A Pryor Love," in *White Girls* (San Francisco: McSweeny's, 2014), 228–29.

7. PHILIP ROTH TELLS THE GREATEST JEWISH JOKE EVER TOLD

1. The last words of *Portnoy's Complaint* are: "PUNCH LINE: So [*said the doctor*]. Now vee may perhaps to begin. Yes?" Philip Roth, *Portnoy's Complaint* (New York: Vintage, 1994 [1969]), 274.

2. He denies any explicit debt to Lenny Bruce in an interview with George Plimpton in 1969. Philip Roth, *Reading Myself and Others* (New York: Vintage, 2001), 18. In retrospect, however, it is difficult not to speculate some kind of connection.

3. Roth, *Portnoy's Complaint,* 19. He also does it to a piece of liver that is later eaten by his family: "So. Now you know the worst thing I have ever done. I fucked my own family's dinner" (134).

4. Roth, 102.

5. It is deeply rooted in American literary traditions, as Bernard Rodgers explains: "Roth's exercise of style as a means to freedom of consciousness and expression, then, is in the American grain; and so is the subject which that style is meant to expose and explore—Portnoy's *complaint.* For like his American forebears, Alexander Portnoy wants most of all to be free—of his past and its burdens, of the weight of a culturally formed conscience and consciousness." Bernard F. Rodgers Jr., "In the American Grain (*Portnoy's Complaint*)," in Harold Bloom, ed., *Philip Roth's Portnoy's Complaint* (Philadelphia: Chelsea House, 2004), 36.

6. Roth articulated a similar approach to literature in his 1963 response to critics of *Goodbye, Columbus:*

> Fiction is not written to affirm the principles and beliefs that everybody seems to hold, nor does it seek to guarantee the appropriateness of our feelings. The world of fiction, in fact, frees us from the circumscriptions that society places upon feeling; one of the greatnesses of the art is that it allows both the writer and the reader to respond to experience in ways not always available in day-to-day conduct; or, if they are available, they are not possible, or manageable, or

legal, or advisable, or even necessary to the business of living. We may not even know that we have such a range of feelings and responses *until* we have come into contact with the work of fiction. This does not mean that either reader or writer no longer brings any judgment to bear upon human action. Rather, we judge at a different level of our being, for not only are we judging with the aid of new feelings but without the necessity of having to act upon judgment. Ceasing for a while to be upright citizens, we drop into another layer of consciousness. And this expansion of moral consciousness, this exploration of moral fantasy, is of considerable value to a man and to society.

> (Roth, "Writing About Jews," in *Reading Myself and Others,* 195)

7. Roth, *Portnoy's Complaint,* 3.

8. Roth, 4.

9. On the other hand, a negative stereotype of the "Jewish mother" is certainly among the flammable materials that Roth is playing with in this novel. The Jewish mother stereotype has a complex history, which has received insightful and comprehensive attention in Joyce Antler, *You Never Call! You Never Write! A History of the Jewish Mother* (New York: Oxford University Press, 2007), especially 143, 171. See also Martha A. Ravitz, "The Jewish Mother: Comedy and Controversy in American Popular Culture," in Bloom, *Philip Roth's Portnoy's Complaint,* 163–87.

10. Roth, *Portnoy's Complaint,* 4.

11. I am not the first person to make this connection: in a review of a book by Gershom Scholem (who, by the way, detested *Portnoy's Complaint* and called it "the book for which all anti-Semites have been praying"), a Rabbi Robert Saks wrote, "Roth, I believe, makes it very clear that the Jewish Mother, the Jewish God, and the Jewish laws are of one mold for [Portnoy]." Quoted in Alan Cooper, *Philip Roth and the Jews* (New York: State University of New York Press, 1996), 156.

12. It is also perceptible in his descriptions of her power and energy: "It was my mother who could accomplish anything." Roth, *Portnoy's Complaint,* 11. A similar structure is evident in the leitmotif of "eyes" in Woody Allen's *Crimes and Misdemeanors.*

13. Roth has said that he conceived *Portnoy's Complaint* in part as an alternative to popular works by Leon Uris and Harry Golden, which depicted Jews either as noble fighters for their God-given land or dignified American successes whose idealized family life was thick with "Old World" schmaltz. Roth's own reflections on the development of his idea for the Portnoy family, to my ears, also demonstrates a bit of this quasi secularization:

> here were the fallible, oversized, anthropomorphic gods who had reigned over the households of my neighborhood; here was the legendary Jewish family dwelling on high, whose squabbles over French-fried potatoes, synagogue attendance, and shiksas were, admittedly, of Olympian magnitude and splendor, but by whose terrifying kitchen lightning storms were illuminated the values, dreams, fears, and aspirations by which we mortal Jews lived somewhat less vividly down below.

Philip Roth, "In Response to Those Who Have Asked Me: 'How Did You Come to Write That Book, Anyway?'" in *Reading Myself and Others*, 35. See also "Some New Jewish Stereotypes" in the same volume, pp. 183–92. Perhaps some of the difference between Philip Roth and Alexander Portnoy is revealed in the fact that Alex is stuck in the structure and concepts of Jewishness, while Roth is stuck enough in Jewishness to conceive of Alex, but is, in his own voice, also apt to think in terms of gods, legends, and Olympus.

14.   Roth, *Portnoy's Complaint*, 16.

15.   Roth, 80.

16.   Roth, 80. Interesting to see the father also intermingled with the divine in this case.

17.   Roth, 32–33.

18.   Roth, 81–82.

19.   And why should he argue with the reasoning behind his parents' *kashrut*: "he sucks one night on a lobster's claw and within the hour his cock is out and aimed at a *shikse* on a Public Service bus. And his superior Jewish brain might as well be *made of matzoh brei!*" (Roth, 82). Note his inescapable mode of explanation: whether or not he believes that eating lobster incited his adult perversion—he does not, of course—he cannot help but narrate it this way!

20.   Roth, 95.

21.   Roth, 17. Lest we assume that Sophie is drawn merely as an hysterical woman, it seems worth noting that the God of Israel is no less tempestuous and wrathful.

22.   Roth, 93.

23.   Roth, 93.

24.   See, for instance, Roth, 101.

25.   Roth, 8–9.

26.   Roth, 5.

27.   Roth, 5.

28.   Roth, 6.

29.   Roth, 7. Notice that he clings to a moral justification for his work. But this doesn't stop him from referring to "these niggers" in a denigrating tone when he is frustrated by their disinterest in insurance (10). His mother, for her part, is also constantly aggrandizing her own moral fastidiousness. Referring to the housekeeper:

> "I'm the only one who's good to her. I'm the only one who gives her a whole can of tuna for lunch, and I'm not talking *dreck*, either. I'm talking Chicken of the Sea, Alex. I'm sorry, I can't be a stingy person. Excuse me, but I can't live like that, even if it is 2 for 49. Esther Wasserberg leaves twenty-five cents in nickels around the house when Dorothy comes, and counts up afterwards to see it's all there. Maybe I'm too good," she whispers to me, meanwhile running scalding water over the dish from which the cleaning lady has just eaten her lunch, alone like a leper, "but I couldn't do a thing like that."
>
> (Roth, 13)

This again points to the contradictions that embroil Alex's world of primordially important stuff.

30. Roth, 7.
31. He particularly despised N. Everett Lindabury, its president (Roth, 8).
32. Roth, 39.
33. Roth, 40.
34. In "Imagining Jews," Roth describes Jack Portnoy as Alex's "well-intentioned Bober-ish father," referring to the character of Morris Bober in Malamud's *The Assistant*, who is clearly identifiable as a kind of moral schlemiel. Roth, *Reading Myself and Others*, 277.
35. Howe reflected, "[My] growing interest in Yiddish must to some extent be stirred by . . . the growing concern about the Holocaust. . . . You *were* a Jew! That was the crucial fact which in a way the Holocaust made clear. . . . [For me] this new feeling about being Jew-ish had a reciprocal relationship with working in Yiddish literature." Quoted in How-ard M. Sachar, *A History of the Jews in America* (New York: Vintage, 1992), 857.
36. This is the way Howe's intentions are described by Edward Alexander in *Irving Howe: Socialist, Critic, Jew* (Bloomington: Indiana University Press, 1998), 78. David Roskies writes,

> Howe's task was to rescue the very best of a culture that had just been dealt its death blow and to make that saving remnant palatable to a cosmopolitan crowd not much prone to tradition or ethnicity. The measure of Howe's success and of the need for this rescue operation is the large numbers of students of Jewish lit-erature whose familiarity with Yiddish rests solely on the introduction to *A Treasury of Yiddish Stories* and the subsequent anthologies that drew their Yid-dish materials exclusively from that collection.

David G. Roskies, "The Treasures of Howe and Greenberg," *Prooftexts* 3, no. 1 (Janu-ary 1983): 110.
37. Alexander, *Irving Howe*, 86. While the introduction is signed by both editors, Alexan-der reports that Howe wrote it (79).
38. Alexander, 85.
39. *Dos Kleine Mentshele* is also the title and theme of Sholem Yankev Abramovitch aka Mendele Mocher Sforim's first novel, which is sometimes said to be the first modern Yiddish novel.
40. Irving Howe and Eliezer Greenberg, eds., *A Treasury of Yiddish Stories* (New York: Pen-guin, 1953), 40.
41. Howe and Greenberg, 42.
42. The literal meaning is "homeyness." "In the introduction to the American edition of his works, Sholem Aleichem derides this concept of *heymishkeyt* [homeyness, like-home] as the last idea of Jewishness assimilated American Jews stick to: 'A *heymisher nign, a heymisher shidekh, a heymisher khazn, a heymish maykhl, a heymish broyt, heymishe fish, heymisher khrey mit rosl, a heymisher tsimes,—ikh hob geton mit mayn kind a heymishn shidekch*.' [A homey melody, a homey betrothal, a homey cantor, a homey dish, a homey bread, homey fish, homey horseradish with pot roast, homey tsimes—Thank God, I made a homey match for my child]." Delphine Bechtel, "America

and the Shtetl in Sholem Aleichem's Di Goldgreber [The Golddiggers]," *Melus* 17, no. 3 (Autumn 1991): 79.

43. Howe and Greenberg, "Introduction," in *A Treasury of Yiddish Stories*, 40.

44. Howe and Greenberg, 40.

45. Howe and Greenberg, 25.

46. Howe and Greenberg, 26.

47. Gerald Sorin has suggested that Howe's image of the communities represented in Yiddish fiction reflects his socialist sensibility. "The shtetl community, while not quite Howe's socialist utopia projected onto the past, contained for him a tradition of fraternity and communal responsibility worth salvaging and promoting." Gerald Sorin, *Irving Howe: A Life of Passionate Dissent* (New York: New York University Press, 2005), 135. Already following the immigration restrictions of 1924, no longer experiencing the replenishment of real Eastern European Jewish immigrants, American Jews went into overdrive imagining their lost, rooted, Old World community: "The place of the shtetl in the self-understanding of millions of American Jews now became fixed for all time. The shtetl was reclaimed as the place of common origin (even when it wasn't), the source of a collective folk identity rooted in a particular historical past and, most importantly, as the locus of a new, secular, covenant." David G. Roskies, "The Shtetl in Jewish Collective Memory," in *The Jewish Search for a Usable Past* (Bloomington: Indiana University Press, 1999), 57. Howe was no doubt influenced by this proliferation and romanticization of shtetl images.

48. Howe and Greenberg, "Introduction," 34.

49. Howe and Greenberg, 35.

50. Howe and Greenberg, 35.

51. Sorin, *Irving Howe*, 284.

52. Despite his admiration for the "long-suffering, persistent, lovingly ironic" domestic antihero, Howe does not fail to note a contrary strain in the literature. The gentleness and delicacy that characterized early stories by Mendele Mocher Sforim and Sholom Aleichem echoed the refined pacific values of the wise Jewish scholar (*talmud khokhum*) and the young men of the yeshiva (*yeshiva bokhurs*); these hang together in the value of *edelkayt*. Daniel Boyarin writes: "The alternative Jewish form of maleness was known as *Edelkayt* (literally, 'nobility,' but in Yiddish 'gentleness and delicacy'!); its ideal subject was the *Yeshiva-Bokhur* (the man devoting his life to the study of Torah) and his secularized younger brother, the *Mentsh*." Daniel Boyarin, *Unheroic Conduct: The Rise of Heterosexuality and the Invention of the Jewish Man* (Berkely: University of California Press, 1997), 23. The next generation of Yiddish writers, like Sholem Asch, I. M. Weissenberg, and Zalman Schneour, abandoned, indeed repudiated, *edelkayt* entirely; "These writers felt that the time had come to put blood and muscle into Jewish life, to revive the idea of heroism and battle." Howe and Greenberg, "Introduction," 62. Howe associates this shift with the rising popularity of socialism and Zionism (45).

53. Howe and Greenberg, 38.

54. In 1971 Ruth R. Wisse further codified this convention as a tradition in *The Schlemiel as Modern Hero* (Chicago: University of Chicago Press, 1971). Sidra DeKoven Ezrahi writes, "Ruth Wisse's *Schlemiel as Modern Hero* and the discourse that it generated

define not only the place of a major Yiddish trope, but also the centrality of the schle-miel as radical diasporic alternative to the cultures of power in which Jews have lived." Sidra DeKoven Ezrahi, *Booking Passage: Exile and Homecoming in the Modern Jewish Imagination* (Berkeley: University of California Press, 2000), 314n11.

55.   Esther Romeyn and Jack Kugelmass, *Let There Be Laughter! Jewish Humor in America* (Chicago: Spertus Press, 1997), 66–67.

56.   Romeyn and Kugelmass, 219.

57.   Romeyn and Kugelmass, 217.

58.   His nicknames for the women in his life have a patronizing quality. It is almost as though he squashes them into narrative puppets with his pithy nominal reductions. On the other hand, his description of Kay Campbell—"the Pumpkin"—suggests that his pet names are no obstacle to sincere admiration.

59.   Roth, *Portnoy's Complaint*, 115.

60.   Roth, 241.

61.   Paul Breines, *Tough Jews: Political Fantasies and the Moral Dilemma of American Jewry* (New York: Basic Books, 1990).

62.   Max Nordau, "Jewry of Muscle," in Paul Mendes-Flohr and Jehuda Reinharz, eds., *The Jew in the Modern World: A Documentary History* (Oxford: Oxford University Press, 1995), 547–48.

63.   Breines, *Tough Jews*, 50.

64.   Breines specifically excludes Alex Portnoy from his catalogue of "tough Jews," listing him instead with Woody Allen's characters as a schlemiel insurmountably neurotic about sex (199). On the other hand, Warren Rosenberg sees Portnoy as quintessentially aggressive. Warren Rosenberg, *Legacy of Rage: Jewish Masculinity, Violence, and Culture* (Amherst: University of Massachusetts Press, 2001), 185–206.

65.   Breines, *Tough Jews*, 13.

66.   Roth, *Portnoy's Complaint*, 235. These passages may reflect Roth's place solidly within the American literary tradition, as much as they clearly introduce a new sensibility into this tradition: "In the way he confronts the question of love, Portnoy, it is important to remember, is not alone as a character in either Jewish novels or in American literature. The themes of the overvaluation of the sex object, the transference of this form of idealization on to the image and symbol of America and the related problems of love, sexuality, and moral development are all intrinsic to American literature and culture." Sam B. Girgus, "Portnoy's Prayer: Philip Roth and the American Unconscious," in Bloom, *Philip Roth's Portnoy's Complaint*, 51.

67.   There is a historical basis for connecting the preoccupations of Roth and Fanon. The historian Susan Glenn writes, "By the end of the 1940s, a growing body of work—social scientific, philosophical, and literary—on the effects of prejudice on minority group self-consciousness created an intellectual convergence zone in which the figure of the 'self-hating Jew' and his black counterpart the 'negrophobic negro' were imagined, in Martiniquean psychiatrist Frantz Fanon's phrasing, as 'brother[s] in misery.'" Susan A. Glenn, "The Vogue of Jewish Self-Hatred in Post-World War II America," *Jewish Social Studies* 12, no. 3 (Spring-Summer 2006): 100–1.

68.   Roth, *Portnoy's Complaint*, 47.

69. Roth, 49.

70. Roth, 50.

71. Roth, 41–42.

72. Roth, 50. He does also express admiration for his father's arms (122).

73. Reflecting on Marie Syrkin's attack on *Portnoy's Complaint* as functionally equivalent to anti-Semitic propaganda, Roth writes: "to Syrkin, for a Jew to have the kind of sexual desires Alexander Portnoy has (conflict-laden and self-defeating as they frequently are) is unimaginable to anyone but a Nazi"; "it does not occur to [Syrkin] that sexual entanglements between Jewish men and Gentile women might themselves be marked, in any number of instances, by the history of anti-Semitism that so obviously determines her own rhetoric and point of view, at least in this letter." Roth, *Reading Myself and Others*, 278–79.

74. Roth, *Portnoy's Complaint*, 27.

75. Roth, 27.

76. Roth, 29–30.

77. Roth, 94–95.

78. Roth, 149.

79. Roth, 150. Sander Gilman has written, "It is being visible in 'the body that betrays,' that the Jew is most uncomfortable. For visibility means being seen not as an individual but as an Other, one of the 'ugly' race." Sander Gilman, "The Jewish Nose: Are Jews White? Or, The History of the Nose Job," in *The Jew's Body* (New York: Routledge, 1991), 193.

80. Roth, *Portnoy's Complaint*, 153. See also p. 162.

81. Roth, 228.

82. Roth, 225.

83. Roth, 230.

84. Roth, 231.

85. Roth, 231.

86. In the end, he laments the loss of The Pumpkin. Roth, 219. See also p. 251.

87. Heine is often quoted as saying that "Judaism is not a religion; it is a misfortune." However, this is no more representative of Heine's complex ambivalence in relation to Jewishness than it is of Roth's.

88. This is even more clear in *Zuckerman Unbound* and *The Anatomy Lesson*, where the character of Nathan Zuckerman must cope with accusations of "self-hatred" for his shockingly lewd best-selling novel about a Jewish boy growing up in Newark entitled *Carnovsky*; Sander Gilman makes a similar point about the Zuckerman books in Sander L. Gilman, *Jewish Self-Hatred: Anti-Semitism and the Secret Language of the Jews* (Baltimore: Johns Hopkins University Press, 1986), 379–92.

89. Roth, *Portnoy's Complaint*, 124.

90. Roth, 251. In this regard, David Biale aptly describes Alex as a "sexual shlemiel." Biale, *Eros and the Jews*, 204–7.

91. Roth, *Portnoy's Complaint*, 33.

92. Roth, 69, 71.

93. Roth, 72.

94. Roth, 118–19.

95. *Sabbath's Theater* plays with similar ideas and emotions. The last line, after Mickey Sabbath refuses his last chance to take his own life, which he has imagined he wants to do: "And he couldn't do it. He could not fucking die. How could he leave? How could he go? Everything he hated was here." Philip Roth, *Sabbath's Theater* (New York: Vintage, 1995), 451.

96. Roth, *Portnoy's Complaint*, 244. He also relishes their bodies: "Belly! Muscle! Forearms black with hair! Bald domes!" (241). These are not big, hardened muscular men or soft, pale waifish yeshiva bukhers. These are the men of the shvitz, alive: these are the energetic and thriving but *still Jewish* and balding and hairy and belly-fatted Jewish men that Alex actually admires. Fascinatingly, the idea of a distinct Jewish American mixing of clowning and sports is not a mere contrivance of Roth's or something idiosyncratic to his imagination. See Rebecca T. Alpert's invaluable analysis of "The Conflict Over Baseball Comedy" in *Out of Left Field: Jews and Black Baseball* (New York: Oxford University Press, 2011), 91–132.

97. Roth, *Portnoy's Complaint*, 245. "It is this reconciliation with memory," writes David Biale, "and not the projection of fantasies, whether onto the State of Israel or elsewhere— that suggest the hope of psychic repair." Biale, *Eros and the Jews*, 228.

98. Roth, *Portnoy's Complaint*, 245. By the way, his vision of healthy Jewish masculinity, of the kind of person that he wants to be (when he's in this mood, anyway), includes going home after the game "to *my* wife and *my* children, to a family of my own" (246). Contrast this to his thoughts, in a very different mood, about the "love" of marriage: "Isn't it something more like weakness? Isn't it rather convenience and apathy and guilt? Isn't it rather fear and exhaustion and inertia, gutlessness plain and simple, far far more than that 'love' that the marriage counselors and the songwriters and the psychotherapists are forever dreaming about?" (104–5). Neither mood is the "standard meter in Paris" to measure Alexander Portnoy's soul, of course.

99. On Lincoln, see Roth, 251.

100. Along these lines, Jeffrey Berman has written: "The novel is less a complaint than a celebration. Why should Portnoy be cured of fantasies that are so entertaining? The exuberance of his language works against his claims for deliverance. The voice never assumes the flatness, fatigue, or disconnectedness that is symptomatic of depression." Jeffrey Berman, "Philip Roth's Psychoanalysts," in Bloom, *Philip Roth's Portnoy's Complaint*, 21.

101. Roth, *Portnoy's Complaint*, 111–12. Sam Levenson and Myron Cohen were comedians. Ruth Wisse has written of Roth's approach to Jewish humor in *Portnoy's Complaint*: "He demonstrates that the very techniques of joking presumed to help alleviate anxiety and stress may be generating anxiety and stress. In other words, Roth is not just ratcheting up Jewish humor to new levels of intensity, but asking whether humor is really the wonder-drug it was cut out to be. With mounting hysteria, and all the while exploiting that hysteria, Portnoy asks the analyst to relieve him not only of the pressure of his family, but of the pressure of joking." Ruth R. Wisse, *Some Serious Thoughts About Jewish Humor*, Leo Baeck Memorial Lecture 45 (New York: Leo Baeck Institute, 2001), 18.

102. Roth actually had the idea for the character after seeing him pop up as a kind of ubiq-
      uitous myth in the stories of young Jewish writers that he taught at the state university
      of Iowa. Roth, *Reading Myself and Others*, 34–35.

103. I draw these terms from Wayne Booth.

> Even the most naïve listener attending with total concentration to the simplest
> tale can be seen, on analysis, to be re-creating and responding to at least three
> different voices: that of the immediate teller, or narrator, who takes the whole tale
> straight and who expects the listener to do the same (the "time" in "once upon
> a time" is real time); that of the implied author, who knows that the telling is in
> one sense an artificial construct but who takes responsibility for it, for whatever
> values or norms it implies, and for the suggestion that "in responding to *me* you
> respond to a real person"; and the inferable voice of the flesh-and-blood person
> for whom this telling is only one concentrated moment selected from the infi-
> nite complexities of "real" life.
>
> (Booth, *The Company We Keep*, 125)

104. Ruth Wisse has written, "American Jewish literature was not merely centered on the
      family, as its critics have often observed, but on perpetual children, the sons and daugh-
      ters who could not or did not want to evolve into Jewish parents." Wisse, *The Modern
      Jewish Canon*, 269. She describes Roth in particular, in his early work especially, hav-
      ing "fix[ed] American Jewish manhood in the image of the raunchy adolescent;" and,
      "Roth wrote from the angle of someone in the protective custody of a culture for which
      he assumes no adult responsibility" (317).

105. Jeffrey Alexander describes Philip Roth's "choice to go public with the once-denigrated
      qualities of Jewish life" as an example of the "multicultural mode of Jewish incorpora-
      tion" into American society. Jeffrey C. Alexander, *The Civil Sphere* (New York: Oxford
      University Press, 2006), 539, 530. He describes a process that resulted in the following
      social transformation by the early 1960s: "Rather than simply being open to full par-
      ticipation by Jewish persons and tolerating Jewish qualities, Christian Americans began
      to find Jewish qualities attractive in themselves. American primordiality was being
      opened to 'Jewishness.' In the nations elite popular culture, in matters of emotion, ideas,
      and aesthetics, communicative institutions played the chords of civil discourse in a new
      key" (532).

106. Dean Franco makes a relevant connection to Eldridge Cleaver: "Roth's novel is come-
      dic, but it relies structurally on the same symbolic economy of race and sexuality as
      Cleaver's justification for his crime. Like Cleaver, Portnoy longs for white women and
      becomes aware of his own racial distinctness through contiguity. Also as with Cleaver,
      Portnoy's desire is masochistic, bringing him moral 'pain.' And finally, again like
      Cleaver, Portnoy turns that masochism outward, deflecting it or displacing it onto the
      women he ravishes." Dean J. Franco, *Race, Rights, and Recognition: Jewish American
      Literature Since 1969* (Ithaca, NY: Cornell University Press, 2012), 42.

107. It is also possible to see how Alex might be described as "trapped in a vicious circle" in
      his relation to obscenity. As Bernard Rodgers explains, "*To Portnoy obscenity is an*

achievement—and a weapon. He uses it *because*, like his parents and the society whose sexual conventions he is struggling so hard to violate, *he* thinks it is 'dirty' too." Rodgers, "In the American Grain," 40.

108. It is interesting to consider the limits and possibilities of metaperspectival intimacy for female readers. I read Erica Jong's *Fear of Flying* (New York: New American Library, 2003 [1973]) as proof that *Portnoy's Complaint* is not closed to metaperspectival intimacy with female readers. Jong, in fact, invites her readers to view their bourgeoning relationship with *Fear of Flying* as connected to a preexisting relationship between the implied author of *Fear of Flying* and *Portnoy's Complaint*. See especially *Fear of Flying*, 201.

109. Dan Colson has offered a contrary view:

> Roth's novel is fully implicated in the discourse around sexuality, no matter how strongly it undermines social norms. *Portnoy's Complaint* may function as a discursive pleasure (the pleasure of writing and of reading) but not as bodily pleasure. In other words, the novel can never realize the bodily presence outside of the discourse toward which Foucault gestures. Because it is always already inscribed within a discourse, it can only generate a knowledge that points toward bodily pleasure—it can never liberate.

Dan Colson, "Impotence and the Futility of Liberation in *Portnoy's Complaint*," *Philip Roth Studies* 3, no. 2 (Fall 2007): 141.

8. *ALL IN THE FAMILY* IN THE MORAL
HISTORY OF AMERICA

1. Donna McCrohan, *Archie and Edith, Mike and Gloria: The Tumultuous History of* All in the Family (New York: Workman, 1987), 263.

2. Digby Diehl, "Q&A: Norman Lear," *Los Angeles Times*, July 30, 1972, W16.

3. David Farber, "The Torch Had Fallen," in Beth Bailey and David Farber, eds., *America in the 70s* (Lawrence: University Press of Kansas, 2004), 10.

4. Eric Porter, "Affirming and Disaffirming Actions: Remaking Race in the 1970s," in Bailey and Farber, *America in the 70s*, 65.

5. Barbara Ehrenreich, *Fear of Falling: The Inner Life of the Middle Class* (New York: Pantheon, 1989), 98.

6. Ehrenreich, 99.

7. Ehrenreich, 100. Edith Efron would go on to write *The News Twisters*, published in 1971, claiming liberal media bias in the coverage of the 1968 presidential election.

8. Ehrenreich, 101–2.

9. Ehrenreich explains, "blue-collar Americans were not, at the time of their discovery, shifting to the right. Nor was much of anybody, except perhaps the media people who were now so anxious to document a surge of right-wing populism" (123). Jefferson Cowie notes, however, that by the 1972 presidential election the majority of white working-class voters voted for Nixon "over the most pro-labor candidate ever produced by the

American two-part system." Jefferson Cowie, *Stayin' Alive: The 1970s and the Last Days of the Working Class* (New York: New Press, 2010), 7.

10. Ehrenreich, 108–9. Ehrenreich identifies Seymour Martin Lipset's essay, "Working-Class Authoritarianism" (1959) as an early contributor to the image of the blue-color reactionary that would emerge in the 1970s.

11. Ehrenreich, 101. See also Cowie, *Stayin' Alive*, 189.

12. Ehrenreich, 130.

13. Ehrenreich, 132.

14. Ehrenreich, 142–43.

15. Cowie, *Stayin' Alive,* 190. Cowie cites specifically the 1970 film *Joe*, with Peter Boyle. On the other hand, Cowie also writes about Ehrenreich, "In her zeal to protect workers, she overlooks the genuine sources of some of the caricature of blue-collar behavior and fails to see that much of the most mean spirited of the genre that she wants to pin solely on middle-class values was simultaneously a byproduct of the failures of the New Left and the real limits of working-class identity" (190).

16. Ehrenreich, *Fear of Falling*, 114.

17. Cowie, *Stayin' Alive*, 10.

18. Ehrenreich, *Fear of Falling*, 115.

19. Cowie, *Stayin' Alive*, 194.

20. Cowie, 194–95.

21. Josh Ozersky, *Archie Bunker's America: TV in an Era of Change, 1968–1978* (Carbondale: Southern Illinois University Press, 2003), 72.

22. McCrohan, *Archie & Edith, Mike & Gloria*, 184.

23. Quoted in McCrohan, 185.

24. Nat Hentoff, "You know you're going to laugh," *Village Voice*, October 14, 1971, 46.

25. McCrohan, *Archie & Edith, Mike & Gloria*, 184.

26. That is, the 1920s to the 1940s. McCrohan, *Archie & Edith, Mike & Gloria*, 185.

27. McCrohan, *Archie & Edith, Mike & Gloria*, 187.

28. McCrohan, 188.

29. McCrohan, 192.

30. McCrohan, 189.

31. McCrohan, 189–90.

32. Charles L. Sanders, "Is Archie Bunker the Real White America?" *Ebony* 27, no. 8 (June 1972): 190.

33. Sanders, 190.

34. Pamela Haynes, "New TV Comedy Takes Hard, Realistic Poke at Bigotry," *Los Angeles Sentinel,* January 28, 1971, in Richard P. Adler, ed., *All in the Family: A Critical Appraisal* (Santa Barbara, CA: Praeger, 1979), 84–85.

35. Mark Crispin Miller, "Deride and Conquer," in Todd Gitlin, ed., *Watching Television: A Pantheon Guide to Popular Culture* (New York: Pantheon, 1986), 183–228.

36. Miller,196.

37. Miller, 207.

38. Miller, 218.

39. Miller, 223.

40. Todd Gitlin, *Inside Prime Time* (Berkeley: University of California Press, 2000), 269.

41. Richard Butsch, "Ralph, Fred, Archie, Homer, and the King of Queens: Why Television Keeps Re-Creating the Male Working-Class Buffoon," in Gail Dines and Jean M Humez, eds., *Gender, Race, and Class in Media: A Critical Reader* (Los Angeles: Sage, 2011), 101. According to his research, of the four hundred domestic situation comedies appearing on network television between 1946 and 2004, only 10 percent of "heads of house" were portrayed as working class (101).

42. Ozersky, *Archie Bunker's America*, 77–78.

43. Saul Austerlitz, *Sitcom: A History in Twenty-four Episodes from* I Love Lucy *to* Community (Chicago: Chicago Review Press, 2014), 123.

44. Austerlitz, 127.

45. Gitlin, *Inside Prime Time*, 211.

46. Gitlin, 212. Contrary to Lear's hope that the show would be funny by virtue of the level of concern that it provoked, Roger Rosenblatt found it mired in presentist, staccato joking about the familiar: "There is nothing intense and nothing to care for. The family are bunkers against our caring." Roger Rosenblatt, "Roger Rosenblatt on Television: All in the Family," *New Republic* (May 24, 1975): 31.

47. Norman Lear, *Even This I Get to Experience* (New York: Penguin, 2014), 245. Several social scientific studies were done in the 1970s in order to determine the likely consequences of large numbers of people watching *All in the Family*. See McCrohan, *Archie & Edith, Mike & Gloria*, 195–96. Cowie characterizes the results of these studies appropriately, writing "limited evidence suggests that *All in the Family* was a bit of a political Rorschach test—viewers sided with whomever they already believed in." Cowie, *Stayin' Alive*, 194.

48. Laura Z. Hobson, "As I listened to Archie Say 'Hebe' . . .," *New York Times*, September 12, 1971, reprinted in Richard P. Adler, ed., *All in the Family: A Critical Appraisal* (New York: Praeger, 1979), 97.

49. Hobson, 97.

50. Hobson, 99.

51. Hobson, 102.

52. Hobson, 102.

53. Hobson, 102.

54. Hobson, 103.

55. Hobson, 103.

56. In point of fact, Lear resisted making Archie Irish Catholic, even though he felt that this would be seen as the natural way to position Carroll O'Connor. He didn't want to associate Archie's bigotry too tightly with any particular national or religious group. Arguably, this is further evidence that he wanted to play with "whiteness" more generally. Lear, *Even This I Get to Experience*, 249.

57. Hobson, "As I listened to Archie Say 'Hebe' . . .," 103

58. Hobson, 103–4.

59. Hobson, 104.

60. Hobson, 104.

61. Hobson, 105.

62. Norman Lear, "As I Read How Laura Saw Archie . . .," *New York Times,* October 10, 1971, reprinted in Adler, *All in the Family,* 107.

63. Lear, 108.

64. Lear, 110.

65. Lear, 110.

66. Lear, 108.

67. Lear, 108.

68. Lear, 108.

69. Lear, 109.

70. Lear, 106.

71. Lear, 109–10.

72. Lear, 110.

73. On *Day at Night with James Day, January 23, 1974,* Lear explains that his father was a "lovable bigot" and that his being Jewish didn't make him any less likely to become a bigot. *Day at Night,* January 23, 1974, http://www.cuny.tv/show/dayatnight/PR1010375.

74. McCrohan, *Archie & Edith, Mike & Gloria,* 11, 7. After reading the blurb in *Variety* about *Till Death Us Do Part,* Lear recalls: "'Oh, my God,' I thought instantly, 'my dad and me.'" Lear, *Even This I Get to Experience,* 221.

75. Jeffrey Shandler, "At Home on the Small Screen: Television's New York Jews," in J. Hoberman and Jeffrey Shandler, *Entertaining America: Jews, Movies, and Broadcasting* (New York: Jewish Museum, 2003), 247.

76. Lear, *Even This I Get to Experience,* 49.

77. Lear, 50.

78. Lear, 51.

79. Lear, 54.

80. I'm thinking in particular of Alex's Thanksgiving visit to the home of his college girlfriend Kay Campbell. Philip Roth, *Portnoy's Complaint* (New York: Vintage, 1994 [1969]), 224–30.

81. Lear, *Even This I Get to Experience,* 54–55.

82. Lear, 59.

83. Lear, 106.

84. Lear, 221.

85. Defending the show in the *New York Times* five months before his response to Hobson, Lear wrote,

> What it attempts to do and, according to much of the mail we receive, succeeds in doing, is to hold a mirror up to our prejudices. We are laughing while we face them, which means that we are not forced to think about it now. It's not jammed at us and forced down our throats. We laugh now, swallowing just the littlest bit of truth about ourselves and it sits there for the unconscious to toss about later. Ask me how I can make such self-serving statements. I'm glad you asked. I can make them because I can see myself in Archie Bunker. "You see yourself, Norman Lear, in Archie Bunker?" Yes, I do.

Norman Lear, "Laughing While We Face Our Prejudices," *New York Times*, April 11, 1971, D22.

86. McCrohan, *Archie & Edith, Mike & Gloria*, 33.

87. This plot device is actually taken from Lear's personal life. For his parents' fifteenth wedding anniversary, Lear wrote a poem for his mother that his father delivered to her as his own. The poem that is read aloud in the first episode of the show is the very poem that Lear wrote as a kid for his mother, in his father's name. Lear, *Even This I Get to Experience*, 37–38.

88. James Baldwin, "My Dungeon Shook," from *The Fire Next Time*, in *Baldwin: Collected Essays* (New York: Library of America, 1998), 292.

89. Baldwin, 294.

90. Quoted in David Zurawik, "O'Connor, 'Family's' lovable bigot, dies at 76," *Baltimore Sun*, June 22, 2001.

91. Archie is capable of such language, though. In season 1, episode 13, Archie is furious when he finds out that Edith has accepted an invitation from Lionel's parents, George and Louise Jefferson, for dinner at their house. Archie says, "I ain't havin dinner with no jungle bunnies," and "Those people are inferior to us people," and "it's my God-given right not to sit down and break bread with my inferiors." This is certainly Archie at his worst. While it is not appropriate or necessary to try to hold a television series to consistency throughout the entirety of its run, it is worth noting that there is nothing in this last episode of the first season that makes Archie come off as "lovable." The show is not afraid to reveal the real ugliness of Archie's character.

92. Gitlin, *Inside Prime Time*, 212.

93. Season 1, episode 11.

94. Lisa Woolfork has written, "Lionel is more than an object of prejudice, more than a neighborhood kid doing odd jobs. . . . Lionel is incorporated into this family and is part of its process of making, unmaking, and remaking whiteness in the Bunker family." Lisa Woolfork, "Looking for Lionel: Making Whiteness and Blackness in *All in the Family* and *The Jeffersons*," in David Leonard and Lisa Guerrero, eds., *African Americans on Television: Race-ing for Ratings* (Santa Barbara, CA: ABC-CLIO, 2013), 50. In general, "Lionel relishes his role as the trickster enabler of the 'lovable bigot'" (53).

95. Gitlin, *Inside Prime Time*, 213–14.

96. *All in the Family* can sometimes seem to blur the line that should separate it as play from politics. The episode entitled "Mike Comes Into Money" (season 3, episode 8), for instance, shows the family arguing explicitly about the 1972 presidential election. It might be tempting to interpret this episode as legitimizing Archie's sensibility as one of two serious political positions, each deserving of equal time, which were on the ballot. But I think the play frame is well crafted and sturdy in this episode. The tension is particularly thick as Archie pressures Mike to hand over money that he has just inherited for Archie's expenses (since Mike and Gloria are living at the house without paying Archie anything). Mike would rather give it to the McGovern campaign. More than any other episode that I've seen, the audience laughter at Gloria, Edith, Archie and Mike screaming at each other seems incongruous. And yet, as fraught as this episode is, after

the last commercial break we find the whole family sitting in their usual spots around the television making gentle jabs at each other while they watch the election results come in. Nothing is resolved. This episode aired on November 4, just days before the presidential election. I don't think viewers who started watching this episode leaning toward Nixon or McGovern could possibly have been influenced to change their vote by the end. Instead, they would have felt the fraught unresolvable emotions of a divided American society in a context that serves no inherent instrumental goal at all. If this episode communicates anything, it communicates the possibility of sitting together as Americans around the television to watch the coming election results that we will have to endure as a nation.

EPILOGUE

1. Key texts for the critique of the category of religion include Wilfred Cantwell Smith, *The Meaning and End of Religion* (Minneapolis: Fortress, 1991 [1962]); Jonathan Z. Smith, *Imagining Religion: From Babylon to Jonestown* (Chicago: University of Chicago Press, 1982) and "Religion, Religions, Religious," in Mark C. Taylor, ed., *Critical Terms for Religious Studies* (Chicago: University of Chicago Press, 1998); Talal Asad, "Religion as an Anthropological Category," in *Genealogies of Religion: Discipline and Reasons of Power in Christianity and Islam* (Baltimore: Johns Hopkins University Press, 1993); Tomoko Masuzawa, *The Invention of World Religions* (Chicago: University of Chicago Press, 2005); Jason Ānanda Josephson, *The Invention of Religion in Japan* (Chicago: University of Chicago Press, 2012). For a clear and concise introduction to this critique, see Brent Nongbri, *Before Religion: A History of a Modern Concept* (New Haven: Yale University Press, 2013).
2. Smith, *The Meaning and End of Religion*, 50.
3. Winnifred Fallers Sullivan, *The Impossibility of Religious Freedom* (Princeton: Princeton University Press, 2005), 8. See also Elizabeth Shakman Hurd, *Beyond Religious Freedom: The New Global Politics of Religion* (Princeton: Princeton University Press, 2015); and Winnifred Fallers Sullivan, Elizabeth Shakman Hurd, Saba Mahmood, and Peter G. Danchin, eds., *Politics of Religious Freedom* (Chicago: University of Chicago Press, 2015).
4. Historically, the Protestant paradigm has been more definitive and the Catholic paradigm has been stigmatized.
5. Sullivan, *The Impossibility of Religious Freedom*, 138.
6. Along with the books cited in footnote 775 above, see Martha C. Nussbaum, *Liberty of Conscience: In Defense of America's Tradition of Religious Equality* (New York: Basic Books, 2008); Christopher L. Eisgruber and Lawrence G. Sager, *Religious Freedom and the Constitution* (Cambridge: Harvard University Press, 2007); Brian Leiter, *Why Tolerate Religion?* (Princeton: Princeton University Press, 2013); Andrew Koppelman, *Defending American Religious Neutrality* (Cambridge: Harvard University Press, 2013).

7. To be clear, I do not want to suggest that the term *religion* ought to be somehow banned or anything like that. In the background culture, it may be a part of a person's non-public project to promote the idea that there are special things that count as "religion," and they are distinctly beneficial to society or distinctly harmful to society. And I will happily admit that *playing* with the category of religion in the classroom is one of my favorite ways to play. I tend to identify with Jonathan Z. Smith when he argues that the scholar of religion is trained, above all, to employ artfully her self-consciousness about the historical construction of religion as a distinct category. Smith has long insisted that scholars of religion recognize "the cognitive power of distortion, along with the concomitant choice of the map over the territory." Jonathan Z. Smith, "When the Chips Are Down," *Relating Religion: Essays in the Study of Religion* (Chicago: University of Chicago Press, 2004), 31. The point is not to exclude the category of religion from the scholarly toolkit, but to study it as an intellectually fruitful distortion.

8. Roy, *Holy Ignorance*, 82.

9. The problem is *not* that the political state shapes the way we think about ourselves through the categories that it hypostatizes. Setting up any kind of governing body will end up shaping the lives of the governed, usually in unpredictable ways. I consider it the task of political thought not to avoid this sort of "shaping," but to take responsibility for it and to offer persuasive reasons why shaping this way might be better than shaping that way. This book reflects my hope that we can start shaping things differently in America.

10. Saul Bellow, *Mr. Sammler's Planet* (New York: Penguin, 2004 [1970]), 164.

11. Bellow, 1.

12. See especially Franz Rosenzweig, *Understanding the Sick and the Healthy: A View of World, Man, and God* (Cambridge: Harvard University Press, 1999).

13. Karl Marx, "On the Jewish Question," in Robert C. Tucker, ed., *The Marx-Engels Reader* (New York: Norton, 1978 [1843]), 35.

14. Marx, 35.

15. I realize that this would not likely satisfy the early Marx of "On the Jewish Question." I suppose that my response to Marx would be that our best option is to focus on constructing a better version of "political emancipation" for a while, since we're not all going to agree on what "human emancipation" should look like. After all, Marx did concede: "Political emancipation certainly represents a great progress. It is not, indeed, the final form of human emancipation, but it is the final form of human emancipation within the framework of the prevailing social order" (35).

16. I have only just begun to explore this speculation. On the meaning of war reenactment in general, I have found particularly helpful Jenny Thompson, *War Games: Inside the World of Twentieth-Century War Reenactors* (Washington, DC: Smithsonian, 2004).

17. I have found especially helpful Margot Weiss, *Techniques of Pleasure: BDSM and the Circuits of Sexuality* (Durham, NC: Duke University Press, 2011). This riveting and outstanding work of ethnography and political analysis offers much to challenge my view. But I think it offers some corroboration too. We'll see where it takes me.

18. Both Jenny Thompson and Margot Weiss illustrate how these elements converge in myriad ways in the cases that they analyze.

19. On the blurred boundaries that already characterize our efforts to distinguish religion from play, see David Chidester, *Authentic Fakes: Religion and American Popular Culture* (Berkeley: University of California Press, 2005); Robert M. Geraci, *Virtually Sacred: Myth and Meaning in World of Warcraft and Second Life* (New York: Oxford University Press, 2014); Joseph P. Laycock, *Dangerous Games: What the Moral Panic Over Role-Playing Games Says About Play, Religion, and Imaginable Worlds* (Oakland: University of California Press, 2015).

20. Martha Nussbaum has argued that we ought to embrace distinctly "religious" liberty in the U.S. Constitution, despite its flaws, as a way of protecting vulnerable minorities and valuing "the faculty with which each person searches for the ultimate meaning of life," which is "identified in part by what it does—it reasons, searches, and experiences emotions of longing connected to that search—and in part by its subject matter—it deals with ultimate questions, questions of ultimate meaning." Nussbaum, *Liberty of Conscience*, 168–69.

INDEX

affirmative action, 34

African Americans, 8–9, 100, 103, 304*n*73; *All in the Family* and, 249, 252–53, 255–56, 258–59; black-Jewish alliance, 51; blackness in *Black Skin, White Masks* and, 88–90, 97; black radical liberalism and, 35; Fanon on blackness, 88–90, 94, 97, 304*n*75; Jewish Americans and, 42–43, 51; Jim Crow and, 42; racial epithets of, 15–16, 27, 36, 88, 90, 252–53, 255–56, 258–59; two-faced racism and, 298*n*138

Afro-pessimist, 35–36

Allen, Woody, 196, 222, 339*n*64

All in the Family, 347*n*91; African Americans and, 249, 252–53, 255–56, 258–59; Austerlitz on, 250–51; Baldwin and, 261–62; bigotry in, 252–54; Bruce and, 25, 243; capitalism in, 250; as conservative, 250; emotions provoked in, 255, 264–65, 268–69; fairness in, 262–63; fear in, 254; Haynes on, 250; Hobson on, 252–53, 255; identification in, 264–66; Jewish background of, 256; Lear creating, 25, 243, 247, 250–51, 346*n*85; Lear response to Hobson about, 253–54, 255–56; M. Miller on, 249–50; metaperspectival

intimacy in, 267; play in, 266, 347*n*96; political and social climate during, 243–46, 347*n*96; political conception of justice and, 267; political love and, 243, 259, 269; popularity of, 242, 247; public cultural critic on, 263; public political culture and, 243; racial stereotyping in, 247–48; Sanders on, 248–49; self-awareness and, 265; silent majority in, 259; social change and, 254, 260–61; white working class and, 246–48, 264–65

Altman, Sig, 195

Amalekites, 73, 297*n*134; Wieseltier on, 69, 71

"America" (Ginsberg), 1, 21, 60–61; caring in, 22; play in, 13; political love in, 7, 13–14; racial hierarchy in, 15–16; rough play in, 17; stand-up version of, 14–16

"Andy Hardy" movies routine, 202–3

anthropodenial, 65, 125, 153

antiracist advocacy, 38

anti-Semitism, 5, 44, 224, 313*n*76, 328*n*41; in early twentieth century, 190–92, 193; German Jews and, 77; Lear and racial, 256–57; new, 286*n*18; Nordau on, 76; in *Portnoy's Complaint*, 240